Praise for
THE PRESIDENT AND THE ASSASSIN

Chosen one of "10 Must-Read Summer Books" by The Daily Beast

"Scott Miller vividly traces the intersecting trajectories of the protagonists."
—*The New York Times*

"Very interesting . . . [Miller] has conjoined two kinds of histories to create a portrait of the United States at the turn of the twentieth century as a country divided between worldviews so radically dissimilar that they hardly seemed to be describing the same reality."
—*Los Angeles Times*

"An engaging, entertaining, and revealing portrait of America at a crucial turning point in its history. . . . Miller has a good eye [for] telling details and enriching anecdotes. A panoramic tour de force."
—Washington Independent Review of Books

"Miller deftly weaves a complex tale. . . . Its broad sweep [is] presented in a wonderfully readable way. . . . A real triumph."
—*BookPage*

"This book casts some welcome light on a stretch of American history that has grown dim."
—*St. Louis Post-Dispatch*

"Miller's polished and vivid narrative of these complex, dissimilar men makes this piece of Americana appear fresh and unexpected."
—*Publishers Weekly*

"[Miller] captures the parallel universes of McKinley and Czolgosz—and their sudden, violent convergence—with assurance. . . . [He] gives both men their due in supple and symmetrical fashion."
—*The Star-Ledger*

"A marvelous work of history, wonderfully written, told from the top down and the bottom up."
—FAREED ZAKARIA, host of CNN's *Fareed Zakaria GPS* and editor-at-large, *Time* magazine

"Fast-moving and richly detailed."
—*The Buffalo News*

"Vivid and insightful . . . a fast-paced read about an astonishing time."
—EVAN THOMAS, author of *The War Lovers*

THE PRESIDENT AND
THE ASSASSIN

McKinley, Terror, and Empire at the
Dawn of the American Century

SCOTT MILLER

RANDOM HOUSE TRADE PAPERBACKS
NEW YORK

2013 Random House Trade Paperback Edition

Copyright © 2011 by Scott Miller

Published in the United States by Random House Trade Paperbacks,
an imprint of The Random House Publishing Group,
a division of Random House, Inc., New York.

RANDOM HOUSE TRADE PAPERBACKS and colophon are
trademarks of Random House, Inc.

LIBRARY OF CONGRESS CATALOGING-IN-PUBLICATION DATA
Miller, Scott.
The president and the assassin: McKinley, terror, and empire
at the dawn of the American century / by Scott Miller.
p. cm.
Includes bibliographical references and index.
ISBN 978-0-8129-7928-2
eBook ISBN 978-0-679-60498-3
1. McKinley, William, 1843–1901. 2. McKinley, William, 1843–1901—
Assassination. 3. Czolgosz, Leon F., 1873?–1901. 4. United States—Politics and
government—1897–1901. 5. United States—Social conditions—1865–1918.
6. United States—Territorial expansion—History—19th century.
7. Anarchism—United States—History. I. Title.
E711.M45 2011   973.8'8—dc22   2010038857

Printed in the United States of America

www.atrandom.com

4 6 8 9 7 5 3

Book design by Dana Leigh Blanchette

To Mom

Contents

THE PRESIDENT AND THE ASSASSIN

1

TEMPLE OF MUSIC

They streamed among the manicured flower beds and dewy lawns of Delaware Park that early September morning in Buffalo, New York, a portrait of America in the Gilded Age. Women in full-length skirts and tight-fitting corsets in the fashion of the iconic Gibson Girl shaded themselves with parasols. The men, seeking relief from the sun with jauntily perched straw boaters, fingered coins deep in their pockets, confident in their jobs. Children in sailor suits skipped and laughed and pulled their parents along as fast as they could. The smoky aroma of grilling bratwurst, the echo of chirping piccolos and booming tubas, the bellow of an elephant, all signaled they had nearly reached the grounds of the Pan-American Exposition of 1901.

As the crowds drew nearer, a series of pillars, each topped with a horse and rider, could be discerned through the trees. Beyond them stood massive domed buildings in red and yellow, preceded by the stout Triumphal Bridge. The view was capped by the signature structure of the Expo, the 389-foot-high Electric Tower, lit with power generated by Niagara Falls twenty-five miles away. John M. Carrère, the Expo's lead architect, had carefully orchestrated the scene so that "the spectator, as he approaches the Exposition, will see it develop gradually until he reaches the Bridge, when the entire picture will appear before him and almost burst upon him."[1] Once inside the 350-acre park, visitors marveled at every sort of attraction: a mock Japanese village, a Trip to the Moon exhibit where midgets served green cheese,[2] and, of course, the pachyderm, a nine-ton specimen decorated by Queen Victoria for its service with the British army in Afghanistan.[3]

This was an especially exciting day. The Buffalo papers were reporting that William McKinley, beloved president of the United States, would meet members of the public at the Temple of Music at 4 P.M. The previous day, a record 116,000 people had crowded through the gates to see him deliver what many considered one of his finest speeches, and the prospect of actually exchanging a handshake or a brief word was an experience not to be missed. Such one-on-one encounters were a favorite of the president. Meeting with people individually, he projected a natural sincerity and warmth. So much time did McKinley spend in receiving lines that he perfected his own handshake, the "McKinley grip," to prevent cramping. When confronted with a long reception line, he made a point of extending his hand first and clasping the other's fingers so he couldn't be squeezed back. Then he would grab hold of his visitor's elbow with his left hand and deftly move him along,[4] clocking up to fifty people a minute. "Everyone in that line has a smile and a cheery word," he once said. "They bring no problems with them; only good will. I feel better after the contact."[5]

But plans for this particular meet-and-greet had left McKinley's staff feeling uneasy. The event had been well publicized and raised serious security issues. George B. Cortelyou, the president's personal secretary, had twice removed the Temple of Music reception from McKinley's schedule, and the president had twice demanded that it be reinstated. Though McKinley was the most popular president since Abraham Lincoln four decades earlier, pockets of dangerous radicals lurked in many cities. Only weeks before, his Secret Service agent George Foster, who looked the part of a professional sleuth with his derby hat and a cigar clenched between his teeth, had chased off a shadowy stranger from the McKinleys' private home in Canton, Ohio.

Responding to pleas to be more cautious, the president conceded only to drawing his living room shades at night. Publishing tycoon William Randolph Hearst also tormented McKinley's inner circle with vicious attacks on the president. On April 10, 1901, his *New York Journal* printed an editorial that read in part: "If bad institutions and bad men can be got rid of only by killing, then the killing must be done."[6]

Cortelyou's nerves had been put even more on edge when, on the evening of September 4, 1901, the special three-car train the president and his wife were riding in pulled into the Terrace Station overlooking Lake Erie in Buffalo. Cannons set up by the Coast Guard to salute McKinley had been placed too near the tracks and, when fired, produced a thunderous report that shattered eight windows on the train and sent shards of glass flying inside. In a brief panic on the station platform, a dozen or so people, their minds quickly racing to the most likely assailant, shouted "Anarchists!"[7]

The reaction was understandable. The notorious exploits of anarchists had become, in the minds of many citizens, a very real and horrifying threat to the American way of life. Anarchist newspapers printed directions for making explosives at home and preached the downfall of the U.S. government. Radical believers of the political philosophy that rejected authority in any form had committed a sickening stream of terrorist attacks on European kings and heads of state. In the United States, anarchists had been convicted of bombing the police and nearly succeeded in murdering the manager of the nation's largest steel company. The president, however, had never been one to worry about his own security and brushed aside pleas that he limit his exposure to the public. "No one would wish to hurt me," he chuckled.[8]

On the evening of August 31, 1901, a slightly built young man entered the barroom of John Nowak's saloon at 1078 Broadway on Buffalo's east side and asked for a room. Clad in a gray suit with a black shoestring tie, he carried a telescope-shaped bag in one hand and a brown hat with a yellow ribbon in the other. He struck Nowak as a "fair sort of man" and possessed a dreamy look.[9] The guest paid the rate of two dollars a week. "What name shall I write on the receipt?" Nowak asked. "John Doe," the man replied. Nowak, accustomed to guests of questionable breeding, thought it somewhat odd but didn't care what he called himself as long as he paid in advance. Nowak asked Frank Walkowiak, a clerk at the hotel who was studying law, to show the man to a room on the second floor. Walkowiak was more curious than his boss. "What made you say John Doe?" he asked as they trudged up-stairs.

"Well, I'll tell you, I'm a Polish Jew and I didn't like to tell him or he wouldn't keep me in the house." Pressing the point, Walkowiak asked the guest his real name. "Nieman, Fred Nieman. . . . I'm going to sell souvenirs."[10]

Nobody could figure out what the man who called himself Nieman was really doing in Buffalo. He generally rose early and left the hotel for the day. In the evening he would return with a collection of news-papers tucked under his arm—the *Express,* the *Courier,* the *Times,* the *Commercial*—and head straight to his room. He occasionally bought a cigar or a good whiskey, not the cheap five-cent shots, and stopped once or twice to watch a card game in the barroom, but he hardly ever spoke. The only time anyone paid him any attention was one morning when he noisily searched for a water pitcher, disturbing a retired German army officer trying to sleep in a nearby room.

Stuffed deep in his coat pocket, however, was one artifact that indi-cated a keen interest in world affairs—a neatly folded and well-worn newspaper clipping about the assassination of Italian king Umberto I. An Italian American named Gaetano Bresci, an editor of an anarchist newspaper in New Jersey, had murdered the monarch a year earlier. Nieman read it carefully. Sometime during the first week of Septem-ber he stopped by Walbridge Hardware at 316 Main Street and asked to see a silver-plated Iver Johnson .32-caliber revolver—the same model that Bresci had used against Umberto I. At $4.50, the weapon was priced well above the other handguns that ran closer to $1.50, but he couldn't resist acquiring the premium model. Back in his hotel room, he loaded the weapon with five Smith & Wesson cartridges and prac-ticed wrapping the gun and his right hand in a white handkerchief.

At fifty-eight, McKinley was still handsome enough for his looks to be a campaign asset. His square jaw and strong cheekbones projected an air of confidence and purpose that suited an increasingly ambitious nation. His large head, some political friends thought, resembled that of Napoléon Bonaparte, and they took to referring to him as such. In figure and form McKinley was very much in keeping with amply portioned men of the day. At a scant five feet, six and a half inches—he made a point of insisting the last half inch be recorded—he sometimes seemed that large around. He might have shed a few pounds, but exercise, other than a brisk stroll in the evenings, had never been a priority. Several years before, McKinley had tried to take up golf but gave it up: too much walking.

McKinley's most distinguishing feature, however, was his piercing dark eyes, eyes that conveyed a genuine goodness of spirit. "The habitual expression of the face is one of gravity and kindness," the *Review of Reviews* wrote in 1896. "If the phrase did not sound too sentimental, the fittest words to characterize McKinley's look would be a sweet seriousness."[11] McKinley, the magazine continued, always had a kind word for secretaries or servants and would see off visitors to the door of his Canton home to warn them about the steps. Longtime Republican stalwart and diplomat John Hay would write years later to a friend, "The president was one of the sweetest and quietest natures I have ever known among public men."[12] Journalists, who had the opportunity to see the president on a daily basis from desks set up near his second-floor office, were likewise struck by McKinley's unfailing affability. Frequently stopping for brief chats, one hand in a pants pocket, the other twirling his glasses, he would ask after any who were missing that day and inquire about their health.[13]

McKinley awoke the morning of September 6, 1901, in an energetic mood. Staying at the stately home of Expo president John G. Milburn, he rose early and made certain he was dressed to the teeth: a boiled shirt, iron-starched collar and cuffs, black satin cravat, pique vest, pinstriped trousers, and frock coat. Into his pockets he stuffed enough trinkets to fill a small jewelry box, including a gold watch and pencil, a wallet, $1.20 in small change, three knives, nine keys (several loose, others on two rings), a pair of gloves, and three handkerchiefs, because it was supposed to be a warm day.[14] At 7 A.M., much to the consternation of his security detail, McKinley set off on a twenty-minute walk along Delaware Avenue, one of the most beautiful streets in Buffalo, enjoying the air and the fine homes.[15] Invigorated by the exercise, he and his wife, Ida, then departed on a sightseeing trip to Niagara Falls, where he clambered about like a boy. His hosts, eager to please their esteemed guest, had arranged for a hearty lunch at the International Hotel and left enough time in his schedule for the president to cap the midday meal with a favorite cigar. By midafternoon, he had boarded his train of parlor cars for the trip back to the Expo, relaxing as farmland and fruit trees passed outside his window.

At the Temple of Music, the main concert hall of the Expo, staff had been preparing all morning for the president's arrival. Security and crowd control were top concerns but seemed to have been addressed. Louis Babcock, a Buffalo attorney and grand marshal of the Exposition, had arranged chairs to form a wide aisle to direct people from the east entrance to the dais and then to corral them out the Temple's south doorways. Babcock's men had also constructed a wooden blind behind the dais to protect the president from the rear, upon which they hung a large American flag. Potted bay trees and other small plants were collected from around the Expo and placed on the edge of the stage, where Secret Service agents were to stand as they studied those in line for strange behavior or a hidden weapon. Before getting anywhere near the president, visitors would have to file between two columns of soldiers who were also ordered to scrutinize each individual. At noon, their work complete, Babcock, Buffalo attorney James L. Quackenbush, and another fair organizer gathered for a lunch of sandwiches and pilsner beer, pleased with their preparations. Referring to Theodore Roosevelt, the ambitious vice president, Quackenbush was confident enough to quip: "It would be Roosevelt's luck to have McKinley shot today."[16]

As the three lingered over their meal, a line began to form at the Temple's east entrance, spilling out onto the Esplanade. Well-wishers balanced on swollen feet for hours under a searing sun, avoiding the temptation of the comfortable chairs in the nearby Pabst restaurant where a seltzer and lemon sold for thirty cents. The afternoon was so warm and humid that by three o'clock the Expo ambulance would pick up three cases of heat exhaustion on the fairgrounds.[17]

If Nieman was suffering from the heat, he kept it to himself and arrived early enough to secure a place near the front of the line. He looked, some later said, like a tradesman or mechanic on holiday, though he hardly stood out. Waiting just in front of him was a dark-haired Italian-looking man. Directly behind was James Parker, a slender six-foot-four African-American waiter from Atlanta. Naturally gregarious, Parker tried once or twice to strike up a conversation with Nieman but was rebuffed.[18]

Shortly before four o'clock, McKinley's Victorian carriage pulled up to the Temple of Music and he emerged still unseen by the crowds of people that waited for him at the other entrance.[19] The Temple, which from a distance resembled a red, yellow, and blue Fabergé egg, was an impressive structure. Able to accommodate an audience of more than two thousand, it hosted famous musicians playing daily concerts. Striding toward the dais, the music-loving president might have noticed the building's impressive pipe organ, an $18,000 Emmons Howard that was one of the largest ever made. Shown to his place, McKinley turned to his security men and gave the order: "Let them come."[20] On cue, organist William J. Gomph coaxed the massive organ to life with a tasteful Bach sonata. The doors to the east entrance were thrown open and excitement rippled through the waiting crowd, many murmuring in hushed tones as they shuffled along on the pine floors.

The first to reach the president was Dr. Clinton Colegrove of Holland, New York. "George Washington, Abraham Lincoln, and President McKinley," he declared.[21]

Several children followed. "To every child, the president bent over, shook hands warmly and said some kind words," wrote a young newspaper reporter, John D. Wells. One boy broke from his mother's hand to dash to the president's side. His horrified mother arrived seconds later but McKinley, who loved children, brushed off the breach of protocol and complimented the boy's enthusiasm.

Not far behind, Parker was growing irritated with Nieman, who seemed to be shuffling along. "If you can't go faster, at least let me by," Parker said. Again, he was ignored. All the while nobody—not the police guard, not the soldiers, not the Secret Service—asked Nieman to remove his right hand from his front coat pocket. The Italian-looking man in front of him had captured their attention. With his tousle of dark hair, olive skin, and mustache, he fit the prevailing stereotype of an immigrant anarchist. The suspect created a further distraction when he would not quickly let go of the president's hand and Secret Service agent Samuel Ireland had to intervene.[22] Once extricated, McKinley turned toward Nieman, smiled warmly, and extended his right hand. Nieman took a step forward. Standing only a foot away, he withdrew a bulging handkerchief from his pocket and shoved it toward the president's ribs.[23]

McKinley and the man who called himself Nieman lived in parallel yet vastly different worlds. Each could see that the Industrial Revolution was forever changing a nation that had long been proud of its simple, agrarian roots. Farmers were abandoning their plows for jobs in clanking, hissing factories. Steamy cities powered by desperately hopeful immigrants clawed into the countryside, and lording over it all was a new breed of American, the rapacious Wall Street tycoon.

For McKinley, these were signs of progress—a prosperous nation was a happy one—and he would do what he could to encourage America's growing economic might. The strongest, most fit companies were allowed to gobble up the weakest until vast swaths of the economy were ruled by a handful of men who understood no economic law other than to produce as much as their straining factories could stand. And when there were no longer enough consumers in the United States to soak up everything that filled the shops and new mail-order catalogs, McKinley attempted to help by establishing new markets abroad. The United States proceeded to acquire foreign territories with all the skill and grace of a hungry Labrador retriever eating dinner—at once sloppy, excited, ravenous, clumsy, and oblivious. Under McKinley, the United States lurched at the chance to snatch territory in the Caribbean and the Pacific, annex Hawaii, and begin what would become a familiar pattern of sending troops to foreign shores to "defend American interests." Bursting with confidence and pride, an almost giddy nation realized it was on the cusp of joining the traditional powers—England, France, and more recently Germany—as a nation of first rank, one whose companies would dominate world markets and whose missionaries would spread its Protestant work ethic and way of life to a grateful planet. The concept of running an "empire," long despised in this former colony, came to be coveted by some as a reward bestowed by the Almighty himself on a deserving people.

Yet in all the exuberance, some saw a nation that had turned its back on its values. The United States had become, they felt, a country owned by the rich and governed only with their interests in mind. The expansion depended on a swelling army of low-skilled workers like Nieman, people who toiled at jobs that often didn't provide a subsistence wage, without hope of advancement or much of anything beyond an early grave. The American economy had come to resemble Frankenstein's monster, both in power and incomprehensibility, wrote historian John Garraty. "Workers, businessmen, professional economists, and political leaders could neither control nor even understand the mighty forces they pretended to supervise and employ."[24] This combination of raw suffering in the workers' tenements and indifference in the mansions of the ruling elite created a fertile breeding ground for a class of social radical who came to see the dynamite stick and the pistol as the only way to break the cycle of servitude. The most notorious of these were the anarchists who, sometimes working in small groups, other times alone, were perfectly willing to resort to terror to redress society's evils.

In diametrically opposed ways, McKinley and Nieman heard in these tumultuous times a calling each believed could change history. This is the story of how they answered.

2

"OH GOD, KEEP HIM HUMBLE"

The curious as well as the committed came by the trainload to Canton, Ohio, throughout the summer of 1896 to see the Republican Party's candidate for president. Neatly dressed local volunteers with welcoming smiles assembled the delegations of miners, tradespeople, streetcar drivers, and soldiers, as well as bankers, lawyers, doctors, and college students, and marched through the center of town toward the McKinley home.[1] By the thousands they strutted to the beat of brass bands and patriotic melodies. Chanting, waving banners, and tooting horns, the throngs surged up Market Avenue North "as thick as flies around a railroad pie stand" until they passed beneath the "McKinley Arch," a plaster structure crowned with the candidate's likeness. Down the tree-lined street and past souvenir stands selling buttons, canes, and umbrellas, they made their way toward McKinley's Victorian home at number 723. It was, in the words of one, as if every day were the Fourth of July.[2]

As the din of each delegation grew louder, McKinley would wait in his office just off the downstairs hall and review the day's scheduled visitors, warned of their imminent arrival by a runner who monitored the train station. The candidate would then emerge from the front door, climb atop a sturdy chair, and greet the enthusiastic crowd. It was a deliberately engineered stage, with McKinley's tasteful yet modest home serving as a picture-perfect backdrop.[3] Gingerbread woodwork hung from the high peaked roof. Large windows, shutters thrown open, looked out on a lawn that, at the start of the campaign, was said to be among the most immaculate in town.[4] White urns spilled over with flowers, brilliant red geraniums lined a walk leading to a covered porch that shaded wicker chairs and rockers. McKinley's mother, Nancy, served lemonade with Ida. The candidate would occasionally interrupt a speech to shout a warm greeting across the fence to a neighbor girl, Mary Harter, gawking at the crowds.

The McKinley home quickly filled up with a trove of gifts. Watermelons, cheese, canes, flags, cakes, and clothing were all stored in a back room for the staff to rummage through. Tons of flowers went in the trash heap. A group from Tennessee brought a finely polished tree stump on which McKinley would later deliver campaign speeches; another brought the largest plate of galvanized iron ever rolled in the United States, and yet another brought a record-breaking sheet of tin, sixty feet long, with the names of the candidates on it. Five bald eagles were bestowed, which McKinley hastily gave to the zoo in Nimisilla Park.[5] On one occasion, an army of bicyclists, riding two, four, and six abreast, performed in intricate formations outside McKinley's home, saluting him by dismounting and raising the front wheels of their bikes.[6]

Under the constant drumbeat of feet, the front yard looked by the end of the summer "as if a herd of buffalo had passed that way."[7] Eager visitors completely demolished the fence, as well as the grape arbor. The velvety lawn quickly wore away, balding to clay that was "hard and shiny." Souvenir hunters stripped the front porch.[8] In one day alone, 16 delegations from 12 states arrived. All told, between June 19 and November 2, 1896, nearly 750,000 people in 300 delegations from 30 states made the pilgrimage to the McKinley porch.

The newspapers dubbed it the "Front Porch Campaign." There would be no whistle-stop tours, no speeches in crowded halls, and no heated rallies in borderline states. Voters would have to come to him. The strategy suited McKinley's strengths, as well as his weaknesses. Mark Hanna, his energetic campaign manager, tried to paint the decision to stay home as evidence of McKinley's qualification for office. "Mr. McKinley will continue to conduct himself as a man who appreciates the dignity and importance of the office he seeks. He will not lend himself to any catchpenny scheme for the sake of satisfying the curious or making himself talked about."[9] There was no doubt a large element of truth to Hanna's claim. Proper manners and comportment were as much a part of McKinley as his ample girth. McKinley also saw practical reasons to stay close to home. As a public speaker, he was no match for William Jennings Bryan, his loquacious Democratic rival. "I might just as well put up a trapeze on my front lawn and compete with some professional athlete as go out speaking against Bryan," McKinley told members of his campaign staff. "I have to think when I speak."[10]

That so many people traveled so far to hear him said much about his appeal. As a Republican, McKinley was undeniably the candidate of the nation's moneyed interests, men in top hats and dark European suits who controlled so much wealth. Yet McKinley also possessed a surprising knack for reaching out to the common man, able to speak his language and, maybe most important, able to show they shared the same humble roots.

Born the seventh of nine children in 1843, William McKinley, Jr., started life in Niles, Ohio, far from the corridors of power. About sixty-five miles southeast of Cleveland, Niles was little more than a wide spot in the road, albeit a bucolic one. Farms dotted the rolling hills outside town, where a young McKinley relished the simple pleasures of standing barefoot on earth warmed by a recently resting cow, roaming the woods with a bow and arrow, or flying his beloved kite. The Mosquito Creek, where McKinley and another boy had once nearly drowned, meandered nearby. A tree-lined unpaved street marked the center of the village. Three churches—as many as there were stores—served a population of three hundred.[11]

The McKinley home, a two-story clapboard, graced a corner lot adjoining a grocery store. Regularly whitewashed, with a steeply gabled roof and curtains neatly adorning the windows, it radiated middle-class propriety.[12] McKinley's father, of tough Scottish-Irish stock, was a powerfully built jack-of-all-trades who supported the family by managing the blast furnace that, along with a rolling mill and a nail forge, constituted the backbone of the Niles economy.[13]

As in many frontier households—and Ohio was considered the frontier in those days—it was the woman of the house who assumed the role of parent-in-chief. Mother McKinley, as she was affectionately known among townsfolk, embodied all that was good about the community, taking in visiting Methodist preachers and handling nearly every church duty short of delivering the sermons. "Don't think my bringing up has much to do with making my son [a success]," she said later, displaying trademark modesty. "I had six children and I had all my own work to do. I did the best I could, of course, but I could not devote all my time to him."[14] Still, she held a special place for her young son. William, she hoped, would fulfill her greatest ambition that one of her children would enter the ministry. Reverend Aaron D. Morton also believed that the boy displayed the makings of a man of the cloth. He noted that McKinley was not the "shouting" sort of Methodist, but one who carefully considered his words. "I often noticed him in church," he said. "He was the best listener I ever saw. . . . Many of us thought he would become a minister."[15]

Education took a close second to religion in the McKinley household. Whenever there was some extra money, the family spent it on books, among them David Hume's *History of England,* Edward Gibbon's *The History of the Decline and Fall of the Roman Empire,* and the early works of Charles Dickens. They also subscribed to monthly magazines such as Horace Greeley's *Weekly Tribune* and *The Atlantic Monthly,* William's favorite. Unusual for the time, the elder McKinley preferred to eat dinner in the evening, not at noon, so as to spend time with his family. For an hour each evening they would gather in the sitting room, children on the floor, parents on creaking wooden chairs, reading aloud to one another.[16]

As a student in Niles's one-room schoolhouse, McKinley was more dedicated and hardworking than brilliant. Eager to please, he threw himself into memorizing dates for history tests, or copying and reciting texts. Later, after the family had moved to Poland, Ohio, so as to take advantage of better schools, McKinley displayed his characteristic work ethic by engaging in a friendly competition with a boy across the street to see who would be the last to turn his lamp off in the evening and the first one up in the morning. Though gifted in mathematics, he thrived on languages, including Latin, Greek, and a favorite, Hebrew. "It was seldom that his head was not in a book," one acquaintance noted.[17]

McKinley would have made a fine university student and did briefly attend Allegheny College in Meadville, Pennsylvania, where he was noted for his debating skills and "winsome" personality. Deft at putting faces with names, he collected friends easily. But his education was cut short by a nervous ailment—the details remain unclear—and he returned home to convalesce before the end of his first term. It was a devastating setback for the promising young scholar. "I felt so much discouraged," he said, "that it seemed I never would look forward to anything again. . . . I was discontented for many months. It seemed to me that my whole life was to be spoiled by my unfortunate nervousness."[18] His hopes for returning to his studies were dealt a further blow when his father was obliged to take on debts run up by a brother. Not only would there be no money for his education, but William was forced to take jobs as a schoolteacher and at the post office to help make ends meet.

McKinley might well have found a way back to the classroom eventually, but like most men of his generation, his life story made an abrupt turn with the coming of the Civil War. Partly out of peer pressure from patriotic neighbors, and partly out of admiration for President Lincoln, McKinley decided to enlist and in June 1861 joined the Twenty-third Ohio Volunteer Infantry Regiment.

For a mama's boy who had never been away from home longer than a few months, McKinley found military life surprisingly agreeable. His comrades noted that he took to soldiering naturally and mastered *Hardee's Tactics,* the army's standard infantry manual, "with little effort." Each morning he rose at four thirty to help make breakfast— simple fare such as biscuits, bacon, and black coffee—and was a stalwart in the regimental religious group known as "the psalm-singers of the western reserve."[19] Although army life offered many temptations for a young man, McKinley apparently remained steadfast to the strict religious teachings of his mother. In one letter home he wrote: "It is by no means essential that an individual who has enlisted to defend his country should forget his early teachings and bury his parents' instruction in oblivion. No—he can continually keep them before his mind, even remembering that they are like 'burning glasses, whose collected rays point with warmth and quickness to the heart.' "[20]

After just a few months in uniform, the handsome young soldier was promoted to the rank of commissary sergeant, a position of considerable responsibility in acquiring and preparing food for up to one thousand men. Yet the duty was a rear-echelon job that offered more in the way of creature comforts—a wagon that transported his personal belongings, plenty of food, and the ability to hobnob with officers—than any chance of battlefield glory. Clearly McKinley wanted more from the war. When an opportunity to see action came along, on September 17, 1862, he seized it. Civil War veterans would long remember the date with a cold shudder, for it marked the Battle of Antietam—the bloodiest one-day battle in American history.

Men of the Twenty-third began their day well before dawn and they made their way through woods and open fields until midafternoon, when the advance stalled near Rohrbach Bridge (later known as Burnside's Bridge), a three-arched stone structure that spanned Antietam Creek near Sharpsburg, Maryland. For the troops, it promised to be a long and uncomfortable evening. Their haversacks were for the most part empty of food and water, and many had not even had time for breakfast that morning. Yet resupply looked like a suicide mission.

McKinley, however, was not one to be easily deterred from his duties. Ignoring the warnings of two officers, he loaded his chuck wagon with cooked meat, beans, crackers, and a barrel of coffee, climbed aboard, and whipped his team of mules over a shallow hill and directly into enemy fire. One hungry soldier later described the wagon approaching the creek at "breakneck speed, through a terrific fire of musketry and artillery that seemed to threaten annihilation to everything within its range." Yet McKinley pushed on, making it to the sloping bank that sheltered the Union troops, where he triumphantly jumped down from his seat to a boisterous welcome. One severely wounded soldier was heard to say "God bless the lad."[21]

Impressed, too, was Rutherford B. Hayes, a senior officer in McKinley's regiment. Hayes advised a fellow officer to "keep your eye on that young man. There is something in him." And so was born a formative relationship with a valuable mentor. Hayes saw to it that McKinley was granted a commission; he would later make him a member of his staff. In 1877, after McKinley worked for a time as a lawyer in Canton, both men went to Washington—Hayes as the newly elected president of the United States and McKinley as a freshman congressman.

War hero, self-made man, a good Christian—these were qualities that attracted the men and women marching up Market Avenue North that summer. There was another topic, however, that consumed even more of their thinking: the economy. The advance of American industry was everywhere to see. Each day, factories stretched farther into the countryside, new smokestacks pierced the sky, and the carriages of freshly minted moguls rattled down the streets, their occupants engrossed in the morning's *Wall Street Journal*.

No manifestation of the changes sweeping the county was greater than the spread of railroads. Where prior to the Civil War, when iron rails timidly penetrated the interior of the continent, by the 1890s virtually everyone lived within earshot of a train whistle. In 1890, the tracks stretched 164,000 miles, nearly five times their length in 1865.[22] Railroads were the largest companies, the biggest employers, and the hungriest consumers of key resources such as steel and coal and land. Completing the transcontinental railroad was one of the most celebrated symbols of American achievement. Telegraphs carried blow-by-blow reports from Promontory Summit, Utah, on May 10, 1869, when railroad tycoon Leland Stanford, who would later found a San Francisco Bay Area university of some note, pounded a golden spike into tracks connecting the Pacific and Atlantic coasts. Soon, strings of telegraph wire suspended above the tracks buzzed with everything from birthday greetings to purchase orders. By 1883, Western Union's network included 400,000 miles of wire carrying forty million messages a year.[23]

Steel output, the other major barometer of national economic prowess in the late nineteenth century, likewise provided ample evidence of America's growing might. About one hundred years had passed since, according to legend, hunter Necho Allen had discovered anthracite coal in Pennsylvania when his campfire ignited the rocks around it. Now, Pittsburgh looked like "hell with the lid off" as the fires of hundreds of furnaces—glass factories, iron mills, steel rolling mills, lead factories, and oil refineries—illuminated the evening sky.[24] Between 1860 and 1896, output of bituminous coal alone skyrocketed from 9 million tons to 138 million.[25]

Maybe it was the sheer thrill of watching their country being transformed on an almost daily basis, but there was also something about this period that seemed to capture the imaginations of ordinary Americans. At no time in the nation's history had there been such a flowering of new products.

Consumer goods that debuted during the era still fill store shelves: Cream of Wheat, Aunt Jemima pancake mix, Kellogg's Shredded Wheat, Juicy Fruit gum, Pabst Blue Ribbon beer, Coca-Cola, and Quaker Oats. Mass production led to standardized brands and massive ad campaigns that created the consumer society as we now know it. H. J. Heinz erected a fifty-foot electric pickle in Times Square in 1896 in an effort to become a household name. Cincinnati's Procter & Gamble rescued housewives from hours of boiling animal fat when it launched a nationwide $11,000 advertising blitz to promote Ivory Soap. Technology helped build bigger markets as well. Thanks to speedy delivery by newly introduced railway refrigerator cars, New Yorkers could regularly savor steaks from the slaughterhouses of Chicago. James Bonsack's automatic cigarette-making machine enabled James Duke's factory to turn America into a nation of smokers, puffing some four billion cigarettes per year by 1900.

European tourists marveled at the inventive spirit they encountered. Whether streetcars, farm implements, or bathroom conveniences, American products seemed more cunning and resourceful. Writing in *McClure's Magazine*, British journalist Henry Norman observed, "On this visit, I noticed a new fitting on the wall of the bathroom. It was an electric heater for curling irons! To you this perhaps seems to be a very ordinary kind of thing. I stood before it in amazement." He continued: "In Europe when we have a certain 'fitment' in house or office that serves its purpose well, we are satisfied with it and go on with our work. If anybody comes along with something better we look upon him as something of a nuisance. The thing we have is quite good enough. In America it seems that a man will try an object one day and throw it away the next for something a trifle more convenient or expeditious."

New ideas abounded: baseball cards, carpet sweepers, safety razors with disposable blades. Bicycling, once a pastime for the well-to-do, became an everyman activity in 1890 when the "safety bike" came out with two wheels the same size. Montgomery Ward, who started as a Chicago hardware salesman, pioneered the mail-order business and transformed how Middle America shopped. Crammed into the 623-page 1895 edition of his catalog was everything from Windsor pianos to saddles to ladies' summer cloaks in more than forty styles.[26]

Perhaps there was no more precise measure of American ingenuity than the patents registry. The total number of filings soared sixfold from 12,688 in 1871 to 72,470 in 1896, the year of the election.[27] All told, output of manufactured goods had nearly tripled in the twenty years since the Civil War.[28] While the volume of U.S. manufactured output ranked fourth in the world in 1860, it had climbed to first place by 1894.[29] The United States had now replaced Britain as the "workshop of the world." Henry Adams, the writer and historian, observed that so much change was concentrated in the second half of the century that "the American boy of 1854 stood nearer the year 1 than to the year 1900."

Inevitably, such dramatic expansion made a lot of people rich. This new wealth bred such crazy excesses that economist Thorstein Veblen was driven to coin the term "conspicuous consumption" to make sense of what he saw around him. Up and down New York's Fifth Avenue, captains of industry and their wives busily attempted to best one another with a building boom that transformed the boulevard into a crass approximation of the Loire Valley as one mansion after another was erected in the style of French chateaux. Dubbed "millionaire's row," Fifth Avenue became one of New York's prime tourist attractions. Horse-drawn omnibuses filled with gawking visitors clattered down the well-worn cobblestones as drivers pointed out landmark abodes. One of the most popular sights stood between Fifty-seventh and Fifty-eighth streets. There loomed the imposing home of Cornelius Vanderbilt II. Designed by the coveted architect George B. Post, the chateau built in the style of Henry IV's housed a dining room stretching forty-five feet. The ceiling was made of opalescent glass and was studded with jewels. Oak beams were inlaid with mother-of-pearl.[30] French prime minister Georges Clemenceau, who lived for a time in New York and New England, was aghast at what he saw. He would remark that the United States had gone from a stage of barbarism to one of decadence without achieving any civilization between the two.[31]

For better and for worse, enabling this economic miracle had been McKinley's most important mission since he first entered Congress. For him, business was not something distinct from the rest of society that had to be regulated and controlled. Industry *was* America. It was how people secured their livelihoods, it drove innovation and improved standards of living, and it was making the nation great. McKinley chose to promote this agenda by mastering perhaps the most important industrial issue of the 1880s—tariffs. Though Democrats saw trade barriers as causing higher prices and therefore harmful to the common man, for McKinley they offered a vital means to protect young American companies from the ravages of established European rivals.

He seemed fated for the job. McKinley's hometown, Niles, Ohio, had been named for Hezekiah Niles, a pioneer of American protectionism.[32] And as he grew older, the symbolism took on more tangible forms. The Ohio counties of Stark, Mahoning, and Columbiana were peppered with furnace mills and other industries that had flourished under, even owed their existence to, long-standing trade barriers.[33] With his maiden speech before Congress in April 1878, McKinley firmly established his protectionist credentials. "We ought to take care of our own Nation and her industries first. We ought to produce for ourselves as far as practicable, and then send as much abroad as is possible—the more the better. If our friends abroad think this position illiberal, they have only to bring their capital and energy to this country, and then they will share with us equally in all things."[34] Twelve years later, in 1890, the same thinking catapulted McKinley into the national spotlight when he authored the most protective collection of trade barriers in American history to that time—legislation that would become known as the McKinley Tariff.

What truly marked McKinley as an ally of business, however, was the company he kept—not that he harbored any desire to join the captains of industry as they summered on Long Island or yachted along the Potomac. Neither he nor they would have been comfortable mixing in such a rarefied atmosphere. Rather, it was one man, Mark Hanna, who linked him to Wall Street and would become inseparably intertwined with McKinley for years to come.

Hanna, a fellow Ohioan with a pleasant round face, a thin comb-over, and a snorting laugh, was a self-made man who embodied much of the American spirit of the era, if not a few of its rougher edges. Overweight from an unhealthy diet that included a constant supply of sweets, Hanna strode quickly and purposefully with an inelegant gait, moving about on his short legs with clipped strides that revealed a greater desire to get someplace than concern for how he looked getting there. He disdained fine food and was infamous for his taste for corned beef hash breakfasts prepared according to a recipe he had devised while working in iron ore camps in Duluth years before.[35]

Having earned a fortune in coal and iron, Hanna forged a diverse empire that included a newspaper, *The Cleveland Herald*, a streetcar line (which he rode every day from his house on Franklin Avenue to his office), and a bank, the Union National. Almost on a whim, he also purchased a theater in Cleveland, considered the largest and most handsome in the city. As his biographer Herbert David Croly wrote: "He always played fair, even if he did not always play politely; and when he sat in a game he usually won, and he usually occupied or came to occupy a seat at the head of the table."[36]

One game that Hanna found especially captivating was politics, though true to form it was a contest he entered only at the highest levels. Preferring the role of kingmaker to vying for the crown himself, Hanna adopted upwardly mobile political ingénues the way an heiress supports starving artists. He recognized in McKinley a figure worthy of his attentions.

The two had first met during the Republican convention of 1888 and quickly discovered in each other qualities they admired. Hanna stood in awe of McKinley's political skills and his loyalty. McKinley respected Hanna's business acumen and boundless energy. Indeed, it was Hanna's financial skill that probably saved McKinley's political career three years before the election he now contested. In 1893 McKinley nearly went bankrupt when a friend whose debts he had agreed to back went insolvent. Through no fault of his own other than unwise generosity, McKinley was suddenly on the hook for more than $100,000 (a little over $2.5 million today[37]), a sum he could not possibly pay. Organized by Hanna, McKinley's moneyed political supporters refused to let one admittedly large slipup derail their man and set about raising money to bail the promising future candidate out. Many contributions came from ordinary voters, but the power brokers ultimately saved him. Henry Clay Frick of Carnegie Steel contributed $2,000. The Illinois Steel Company added $10,000; George Pullman, maker of railway cars, chipped in $5,000; and Philip Armour, the meatpacker, ponied up $5,000 as well.[38]

In the years that followed, as the relationship flourished, left-leaning newspapers gleefully savaged McKinley as an unwitting stooge to Hanna the money man. A series of cartoons by Homer Davenport in the *New York Journal* depicted Hanna as a fat, crafty man wearing suits covered with dollar signs, the buttons of his vest straining under a bloated gut. In one cartoon, he grips a bull-snake whip resting on a skull entitled "labor." A dwarfed, grumpy-looking McKinley is tucked in a belt, his feet shackled. "He [Hanna] has McKinley in his clutch as ever did hawk have chicken, and he will carry him whither he chooses," the *New York Journal* wrote. "Hanna and the others will shuffle him and deal him like a deck of cards."[39]

That much the opposite was true mattered not to the Democrats. While McKinley valued Hanna's advice, it was Hanna who took the orders and acted "just a shade obsequious in McKinley's presence." H. H. Kohlsaat, a Chicago newspaperman, wrote that Hanna's attitude was "always that of a big, bashful boy toward the girl he loves." McKinley enjoyed gently teasing Hanna, urging him at a Sunday concert, for example, to sing more loudly, even though he had a terrible voice. At a Yale vs. Princeton football game, Hanna was much impressed when a couple of students pointed in McKinley's direction and asked, "Who is that distinguished looking man, the one that looks like Napoleon?"[40]

———

McKinley may have put great store in the American economy in the latter decades of the nineteenth century, but one unmistakable fact remained that tainted its dazzling achievements. Economic growth came not in a smooth, upward trajectory, but in a series of gut-wrenching collapses and dizzying recoveries that exacted a terrible toll on the workforce. As the presidential campaign of 1896 gathered pace, the country still had not recovered from the latest collapse, the great financial panic of 1893. Ignited by the bankruptcy of the Philadelphia and Reading Railroad, the banking system had nearly imploded. Prices for every manner of consumer good steadily fell, part of the longest and worst spell of deflation the country has ever seen. Hundreds of financial institutions failed, and thousands of businesses went under. Unemployment rose to more than 20 percent in some cities. Tramps seemed to spring from the earth, hopping trains from city to city in search of work, or to flee the scene of a rising number of petty crimes. "Never before," wrote *The Commercial and Financial Chronicle* in August 1893, "has there been such a sudden and striking cessation of industrial activity."[41]

If there was one man who could exploit such economic implosions, it was the Democrat William Jennings Bryan. Where McKinley stood for the establishment, the thirty-six-year-old Bryan was a populist, a westerner from Nebraska, an outsider. For him, the campaign was a moral crusade, one in which he reveled in contrasting the conditions of the working poor with McKinley and the Republicans. "One of the most important duties of government is to put rings in the noses of hogs," he said, referring to the need to control fat-cat Republicans. Speaking from on top of a manure spreader in one farm state, he quipped, "This is the first time I have ever spoken from a Republican platform."[42] He was, his supporters liked to say, their "Nebraska cyclone."

Bryan was so removed from the power circles of his own party that any hope of earning their trust had initially seemed preposterous—until they heard him speak. Introduced to a crowd of twenty thousand delegates at the Democratic Party's national convention on July 9,

1896, Bryan sprinted down the aisle toward the stage, vaulting up the steps to the speaker's rostrum two at a time. With theatrical flair, he tossed his head back, thrust one leg forward, and extended a hand toward the crowd demanding their silence so not a word would be wasted.[43]

In a soft baritone that lent credibility beyond his years, Bryan painted a picture of a desperately unfair social order, one that pitted "idle holders of idle capital" against the "struggling masses." Time and again the audience erupted with cheers and applause, furiously waving handkerchiefs that turned the floor into a sea of white. Attacking McKinley for his defense of the gold standard, which he argued restricted growth in the money supply and drove prices down, Bryan asked what was wrong with backing the dollar with silver as well, a theory that he hoped would generate a healthy level of inflation and aid farmers, who formed the backbone of his constituency. When he reached his closing remarks, Bryan extended his arms as if he were being crucified, froze for what witnesses claimed was a full five seconds, and uttered one of the most famous lines of nineteenth-century politics: "You shall not press down upon the brow of labor this crown of thorns, you shall not crucify mankind upon a cross of gold." The next day, party delegates still hoarse from their thundering ovation gave Bryan the nomination.

As the campaign gathered pace in August, Bryan's youth and energy revealed themselves in ways that McKinley could not hope to match. While McKinley stayed at home, sleeping in his own bed and convincing himself he was dignified and above the fray, Bryan engaged voters on four major campaign trips. Despite a heat wave throughout the Midwest, throngs of eager supporters flocked to railway stations to welcome him. On one trip, crowds were so large in Columbus, Toledo, and South Bend that there weren't buildings large enough to accommodate them, so he delivered his speeches in open fields.[44] Farmers traveled as much as a hundred miles by foot, bicycle, horseback, or carriage to hear him speak. Scores of babies were named after him. On a second foray, his show traveled through the Northeast, where he addressed seventy-five thousand people in Boston.[45] His endurance quickly became legendary. Delivering up to thirty-six speeches a day, he taught himself to fall asleep in minutes, fortifying himself with catnaps on the floor of his train. Unable to take regular baths while on the road, Bryan would strip off his clothes between speeches and rub his body with gin to mask the scent of his own sweat, leaving him smelling "like a wrecked distillery."[46] By the time the campaign was over, Bryan estimated that he had traveled 18,009 miles, delivering six hundred speeches in twenty-seven states to some five million people.[47]

The first polls in 1896 revealed that Bryan had taken the lead and was already projected to hang on to it. Some Republicans feared that McKinley could even lose Ohio, his home state. "We could have beaten an old-fashioned Democratic nomination and ticket without half trying, but the new movement has stolen our thunder," wrote Senator Eugene Hale of Maine.[48]

Hanna pleaded with McKinley to mimic Bryan's stump-speech technique, warning that defeat was imminent if he didn't. Still, McKinley would not budge from Canton. "I am going to stay here and do what campaigning there is to be done," he told Hanna, arguing that Bryan had an unbeatable knack for relating to the common man. "If I took a whole train, Bryan would take a sleeper, if I took a sleeper, Bryan would take a chair car, if I took a chair car, he would ride a freight train. I can't outdo him, and I am not going to try."[49] Stunned at Bryan's popularity, the stock market swooned and McKinley's base of support evaporated. Hanna reported glumly after a fund-raising trip in the August heat of Chicago and New York that the financial outlook for McKinley's campaign was bleak and they would have to scale back their plans.[50] John Hay saw industrialists who should have been working hard for McKinley checking out of the campaign. "[Bryan] has succeeded in scaring the goldbugs out of their five wits," Hay wrote to a friend on September 8, 1896. "If he had scared them a little, they would have come down handsome to Hanna. But he has scared them so blue that they think they had better keep what they have got left in their pockets against the evil day."[51]

With a full white beard and a balding scalp, James Hill roamed the corridors of his home in St. Paul, Minnesota, in the late summer of 1896, stewing over the Republicans' troubles. "Home" for Hill was not a concept many Americans would have understood. The massive red sandstone building at 240 Summit Avenue looked more like a hotel than a house. Some twenty-two fireplaces warmed him during cold Midwestern winters, sixteen crystal chandeliers lit his way to dinner, and thirteen bathrooms stood ready to relieve any sudden calls of nature.

Undeterred by a childhood of modest means and limited education, Hill had built himself into an overachieving businessman. He established a flourishing anthracite coal business in St. Paul, served as a banking executive, and constructed a railroad network, earning the sobriquet "Empire Builder" in local headlines. He personally scouted a rail route over the Rocky and Cascade mountains, traveling by horseback for weeks in the wilderness. The line, finished in 1893, became the Great Northern Railway, running 1,700 miles from St. Paul to Seattle.

A Democrat, Hill watched with growing alarm as his party painted his economic class as greedy tyrants. Bryan, he concluded, simply could not be allowed to become president. And as a man of considerable power, Hill was in a position to do something about it. Although on the opposite end of the political spectrum, he knew Mark Hanna from old business dealings and believed he could help him with McKinley's campaign. Hanna may have been an astute strategist, Hill thought, but he lacked the gravitas needed to convince America's financiers to commit their precious money to McKinley's cause. Hill, on other hand, was a well-known figure on Wall Street, having worked on railroad ventures with men such as J. P. Morgan.

During the week of August 15, 1896, Hill dressed Hanna in a convincing gray suit and led him over the length and breadth of Manhattan. Tracked by a bevy of reporters, the pair stepped out of their carriage at one stately address after another—the House of Morgan, the Pennsylvania Railroad offices, the investment bank Kuhn, Loeb & Co. Among the brass knobs and potted palms and polished wood, Hill assured his peers that the Republicans could still win this election. He reminded bankers, as if any reminder were needed, of one scary piece of the Democratic platform: the inflationary perils of silver. As any good fund-raiser knows, the easiest way to collect money is to have the rich ask one another on your behalf, and soon William Rockefeller was twisting arms from his house in the Hudson Valley. Cornelius Bliss personally traveled in his closed carriage around the southern tip of Manhattan. "The feeling about Mr. H. has changed," wrote Wall Street attorney William Beer to a friend on August 20. "He has made a lot of these people see that he knows what he is doing."[52]

But even more important, indeed pivotal to the election, was Hill's reputation as a devout Democrat. When he and Hanna appeared in corporate boardrooms, they represented much more than the pleadings of the Republican Party. It was a bipartisan effort to fight the silver movement. Suddenly, corporate treasuries that previously had lain untapped in political campaigns because of the split party allegiances of directors—there were, it appears, at least a few Democrats on corporate boards—were thrown open to the benefit of a single party. For the Republicans it was a whole new source of funds that far exceeded private donations.[53]

One by one, Big Business opened the vaults. Standard Oil contributed $250,000, as did J. P. Morgan. The great meatpacking houses of Chicago were reported to have forked over $400,000. Attempting to systematize the contributions, Hill and Hanna convinced banks and trust companies to sign on to a formula by which they would contribute one-quarter of 1 percent of their capital.[54] Officials at the New York Life Insurance Company and the Equitable companies later admitted that they gave large portions of their clients' premiums to the Republican cause. Hanna was emboldened. When a few Wall Street types attempted to get off with only a $1,000 contribution, Hanna barked that the men were a "lot of God-damn sheep" and that it would serve them right if Bryan "kicked them to hell and gone."[55]

As Republican boosters pulled wad after wad of bills out of their office safes, Hanna organized the first comprehensive mass mailing in American political history. Booklets, pamphlets, posters, and ready-to-print newspaper and magazine articles on McKinley were distributed to even the most isolated communities by overflowing train cars. The *Review of Reviews* reported that the 250 million Republican documents printed during this one campaign exceeded the sum of everything produced since the founding of the party by more than 50 percent. Lithographs, cartoons, and posters displayed McKinley as the "advance agent of prosperity," while cartoons in *Harper's Weekly* painted Bryan as an anarchist and an Antichrist.[56] Immigrants were a particular target and materials were prepared in a multitude of languages: German, French, Spanish, Italian, Swedish, Norwegian, Danish, Dutch, Hebrew, and English. Five million families got material once a week, much of it targeted at the West, where the Republicans were weakest. The Republican Party's regional headquarters were showered with money. Lunching with his Chicago campaign manager Charles Dawes in September, Hanna handed over an envelope containing fifty $1,000 bills, the contribution from a single railroad.[57]

Altogether, the Republican Party is thought to have raised $3.5 million, twice what it had collected in 1892.[58]

Now fully engaged in the election, business leaders took innovative and, the Democrats would say, unscrupulous steps to push McKinley's candidacy. Railroads stuffed statements in pay envelopes, warning that business would grind to a stop if Bryan were elected. "Men, vote as you please," the head of the Steinway piano works said, "but if Bryan is elected tomorrow, the whistles will not blow Wednesday morning."[59] On September 5, 1896, the McCormick Machine companies notified employees that they would shut down if Bryan won.[60] Big insurance companies in New York and Connecticut dispatched local agents to individual farmers in Iowa, Indiana, and Illinois to tantalize them with five-year low-interest loan extensions if McKinley prevailed.[61]

Other large companies employed "contingent deals" to aid their candidate, placing orders with manufacturers under the proviso that they would be canceled if McKinley lost. On August 24, 1896, the Sargent & Greenleaf company of Rochester, New York, one of the largest lock and safe manufacturers, received an order for $4,000 on the condition of a McKinley victory. "If Bryan wins, the order is not to be filled," the customer warned. It marked a historic shift in the role of business in American politics. William E. Chandler, a former Republican National Committee chairman, would later write of the 1896 election: "Four years ago for the first time corporations began to make political contributions directly from their corporate treasuries. Prior to that time no such thing would have been tolerated. In every corporation there were minority directors who would have arrested any such contributions by going to law, if necessary."[62]

While the Republican Party was rolling in cash, the Democrats were floundering. On August 22, 1896, Democratic Party national chairman James K. Jones wrote an open letter pleading for funds: "No matter in how small sums, no matter by what humble contributions, let the friends of liberty and national honor contribute all they can to the good cause."[63] His top fund-raiser, William Randolph Hearst, offered to match contributions dollar for dollar but eventually handed over a scant $40,901.20, a drop in the bucket compared to the Republican haul.[64] So short of funds were the Democrats that in the early stages of the campaign, Bryan had to make all his own travel arrangements, ride on normal trains, and even carry his own luggage.[65] "We could have raised $100,000 four years ago easier than we can raise ten now," Senator Henry M. Teller of Colorado said.[66] All told, the Democrats were believed to have collected $425,000.

Around the country, Democrats watched in horror as anecdotal evidence mounted that the Republican strategy was swaying voters. One man entered the Democratic headquarters in Chicago loudly sobbing that he had been threatened with dismissal because he was a leader in the local campaign.[67] "If I were a working man and had nothing but my job, I am afraid when I came to vote I would think of Mollie and the babies," Senator Teller admitted to colleagues. Opinion polls also showed McKinley was closing ground on Bryan and even overtaking him. Iowa, for example, had in early September appeared to be safely in Bryan's hands. But when a second survey was conducted six weeks later—one that followed a massive Republican blitz—it was discovered that McKinley was the state's new most-favored candidate.[68] By late September the betting public had also made up its mind. Oddsmakers Ullman & Ranking installed McKinley as a two-and-a-half-to-one favorite.

On October 31, 1896, just days before the election, New Yorkers witnessed a most unusual street protest. An unlikely army of millionaires, lawyers, journalists, and university professors marched shoulder to shoulder in their bowler hats and overcoats from the Battery in lower Manhattan to Fortieth Street to voice their support for the gold standard. All told, one hundred thousand people made the journey, cheered on by a quarter million spectators lining the sidewalks several rows deep. For a *New York Times* reporter, it was a moving sight, the cream of New York society taking to the streets on behalf of McKinley, accompanied by one hundred bands, chanting like college students and lustily singing favorites such as "The Star-Spangled Banner," "Rally Round the Flag," and "John Brown's Body."

"Never before in the world's history have so many citizens in time of peace in any country rallied to march under the country's flag," the *Times* gushed. "Never before in this nation's history have so many flags been waved as were waved by the army that mustered in the streets of New York City yesterday."[69]

Several days later, on November 3, 1896, Americans eagerly cast their votes in what had become one of the most captivating presidential campaigns in the nation's history. They rushed to the polls in record numbers, so enthusiastic that in many towns and cities most ballots were cast before lunch. Carriages that political parties made available to transport the faithful stood idle by the afternoon, their work done. The *Iowa State Register* noted that Des Moines had "never before witnessed an election in which the voters were got out with so little effort." *The Pittsburgh Post* reported that little business had been transacted that day: "The streets were only sprinkled with people and altogether a sort of Sunday air pervaded the old city and the North side." Not until 1908 would as many ballots be cast in a presidential election again.[70]

As the workday ended and the process of ballot counting commenced, crowds began to gather on street corners and in newspaper offices. In the larger cities, newspapers projected the results onto hastily erected canvas screens with stereopticon projectors. In Chicago, twenty-five thousand people swarmed to the Coliseum to watch an election-night show sponsored by the *Tribune.* In Philadelphia an estimated one hundred thousand people surged up and down its main avenues, one "callow youth" blowing horns with such frequency that "all his neighbors in the crowd wished that they might be transported . . . to some foreign isle." In San Francisco, someone hooked up a steam whistle that, with every report for McKinley, was sounded so that it could be heard for several blocks. In Atlanta, Bryan boosters braved a steady rain, cheering what few reports came in for their candidate.

At McKinley's home on Market Avenue North in Canton, fans packed the yard and the adjoining streets as they had throughout the campaign. Whistles blew insistently; chilled boosters lit small bonfires, boys climbed nearby trees. McKinley came out to acknowledge the throng once, but realizing he couldn't possibly be heard, simply smiled, waved, and went back inside to wait out the night in his office with a few close friends. Outside the door, the house hummed with the clicking of specially installed long-distance telephone lines and telegraph machines. Excited clerks rushed about with the most recent results. As each new report came in, McKinley added the numbers to columns on sheets of light green paper, figuring and refiguring how close he was to winning the election. During lulls, he puffed on cigars or walked across the hall to the parlor where Ida kept a vigil with her knitting.

As expected, McKinley easily carried most of New England and the eastern seaboard down to Maryland. But as the evening wore on, a vast swath of twenty-one states, from North Dakota to Maine and Oregon and California, also fell into his grasp. Bryan, who should have been able to count on a solid result from the South, watched states such as West Virginia and Kentucky tilt Republican. In the electoral college, that added up to a decisive McKinley victory, 271 electoral votes to 176. Still, the election had been uncomfortably close. Bryan received 6.5 million votes, not far behind McKinley's 7.1 million.[71] According to one calculation, a change of 34,000 votes in Ohio, Indiana, and Kentucky could have given Bryan a majority in the electoral college.[72] Only long after friends had phoned in their congratulations did McKinley feel secure enough to go to bed. Before turning in, he and Ida went to Mother McKinley and shared the news. While they thought nobody was looking, they kneeled at her bed, Mother wrapping her arms around her son and daughter-in-law. "Oh God, keep him humble," she prayed.[73]

A QUIET MAN IN THE CORNER

As McKinley was gearing up for his 1896 campaign in Canton, some sixty miles away an enigmatic young man named Leon Czolgosz had become a regular at Dryer's bar, a working-class saloon at Third Avenue and Tod in Cleveland.[1] Standing a slender five foot seven and in his early twenties, Czolgosz—who also went by the name Fred Nieman—would carefully wipe his shoes before entering and take his usual seat by himself in the corner. He would order a meal and a drink from Mr. Dryer, or perhaps his wife, "a big, stout, rough-looking woman,"[2] and spread the daily newspapers out on his table. Eagerly flipping through the pages, he took a particular interest in articles about the labor movement while he slowly sipped his drink, intent on getting his money's worth.

In the view of the Dryers, Czolgosz was strange and difficult to fathom. Though a regular, Czolgosz would have nothing to do with the other patrons. While they laughed and played games, he remained stubbornly in his place, reading his papers or napping. When asked to join the other men for a hand or two of cards, he would demur. Only once, as far as anybody could remember, did he bring a friend to the bar. On days off, Czolgosz might spend all day, "thinking-like" and sleeping.[3] On the rare occasion when he did agree to share a meal with the Dryers, he ate little and barely spoke.

Yet the painfully shy Czolgosz did not draw much sympathy. The Dryers noted an edgy bitterness to him. He would snap at the slightest sign of teasing. When Mr. Dryer once ribbed him for being tight with his money and urged him to spend more freely, Czolgosz barked, "No, I have use for my money."[4] Other times, he displayed scant concern for those around him, even his own family members. One night, just outside the bar, a group of thugs accosted his brother Jake, who was returning from a dance, and threatened him with a knife. Dryer shouted to Czolgosz, "Aren't you going out to help your brother? He is in trouble."

But Czolgosz refused to budge. "No. If he will associate with those Polacks, he'll have to take the consequences," he replied, and returned to his paper. It was all too easy, the Dryers found, to dismiss Czolgosz as "rather stupid" and "dull-like."[5]

Yet such an assessment was mistaken. Czolgosz had remained in school until he was a teenager, longer than many of his social class. He was even ambitious enough to attend the Union Street School, a night program in Cleveland, for a time.[6] His boss at work had nothing but good things to say about his performance, and promotions had even come his way. While never destined to become rich, he was earning a respectable living. There was yet another quality that Czolgosz possessed that the Dryers failed to notice: He had developed an inquiring mind, and what he observed about his country moved him greatly.

For every tycoon smoking cigars wrapped in hundred-dollar bills, for every society woman who strapped a diamond-encrusted collar on her dog, for every playboy who spent the summer sailing Daddy's yacht, there were tens of thousands of seamstresses, coal miners, and assembly line workers for whom life was simply a battle for existence. Armies of exhausted men, women, and children—entire families in many cases—trudged through factory gates six and seven days a week, performing the same mind-numbing tasks for 10, 12, 14, and even 16 hours. Daily salaries were counted in quarters and dimes. One observer of life in the Pennsylvania coal mines described conditions as "one of unmitigated serfdom. Life is scarcely worth having under such circumstances."[7]

A startlingly high share of families struggled through such appalling conditions. By the end of the 1880s, a working-class family of five needed an annual income on the order of $500 to manage a respectable living. Skilled factory hands such as glass blowers and iron rollers could easily manage that threshold, some making more than $1,000 a year. Carpenters and machinists couldn't bring home such a paycheck yet managed to survive right around the subsistence point. For a staggering 40 percent of the workforce, however, those who toiled in factories without special skills, life was lived below the poverty level, a never-ending struggle to make ends meet.[8] A cigar maker in Cincinnati was asked how he, his wife, and three children lived on his earnings of $5 a week. "I don't live," he replied. "I am literally starving. We get meat once a week, and the rest of the week we have dry bread and black coffee."[9]

Just how so many people had deteriorated to this miserable state was hardly a mystery. Great leaps in industrial progress were partly to blame. New inventions and manufacturing techniques made it possible to produce more and more with fewer and fewer workers. In flour mills in the mid-1880s, for example, one person was able to do the work of what four men accomplished a few decades earlier. In machine tooling, a single boy had replaced ten skilled men. And in one Ohio mine, a manager stated that improved machines enabled 160 men to perform the work of 500.[10] At the same time, thousands of immigrants speaking German, Italian, Polish, Chinese, and other tongues emerged from the holds of ships at American seaports every week. In the thirty years prior to 1900, the number of wage workers in the United States more than doubled to eighteen million.

For factory managers facing severe competition in largely unregulated markets, workers represented nothing more than interchangeable cogs in the production process. As long as there was one person waiting for a job, managers concluded they were paying too much to the person already employed. Wages, not surprisingly, steadily declined. The earnings of furniture makers dropped 40 to 60 percent between 1873 and 1877. Textile workers saw their incomes drop 45 percent between 1873 and 1880. Most disheartening, there was little that working men and women could do about it. Standing up to the boss was a risky proposition. "I can hire one half of the work class to kill the other half," Jay Gould once boasted. With a personal fortune of $77 million at the time of his death, he was probably right.[11]

Unprotected by the government and ignored by their employers, workers were subject to every manner of danger. Lint-filled air in the textile mills of New England caused lung disease. Toxic chemicals were used with little safeguards. Bosses frequently locked seamstresses in stifling rooms, blithely ignoring the terrible risk of fire.[12] Outmoded safety equipment on trains made working on railroads one of the most dangerous jobs in the country, leaving thousands of men with crushed limbs or feet sliced off by rolling stock. In one textile mill, fines were imposed for being late, eating at the loom, washing hands, sitting down, and even taking a drink of water.

Most distressing was the plight of children. Families desperate for money sent their young ones to work rather than teach them to read and write. A New Jersey report in 1885 showed that of the 343,897 school-age children in the state, 89,254 received no formal education at all.[13] At textile mills, children were prized for their small fingers because they could more easily fix bobbins than adults. Nor did children receive any special consideration in the length of their workday. In the mills of Yorkville, New York, children under fourteen labored eleven hours a day. And in bakeries, kids as young as nine began work at 11 P.M. and helped prepare bread until 4 A.M.[14] Eight-year-olds were sent deep underground to work the coal mines of Pennsylvania and West Virginia and perished at an appalling rate. *The Luzerne Union* newspaper in Pennsylvania reported in January 1876 that "During the past week nearly one boy a day has been killed, and the public has become so familiar with these calamities that no attention is given them after the first announcement through a newspaper or a neighbor."[15]

Living conditions for the lowest rung of American workers were as miserable as the jobs they performed. Hundreds of thousands squeezed into ramshackle tenements that infested major cities—neighborhoods with names such as Kerosene Row, Poverty Gap, Hell's

Kitchen, and Bone Alley. All told, some 70 percent of New York City's population would squeeze into thirty-two thousand slum tenements by the end of the nineteenth century.[16]

The most noxious was New York's notorious Five Points neighborhood around the intersection of Anthony, Orange, and Cross streets in lower Manhattan. The stench alone was enough to overpower any stranger who took a wrong turn, what with the open sewers and dog and horse excrement that fouled the air. Rotting garbage slickened the sidewalks. The buildings, a warren of three- and five-story structures, were packed with grimy, sick, and desperate people. As many as a dozen might share a room less than ten feet square, often under roofs that leaked rain and snow.[17] Whether to save money or for fear of fire, landlords refused to install gas lighting in many of the buildings, leaving the interiors and steep staircases so dark that inhabitants had to light matches to walk in their own buildings.[18] In many dwellings, beds were little more than piles of rags or straw covered with a sheet. Those that did have bunks had to share them, sleeping head to toe and fighting over the covers. Sanitation and disease were terrible. Brick sewers were clogged for years at a time and drained into the soil. Hand pumps drew water from wells adjacent to backyard privies.[19]

The institutions that might protect workers were either unable or unwilling to grapple with the scale of the problem. Labor unions were still weak and ineffective. They flourished when the economy prospered and employees had bargaining power. Yet as soon as times turned tough again, employers used every means to break them. Where there had been thirty national unions before the financial panic of 1873, only nine would exist four years later.[20]

From their mahogany-lined boardrooms, the rich and powerful failed to see anything wrong in the disparity between rich and poor, or even to recognize the magnitude of the gulf. Andrew Carnegie, speaking at the Nineteenth Century Club at the end of 1887, said: "I defy any man to show that there is pauperism" in the United States. William Graham Sumner agreed that American wage earners could not be considered destitute. "It is constantly alleged in vague and declamatory terms that artisans and unskilled laborers are in distress and misery or are under oppression. No facts to bear out these assertions are offered."[21] Sugar magnate Henry Osborne Havemeyer summed up the feeling of many captains of industry when he described the country as being divided into two classes, "the industrious and those who wish to live on the industry of others. It is they who are without capital who are hostile to it."[22]

Czolgosz, like millions of working-class men, would have read such remarks with a disdainful snarl. His own life story, and that of his family, was one of hard work and risk taking. Yet they remained solidly anchored in the lower strata of American society with little prospect for ever breaking out.

Czolgosz's father, Paul, had been a member of the first big wave of ethnic Poles to immigrate to the United States, trudging off in the winter of 1872 from his home near the village of Gora, Prussia, leaving behind his wife, Mary, and three children until he got on his feet.[23]

There were plenty of reasons for Paul to think his lot would be improved in America. His brother had gone before him to Detroit and wrote that jobs abounded. Willing hands and backs were needed for a constantly expanding industrial base and, it must be noted, to replace striking American laborers who refused to accept ever lower wages. Shipping agents, anxious to recruit passengers, dazzled European peasants with tales of the new life that awaited them. Incredibly, they learned, land was virtually free for the taking in the West thanks to the Homestead Act of 1862.[24] States such as Michigan and Wisconsin even established European colonization bureaus to explain the practicalities of embarking on their new venture.[25]

While the Irish would later congregate in Boston and the Swedes in Minnesota and the Pacific Northwest, the Poles descended on the Midwest, especially its big cities, where the miseries of rural life could be forgotten and where massive factories were sucking in every able body they could find.

Bundled against the icy North Atlantic, Paul spent much of the voyage belowdecks in the company of his countrymen, playing cards and preparing for New Year's Eve, the last evening the passengers would spend together before arriving in the United States. One can only wonder what anxious thoughts passed through his mind as he made such a giant leap into the unknown. Paul spoke no English and offered no tangible skills. Yet true to his brother's letters, there were indeed jobs in Detroit. Within a couple of months, he found employment and an apartment in a three-story building at 141 Benton Street and was confident enough to send for Mary and their three children. Leon was born only a month after his mother waddled down the ship's gangway.

The Czolgosz family had it relatively good. Unlike the horrific crowding of New York tenement houses, they enjoyed at least a little elbow room at Benton Street in one of only two brick houses in the area. The Czolgoszes and their four children inhabited the first floor, a family named Smith the second, and the owner, a Mrs. Mincel and her mother, Mrs. Munro, lived on the third floor. Across the street the family could reminisce about folks back home with Jacob J. Lorkowski, who came from the same area.[26]

Paul, noted in the neighborhood as a good storyteller and skilled cardplayer, managed to secure jobs a step above the mindless factory work so many new arrivals fell into. He arose early each morning and headed off to what would become a variety of positions such as working on the loading docks. Mary, too, was spared the worst of the Industrial Revolution's horrors and would remain at home, taking in other people's laundry. Each morning she would descend the steps of their building and call on vegetable shops, butchers, and bakers, greeting neighbors in Polish, many of whom she would have seen in church the previous Sunday at the new St. Albertus parish.

Located on the western side of St. Aubin Street, the church was the pride of Detroit's fast-growing Polish community. Construction of the wood-framed building with its tall bell tower had begun in June 1872, paid for with $600 raised by the community's St. Stanislaus Kostka Society. Here Mary and Paul brought their new baby Leon to meet Father Gerick and be baptized into a life of assumed devotion to the Catholic Church.[27]

One day, perhaps in a copy of the *Detroiter Abend-Post,* Paul's glance rested on an advertisement for an opportunity to secure his own piece of land. Jobs were on offer in a place called Rogers City. And so began what would become a nomadic existence for young Leon that demonstrated his father's determination to realize the American dream.

Over the next two decades, the growing family would move time and again, from Rogers City to Alpena, Michigan, to Posen, Michigan, and then back to Alpena; to an area near Pittsburgh, to Cleveland, and finally to a farm in Warrensville, Ohio. Life was no doubt hard. In Alpena, a prosperous community of five thousand on Lake Huron's Thunder Bay, Paul held a number of jobs, working in a lumberyard, on the docks, and for a man named Fletcher, a member of one of the most prominent families in town. But his wages were a paltry 25 to 30 cents an hour.[28] That would have left the family with an income of between $520 and $624 a year by the time seasonal layoffs were taken into account, well below the $700 estimated to be a satisfactory wage for a family his size to live on.[29]

In Posen, less than thirty miles away on modern roads, prospects for the family must have seemed brighter. There, Polish immigrants like themselves were building up a new town from scratch. Despite the hardships of bitterly cold winters and exhausting physical work, these were happy times. Mary lost one baby, the little one lasting only a few weeks, but the family had grown to nine and was otherwise scarcely touched by tragedies of prolonged unemployment or disability that haunted so many immigrants. They might have stayed in the content little community, but death loomed over the family a second time.

One day in 1883, Mary, pregnant for the tenth time, felt the first contractions that signaled her baby was on its way.[30] Posen, little more than a hamlet, possessed scant medical facilities, but this was of little concern for Mary, who had been through this so many times before. Yet something went wrong. Although the baby, named Victoria, was born healthy and grew to be an attractive young woman, complications arose in the delivery.

Paul rushed his wife to Alpena where doctors performed increasingly futile examinations. At times Mary was well enough to climb out of bed and walk around, but family members often heard her talking to herself, saying once, for example, "My children, the time will come when you will have greater understanding and be more learned."[31] Unable to arrest her decline, doctors and her family watched helplessly as she steadily weakened. Finally, six weeks after Victoria's birth, Mary died.

Leon, by now ten years old, was a fast-growing boy. Despite being described as pale and of soft skin, he possessed a hearty constitution and was seldom sick. By all accounts, he was a bright youngster. His older brother Waldek would later say that at one school, Leon was "the best scholar of them all."[32] At home, he was obedient and well-behaved. Almost never, his father said, did Leon protest when he was reprimanded for some transgression. More than most people, his father thought, Leon seemed to think about his punishments.[33] The boy was also developing another personality trait. From even these early years, he preferred to keep his own company. While other boys might fish or play in the snow, Leon was inclined to remain very much to himself. As far as his father could tell, Leon did not have a single close playmate.[34]

═══╪═══

"THERE WILL BE NO JINGO NONSENSE"

President-elect McKinley and a cortege of family members and dignitaries followed black-robed Supreme Court justices along the marble
hallways leading from the Senate gallery to the east front of the Capitol building shortly after 1 P.M. on March 4, 1897. As the somber line
neared the doors, hearty cheering filled the corridor, growing to a
"great roar" as McKinley stepped out into the brilliant sunshine to take
the oath of office. Before him thirty to forty thousand people were
gathered on the plaza, some having waited for over three hours. So
dense was the crowd that it seemed to sway back and forth in unison
like "a great body of water."[1] Some of the more adventurous found
vantage points by sneaking onto the Capitol's stairs, lining up along
the roof, and even perching in leafless trees.

Striding the wooden steps of a temporary stage, McKinley made his
way to the rostrum, where a stiff breeze pulled at the flag bunting. His
brother Abner rushed about directing operators of kinetoscopes, Edison's latest invention, in an attempt to capture the inauguration in

moving pictures. As always, McKinley was supremely decked out for the occasion, although this time his clothes were chosen with symbolism in mind: His frock coat was made of domestic worsted wool, not imported, the newspapers were told. A Canton cobbler who had been a drummer boy at Gettysburg crafted his shoes.

McKinley took a seat in a red leather chair and turned to make sure members of his group were comfortable. Mother McKinley, spry and wiry at age eighty-seven, clutched a bouquet of roses. Unimpressed with the pomp and ceremony, she remained convinced that her precious son would have been better off joining the church and becoming a bishop. One sharp-eared bystander overheard McKinley's brother Abner remark the morning before the inauguration: "Mother, this is better than a bishopric."[2] President Cleveland, nursing his gout, was seated just to McKinley's right, his foot wrapped in a soft shoe.

Ida appeared unwell and failed to do justice to her royal-blue velvet grown and short sealskin cape. In fact, she nearly fell making her way to her seat and had to be supported by a member of the inauguration party. A *New York Times* reporter who watched her progress dismissed her difficulties as fatigue from the trip from Canton.[3] Her problems, however, ran much deeper.

The curious illness of Ida McKinley began in the spring of 1873, shortly before her second child was due. From the fine home where her parents lived on Market Avenue South, just down the road from her own house, word reached her on March 14 that her mother had died. Ida was staggered by the news and suffered through the remaining weeks of her pregnancy in despair. Weak and emotionally spent, Ida delivered her second daughter and family members hoped the new arrival would buoy her spirits. The baby, however, brought only more heartache when doctors discovered she suffered some sort of physical ailment that, as the weeks passed, became increasingly severe. The infant died five months later. Having lost two family members in short order, Ida descended into a black hole of depression and confusion. Why was God inflicting so much pain upon her? Seeking solace, she clung to her two remaining family members with all her emotional strength. She could not stand to be away from her husband for more than a few hours, and became ever more protective of her lovely first daughter, Katherine. Born on Christmas Day in 1871, Katie, as her parents called her, was a fair-haired girl with a serious face, and had become the focal point of the family. On warm summer evenings back in Canton before supper she would wait on the gate for her father to come, and she liked to sit on his lap listening to boyhood stories. Ida hired a photographer as well as a painter to capture her in oils.

No amount of parental protectiveness, however, could save a child from the many diseases crisscrossing the United States at the time, not the least of which was typhoid. With relentless savagery it swept through Canton and sent young Katie to her grave before her fourth birthday.[4]

The weight of three deaths was more than Ida could bear, leaving her physically and emotionally wrecked. For much of the rest of her life, fits and convulsions would strike without warning, the gruesome attacks including frothing at the mouth, incontinence, memory loss, and infantile behavior.[5] It is unclear to this day what exactly was wrong with Ida. Some historians have speculated a latent form of epilepsy was to blame, or perhaps the trauma of the three deaths had produced an emotional disorder that resulted in seizures. It is also not impossible that Ida exaggerated her ailment from time to time to excuse herself from unpleasant social obligations.

Whatever the cause, through the years, McKinley learned how to make the best he could of Ida's illness. In receiving lines, she sometimes sat rather than stood, "looking rather blankly at the procession passing in front of her." Ignoring protocol at official dinners, McKinley insisted that his wife be seated next to him so that he could help in the event of a sudden attack. These he handled with stunning calm. William Howard Taft remembered talking with the couple one day when he noted "a peculiar hissing sound" coming from Ida. McKinley quickly removed a handkerchief from his pocket and draped it over her face, continuing the conversation as if nothing had happened.[6] No expense was spared in looking for cures. At various times, Ida tried osteopathy, was sent to New York for a course of intensive medical treatment, and took bromides, the contemporary treatment for epilepsy.[7] The only thing that seemed to ease Ida's suffering was the company of her husband.

"Charming, beautiful and cultured when well, she seemed to be the ideal wife," wrote McKinley biographer H. Wayne Morgan.[8] "But an attack of nervous illness, however slight, made her pathetic and irritable, and at such times she was demandingly dependent on her husband." While McKinley was a congressman, visitors to his office at the Ebbitt House became accustomed to Ida calling him out of meetings on such trivial pretexts as soliciting his opinion on her clothes. She asked McKinley to sit for a portrait, which she hung near her bed so as to always be able to see him. Ever attentive to her needs, McKinley did all he could to feed her obsession. He would send her notes if detained on Capitol Hill and wrote her at least once a day when traveling outside Washington.[9] Even as president, McKinley made a point to see her several times in the morning and the afternoon and often had lunch with her.

The possessiveness bred no small amount of hostility toward anyone other than her husband and a small collection of family members and friends. On one occasion, an English visitor remarked to Ida that she liked America but preferred her native country. To that Ida answered icily, "Do you mean to say that you would prefer England to a country ruled over by my husband?"[10]

Despite the great burden that McKinley's wife had become, their love for each other never wavered. "The relationship between them was one of those rare and beautiful things that live only in tradition," friend Jennie Hobart wrote.[11] McKinley referred to Ida with such terms of endearment as "my precious love."[12] He also took time to learn about laces and jewelry and to share Ida's passion for flowers, though he preferred pink carnations to Ida's favorite, the rose. Many a night McKinley sat up with his wife in her stuffy room and gently read to her as she rested in an ornately carved rocking chair that she had treasured since childhood. On days when she felt better but unable to go out, he would quietly read the newspaper as she knitted, a hobby she pursued with such enthusiasm that over her lifetime she produced some five thousand pairs of socks.[13] Warning a guest what to expect before meeting Ida, McKinley once said, "Ida was the most beautiful creature I ever saw and the most gifted when I fell in love with her, a girl of almost twenty, and she married me. She is beautiful to me now."[14]

With Ida carefully watched over by friends on the rostrum, McKinley repeated the oath of office after Chief Justice Melville Fuller, resting his hand on a bible made of Ohio paper, bound in dark blue with a "fine line of gold around the outer edge."[15] Removing his top hat and frock coat, McKinley then turned to the expectant crowd. Affixing his glasses to his nose, a rare public admission of an imperfection, he reached into his coat pocket and retrieved the rolled text of his speech. Appearing "slightly nervous," a *New York Times* reporter thought, he referred cautiously to his notes as he began speaking.[16]

Gradually McKinley seemed to gain confidence and raised his voice so that the greater part of the tens of thousands gathered there could hear him. Not until midway through, however, did he mention the issue that would dominate his presidency. The country would "aim to pursue a firm and dignified foreign policy, which shall be just, impartial, ever watchful of our national honor." But, he added, "We want no wars of conquest; we must avoid the temptation of territorial aggression. War should never be entered upon until every agency of peace has failed; peace is preferable to war in almost every contingency."[17]

It was daring for an American president to speak of a "dignified foreign policy" with a straight face. The tradition of isolationism that had begun with George Washington and his warning against foreign entanglements retained a strong pull on the American psyche. The closest the United States came to defining a coherent international strategy was the Monroe Doctrine of 1823, which stipulated that any move by the Europeans to colonize in the Americas or interfere with countries there would be treated as an act of aggression by the United States.

Even that, however, amounted to little more than the hollow threats of a ninety-eight-pound weakling, which is how the rest of the world treated the United States. As late as the 1880s, foreign diplomats considered a posting in Washington a career ender. One German diplomat in Washington offered to take a pay cut if the foreign ministry would transfer him to Spain. Russia didn't even bother having an office in the United States for two years.[18] The U.S. Navy had long been a laughingstock. America's collection of ships, smaller than in 1799,[19] ranked twelfth largest in the world, trailing the likes of Turkey, Sweden and Austria.

This indifference seemed set to continue under McKinley. The new president had learned to conjugate a few foreign verbs as a student, but that was about as far as his interest in international affairs had ever gone. More important, McKinley seemed to completely lack the aggressive gene that drove the foreign policies of most European capitals in the nineteenth century. Many who had worked shoulder to shoulder with him in the House of Representatives over the years believed he was simply too amiable for the rough-and-tumble game of geopolitics.

The new congressman first arrived in Washington in 1876 and, along with Ida, settled into a modest two-bedroom suite at the Ebbitt House at the corner of Fourteenth and F streets. Even among the hotel's other residents who seldom saw him, McKinley quickly attained a reputation for earnest sobriety. He was typically the first one downstairs in the morning, striding through the lobby with a distinctive ramrod-straight posture to collect the newspapers and mail. Along the way, he would greet fellow residents and staff with his trademark friendliness. Everyone, it seemed, liked this new man from Ohio. Journalist Orlando Stealey, who lived across from McKinley at the Ebbitt House, later wrote of his unfailing good nature in almost biblical terms. "He was of kindly disposition, of no hatreds, and mistreated no one."[20]

Whether through Ida's influence or his own maturing sense of proper comportment, McKinley had acquired a taste for fine clothes and was always seen immaculately attired in a dark suit, a carnation in the lapel, and neatly ironed cuffs and collar. Glasses hung around his neck on a black string, though he was seldom caught with them on in photographs. In an age when most politicians and business figures wore a beard or mustache, he started each day ambidextrously shaving his face clean while hardly looking in the mirror, a skill he had learned in the army. After a hearty breakfast together, McKinley would offer an unwelcome good-bye to Ida and head off toward the Capitol.

The walk usually began in pursuit of his one real vice—a love for cigars. He would stop at the newsstand in front of his building to purchase a daily supply, an order that the newsboys learned to have ready in ample number.[21] One estimated that McKinley went through as many as fifty a week, more if Congress was keeping late hours. When not actually smoking, McKinley enjoyed chewing on a broken half and spitting out the remnants, a habit so frequently practiced that he excelled at hitting a cuspidor.

Unfailingly good-natured, McKinley quickly became one of the more popular members of the House. He reveled in swapping stories, as long as they were not dirty, prompting barbers to vie with one another to give him a trim.[22] He genuinely enjoyed jokes delivered at his own expense and gleefully poked fun at the profession of politics. One favorite was the politician who refused to be baptized by immersion because he didn't want to be out of the public's view that long. Only rarely did he publicly display what close friends claimed was a fine wit. Yet he could not always resist. In one debate, an opponent asserted that Republicans had rigged the economy so that any fool could get rich. "Permit me to inquire further, Doctor," McKinley asked, "why you are not a wealthy man?"

Such remarks were rare, however. McKinley's overriding trait was an unstinting affability. Even McKinley's adversaries found it hard to dislike the man. "My opponents in Congress go at me tooth and nail," said fellow congressman Tom Reed, "but they always apologize to William when they are going to call him names."[23] Rather than throwing himself into acrimonious posturing, a frequent tactic of ambitious young congressmen, McKinley seemed content simply to sit and listen. When debates became particularly heated, he would drop by the desk of a rival to offer a kind word and, later in his career, would rein in new members who he felt were excessively combative. Once, watching junior congressman John S. Wise erupt on the House floor, he urged caution. "Don't allow them to draw you into such controversies," he told Wise. "No good can come from it."[24]

As governor of Ohio between 1892 and 1896, a state notorious for its rough-and-tumble politics, McKinley stood out for his open mind and genteel demeanor. Confronted with labor unrest, so common in the decade, McKinley did not come down blindly in favor of industry as other Republicans might have, but encouraged business and labor leaders to negotiate.

——

As McKinley prepared for the White House in early 1897, all indications were that the same nonconfrontational, consensus-seeking habits would govern how he dealt with affairs of state. John Sherman, his selection for the post of secretary of state, had once been a powerful force in the Senate but was a shell of his former self, lacking both mental fortitude and a desire for adventures abroad. At age seventy-four, Sherman had devolved into a cranky old man whose fading hearing and memory made him an embarrassing choice for America's top diplomat. Indeed, it was an open secret around Washington that McKinley had selected the aging gentleman for political purposes—in order to open a Senate seat in his home state of Ohio, the job that Hanna had been eyeing and eventually received.

Foreign diplomats and members of Congress would soon learn that the real seat of power in American foreign policy belonged to the number two man in the State Department, a man who still possessed all his faculties but seemed no more ambitious. Exuding the appearance of a university professor, William R. Day was an old McKinley friend from Canton, a judge and country lawyer with no diplomatic experience and who had never traveled abroad. Day hadn't even wanted the job for fear it would pose a strain on his delicate health. He was well aware of his shortcomings.[25] "I see that the newspapers talk about the diplomacy of this administration as 'amateurish,' " Day once said, partly tongue in check. "And I must confess that it is."[26]

McKinley's single foray into the ranks of bolder men was made under duress and with serious misgivings. No sooner had he won the election than friends began pushing him to appoint a young aristocrat from New York for the important job of assistant secretary of the navy. The candidate, Theodore Roosevelt, was immaculately connected and possessed an undeniable interest in the job. He had written a book on the role the navy had played in the War of 1812 and had campaigned for McKinley in 1896. What's more, Roosevelt was dying to do anything other than his current job as president of the board of New York City police commissioners.

The thought of Roosevelt in such a plum position made McKinley shudder. "I want peace," he told a mutual friend when she lobbied him for Roosevelt. "And I am told that your friend Theodore—whom I know only slightly—is always getting into rows with everybody."[27]

Roosevelt also belonged to a group of jingoists who advocated a more aggressive approach to foreign affairs and encouraged the more prickly America that from time to time was starting to emerge. Only two years previously, Roosevelt had taken a view that McKinley abhorred. In 1895 the United States waded into a long-simmering dispute between Britain and Venezuela over who owned the resource-rich area around the Orinoco River separating Venezuela from the British colony of British Guiana. Outraged by the idea of the British throwing their weight around in the hemisphere, President Cleveland stated to Congress that the United States would consider it a "willful aggression upon its rights and interests" if Britain tried to occupy parts of Venezuela. Eager for the United States to enter a war, Roosevelt wrote a friend, "I don't care whether our sea coast cities are bombarded or not; we would take Canada." Later, responding to the reticence of bankers and industrial leaders who feared their business dealings would suffer in a war with Britain, Roosevelt added, "The antics of the bankers, brokers and Anglo-maniacs generally are humiliating to a degree. . . . Personally I rather hope the fight will come soon. The clamor of the peace faction has convinced me that this country needs a war."[28]

Ultimately it would take the combined lobbying of no fewer than twenty-five people to win Roosevelt the nomination, including Senator Henry Cabot Lodge and even Vice President Garret Hobart.[29]

Meeting with Carl Schurz, an avowed anti-imperialist, in the spring of 1897 at New York's Windsor Hotel, McKinley seemed to confirm a benign foreign policy. McKinley said, "Ah, you may be sure that there will be no jingo nonsense under my administration. . . . You need not borrow any trouble on that account."[30] He would also later remark that aggressive bullying such as forced annexation of foreign territory was nothing more than "criminal aggression." Just as at home, government of foreign lands depended on the consent of the governed. "Human rights and constitutional privileges must not be forgotten in the race for wealth and commercial supremacy," he said.[31]

Such remarks clearly were born of the president's predilections and upbringing. Yet ever a keen student of the public's mood, the president

understood that the ground upon which the country's historical isolationism stood was starting to shift. In the late 1880s there had been a
testy exchange with Germany over Samoa. In 1891, there had been
whispers of war with Chile over what had begun as a barroom brawl
in which American sailors had been killed. Filled with a growing sense
of its own importance, the United States was starting to develop an interest in what happened abroad.

It was, in fact, a continuation of the same forces that had helped
propel Americans across the North American continent. In 1845, journalist John O'Sullivan attached a name to America's relentless push
outward: Manifest Destiny. The idea that the Almighty had ordained
America for great things motivated leaders of the wagon trains headed
west. God, now the popular thinking went, had selected the United
States to lead the world out of the oppression of European monarchies
and the backwardness of still-developing countries into a new, enlightened age based on such values as freedom, a robust market economy,
and the teachings of the Protestant church. In circular fashion, one
display of American greatness reinforced another. Charles Darwin
ratified such thinking in 1871 in his book *Descent of Man*. "There is apparently much truth in the belief that the wonderful progress of the
United States, as well as the character of the people, are the results of
natural selection; for the more energetic, restless and courageous men
from all parts of Europe have emigrated during the last ten or twelve
generations to that great country, and have there succeeded best."[32]

Historian John Fiske, enamored with the theory of evolution as a
student at Harvard, gained a wide following after he wrote an article
for *Harper's New Monthly Magazine* in 1885 entitled "Manifest Destiny."
In it, he argued that the United States must take the torch from the
British in spreading Anglo-Saxon traditions around the world. "It is
enough to point to the general conclusion that the work which the English race began when it colonized North America is destined to go on
until every land on the earth's surface that is not already the seat of an
old civilization shall become English in its Language, in its religion, in
its political habits and traditions and to a predominate extent in the
blood of its people," he wrote.[33]

Congregational clergyman Josiah Strong captured the mood in his
1885 bestseller, *Our Country: Its Possible Future and Its Present Crisis.*

Strong had traveled widely throughout the American West as a member of the Home Missionary Society and developed a theory that there was a geographic force behind the world's great nations. Each new empire, he noted, seemed to move farther and farther west. The culmination of that march would be in the United States. Anglo-Saxon nations, he argued, possessed a genius for colonizing, and their native energy and belief in a Christian God ensured their dominance. As scientific theory, it was hardly watertight. Strong, for example, pointed to the fact that the relatively large size of Americans, and not just in height, indicated that they possessed the "physical basis" needed to achieve a higher civilization. "Is there room for reasonable doubt that this race, unless devitalized by alcohol and tobacco, is destined to dispossess many weaker races, assimilate others, and mold the remainder, until, in a very true and important sense, it has Anglo-Saxonized mankind?"[34]

Skilled though such men were at making the hearts of patriotic Americans race, they operated largely in the realm of rhetoric and theory. What they needed to achieve their lofty ambitions was a credible, detailed vision for what an American empire might look like. That would arrive five years later from an unlikely source—naval officer Alfred Thayer Mahan.

Mahan had through much of his career hardly been the pride of the American navy. Though he did rise to captain his own ship, his seamanship was shaky at best. Indeed, he much preferred the quiet of a good book to the duties of leading a fighting ship, and always made sure to bring plenty of volumes with him on long voyages. True to form, during one deployment to Peru, he made time to leave ship and visit a local library. There he picked up a copy of Theodor Mommsen's *History of Rome* and, flipping through its pages, was struck by a revelation. Sea power, not land armies, had been the deciding factor in the rise of great empires. The topic, he concluded, would make a fine subject for a series of lectures he was to give at the Naval War College.[35]

When Mahan turned his lectures into a book published in 1890 called *The Influence of Sea Power Upon History, 1660 to 1783,* it became one of the most important and famous works ever written on naval matters. Turning conventional thinking on its head, Mahan argued that the seas should not be seen as a buffer, protecting the United

States from foreign aggression, but as a "great highway" upon which Americans could cruise beyond their borders. Although many of his ideas were not new then, and appear obvious now, Mahan articulated an argument that many instinctively felt: As an industrializing power, the United States would eventually have to seek new markets and sources of raw materials. It followed, he said, that the country must do everything possible to protect its sea lanes, build a strong navy, and acquire territory. "Whether they will or no, Americans must now begin to look outward. The growing production of the country demands it," he wrote. "Having therefore no foreign establishments, either colonial or military, the ships of war of the United States, in war, will be like land birds, unable to fly far from their own shores. To provide resting-places for them, where they can coal and repair, would be one of the first duties of a government proposing to itself the development of the power of the nation at sea."[36]

Roosevelt, for one, devoured the book in a weekend and dashed off a letter to its author. "During the last two days I have spent half my time, busy as I am, in reading your book; and that I found it interesting is shown by the fact that having taken it up, I have gone straight through it. . . . It is a very good book—admirable, and I am greatly in error if it does not become a naval classic."[37]

Roosevelt and others who shared his views—John Hay, Senator Henry Cabot Lodge, and journalist-historian Brooks Adams—began meeting in Washington's finest restaurants to discuss Mahan's theory and to quietly cheer on an expansionist agenda, waiting for some spark that would unite the country behind their thinking.

When it finally came, hardly anyone noticed.

Three miles off the coast of Cuba on the night of April 10, 1895, the German freighter *Nordstrand* crashed through rolling waves. Six men had paid the captain $1,000 to drop them in a small boat outside Cuban territorial waters, a point from which they planned to row themselves ashore. Their plan was foolish. It was impossible to see land through a driving rain and gloom. Nor could anyone make out the stars or the moon, the next best navigational aids.

But they had paid their money and insisted that the captain lower their four-oared boat into the choppy sea. Pulling hard in what they believed to be the direction of land, the six braved salty spray lashing their faces and waves that threatened to swamp the craft, one so powerful that it ripped the rudder off the transom. Then luck smiled on them, and a red tropical moon peeked through the clouds. Scanning the horizon, José Julián Martí y Pérez noticed two lights and the silhouette of a hilly countryside. The way now clear, he urged the crew to put their backs into it and they reached a secluded beach. Martí, wiry and with a bushy mustache, watched as the other five jumped from the boat onto a rocky shore, their feet crunching pebbles as they landed. Then he climbed out himself feeling, he would say later, "great joy." Founder of the Cuban Revolutionary Party and leader of the Cuban resistance movement, Martí had arrived to lead a rebellion that he hoped would end Spain's four-hundred-year rule over his homeland.

5

"THE GOVERNMENT IS BEST
WHICH GOVERNS LEAST"

Few places in the country in the 1890s attracted ambitious ethnic Poles as did the area around Cleveland. They found its thriving steel mills well suited to the qualities they brought to the New World, especially a willingness for long, uncomplaining labor. Though conditions might have been tough, they were nothing the Polish work ethic could not handle and were better than what they had known back home, slaving behind plows and caring for a few meager livestock during winters that were out of the ice ages. Even in their leisure hours, it seemed Poles could not sit still, and were often seen around Cleveland carrying lumber on their backs that they used to construct tidy homes.[1]

One mill in particular—the Cleveland Rolling Mill Company—actively sought Polish immigrants. Henry Chisholm, who happened to be a friend of Hanna, had built the firm into one of the world's largest wire mills by devising new technologies—such as an ingenious method of producing wire from Bessemer steel ingots—and by reducing the cost of nails made from steel wire. Those technological advances, combined with booming demand throughout the second half of the 1880s and early 1890s, had made the company a tremendously profitable enterprise and one constantly in search of new workers.[2] Chisholm had even dispatched a subordinate named Charley Frank, who spoke five languages, to New York in the early 1880s with the express purpose of recruiting Poles and other Slavs as soon as they stepped off ships from Europe.[3] It was no surprise then that when Leon Czolgosz showed up with some factory experience, he was quickly offered a job.

Czolgosz, about seventeen, had moved to the Cleveland suburb of Newburgh and already fully understood the demands of factory work. The playful days of his youth had ended about age fourteen when, then living near Pittsburgh, Czolgosz got his first job. There he toiled at a glass factory, carrying red-hot bottles to cooling areas, a task that required a steady hand and steely nerves. His salary was seventy-five cents a day.

He must have learned some valuable lessons, however, because Czolgosz soon was impressing his bosses in Cleveland. The young man so excelled at making fence wire that he graduated to finer, trickier grades. Shifts were long. Each month he worked ten hours during the day for two weeks, then twelve hours at night for two weeks, earning around seventeen dollars for the daytime fortnight and around twenty-four for his two weeks on the night shift. It was a respectable sum for a single young man and an important contribution to the family, with father Paul trying his hand at being a barkeep, having invested the family's savings in a Newburgh saloon.[4]

The financial collapse of 1893, however, shattered any dreams that Czolgosz may have harbored about riding the expanding American economy to a prosperous middle-class life. As a semi-skilled laborer, Czolgosz could only helplessly watch as the rapidly contracting economy pulled his future down with it, the depth of the plunge amplified by the fact that he happened to work at a steel mill—a sector of the economy dependent on the once booming and overextended construction and railroad industries. As the economy contracted, some twenty-one wire nail companies failed or closed and prices plunged.[5]

Cleveland Rolling would survive, but not without costs for the workforce. Chief executive William Chisholm, Harry's son, temporarily shut the factory to upgrade his equipment and at the same time made plans to reduce wage costs when he reopened, aiming to slash costs to those prevailing in Pittsburgh, which set the industry standard in efficiency.[6]

The months that followed at Cleveland Rolling played out with a sickening ring of predictability. Faced with a cut in wages, steel unions called a strike, as expected. Yet well aware that there were plenty of people desperate for jobs, Chisholm responded with the well-practiced countermeasure of an American industrialist and promptly announced that the company didn't want them anyway and that anyone who walked off the job could count on his name joining a lengthy blacklist that would make rehiring an impossibility.[7] Among those added to the list was Czolgosz.

For weeks on end, Czolgosz watched as the strike decimated his once prosperous community. Former coworkers packed up their belongings and made their way to the train station, hopping boxcars for parts unknown in search of work. Those who remained would gather on street corners to swap rumors of potential work, watching enviously as horse-drawn carts clattered past with goods they could not afford. The local butchers and vegetable stalls that the Czolgosz family frequented stood empty.

Losing his job was a deep psychological and emotional blow for Czolgosz that brought home injustices he had only read about in the newspapers. His brother Waldek would later say that Czolgosz "got quiet and not so happy" and soon began to question the institutions that formed the basis of immigrant life.[8] Brought up in a household of devout Catholics, where crucifixes and likenesses of Mary would have adorned the walls, he turned first to religion for help. Sitting in church on Sunday mornings at St. Stanislaus parish, the largest Polish church in the area, he inhaled the scent of candles and incense, gazed upon the priest in his fine robes, and earnestly prayed for relief. He and his brother purchased a Polish bible that they read at least four times, studying the well-turned pages for overlooked messages that would help them make sense of their troubles.[9] Yet none appeared.

Czolgosz grew increasingly frustrated as priests urged their congregations to remain strong yet failed to help working people put bread on the table. He slowly grew to distrust them. Priests were, he became convinced, nothing more than phonies who asked for obedience but gave nothing in return. Once, he and his brother went to visit a priest and asked for proof that God would help them. The priest encouraged the pair to pray harder, something they did without result. Frustrated, Czolgosz told his brother that "the priest's trade was the same as the shoemaker's or any other."[10] Introverted and brooding, he spent more and more time studying newspapers, pamphlets, and books—anything he could get his hands on that would help him come to grips with what was happening in the country.

Stories of labor unrest that year were hard to miss. A wildcat strike at the Pullman Palace Car Company, long a model of labor-management relations complete with a company town, captured headlines for weeks when the company's founder, George Pullman, announced plans to cut wages but not the prices he charged employees for rent in his houses.[11] Outraged by such egregious treatment, more than a quarter of a million railroad workers walked off the job in twenty-seven states and territories in what *The New York Times* called "the greatest battle between labor and capital that has ever been inaugurated in the United States." The *Chicago Tribune* added that the strike had attained the "dignity of an insurrection."[12] Only pitched battles between strikers and thousands of federal troops ended the standoff, but not before thirteen people were killed and fifty-three were seriously injured.

Increasingly distressed by the turmoil around him, Czolgosz began to order books about religion from New York, frequently ones that criticized the scriptures.[13] He became interested in astrology and favored the *Peruna Almanac* because it purported to forecast his lucky days. Perhaps the book most influential on his state of mind was a Polish translation of Edward Bellamy's *Looking Backward, 2000–1887*.[14]

Bellamy, the son of a Baptist minister, had written one of the most talked-about novels of the nineteenth century, leaving many wishing they could trade places with Julian West, the book's hero. In the opening chapter, set in 1887, the prosperous thirty-year-old Bostonian decides to treat persistent insomnia by medicating himself in a special underground sleeping chamber. His house then burns down and his presence is forgotten until 2000, when he is discovered by a building crew and brought out of his slumber. When West awakens, he finds a utopian world where government has taken over control of industry and runs it for the welfare of society. Everyone is educated until age twenty-one and the notion of child labor has been relegated to the history books. Money is no longer used and everyone receives an equal share of the nation's products. Militaries are disbanded and crime is nearly nonexistent.

With surprising accuracy, Bellamy described inventions of the early twenty-first century. He foresaw devices similar to radios and televisions, the airplane, and power-drawn plows. A full century before the development of the Internet, Bellamy imagined that music could be distributed over phone lines.

In Bellamy's own words, recorded in a postscript to later editions of the novel, the book was "intended, in all seriousness, as a forecast, in accordance with the principles of evolution, of the next stage in industrial and social development of humanity." He believed that "the dawn of the new era is already near at hand," and that "the full day will swiftly follow."[15] The novel was an instant bestseller; hundreds of thousands of copies and dozens of editions, some in foreign languages, were printed in five years.[16] Bellamy clubs sprang up worldwide, and by 1891 there were 162 in the United States alone.

Around this time Czolgosz began a quest that would last the rest of his life. He wanted to make the acquaintance—"friends" would be going too far for him—of people who shared his concerns. His first social forays were with the tamest of groups. He joined, for example, the Golden Eagle Society, a respectable workingman's association, albeit one with socialist, anti-Catholic leanings. One club member, a Mr. Page, who also happened to be Czolgosz's foreman at work, thought it strange that Czolgosz chose this club as it was mostly made up of men of higher social standing than those from the Polish community. Page presumed he was striving to improve his place in the community.[17] But Czolgosz never really fit in, remaining quiet and withdrawn during the club's discussions. He apparently had hoped for more radical solutions to society's ills than the Golden Eagle offered.

In 1894, perhaps at the Golden Eagle Hall, Czolgosz met someone who was more to his liking, a young man who would "open his eyes" to the evils of the American government and introduce him to the like-minded. Anton Zwolinski was an upholsterer from Cleveland and a member of a Polish "educational club" known as Sila, or "The Force."[18] Sila consisted of an eclectic group of social radicals who wanted to crack an American political system that favored big business. In angry speeches that tended to be exercises in preaching to the choir, its members demanded that working people receive a fair share of what they produced. "I came to the opinion that our form of voting was not right," Czolgosz said. "I discussed it and began to talk it over with the people that belonged to [Zwolinski's] circle. That was the beginning of my thought about the subject."[19]

How far Czolgosz's thinking on the social issues evolved during the vitriolic meetings of the Sila is open to question. Many of the beer-fueled men who ranted and stirred up its gatherings were more interested in attacking current American institutions than political theory. Yet among the ideologies embraced by hard-core social radicals around Cleveland was one that would have held special appeal for men like Czolgosz: anarchy.

The anarchist movement in its modern form can be traced back to a spartan room in London's Titchfield Street in the late eighteenth century. There William Godwin, a struggling writer desperate to make his mark in the world, spent countless isolated hours in 1792 casting and recasting a treatise about political theory. It was slow going for the unaccomplished writer, and the effort sounded like a snore: "An Enquiry Concerning Political Justice and Its Influence on General Virtue and Happiness."

Godwin's conclusions, however, floored his readers. All obstacles to the pursuit of personal liberty, he boldly wrote, should be eliminated. There were no qualifications, no shades of gray. Man, he said, must be his own master. "Everything that is usually understood by the term cooperation is to some degree an evil. . . . If I be expected to eat and work in conjunction with my neighbor, it must either be at a time most convenient to me, or to him, or to neither of us. We cannot be reduced to clockwork uniformity."[20] Institutions such as the family and marriage restricted the pursuit of individual perfection. Music composed by someone else involved a level of suppression. Even sex was an unwelcome distraction. But worst of all, in his view, was government.

The notion that all authority should be eliminated had appeared in Western philosophy as early as the third century B.C., when Greek philosopher Zeno of Citium argued that reason should replace authority. During the Middle Ages, anarchism was elevated to the status of a religious movement by numerous groups with such uplifting names as the Brothers and Sisters of the Free Spirit. And although he claimed it was a satire, Edmund Burke wrote of the tyranny of government in 1756 when he published *A Vindication of Natural Society*, in which he argued that all forms of government are to some degree oppressive. Whether or not in jest, Burke wrote in one passage: "Parties in religion and politics make sufficient discoveries concerning each other, to give a sober man a proper caution against them all. . . . The monarchic, and aristocratical and popular partisans, have been jointly laying their axes to the root of all government, and have, in their turns, proved each other absurd and inconvenient."[21]

Godwin's work encapsulated much of the classic theory on anarchism that had been passed down over millennia. Although he made more than a few assumptions, his was a tidy, sequential argument. One: Man's actions are shaped by experiences and education. Two: Man will always act according to reason. Three: Fill him with the proper experiences and education and man will always act in a reasonable way. Four: In a world where each of us acts rationally, there is no need for authority.

Monarchy represented the greatest threat to personal liberty, he concluded. But democracy wasn't much better. Even with the right to choose their government, people are obliged to follow the will of a majority, whether it is right or not—what Godwin called "an intolerable insult upon all reason and justice." Moreover, government to him was overly oriented toward superficial material values in its focus on protecting property. The "true perfection of man," he wrote, "is to divest himself of the influence of passions; that he must have no artificial wants, no sensuality and no fear."[22]

Although he didn't refer to anarchy by name, Godwin's philosophy came to describe something close to a paradise on earth. People would be able to live in complete freedom to do as they wanted without fear of punishment. Material desires would be met, not necessarily because of a new economic system, but because people would realize they needed less. Freed from their oppressors, political or corporate, the poor would finally be able to enjoy the fruits of their labor. And liberated from earthly wants, mankind would finally be able to achieve true happiness, the kind that comes from the pursuit of reason.

The United States provided fertile ground for Godwin's ideas. Men and women of the frontier, whether hunters, gold miners, or isolated family farmers, lived with little or no authority imposed upon them. And when they did interact with others, it was often in ad hoc communal projects of which anarchist philosophers would have enthusiastically approved. The experience of life under British rule didn't make government seem any more attractive. Propagandists such as Thomas Paine not only turned their pens against colonial rule, but against government in general. In his famous work *Common Sense,* Paine wrote: "Government, even in its best state, is but a necessary evil; in its worst state an intolerable one."[23] Some of the founding fathers shared Paine's beliefs. Famously declaring that "the government is best which governs least," Thomas Jefferson argued that people had the right to veto the decisions of their government, even if that meant the occasional small revolt.[24]

Several leading American writers expressed similar views. Ralph Waldo Emerson, the poet-philosopher, wrote that nothing truly great is produced by government and in most cases comes about in opposition to it. The state, Emerson wrote, was often the enemy of liberty. "Every actual State is corrupt. Good men must not obey the laws too well."[25] From his self-imposed exile from society at Walden in Massachusetts, Emerson's friend Henry David Thoreau arrived at similar conclusions, writing tracts that would strongly echo the sentiments of confirmed anarchists. After spending a night in jail for refusing to pay taxes that, he reasoned, would be used to support a war with Mexico, Thoreau wrote *On the Duty of Civil Disobedience,* which included one of his most memorable lines: "That government is best which governs not at all."[26]

These were appealing sentiments for radical Americans who, knowing the government of the United States was unlikely to adopt the beliefs of Thoreau and Emerson, tried to create their own communities that would. Over the course of the nineteenth century, dreamers, idealists, and the odd charlatan would establish more than one hundred utopian communities around the country.[27] Some were religious, others were based on socialist values, and a number drew on the theories of anarchy.

If there ever were a man of his convictions, it was Josiah Warren. A member of one of Boston's more prominent families, he had given up a prosperous lamp factory in 1825 and taken his family to join an experimental utopian community in Indiana known as New Harmony. The brainchild of the famed Welsh social reformer Robert Owen, New Harmony was a massive undertaking consisting of 180 buildings standing on twenty thousand acres.[28] Yet few communities in American history have been as inaptly named. In April 1825, Owen imposed the first of several different constitutions, replete with conflicting regulations that said nothing about how an individual's work would be counted toward what he could consume. Many of the rules flouted the spirit of a utopian enterprise. One stated that anyone who invested financially in the community would be considered a "non-laboring" member.[29] Perhaps worst of all, Owen hadn't screened his recruits very well, and they came to include a diverse collection of loafers, malcontents, and intolerant disciples of several different religions. It didn't take long before the community fell into a tangle of bitter factions where just 140 adults out of the total population of 800 worked in crafts and industry and only 36 in the fields. Financial ruin followed, and a disheartened Warren took his family and left.[30]

Time and again, Warren turned over in his mind what had gone wrong. He could find only one explanation: The individual freedoms of New Harmony's members had been suppressed by the authority of Owen. Just as no two people are physically identical, so, too, are no two people identical in character and temperament, he wrote. It fol-

lowed that forcing unique individuals to behave in an identical way
must inevitably make man unhappy. "Man seeks freedom as the mag-
net seeks the pole or water its level, and society can have no peace until
every member is really free," he would later write.[31]

In the years that followed, Warren devoted himself to perfecting his
theories and promoting his ideal way of life. In 1827, he opened a store
in Cincinnati where customers paid not in cash, but with promises to
trade their labor for goods. It grew to be one of the most successful enterprises in town. Five years later, Warren began publishing what
many consider the first anarchist newspaper anywhere, *The Peaceful
Revolutionist,* a four-page weekly.[32]

What Warren really craved, however, was a chance to put his theories to a live test. Twice he attempted to found utopian communities
based on anarchist principles, with mixed success. One community in
Tuscarawas County, Ohio, was built near an area heavily populated
with mosquitoes that spread malaria among the colonists.

Warren's third and final attempt at a working utopia, optimistically
named Modern Times, was a community of thirty-seven families on
Long Island not far from New York City. Starting work in 1850,[33] Warren and the first settlers built a picture-perfect community in which
neat cottages trimmed with strawberry plants and tidy gardens dotted
streets lined with fruit trees.[34] A true anarchist's enclave, here one rule
prevailed: Mind your own business. There were no police, no court, no
jail. No restrictions were placed on moral or religious beliefs. All social
interaction was strictly voluntary, and economic transactions were
based on Warren's labor-exchange principles, though all were free to
hold normal jobs outside the community. It all seemed to work. Crime
and violence were nonexistent. Citizens wrote glowing letters of their
experiences.

Modern Times soon became home to an eccentric group. One po-
lygamist joined the village and published a paper to support his penchant for multiple wives. A nudist forced the practice on his
embarrassed children. One woman adopted a masculine style of attire,
prompting one newspaper to write that the "women of Modern
Times dressed in men's clothes and looked hideous." Yet another
woman tried to live on a diet that consisted exclusively of beans. She
died within a year.[35]

Even more titillating for newspaper readers, the community developed a reputation as a center of "free love" where quaint institutions such as marriage were not necessarily observed. "Marriage! Well, folks ask no questions in regard to that among us. We, or at least some of us, do not believe in life partnerships when parties cannot live happily. Every person here is supposed to know his or her own interest best," one member said.[36]

While life at Modern Times seemed free and easy, utopian communities by their very nature remained fragile enterprises. The micro-economy that Warren had created was largely based on agriculture, which left the community's inhabitants decidedly less well off than city dwellers. Attempts to establish some sort of light industry constantly foundered on an inability to receive financing from bank loan officers who chuckled at the community's labor vouchers. And if such problems were not enough, there was the little matter of the Civil War. Just as the conflict split the nation, so, too, did it sow conflict among members of the community—a tension that was exacerbated by speculation of a hefty increase in taxes and a military draft. Warren himself added to the disquiet when he left Modern Times in February 1863 and never returned. The same year, other original members moved away.[37] Modern Times would continue to limp along in various forms for several more years but never again served as a model anarchist experiment.

For anarchy's most ardent believers, however, the communes failed on one more score: They were anomalies with no power to reshape society. It was a shortcoming that future generations of anarchists including Czolgosz would attempt to address in their own way.

6

THE HAWAIIAN ANVIL

McKinley was still enjoying a respite in Canton before moving to Washington in early 1897 when a portent of his presidency literally landed on his doorstep. Among the throngs of office seekers, well-wishers, and old friends who descended on his front porch was an Indiana lawyer named Henry Ernest Cooper.[1]

Cooper had left the United States six years previously for what was now the Republic of Hawaii and—advancement in the islands came quickly to ambitious transplants—served as its foreign minister. With a certain level of detachment, McKinley listened as his decidedly un-Polynesian guest warned the president of a pending crisis.

Cooper told McKinley that "Orientals," by which he meant Japanese, were pouring into the islands at an alarming rate, so much so that the balance of the population was tilting "dangerously" in their favor. The statistics were indeed eye-opening. Whereas in 1884 there had been only 116 Japanese in the islands, there were more than 24,000 by 1897, nearly a quarter of the total population of 109,020.[2] By contrast, only some 3,000 residents were of American ancestry. Immigrants from Germany, France, Norway, and Portugal brought the total of non-Asian, nonnative Hawaiians to 15,000.[3] If the influx remained unchecked, it seemed only a matter of time until the heavily outnumbered pro-American government would be displaced. Efforts to stem the flow of Japanese immigrants, he continued, had offended the Japanese government, and now he feared Tokyo would send warships. Would McKinley, Cooper wanted to know, please, finally, annex Hawaii?

Hawaii had long posed vexing moral and political problems for the United States. On the one hand, there were unmistakable historical and cultural ties. From the first American whalers who built lean-tos on their palm-fringed shores, to the earnest missionaries establishing churches and schools and the sugar barons who bought up the land, an American character permeated the islands. With its clapboard storefronts and hitching posts, Honolulu looked like a typical western boomtown. Every year, the Fourth of July and Thanksgiving were celebrated as joyfully as on the mainland.[4] The United States and Hawaii had also, with varying degrees of happiness, entered into a series of trade pacts that closely bound their economies. And now the islands were governed by a collection of transplants, mostly Americans, led by Sanford Dole, a relation of the founders of the fruit empire of the same name.

The problem was that Dole and the rest of the Americans who ran the government had taken power from the native Hawaiians in rather awkward fashion. In 1893 the power brokers, backed by a militia known as the Honolulu Rifles, had successfully led a coup against the cultured and headstrong Hawaiian monarch, Queen Liliuokalani, hoping that once they controlled the government, they could convince Washington to annex the islands. But to the supreme embarrassment of President Cleveland, who had only recently taken office, an investigation into the coup revealed that the plot had been aided in no small part by the U.S. Navy. Captain G. C. Wiltse of the USS *Boston* had at a critical moment in the overthrow dispatched 154 of his men ashore, giving the appearance that plotters had official American backing.[5] Annoyed by the navy's role in aiding a coup, Cleveland promptly announced that Hawaii's new government could forget about joining the Union.

In the years since, a debate about what to do with Hawaii had burned with irregular intensity. American sugar interests, which included sugar processors, beet sugar growers, and the sugar trust that controlled the U.S. market, quarreled among themselves over who stood to gain and lose from annexing the islands. The proponents of a larger navy and anti-expansionists bickered over the ethics of taking a possession so far from the American mainland.

McKinley listened politely as Cooper finished his plea, thanked him for coming, and sent him on his way without offering any clues about his thinking—as was his habit. The Dole government may have taken the islands in usavory fashion, but McKinley knew he faced bigger issues now. He was struggling to prevent an economic calamity at home and saw in Hawaii the hint of a solution.

At the turn of the century, economists and laborers alike referred to McKinley's economic problem as "the surplus."

The American economy, the thinking went, simply produced too much stuff. Where once factory managers would have tailored output to meet consumption, many now believed that mass production and mass investments demanded that the marketplace be viewed in new ways. What became known as "running full" was the new goal of all factory managers—that is, producing to the utmost of their capacity to get the most of their investments, no matter if there were enough consumers or not. Andrew Carnegie, always keen to show himself a modern thinker, stated flat out that the old laws of supply and demand no longer applied in an industrial economy. "This was true when Adam Smith wrote," Carnegie argued, "but it is not quite true today" when "manufacturing is carried on in enormous establishments." Now, Carnegie said, "it cost the manufacturer much less to run at a loss for a ton or yard than to check his production."[6]

From one industry to another, chief executives adopted this logic with almost religious conviction. In the 1880s, sugar producers led by Henry Osborne Havemeyer engaged in a production war, investing heavily in their mills to make them as efficient as possible. Prices and profits plunged, but production was kept up because the alternative of letting expensive plants and equipment sit idle was unthinkable. By 1887, following five years of price cutting, refining capacity stood 20 percent above demand.[7] Newsprint manufacturer G. W. Knowlton wrote in the early 1890s that "prices are low and if a mill does not make big runs there is little in it in the way of margin," adding later, "It is the last ton or two that pays the profit."[8] The Illinois Steel Company summed up this thinking in its annual report for the year ending in 1897. "For many years American manufacturers attempted to do business on the basis of large profits for comparatively small tonnage; but there has been a revolution in this condition of affairs, and it seems to have been demonstrated that for the future the policy of small profits on large tonnage furnishes the best assurances of success."[9]

There seemed to be no end to the absurdity of production. In the wire nail industry, American factories were thought to be able to produce four times as much as Americans would buy. The same went for rail mills, locomotive producers, and glass factories. In 1890, the United States produced three million more bales of cotton than the entire world could consume.[10] The burgeoning consumer economy also showed the signs of the output glut. According to *The New York Times*, U.S. factories were capable of producing one million bikes by 1896, where there were but 600,000 to 700,000 customers. The result was a plunge in prices. Bikes that once went for $100 sold in department stores for as little as $24.[11]

Too many bikes, too much steel, too much cotton. The self-inflicted predicament unfolded upon American businessmen as a nightmare of catastrophic proportion. In the economic logic of the day, this was no business cycle; it was a crisis that spoke to the very core of the economy and, more than a few felt, threatened even the democratic principles on which the country was founded.

In 1895, the year before the election, representatives of some three hundred companies gathered in a Cincinnati conference hall with the problem of overproduction very much on their minds. To restrict output, they believed, might not only be difficult, but disastrous. Huge numbers of workers would have to be laid off and few wanted to contemplate the mass strikes and violent protests that seemed sure to follow. If reducing production was unthinkable and there were no new American consumers, that left one alternative—to find new customers abroad. Forming what would become the National Association of Manufacturers, the executives concluded that U.S. companies had "outgrown or are outgrowing the home market" and that the "expansion of foreign trade is [the] only promise of relief."[12]

In the years that followed, captains of American industry obsessed over the need to find foreign markets. Business pages burst with exhortations of the vast possibilities that existed beyond American shores. Speaking in January 1896 at the National Convention of American Manufacturers in Chicago, Ulysses D. Eddy, president of Flint, Eddy & Co., bemoaned the fact that six months of production in most factories now supplied twelve months of consumption. "This condition cannot continue," Eddy said. "We are beginning to recognize that the 1,400,000,000 people living outside our borders represent a vast commerce and that one billion of them live in non-manufacturing countries."[13] Senator Albert Beveridge, as chest thumping a patriot as there was in those days, wrote in April 1897 with characteristic gusto: "Fate has written our policy for us; the trade of the world must and shall be ours."[14]

McKinley marched not more than a step behind such men. No stranger to the importance of trade after all his work on tariffs, he had watched the "surplus problem" for years with a growing sense of alarm. Speaking well before his presidential campaign, he had said that industry "cannot be kept in motion without markets," adding that foreign markets were essential "for our surplus products." In the White House, he appeared to remain as convinced of the value of exports as ever. His friend H. H. Kohlsaat believed that McKinley's "greatest ambition was to create new markets for American producers and manufacturers."[15]

As McKinley and others opened their atlases and studied economic statistics, one market alone seemed to offer opportunities on the scale that the United States needed to relieve the pressure building within its swelling warehouses. Europe was already crowded with fierce competitors and South America was too small. Asia, however, was a region of vast wealth. Here the future of great nations would be decided, or at least that was the fashionable belief of many commentators. "Our geographical position, our wealth, and our energy pre-eminently fit us to enter upon the development of eastern Asia, and to reduce it to part of our economic system," Brooks Adams wrote.[16]

When Adams and others spoke of Asia, they meant one country in particular—China. Its size alone was staggering. At four hundred million people, its population matched all of Europe and was more than five times that of the United States, with seventy-six million. Unlike other national markets such as England and Germany, where Americans faced daunting, homegrown competition, China was wide open. It lacked modern factories, and many recent inventions had not yet found their way across the Pacific. Best of all, it appeared to be an untapped market. U.S. exports to China amounted to a scant $7 million, only 1 percent of total U.S. trade.

China, *Harper's Magazine* later wrote, was poised to explode. The country sprawled over four million square miles yet there existed only four hundred miles of railroads and very few roads. In the near future, the magazine assured its readers, the country would need forty thousand miles of track. A back-of-the-napkin calculation promised untold riches. By Harper's estimate, China's foreign trade amounted to a single dollar per person of her population. That figure, if the pattern seen in other countries held true, would quickly swell to five dollars per head. "If we multiply China's population of 400,000,000 by $5, we have a reasonable possibility of $2,000,000,000 per annum, compared with a current figure of $43,000,000. . . . We can never afford to retreat from such possibilities," the magazine wrote. And that was to say nothing of the potential for trade with Japan, the Dutch East Indies, Siberia, Siam, and Korea.[17]

China also held an almost magical grip on the imaginations of Americans. Many a young child had read thrilling accounts of the old China trade—clipper ships dropping anchor in exotic ports where untold riches seemed ripe for the taking. Travelers wrote in wonder of the scene that opened before them as their ships rounded a bend in the

Pearl River at the trading center of Whampoa.[18] There, stretched for three miles, stood a forest of masts from dozens of sailing vessels from all over the world. The voices of sailors shouting in German, French, Dutch, Swedish, Danish, and, above all, British-accented English, carried across the slow-moving river. Slipping among the ships was every manner of waterborne craft. Mandarin boats, decorated with gray silk pennants and propelled by double banks of oars, glided up and down the river. Hundreds of filthy sampans, their decks covered with pots, pans, and pens containing live ducks or rabbits, were tied up two and three deep along the shore. Half-naked coolies, their sinewy bodies glistening with sweat, powered the paddle wheels on river junks.[19]

Dynasties such as the Forbes, Delano, and Astor families were born in China. Warren Delano II, grandfather of future president Franklin Delano Roosevelt, made two fortunes there, having been forced to return to Canton after he blew the earnings from his first stint on an ill-advised real estate deal in Massachusetts. Several members of the Forbes clan were to forge a lifelong relationship with Houqua, their Chinese agent in Canton, said to be one of the richest men in the world. For years the family kept above the fireplace of their Long Island estate a portrait of the old man with a white wisp of hair on his chin. John Jacob Astor, the first American millionaire, made his fortune in China as well, in the process founding a trading outpost on the coast of Oregon that now bears his name. Samuel Russell, whose family helped found Yale College and its secret society Skull and Bones, was the most successful of all. A reclusive workaholic orphaned at age twelve, Russell assembled a who's who of investors, traders, and sea captains to establish the most prominent American trading company in China through the 1890s.[20]

By the time McKinley was elected, American companies had established small but promising footholds in China. China bought nearly half of all U.S. cotton exports, and demand was soaring, climbing 121 percent between 1887 and 1897.[21] Cotton spinners in South Carolina were moved to write their congressmen: "You can at once see what the importance of the China trade is to us. It is everything. The prosperity of the cotton-mill business of South Carolina depends in our opinion upon the China trade."[22] Standard Oil found in China a huge market for its kerosene, just as demand was starting to shrink at home with the spread of the electric lightbulb. Chinese consumers flocked to kerosene from the moment Standard introduced it in 1879, abandoning their own vegetable-based lighting fuel that burned dim and smoky and cost twice as much. By 1882, one house out of six in Shanghai burned American kerosene, the streets were lighted with it, and the highest-ranking Chinese official in the city used it in his office.

Still learning his way around the executive mansion in the spring of 1897, McKinley recognized Hawaii's pivotal role in the health of the U.S. economy. If China was to supply the markets, he needed safe passage through the Pacific. Undisputed access to Hawaii's wonderful anchorage at Pearl Harbor would allow merchant ships to refuel and refurbish along the way. In short, Hawaii was to be a stepping stone for American commerce, one that McKinley must protect from other powers. For naval strategist Alfred Thayer Mahan, Hawaii represented America's "first fruit."[23]

Meeting with Senator George Hoar, McKinley said: "We cannot let those islands go to Japan. Japan has her eye on them. Her people are crowding in there. I am satisfied they do not go there voluntarily, as ordinary immigrants, but that Japan is pressing them in there, in order to get possession before anybody can interfere. . . . Japan is doubtless awaiting her opportunity."[24] On July 10, 1897, a cipher was sent to the new minister in Honolulu, Harold M. Sewall. If Japan resorted to force, he was to declare an American protectorate over the islands.[25] Mahan weighed in, not surprisingly advising the Navy Department to seize Hawaii at once.

By early summer, McKinley would demonstrate qualities that his critics claimed he lacked. When events demanded it, he was capable of decisive and even unpopular action. Without taking the time to consult with many of his staff, including an outraged Secretary of State Sherman, he ordered that a treaty to annex Hawaii be prepared.[26] A few days later, on June 16, 1897, McKinley sent it to the Senate, knowing full well that he was getting himself into what promised to be a most difficult battle over ratification that, incredibly, cast him in the role of imperialist.[27]

Schurz, the man to whom McKinley had once forsworn "jingo nonsense," would soon write that the move to annex Hawaii left him "with a heart heavy with evil forebodings."[28]

‖⹀‖

AN UNLIKELY ANARCHIST

Leon Czolgosz slipped into presentable clothes and made his way along the familiar streets between his home and his old employer, the Cleveland Rolling Mill Company, harboring a bitter sense of defeat. The 1893 strike had left him idle for six months, vainly hoping that the mill's managers would give in to the workers' demands. Yet Cleveland Rolling had yet to show any sign of surrendering. It was time to swallow his pride and accept a meager paycheck rather than earn nothing at all.

By rights Czolgosz should have made it no further than the front gate. His name, like that of all the strikers, had been added to a blacklist of men the mill refused to rehire, retribution for walking out in the first place. The mill, however, had recently let Czolgosz's old boss go. At a time when standards of identification had not yet evolved—no picture ID, no Social Security numbers—all Czolgosz had to do was supply a new name. He introduced himself to his prospective new managers as Fred C. Nieman. The foreman likely guessed that he was now face-to-face with a striker, yet the company needed bodies. Anyone willing to pitch in would be welcome. Czolgosz was hired and thereby adopted a new identity that he would periodically turn to for the rest of his life.

Though Czolgosz resented the humiliating wages, he masked it carefully while on the job. His supervisor quickly noted his diligence and soon trusted him with additional responsibilities. He became a wire winder, which required considerable skill, and rose to the post of assistant superintendent of some of the machines. While most men were fined for various lapses at work, Czolgosz received only a handful of such reprimands for minor transgressions.

Czolgosz may have changed his name, but he retained his rather quirky personality. He continued to lead a solitary, almost sullen existence. During lunch, he would often find a place apart, remove a sandwich from his pail, and quietly observe the conversations and friendly banter of the other men as he munched his food. After work, when colleagues made plans to meet up for a beer or a game of cards, he slipped out of the factory gates alone, heading to his usual place in the saloon at the corner of Third and Tod or straight home to read.

Why Czolgosz led such an antisocial lifestyle is not easily explained by anything in his upbringing. His siblings didn't seem to share the trait. And although he had lost his mother at a tender age, so had multitudes of American children of the era without withdrawing into themselves. Normal social interaction simply seemed beyond his abilities. When he did find himself with a group of people, he was reserved and behaved awkwardly, as if he lacked self-confidence and attempted to protect his ego and emotions by shutting himself off from anyone who might discover his weaknesses.

Nevertheless, Czolgosz increasingly found himself drawn to men such as Zwolinski, the social radical who first introduced him to the political ideology of the underclass. He began to attend meetings around Cleveland organized by people who dared to utter their discontent with authority. Typically held in bars or small halls, the gatherings were poorly organized and primarily allowed angry workers to let off steam with bitter attacks on local industrialists, William Chisholm no doubt heading the list.

Czolgosz began to find company among these men. One was a short, plump cigar salesman with an iron-gray mustache named Walter Nowak. The two became friendly and began attending meetings together, and in a remarkable social stretch for Czolgosz, even went to the theater on occasion.[1] Another new friend, Frank Dalzer, was also a foreman at the plant and was very impressed by how frequently Czolgosz attended socialist and anarchist meetings.[2] Yet even among these like-minded comrades, Czolgosz was hopelessly out of step. He would alternately sit quietly in the back of the room while a speaker riled a whooping audience with attacks on capitalism and government, or awkwardly spew his own views in free-flowing rambles.

One victim of Czolgosz's outbursts was the Catholic church. The Reverend Benedict Rosinski, pastor of St. Stanislaus Church in Cleveland, met with Czolgosz around 1897 when he asked him for a contribution for the parish. "He surprised me by refusing to give it," the reverend later said. "I asked him why he would not contribute, and he said he was an Anarchist. I always supposed that he was a Catholic and that was why I had approached him on the subject of contributions. He told me he had no religion and that he did [not] wish to help churches. He said anarchy was his religion. I tried to argue with him and drive the anarchistic principles out of his head, but it was to no purpose. I believe that he was mentally unbalanced."[3]

The fact is that by the final decade of the century, anybody who seemed to support anarchy was likely to be considered "mentally unbalanced." Americans had seen plenty of those who subscribed to the theory and recoiled at even the mention of their names.

Two of these towered over the landscape of American social revolution. Though they never met each other, Albert Parsons and Emma Goldman had through their appetite for self-sacrifice and willingness to flirt with the law made anarchy a household word. Parsons would transform it from the intellectual parlor game of the overeducated and underemployed into one of the most feared and hated movements in the nation. Inspired by his example, a teenage Goldman eagerly took up Parson's torch when he was ultimately sent to the gallows for his beliefs. The so-called Red Emma, the high priestess of anarchism, was a force of nature who discovered she could inspire by words as easily as others did by deeds. Together Parsons and Goldman formed a lineage that was passed on to Czolgosz almost as surely as if he had been their biological son. It is impossible to comprehend Czolgosz without understanding the stories of Parsons and Goldman and the worlds they hoped to create.

Little about Parsons suggested social revolution. In contrast to the shaggy-haired, amply proportioned Germans that typically populated the movement, Parsons was a Texan, and a bit of a dandy at that. His build was that of a long-distance runner. He kept his hair and mustache finely clipped and black with regular coloring, and with his keen, dark eyes had the look of a terrier about him. He would not be caught wearing the rumpled-suit uniform of a socialist, always making sure his attire was fashionable and crisply pressed. Perhaps most surprising was his family background. Parsons could not have come from more respectable and stable stock. His forefathers had been among North America's earliest settlers.[4] Later generations had fought in the Revolutionary War, and one relative on his mother's side had served General George Washington as a bodyguard.

Raised by a much older brother from age five in the Texas frontier after his parents died, Parsons seemed destined to become a respected southern gentleman. At age thirteen he enlisted with the local volunteers, the Lone Star Grays, and headed off to fight the Yankees. He later attended Waco University, now Baylor, and worked in Waco at a printing shop where he won the respect of the city's elders.

Yet Parsons was not the man his friends and neighbors in Waco thought they knew. Deep within him burned a hatred for the ideals he had risked his life for fighting the Civil War—white supremacy and slavery. He had joined the military, he later would say, for the adventure of it, not the principles. Yet when he returned home, he could not reconcile the war's aims with the loving fondness he felt for his "old

Aunt Esther," a former slave who had helped raise him with "great kindness and a mother's love." It was a shame that tormented him. At age nineteen, employing his printing skills and his brief university education, Parsons founded a newspaper called *The Spectator* to champion the rights of former slaves and began traveling around the state encouraging them to vote.[5]

It was an unpopular choice of occupations—one that ruined friendships and turned the upper crust of Waco against him. In various attacks he was beaten, shot in the leg, kicked down a flight of stairs, and threatened with lynching. He even made the local newspaper, which reported that Parsons was a "violent agitator," ever ready to stir up the "worst class of Negros."[6] Confirmation that Parsons had really lost his head, townspeople felt, came when word got out that he had married a mysterious woman named Lucy, who claimed to be the daughter of a Mexican and an Indian. Yet her dark complexion and kinky hair led the townspeople to whisper that she was actually black.[7] Equally enigmatic were details about her early life. She offered several different family names for herself as well as conflicting places of birth.

Whatever Lucy's origin, there was no place left for Parsons in Texas as long as he was married to her and continued to spread his unorthodox views about race and politics. "He was practically a political exile," his brother once noted. "He had either to fight every day, or leave."[8] Leave he did, for Chicago, where he hoped his marriage, and his political views, would be more readily accepted.

Parsons and Lucy arrived in Chicago in the winter of 1873, one of the low points in the city's history, as the country suffered the first in a string of financial panics that would ravage the economy with increasing and maddening regularity through the end of the century. Triggered by the collapse of a pillar of American finance, Jay Cooke and Company, the financial system melted down, taking the rest of the economy with it.

Life was particularly brutal in Chicago. For two years, immigrants had been flocking by the trainload for jobs rebuilding the city after the great fire of 1871—Czechs, Poles, Scandinavians, and especially Germans. There were enough to support one hundred saloons and beer gardens, including tradespeople from Bavaria, German Jews, and more than a few political exiles.[9]

With banks no longer able to finance the reconstruction, building companies locked up their hammers, saws, and shovels and laid off their workers. In a matter of weeks, Chicago was awash in desperate foreign-born men who felt more than a little resentful about the circumstances that had led them to where they were. "The lumberyards, vacant buildings, sheds, railroad depots and all public places were thronged with idlers," a journalist later wrote, adding that it was getting dangerous to go out after dark.[10]

The disparity Parsons saw all around him echoed the pain of the former slaves he had tried to help in Texas. Just as blacks had suffered under the stinging whip of the cotton farmer, workers in Chicago were enslaved by robber barons who demanded obscenely long hours for obscenely small pay. Parsons began reading socialist materials, including *The Communist Manifesto*. He joined the Typographical Union Number 16 and the Social Democratic Party. And he discovered that, combining humor, statistics, and a gift for mimicking his opponents, he could deliver a moving speech. By May 1876, Parsons and his cohorts had become in the words of the *Chicago Tribune* "a parcel of blatant communist demagogues."[11] There was, however, much more to Parsons than demagogy, as the city would soon find out.

In the summer of 1877 it was known simply as the Great Railroad Strike. A decision by the Pennsylvania Railroad in May to cut wages by 10 percent, a step quickly mimicked by other railroads, lit the fuse. For several weeks, railroad workers in seventeen states walked off their jobs in protest, by some measures the largest labor uprising of the nineteenth century to that point.[12] By the strike's end, tens of thousands of militia and federal troops had been called upon, more than one hundred people had been killed, and millions would fear for their safety.

Pittsburgh was the scene of the bloodiest and most destructive clashes. On the warm afternoon of July 19, 1877, some six hundred militia troops were called in from Philadelphia, after the Pittsburgh troops sided with the strikers, and forcibly tried to remove five thousand to seven thousand protesters, "greasy and ragged outlaws from the coal regions," including a few women "with the faces of demons," who had blocked traffic at the rail yard. When the Philadelphians bayoneted and shot into the ranks of demonstrators, Pittsburgh melted into a postapocalyptic scene of lawlessness and violence. Mobs roamed the streets, breaking into gun shops and threatening the armory in a quest to find weapons that could pry the militiamen out of the sturdy brick railroad buildings in which they had sought refuge. In a battle that lasted until the wee hours of the morning, the mob fired rifles and pistols at anything that moved, rolled a flaming railroad car into one building, and tried to blow a hole in another with a stolen cannon.

Similar scenes played out around the nation. In Baltimore, a 180-man state militia fought their way from the Sixth Armory to Camden Station, where they had been ordered to protect the trains. The angry crowd hurled stones and hunks of roadway at them, screaming insults and threats as they did so. Despite orders to hold their fire, the troops, many still teenagers, and terrified ones at that, began to take aim at anything that might have been a rioter, the flash of their rifles eerily pretty in the night air. Innocent shoppers fell writhing on the sidewalks. Shopkeepers slammed their doors shut and ran for the back rooms, while friends dragged wounded comrades behind sturdy wagons, sheltering themselves from flying splinters.[13]

So fast-moving and violent were the strikes that newspapers began to wonder whether they might be witnessing the first throes of a nationwide revolution. In every town, the work of radical agitators, socialists, or communists (little distinction was made) was suspected. A headline in *The New York World* asked RIOT OR REVOLUTION? The *New-Orleans Times* wrote: "War between labor and capital has begun in earnest. . . . America's first experience in communism is now the most significant episode of the most extraordinary year in our political history."

Most shocking was that the government seemed powerless to stop it. The police were hopelessly overwhelmed while the boys and old men who made up local militias had no stomach for this kind of fighting—and many sided with the strikers anyway. President Rutherford Hayes was so worried that he dispatched the ironclad *Monitor*—a heavily armed, low-profile navy vessel—to watch over the Treasury Building in New York from offshore and saw to it that postal employees were provided with rifles so that they might guard federal buildings in Washington, D.C.[14]

City by city, state by state, the strike spread through Cleveland, Cincinnati, Columbus, Indianapolis, and inevitably to Chicago, home to the greatest railway hub in the American West.

City leaders looked on in horror as the revolt, with the savagery and inevitability of a tsunami, worked its way toward them. Albert Day, a grain merchant, feared that "the mob" would attack "the best residence sections of the city." In the Eighteenth Ward, financiers, storekeepers, and lawyers were sworn in as special police and received U.S. Army muskets.[15] Marshall Field, the department store magnate, joined the makeshift force and lent delivery wagons and horses to the police department. Private militia companies, veteran groups, and citizens' cavalry companies similarly prepared to defend the city from lawlessness. Mayor Monroe Heath, who had seen that local militias in other cities often sided with the strikers, persuaded President Hayes to dispatch six companies of the Ninth Infantry and two more companies from the Dakota Territory.

Parsons found that his popularity and notoriety increased the closer the strike drew to Chicago. Where before he was happy speaking before twenty or thirty people, now thousands clamored for him. On Saturday afternoon, July 21, 1877, crowds packed into Sack's Hall to hear him deliver a speech savaging media moguls and railroad tycoons. "If the proprietor has a right to fix the wages and say what labor is worth," he said, "then we are bound hand and foot—slaves—and we should be perfectly happy: content with a bowl of rice and a rat a week apiece."[16] The delirious crowd answered back: "No! No!"

Two evenings later, some ten to fifteen thousand workers marched in a torchlight procession to Market Square, an open area at the intersection of Market and Madison streets, to hear him again. Hoisting banners and placards in English, German, and French that read WE

WANT WORK, NOT CHARITY and LIFE BY LABOR OR DEATH BY FIGHT, they thundered with cheers when Parsons began to speak. Railroad barons Tom Scott, Jay Gould, and Cornelius Vanderbilt were assailed for paying their workers ninety cents a day. He attacked newspaper editors for devoting their pages to titillating crime stories rather than offering real journalism about working conditions. He urged the crowd not to resort to violence, yet not to back down in the face of oppression either. "Enroll your names in the Grand Army of Labor," Parsons exhorted the roaring crowd, "and if the capitalist engages in warfare against our rights, then we shall resist him with all the means that God has given us."[17]

With those words, Parsons forged the first link in a chain of events that would span two decades and fundamentally shape the destiny of Leon Czolgosz.

AN OPEN CASK OF GUNPOWDER

Fitzhugh Lee, the American consul general to Cuba, cut a comic figure on the streets of Havana in the spring of 1897. Appointed by President Cleveland the year before, Lee roamed the city's bars in white suits that stretched around an ample frame. A Panama hat topped his round head, and around one leg was occasionally strapped a sidearm, no doubt ensuring a level of authority that he, unable to speak Spanish, might not have otherwise commanded.

A West Point graduate, Lee was remembered more for his pranks, his horsemanship, and for being the nephew of Confederate general Robert E. Lee than for his scholarly ability, graduating near the bottom of his class. Not that Havana posed much of an intellectual challenge. In fact, Lee found plenty of time for pursuits other than those of the government, most notably private business ventures on the island. Finding investors to launch a streetcar line in Havana was one cherished dream.[1]

Lee's attempts to curry favor among his new bosses in the McKinley administration were typical of his heavy-handed approach to dealing with people. In one dispatch to Washington shortly after McKinley's election, he tried to assure his superiors that he was trustworthy, saying that he could be absolutely depended upon and that he was not prone to hasty decisions. "I never get excited or bewildered," he boasted.[2]

Yet there was more to Lee than a flamboyant rogue playing at diplomat. His analysis of the situation in Cuba had for the most part been dead-on. The uprising launched when José Martí and his crew landed their small boat on a Cuban beach in 1895, he wrote, was spinning out of control. Innocent civilians were dying by the thousands and American business on the island was getting caught in the cross fire.

Cuba, then an island of 1.5 million people, was along with Puerto Rico virtually all that remained of Spain's once magnificent empire in the Americas. Rich in resources and agricultural wealth—it was the world's largest producer of sugar—the four-hundred-year-old colony held a romantic place in the hearts of many Spaniards, who knew it as "the ever faithful isle." Cuba was, for the Spanish, more than just an island. It was part of an empire that made them great, a reward from God, as legend had it, for liberating the Iberian Peninsula from Islam in the fifteenth century. As French journalist Charles Benoit put it: "Cuba—it is the flesh of the flesh of Spain; it is part of the history, the glory, and the grandeur of Spain."[3]

Yet this conception of Cuba as an "ever faithful isle" did not fit with reality, so often had Spain faced revolts. As recently as the 1870s, Cuban rebels seeking independence had battled the Spanish before finally giving in to exhaustion and promises of reforms. Now, convinced that Spain had never delivered on its pledges, they were trying again. Rebel military leader Máximo Gómez y Báez, exhibiting an astonishing disregard for the poor Cubans in whose name he fought, employed a strategy to destroy Cuba's economy to the point that the Spanish wouldn't want it. By turning Cuba into an "economic desert," Gómez figured he could both bleed the Spanish of the resources to prosecute the war and raise doubts about whether it was worth the effort.[4] His armies, a collection of twenty-five thousand or so machete-wielding peasants, crisscrossed the island laying waste to anything of value, burning cane fields and sugar mills, dynamiting railroad trestles, and cutting telegraph wires. He dictated that all sugar plantations, the backbone of the economy, had to be leveled and the men who worked on them shot as traitors.[5] Harsh though his tactics were, Gómez succeeded in his most immediate objective. Sugar production plunged and with it Cuba's economic fortunes. In 1894, the value of the sugar crop had stood at $62.1 million. In 1895, the first year of the uprising, it declined to $45.4 million, and in 1896 it plunged to $13 million.[6]

Spain, Lee noted with some anguish, responded to the rebellion in February 1896 by assigning its most ruthless commander to the island. Valeriano Weyler Nicolau, a Spaniard of German ancestry, was a soldier's soldier who didn't fuss much about his appearance, a novel trait among the peacocks of the Spanish officer corps. He slept in a hammock on campaigns and ate enlisted men's rations of bread, sardines, and red wine.[7] Refusing to smoke or drink liquor, he looked fit and youthful, with short hair, muttonchops, and a mustache.

But it was Weyler's cold heart that had made him famous. A veteran of Madrid's colonial wars, he had earned a fearsome reputation as "the Butcher" for his ruthless methods. In an article that appeared on February 23, 1896, *The New York Journal* reached deep into its bag of villainous adjectives to describe him as a "fiendish despot" who was "pitiless" and a "brute," as well as an "exterminator of men." "There is nothing to prevent his carnal, animal brain from running riot with itself in inventing tortures and infamies of bloody debauchery."[8]

Weyler didn't disappoint his critics when he revealed his strategy for crushing the rebellion. Recognizing that he couldn't keep up with the rebels' hit-and-run tactics, he decided to cut off their network of support among the peasants. In a massive relocation program infamously known as La Reconcentración, Weyler swept the countryside of every man, woman, and child his troops could find, relocating some four hundred to six hundred thousand people to encampments where they could be watched.[9]

Without jobs, enough to eat, or even in some cases a place to sleep, the uprooted peasants were plunged into a hellish existence of deprivation and cruelty. Emaciated and sick, thousands wandered the dirty cobblestone streets of Cuban cities begging for scraps and fighting over morsels of food like animals, their children's stomachs bloated from malnutrition, their teenage daughters offering furtive glances at Spanish soldiers, hoping to earn some quick money for their families.

Those who hid in the countryside met an even worse fate. Spanish scouts patrolled the arid, rocky hills, poisoning water supplies and shipping off anyone they found to a notorious penal colony at Ceuta in Africa. Estimates of the death toll vary widely, but even by conservative accounts, the carnage was horrific—one scholar has estimated that around one hundred thousand had died by 1898.[10]

The remorseless Weyler dismissed their plight as the price of doing business. "How do they want me to wage war?" he once snarled. "With bishops, pastorals and presents of sweets and honey?"[11] Trapped between the rebels and the Spanish army, Cuban peasants didn't stand a chance. "On the whole," said Nicolas de Truffin, the Russian consul in Havana, "it looks as if the two sides, equally aloof from the desire to make concessions, have sworn to lay waste to this unfortunate country."

The uprising would normally have been of little consequence to most Americans. Colonial wars had been waged for decades in the four corners of the globe with the United States taking little notice. Yet this insurgency offered a riveting cocktail of politics, economics, and religion. Equally important, Americans could track its gruesome developments almost daily from their breakfast tables. It just so happened that the two greatest newspaper moguls of the era had decided to use Cuba as their battleground for media supremacy.

William Randolph Hearst and Joseph Pulitzer: Their own inventive reporters could not have scripted a more compelling pair of rivals. For starters, the two came from opposite ends of the economic spectrum. Hearst, the son of a salty California millionaire and U.S. senator, had been given the struggling *San Francisco Examiner* almost as a toy, a project to run when his father couldn't figure out what to do with it. Quickly displaying an ability for publishing, the young Hearst rescued the paper and began looking for a fresh challenge, heading east in 1895 with a fat check from his mother and a burning ambition to make himself the nation's most influential and richest newspaper tycoon.[12] A year later, he purchased the struggling *New York Morning Journal* and hired star reporters such as Stephen Crane and Julian Hawthorne to boost circulation.

Pulitzer, by contrast, was a self-made man, a classic American success story. A Hungarian adventurer, he came to the United States on the promise of earning $500 to fight in the Union army. He cut his teeth as a reporter on a German-language newspaper in St. Louis and climbed to the upper strata of American media as publisher of *The New York World*, even though he rarely set foot in the newsroom, suffering from near blindness and a hypersensitivity to any sort of noise.

Yet the two had much in common. Both were at heart bareknuckled street fighters determined to give the people what they wanted—scandal, titillation, and the kind of journalism that never let the facts get in the way of a good story.

The unfolding events in Cuba provided all the inspiration they would need to promote their papers. To this day, journalism school students snicker at one oft-repeated but unconfirmed exchange between Hearst and sketch artist Frederic Remington. According to legend, Remington once telegrammed his boss from Havana to tell him all was quiet on the island and "there will be no war." Hearst supposedly replied, "Please remain. You furnish the pictures and I'll furnish the war."[13]

Everywhere the reporters and artists of Hearst's *Journal* and Pulitzer's *World* turned, they managed to find the nugget of a story that, embellished just right, was sure to land them on the front page.

The rebels' female combatants were a godsend, providing an excuse to combine sex and violence in page-turning tales. Describing the women as beautiful "Amazons" unafraid to charge their horses into Spanish troops, the journalists let their imaginations and the hyperbole run unchecked. As the *World* reported on April 5, 1896: "Nothing more dreadful has ever been conceived by mortal man than the behavior of the women who fight in Cuba. Most of them are beautiful, judged by ordinary standards. . . . In battle they show no mercy; they hack, hew with their machetes, and shout in such a way as to alarm any opponent, and yet, when the fight is over, they are as tender to their foes as to their friends."[14]

On other occasions, the papers thrust themselves squarely into the middle of the story. One series of reports in 1897 ranks as one of the most enterprising attempts made by any American media organization to score a headline. It came in August, when the *New York Journal* took up the cause of the beautiful Evangelina Cosio y Cisneros, the eighteen-year-old niece of a Cuban rebel leader. While she stood trial in Havana for revolutionary activity, a *Journal* reporter, Marion Kendrick, wrote a series of articles in her defense. One entitled "The Cuban Girl Martyr" was a spine-tingling account of the horrors that surely awaited her in a Spanish jail on a small island near Gibraltar. The paper then organized a petition on her behalf, collecting fifteen thousand signatures, including those of Clara Barton and Mother McKinley.

The story reached its climax when a man working for the *Journal* in Havana, one Karl Decker, rented a house across an alley from Evangelina's cell. From his window he stretched a ladder over a twelve-foot gap, cut the bars to her cell, and spirited the prisoner away. She would eventually escape Cuba dressed as a boy in a sailor suit complete with flowing tie, coat, and trousers, her hair stuffed under a large hat.[15]

Stories like Evangelina's filled readers with both sympathy and rage. In the Cubans, Americans saw images of themselves from a century earlier: oppressed, thirsting for freedom, and eager to throw off a European master. In the Spanish, they saw a country that was the epitome of the old order they detested: fiscally bankrupt, a monarchy, a land from which nothing new or valuable seemed to come. "Spain has run her course," Congressman William Sulzer of New York bellowed to Congress in 1896. "Her days of conquest are passed. She is tottering to-day on the greatness of her own historic ruins."[16]

That so many Americans felt so strongly about Cuba is hardly a surprise when seen through the prism of history and opportunity. Presidents and businessmen had long fantasized about bringing Cuba into the union, casting a covetous eye southward as early as the 1820s. "I have ever looked on Cuba as the most interesting addition which could ever be made to our system of states," Thomas Jefferson wrote in 1823.[17] John Quincy Adams chimed in that it was "scarcely possible to resist the conviction that the annexation of Cuba . . . will be indispensable to the continuance and integrity of the Union itself."[18] President Polk even tried to buy Cuba for $100 million in 1848, an offer rejected by a Spanish minister, who said he would rather see the island sink than sell it.[19]

Reprobation of the Spanish tumbled in from every quarter. Preachers who disdained Catholicism as a holdover from the Middle Ages spoke openly of their desire to raise an army of right-thinking Protestants who would drive the "pope-ridden Spain" out of the Western Hemisphere. Labor leaders saw a land of new recruits. As early as 1896, Samuel Gompers, the founder of the American Federation of Labor and onetime employee in a cigar factory alongside Cubans in New York, helped introduce a resolution at an AFL convention expressing sympathy for the rebels. Only through independence, he argued, could workers in Cuba organize and improve employment conditions. The resolution was overwhelmingly approved.[20] The Spanish colonial government in Cuba stirred up even more hostility by arresting Americans, albeit mostly naturalized former Cubans, who it felt were aiding the rebels.[21]

Churchmen, union leaders, politicians, Cuban expatriates, men on the street—for the rebels, the United States constituted a second front that was almost as important as dynamiting and shooting in Cuba. Finely tailored Cuban revolutionaries established offices in Washington, D.C., and New York, where they directed surprisingly slick fund-raising and public relations campaigns. They organized expatriate Cuban cigar makers into clubs where each member was expected to contribute 10 percent of its income to the revolution.[22] In Washington, D.C., they established an effective network of lobbyists who gained the confidence of members of Congress. And from offices at the Manhattan Life Insurance Building at 66 Broadway across from Trinity Church in New York, they operated a spin machine that would routinely place their cause on the front pages. Most afternoons at 4 P.M., up to forty reporters would meet Horatio Rubens, a young Columbia University–educated lawyer and de facto press officer. Milling around a room known as the Peanut Club for the snacks that Rubens served, the reporters gobbled up news, or at least his version of it, about events in Cuba.[23]

Rubens hoped to achieve two things by luring reporters to his office. There was, of course, the need to raise money to fund the revolution. The bedraggled soldiers fighting in Cuba could not afford even bullets for their guns. The other, more important, objective was to force a change in American policy.[24] As things stood, the federal government was obliged under international law to prevent those considered revolutionaries from smuggling arms from its shores, a duty Washington had taken seriously. Scores of sailings had been intercepted by the navy and the Treasury Department's revenue cutters—predecessors to the Coast Guard. That dragnet would be lifted if the United States would provide diplomatic recognition to the Cuban revolutionary government by granting them legal status of belligerents.[25]

Were it up to Congress, the Cubans could have done whatever they wanted long ago. Any politician with even the faintest measure of the public's pulse could see that sympathy for the insurgents was widely and deeply felt. With an alacrity not often associated with legislators, both houses produced torrents of resolutions expressing support for the insurgents, calling for their independence and for the United States to grant them belligerent status.[26]

But the Cubans also needed the support of President Cleveland, and his backing was proving considerably harder to obtain. McKinley's predecessor had never been convinced that the Cuban revolutionaries were ready to govern. Scratch beneath the movement's urbane public image, he believed, and one would find a hard-bitten group composed of simple peasant stock. Far from members of America's continental army to which they were often compared, soldiers of the insurgent force were not the type to linger over a newspaper's political section or debate the issues at the local town hall. Nor did they seem well organized. The insurgents had written a constitution and referred to themselves as a junta, but did not possess enough power to occupy so much as a single building. It was unclear, meanwhile, if the Cuban army really answered to the movement's political leaders. As Lee said, the single voice of military leader Gómez seemed to dominate the rebel cause.[27]

The Cubans, Cleveland believed, would bring chaos to Cuba and possibly create a power vacuum that a European nation such as Germany would eagerly fill. As long as he was in the White House, all the congressional resolutions in the world were completely useless.

——

The swirling currents of public opinion, history, and national security were enough to make McKinley's head spin. Cuba seemed to offer nothing but risk with little prospect of reward. Quietly, he hoped the whole thing would somehow magically disappear. Meeting with President Cleveland the night before his inauguration, the president-elect confided that he felt conflicted over whether Americans were duty-bound to intervene in the revolution that was gaining strength in Cuba. "He adverted to the horrors of war, and was intensely saddened by the prospect incident to the loss of life, the destruction of property, the blows dealt at the higher morality and the terrible responsibility thrust upon him," Cleveland later said. Preparing to leave, the two shook hands and McKinley added, "Mr. President, if I can go out of office, at the end of my term, with the knowledge that I have done what lay in my power to avert this terrible calamity . . . I shall be the happiest man in the world."[28]

In any other circumstance, such a sentiment would be dismissed as a throwaway expression, an exaggeration. Yet, for this president, there was more than an element of truth to McKinley's dreams of professional bliss.

"Nothing could be simpler and more methodical than President McKinley's daily life in the White House since he came to Washington," wrote a correspondent for *McClure's Magazine*.[29] The pace was relaxed and stately, his schedule full of holes. McKinley began his official day at the very civilized hour of ten o'clock and would knock off around four or five for some fresh air. In between, there was ample reason to think he wasn't overly taxed. It was not uncommon for visitors to see newlywed couples, accompanied by their congressmen, waiting outside the president's office for a brief exchange of pleasantries. If the bride were charming enough, she would receive the red carnation from McKinley's lapel.

Each day, he found time to read a tower of newspapers that might include five or six of the New York dailies, a couple of the Washington and Chicago papers, and half a dozen from other cities, all in addition to regularly reading the *Canton Repository* from his hometown.[30] After lunch, McKinley would sometimes pause to cheer as the office staff played baseball on the south lawn. A pet parrot provided a musical accompaniment to his days when the two would take turns whistling "Yankee Doodle Dandy."[31] Evenings were usually quiet affairs, spent at home with Ida or a small gathering of close friends. Weather permitting, he often slipped out for a constitutional down Pennsylvania or Connecticut avenues. By today's standards, these sojourns were unthinkably casual affairs. The leader of the nation would simply pack up a newspaper, pull on his dark frock coat, and stride out the front door of the executive mansion in his quick-paced, erect manner, nosing at store windows for gifts for Ida, and, if he wandered too far from home, taking a streetcar back.[32] Other times McKinley would ride in a carriage with Ida or a White House guest and explore Washington, favorite routes being the "Soldiers' Home" ground, the National Park, and Arlington. Children quickly learned his habits and would wait on the sidewalk, shouting "Hello, Major!" as he passed, addressing McKinley by his Civil War rank. He would happily respond with a friendly wave, "How do you do, boys?" or "How do you do, girls?" Workmen would doff their caps.[33]

His days regimented, his habits well ingrained, the president sought a dignified presidency, slavishly adhering to proper decorum in policy as well as in personal behavior. This discipline, as it had throughout his professional life, started with his attire. Suits and shirts were made to measure by a New York tailor and delivered to him in Washington by his brother Abner. They did not long remain in the closet. McKinley sometimes changed his vests three or four times a day to keep them from looking wrinkled, a practice that appears less extravagant given the place—Washington, D.C.—and the time—decades before the invention of air-conditioning. Other times, he required a more complete change of wardrobe. He once wore a frock coat and silk hat on a short fishing trip, a decision he must have regretted when, upon seeing his rod arch with a strike, he rocked the boat so violently that it sank.[34]

One facet of presidential life left largely unattended, however, was the sorry condition of the White House. Trampled under the feet of an unchecked horde of visitors, including the curious who simply wandered in off the street, the carpets were worn to a stub in the middle and frayed along the edge. Lightning bolts of cracked paint marked the ceilings. Wallpaper hung dog-eared. Flimsy stair banisters were more ornament than safety device.[35] The floors were so weak that during large parties, staff would rush to the basement to affix support beams and bricks. Not just the structure, but the layout was in desperate need of renovation. The state dining room, for example, accommodated only fifty people, and for larger events the staff was forced to set up tables in the central hall. Food was prepared in the basement, requiring considerable exertion just to transport meals of eight to twelve courses to the tables. Mark Hanna, a frequent visitor, entertained himself by timing how long it took to deliver his meal.[36]

The Army Corp of Engineers did what they could to remedy the executive mansion's shortcomings, putting forward several remodeling plans. Ida submarined them all, complaining she wouldn't be able to stand the hammering. The only improvement was made by Captain Theodore A. Bingham, commissioner of public buildings and grounds, who, frustrated by an almost total lack of storage space for coats and hats, purchased velour curtains at sixty cents a yard and hung them in the entrance hall to hide a recently acquired collection of secondhand racks and boxes.[37] So meager was the White House budget that the president had to pay the salaries for some of his staff out of his own pocket, including forty dollars a month for a cook who specialized in the hearty Midwestern fare that became known around town as "cuisine à la Canton."

Cling though he might to the simple, courtly life of a nineteenth-century president, McKinley could not for long escape the demands that Cuba was exerting on his presidency. Like the walls of a shrinking room, one new problem after another seemed to be closing in upon him, the latest being the plight of American business on the island.

In May 1897, some three hundred prominent American bankers, merchants, manufacturers, and steamships owners who did business in Cuba signed a petition pleading for the president's help. The group believed that the Cuban revolution had already "seriously injured" their businesses, which were "now threatened with total annihilation."[38] Though Cuba hardly topped the ranks of America's trading partners, the "advance agent of prosperity" could not take lightly the worries of American industry anywhere.

Cuba had, in fact, for years been a popular destination for American companies. A New York–based firm ran the largest sugar property in the world in Cuba, the sixty-thousand-acre Constancia plantation. An American company printed most of the money used on the island, and several cork companies and tobacco plantations operated under American control. The Bethlehem Steel Corporation had established the Juragua Iron Company, Ltd., and the Ponupo Manganese Company near Santiago. Three American iron and manganese companies claimed to have investments totaling $6 million of purely American capital. As early as 1882, the U.S. consul Ramon O. Williams was able to write: "De facto, Cuba is already inside the commercial union of the United States."[39]

What exactly the president was supposed to do remained a tricky matter. The petitioners would ask only that he seek an "honorable reconciliation between the parties in conflict." No wonder. For as much as they worried about their Cuban investments and longed for new markets, the specter of war was something that few could bring themselves to contemplate. From the well-padded seats of their carriages to the snooty elegance of their clubs, industrialists sang the chorus in almost perfect harmony. The last thing American balance sheets needed was for their country to be exchanging cannon fire with a European power. Not now, not as the economy was just starting to turn around.

As 1897 wore on, sales of everything from buggy whips to Cracker Jack snacks began to rebound from the depths of the depression that had begun four years before. The terrible bout of deflation that had so ravaged farmers was subsiding. Workers again filed through factory gates. The New York *Commercial Advertiser* published survey results on January 3, 1898, finding that "after three years of waiting and of false starts, the groundswell of demand has at last begun to rise with a steadiness which leaves little doubt that an era of prosperity has appeared."[40] It was starting to look like McKinley, as he had promised from his front porch, was delivering prosperity after all. A military showdown with Spain threatened everything. War would rattle consumer confidence, which was so important to boosting demand. Foreign trade might be disrupted. Corporate investment could be shelved.

——

It is easy to imagine McKinley seated in the chair where he conducted most of his work—at the head of the polished, heavy table in the cabinet room adjoining his office—squirming over the dilemma that taunted him. Studying newspapers with his intent, dark eyes, he would have winced at the sharply conflicting editorials on what he should do about Cuba. Drawing long breaths from his ever present cigar, filling the room with its pungent smoke, he would listen intently as visitors from Cuba, such as American plantation owner Edwin Atkins, pleaded for his help in dealing with the rebels. With some irritation, he might have risen from his seat and walked across the Oriental carpet to spin the large globe in the corner, snarling in frustration as he stopped the rotation when faced with the small outline of an island just off Florida. Always deliberate, always careful, always cautious, McKinley finally decided he needed more information, but not from newspapers nor from Fitzhugh Lee, whom he hardly knew. Somebody he trusted had to go to Cuba to bring back firsthand accounts of the events in the island that seemed so perilous to the United States.

William J. Calhoun, an Illinois Republican and associate of McKinley friend Charles G. Dawes, spent four weeks that spring traveling throughout the island conducting interviews, studying the land, furiously taking notes, and apparently suffering mightily from the climate. Describing his journey to reporters waiting at the base of Wall Street for his return on the steamship *Saratoga,* Calhoun complained that the rain in Cuba came down so hard that he once had to take a carriage to cross a street that had flooded in less than ten minutes.[41]

What he saw of the uprising shocked him as well. With literary flourish, Calhoun described in a letter to McKinley on June 22, 1897, how Weyler had laid waste to the country. "Every house had been burned, banana trees cut down, cane fields swept with fire, and everything in the shape of food destroyed. . . . The country was wrapped in the stillness of death and the silence of desolation."[42] Then Calhoun took a step further by asserting a view that was at odds with American public opinion. It would be, he concluded, neither wise nor feasible to recognize the rebels nor seek Cuban independence.

Echoing reports already made by Lee, Calhoun found the rebels whom he met to be poorly educated and disorganized, wholly unsuited to democratic government. Nearly all the affluent segments of society, be they Spanish or Cuban, preferred annexation by the United States over a government dominated by the insurgents. Like Cleveland, Calhoun feared that instability and chaos seemed the most likely outcome of a rebel victory over the Spanish—a failed state that would invite another European power to take charge. It was a chilling thought: American commerce, one day traveling through the Caribbean, passing directly under the barrels of the Kaiser's guns.

In the days immediately thereafter, McKinley drafted a letter to Madrid.

On the quiet Sunday of August 8, 1897, Spanish prime minister Antonio Cánovas del Castillo and his wife were enjoying a relaxing afternoon at a spa in the resort town of Santa Agueda. The respite was a welcome escape for Cánovas, who was sick of American whining about Cuba and would soon have to meet the new American minister to Madrid, sixty-two-year-old Civil War veteran Stewart Woodford, who was carrying McKinley's letter. Cuba was Spanish business alone, and Cánovas was in no mood to take advice from anybody about how to deal with it, especially upstart Americans who had recently fought a brutal civil war. His own methods were no more harsh, he believed, than those of the Union army that had laid waste to the Confederate South. What's more, Cánovas knew, Spanish public opinion stood solidly behind him. So hostile were the Spanish to American interference that the State Department had warned Woodford and his nervous wife to postpone their arrival in Madrid until after the end of the bullfighting season, when presumably Spanish bloodlust would have been quenched. Plans were made for the Spanish military and the police to take up positions on board Woodford's train to protect it as it traveled through the country and to closely guard the train station when he arrived to deliver McKinley's message.[43]

No doubt feeling relaxed after a morning of treatments and an enjoyable lunch, Cánovas was lingering in the spa's gallery when he noticed a young man approaching. As he neared, the stranger reached inside his coat and withdrew a revolver. In quick succession, three shots echoed throughout the building. The prime minister crumbled to the ground, blood oozing at the feet of his terrified wife. He died two hours later. The assassin was an Italian by the name of Michele Angiolillo, the newspapers reported, and he had killed the Spanish leader in the name of anarchy. In the gilded halls of European capitals, monarchs and heads of state nervously gulped and wondered if they might be next.

In Washington, newspaper headlines elicited a somewhat different reaction. More than one guilty smile crept across the face of State Department staffers as they realized their incredible good fortune.

On September 20th, 1897, McKinley snapped the reins of his fine horse team and, with Theodore Roosevelt seated next to him, drove his carriage out of the White House grounds into the streets of Washington. Roosevelt, thrilled by his recent access to the president, including a dinner the previous Friday, was bursting with excitement at the opportunity to update McKinley on the deployment of American ships. The assistant secretary of the navy believed that the United States was on a collision course with Spain and had strong opinions on what the president should do in case of war. As they bounced over the cobblestones, Roosevelt argued that the United States should be ready to quickly dispatch an expeditionary force to Cuba and that a flying squadron of ships be formed to harass the coast of Spain. And there was one more thing. "Our Asiatic squadron should blockade, and if possible take, Manila," he insisted.[44]

Manila seemed an unlikely place to prosecute a war against the Spanish. The Philippines, Spain's largest colony in the Pacific, was more than nine thousand miles away from Havana and the United States didn't have a quarrel with Spain per se. McKinley simply wanted them to leave Cuba.

American naval planners, however, had linked Cuba and the Philippines ever since Lieutenant W. W. Kimball of the Office of Naval Intelligence first sketched out plans for a possible war with Spain in 1896. Taking the Philippine capital, Kimball theorized, could give the United States an important bargaining chip to bring the Spanish to heel in the Caribbean.[45] By June 1897, American thinking had advanced further. The United States, naval planners wrote, might be able to work in concert with the rebels who had been fighting Spanish forces on the ground, arguing that "we could probably have a controlling voice, as to what should become of the islands, when the final settlement is made."[46]

McKinley listened politely, but still refused to consider any objective other than averting war. Yet as a veteran of the Civil War, McKinley understood that military strategy often called for attacks in unlikely places. Although he could have scotched the plan with a wave of his hand, McKinley kept his peace and let the experts play their war games.

The Spanish summer capital of San Sebastian, perched on beautiful green mountains above the turquoise waters of the Bay of Biscay, was just stirring to life after the siesta on September 18 when U.S. envoy Woodford stepped into his coach and directed the driver to take him to the offices of the foreign ministry. Arriving a few minutes later, at 5 P.M., he put on his most amiable face and proceeded to explain McKinley's hopes for Cuba.

The United States had the right to involve itself on the island, he said. Both economic and humanitarian concerns compelled it to do so. As directions he had received from Washington read: "The chronic condition of trouble . . . causes disturbances in the social and political condition of our peoples. . . . A continuous irritation within our own border injuriously affects the normal functions of business, and tends to delay the condition of prosperity to which this country is entitled."[47]

Yet McKinley had decided, for the time being at least, that he would let the Spanish sort out their uppity colony on their own. There would be no official American demand for Cuban independence. Spain, Woodford said, should offer proposals to end the war that were "honorable to herself" and "just to her Cuban colony and to mankind." Nor would the United States tell the Spanish how to end the fighting, insisting only that they establish peace on the island by November 1.

Had Cánovas still been alive, this would probably have elicited a finger-wagging tirade. Who were the Americans to be giving his government timetables? But the Spanish listened with polite interest. Práxedes Mateo Sagasta, Spain's new prime minister, was a liberal who, as McKinley's luck would have it, had months before championed a kinder, gentler approach to dealing with Cuba. Within weeks, Sagasta's cabinet was well on its way toward implementing the reforms that McKinley had requested. The murderous Weyler was ordered back to Spain. Political prisoners, among them a number of Americans, were freed from Cuban jails. And while Spain would retain control of military and foreign affairs, it would grant Cuba a level of autonomy that it had never seen before.

Spain's acquiesence marked a diplomatic triumph for McKinley. He appeared to have averted a war with Spain and established a level of authority on the island that would safeguard American business interests. In his message to Congress on December 6, 1897, McKinley wrote that Spain should be given "a reasonable chance to realize her expectations and to prove the efficacy of the new order of things to which she stands irrevocably committed."[48] To underscore his commitment to the new order, McKinley contributed $5,000 of his own money to launch an effort to collect private funds to ease the suffering of displaced Cubans. He even felt confident enough to express his own views on the rebels, ones that were sharply at odds with much of the American public, who still favored independence. He now flatly asserted that the insurgents were simply not "capable of the ordinary functions of government towards its own people and other states."[49]

In dusty rebel camps around Cuba that autumn, revolutionaries studied the proposal that Sagasta and McKinley had agreed upon. With some sense of victory, they could smile at news that Weyler was being sent home.

Yet a close reading of the proposal revealed unacceptable provisions. It stated, for example, that the upper house of a new Cuban parliament would be made up of men mostly appointed by Spain's governor-general to the island. The governor also would retain the power to veto legislation and dissolve parliament whenever he saw fit. In short, under this definition of autonomy, Cuba would remain firmly under Spanish rule.[50] Gómez, to whom the ends always justified the means, declared that he would die fighting for independence rather than accept this offer from Spain. Anyone who openly favored autonomy would be subject to court-martial and sentenced to death.[51]

Even more unsettling was the reaction of the *peninsulares,* the Spanish loyalists who made up Cuba's economic and political elite. Reforms that had not gone far enough for the insurgents were wildly radical in the eyes of Spanish soldiers, shopkeepers, and farmers. Madrid, it appeared, had taken steps to hand them over to the unkempt, violent rabble that would stop at nothing to destroy the comfortable lives that they and their forefathers had built. Their reaction to such betrayal could not have been more extreme. One tobacco planter in the Santa Clara Province told Stephen Bonsal of *The New York Herald,* "The only way for Spain to retain her sovereignty over these islands is to exterminate—butcher if you like—every man, woman, and child upon it who is infected with the contagion and dreams of 'Cuba libre.' "[52] Throughout the later part of the year, rallies and meetings were held all over the island denouncing Madrid's autonomist plan. In December, a statement purporting to represent the views of men holding 80 percent of Cuba's wealth was circulated demanding a change in policy.[53] Richard Weightman of *The Washington Post* wrote in December that the *peninsulares* feared that autonomy "would be the death knell of civilized society in Cuba."[54]

None were more upset than the Spanish soldiers based in Cuba, many of whom had not been paid in months and were held together only by their faith in Weyler. The bitter ex-commander could do little to soothe their worries. As his bags were being loaded on a steamship for the trip back to Spain on October 31, 1897, Weyler told well-wishers gathered on the dock that Sagasta didn't have the guts to defend Spain's interests. "I had expected my release from the time of the death of Senior Cánovas, not believing that any political leader would be strong enough to sustain me when the United States and the rebels were together constantly demanding that Spain should come to a settlement." Unwilling to defend an autonomist government without Weyler leading them, scores of officers quit. Those who remained spent the Christmas holidays sipping wine, smoking cigars, and plotting against Weyler's replacement, General Ramon Blanco, all the while cursing the interfering Americans.

The morning of January 12, 1898, Fitzhugh Lee awoke in his room at the Hotel Inglaterra to a disturbance in the streets outside his window. From the narrow alleys and streets below echoed the sound of breaking glass and chants: "Death to Blanco and death to autonomy" and "Viva Weyler." An article in *El Reconcentrado* that morning had infuriated Spanish troops stationed in the city. Entitled "The Flight of the Scoundrels," the article leveled a stinging attack on a subordinate of their hero Weyler. Mobs of riotous Spaniards, most of them soldiers, surged toward the city's leafy central park in numbers that would eventually reach an estimated five thousand. Renegade troops ignored the commands of their superiors. One cavalry commander, ordered to charge into the swelling crowd, asked his superior officer, "Whom shall I charge, Loyal Spaniards for shouting 'Long Live Spain,' and 'Long live the Spanish Generals'?"[55]

This was exactly the sort of lawlessness that Lee had most feared and warned against with increasing passion since November. Unchecked, renegade soldiers might easily attack American citizens or their factories and plantations. Throughout the day, Lee dispatched frenzied, terse notes to Washington that seemed only to raise more questions than they answered. Early that afternoon he wrote: "Mobs, led by Spanish officers, attacked to-day the offices of the four newspapers advocating autonomy. Rioting at this hour, 1 P.M. continues."[56] A few hours later, he scratched out another dispatch. "Much excitement, which may develop into serious disturbances. . . . No rioting at present, but rumors of it are abundant. Palace heavily guarded. Consulate also protected by armed men."[57] The next day, January 13, 1898, Lee wrote that all was quiet, but that business had been suspended and the city was heavily guarded. He had heard protesters shout the day before that they should march on the U.S. consulate. "Presence of ships may be necessary later, but not now."[58] Later that day he added, "Uncertainty exists whether Blanco can control the situation. If demonstrated he cannot maintain order, preserve life, and keep the peace, or if Americans and their interests are in danger, ships must be sent, and to that end should be prepared to move promptly. Excitement and uncertainty predominates everywhere."[59]

No one had lifted a finger against a single American in Havana, yet the reports shocked Washington. Alvey Adee, the State Department's foremost expert on Spanish affairs and the most powerful diplomat after William Day, found Lee's dispatches especially worrying. He had been skeptical of Sagasta's plan to begin with, and now events in Cuba seemed to fulfill his worst expectations. Telegraph operators clicked out frantic messages back to Havana. A warship would be sent, Lee was told, if communications were cut off. On January 12, 1898, Adee wrote: "I think it would be well for our squadrons in the Gulf of Mexico to be ready to enter into action immediately since the emergency could arise at any moment."[60] Secretary of the Navy John Long ordered the naval commanders of the European and Asiatic fleets to retain all seamen whose enlistments were to soon expire.

The New York newspapers fueled the sense of panic with characteristic bombast. *The New York World* wrote: "The riots in Havana mean revolution" and warned of danger to Americans.[61] The *Journal* told its readers that the riots were aimed at Americans and predicted American military intervention within two days. Writing to Madrid on January 16, 1898, Spanish ambassador to Washington Enrique Dupuy de Lôme said that the "Government and Cabinet, although they have said nothing to me, seem to have lost all faith in Spain's success, and, to some extent, to have lost tranquility."[62] Dupuy de Lôme was more right than he knew.

At 10 A.M. on the brisk morning of January 24, 1898, Dupuy de Lôme arrived at the State, War, and Navy Building next door to the White House at Seventeenth Street and Pennsylvania Avenue. The massive gray structure, which took seventeen years to construct, had been designed in the style of the French Second Empire. Yet, built from granite and cast iron, it most closely resembled nothing more elegant than an imposing gray pile of rocks. As Dupuy de Lôme walked along the black-and-white-tiled corridor toward Day's office, he anticipated an uneventful meeting with a representative of a nation he disdained. Urbane and worldly, Dupuy de Lôme was considered imperious and insufferable, even by his own colleagues, who believed he labored under "delusions of grandeur."[63] For him, America was too new, too rough around the edges, too driven by the lowest common denominator to be considered Spain's equal. "Spain represents Europe, a monarchy and a sophisticated civilization; the United States is part of America, a Republic and herself a former rebellious colony,"[64] he once said. America's knee-jerk sympathy for the rebels was a constant source of frustration, no doubt heightened by his own failed attempts to court the American media. "Ignorance is perhaps the biggest defect of this immense country," he wrote. "Here all read but nobody meditates. . . . Trivia is magnified and made important."[65]

Day, the de facto secretary of state, planned to give the haughty Spaniard a rude awakening. McKinley had decided to send a warship, the USS *Maine*, to Havana on what the Spanish would be told was a courtesy call. Yet courtesy had very little to do with it. Secretary Long, writing in his diary, noted the double-sided intention in sending the ship. It was a good time to dispatch an American vessel as a step toward resuming normal relations, "a purely friendly matter." American ships should visit Cuba just like those from other nations to "exchange courtesies and civilities with the Spanish authorities there."[66] On the other hand, the secretary was also interested in having a ship in Havana because "some means of protection should be on hand."

It was a risky move. Spanish officers would be irritated by the sight of a brash Yankee warship anchored outside their bedroom windows. Madrid openly worried about the ramifications of some sort of accident. Even Lee suggested that the United States hold off for a few days. As Mrs. Richard Wainwright, wife of the ship's executive officer, noted from her parlor at home, "You might as well send a lighted candle on a visit to an open cask of gunpowder."[67] In Washington, Mark Hanna shared the sentiment and the explosive metaphor. Sending the *Maine* to Havana, he said, was like "waving a match in an oil-well for fun."[68]

PROPAGANDA OF THE DEED

Around noon on July 24, 1877, Albert Parsons opened the door at 94 Market Street in Chicago and slipped into the offices of the *Chicagoer Arbeiter-Zeitung*, the German-language publication of the Working-Man's Party of the United States. After a tumultuous twelve hours, Parsons needed the sympathetic ear that fellow labor activists were sure to provide. The night before, he had addressed a rally of six thousand workingmen near the crossing of Madison and Market streets, championing state control of the means of production, transportation, and communication.[1] "If capitalists engage in warfare against our rights, we shall resist them with all the means that God has given us," he told the approving crowd.[2] Unwisely for a man who worked at a major newspaper, he also chastised Chicago's media for playing a willing stooge to corporate America. Indeed, on showing up that morning for his day job as a typesetter for *The Chicago Times*, Parsons learned that his message had not gone over well and he was fired. What's worse, his name was added to a blacklist of Chicagoans that no respectable company would employ.

As Parsons related the events of the last twenty-four hours to his activist friends, heavy footsteps on the stairs grew louder outside the door. Two men had come looking for Parsons with a message. Mayor Heath wanted to see him, and he should come now. Parsons didn't resist but accepted the invitation with well-founded trepidation.[3] As he and the mysterious strangers stepped out onto the sidewalk, a gust of wind caught the jacket of one and revealed a sidearm.[4]

Led to a room through a labyrinth of corridors in an old wooden building known as the Rookery, police headquarters since the great fire, Parsons was given a seat before thirty angry men, including police superintendent Michael Hickey.

For two hours the group barked questions and accusations. Why, Hickey wanted to know, was Parsons stirring up so much trouble among working people? Why had he come to Chicago? Where had he been born? Was he married? Parsons would later write that Hickey asked him if he didn't "know better than to come up here from Texas and incite the working people to insurrections."

From the back of the room, shouts of "hang him," "lynch him," and "lock him up" echoed. In a voice raspy from so much public speaking, Parsons explained that the fact that so many people attended his speeches had nothing to do with him personally, but rather their miserable working conditions. He insisted he did not advocate violence; his social agenda was to be won at the ballot box: "Elect good men to make good laws and thus bring about good times."[5]

Unable to find any laws that Parsons had broken and afraid of making a martyr of him, the chief of police gripped Parsons's arm tightly and escorted him to the door. But before releasing the Texan from his grasp, Hickey delivered an ominous warning: "Parsons, your life is in danger. I advise you to leave the city at once. Beware. Everything you say or do is made known to me. I have men on your track who shadow you. Do you know you are liable to be assassinated any moment in the streets?"[6] Parsons later admitted to feeling alone and confused as he was turned out into the hall. It was the last time, for a long time, that the man who would become one of the most notorious American anarchists would feel that way.

By the time police chief Hickey hauled Parsons in for a dressing-down, the Great Railroad Strike was on Chicago's doorstep. Over the next few days, the city would be the scene of one running street battle after another. At the Chicago, Burlington, and Quincy roundhouse, a crowd of eight thousand workers destroyed two locomotives before police chased them off, killing three people in the process. On Blue Island Avenue, leading to the McCormick Reaper Works, police battled one thousand strikers who had been menacing scabs. At the Vorwaerts Turner Hall on West Twelfth Street, police smashed down the door and beat and fired upon a meeting of furniture workers, killing one. At the intersection of Sixteenth and Halsted streets, police charged a boisterous mob of strikers, killing two.[7]

Soon the entire transportation system in the city ground to a halt. Streetcars on the South Side stopped running, longshoremen refused to load ships, furniture workers and tailors abandoned their shops. Ironworkers, brass finishers, carpenters, brick makers, stonemasons, glaziers, and painters all laid down their tools and took to the streets.[8] In two days of fighting, between twenty-five and fifty civilians were killed, and around two hundred were seriously injured.[9]

Unknown to the Chicago strikers, their protests were starting to crack the resolve of railroad bosses. Executives at the Burlington in Chicago were coming to the conclusion that "the only question is whether or not to concede all demands." At the Illinois Central, one top official wrote that the company might have to relent on its cost-cutting demand and restore the recent wages of its switchmen.[10]

Yet the determination of the strikers was weakening even faster. By late July, the heady thrills of closing the rails had given way to stalemate along a number of lines. Many men had families to feed and could not continue the walkout indefinitely. What's more, after getting off to a shaky start, authorities finally seemed to have gained the upper hand, aided in part by the arrival of federal troops. Still shaking off the dust and grime of fighting Indians farther west, troopers were a new and intimidating sight for the railroad workers. These were hard-bitten, well-disciplined men, schooled in military tactics and used to taking orders. They were not going to be intimidated by a rabble of protesters.

The strikers knew they could not repel such firepower. One after another, groups met with their employers and agreed to peace terms. As when a river blasts ever-widening holes in a leaky dam, the entire edifice of the strike collapsed. Securely holding the advantage, many of the railroads set a deadline of July 30, 1877, for workers to return to their jobs without facing punishment. Most of them readily accepted. There were a few isolated examples of railroads making token concessions, but most men were forced to accept the starvation wages they had fought to prevent. It was hard to see the strike as anything other than an overwhelming defeat.

Yet the Great Railroad Strike left a surprising legacy. Even though they had utterly failed to achieve their goals, union and labor leaders got an exhilarating taste of what they could accomplish. Lizzie May Holmes, a friend of Parsons, wrote: "The great railroad strike of 1877 brought out the vague lines between classes distinctly, and forced every thinking man and woman to take a stand on one side or the other."[11] Soon, laborers were turning to strikes in record numbers. In 1880 alone, there were as many strikes and lockouts in the United States as in the previous 140 years combined.[12] In 1881, 129,521 workers participated in 471 strikes, and five years later, nearly half a million people walked off the job in 1,411 strikes.[13] Membership in the Knights of Labor soared.

The same phenomenon was true for Parsons. For a man who had been threatened with murder if he continued to stir up trouble, Parsons emerged with a fierce determination to build on his newfound popularity. He campaigned for an eight-hour workday. He ran for public office in Chicago, including alderman and county clerk, never winning, but putting in respectable showings. He served as president of the Trades Assembly of Chicago. He worked as an editor on the Socialist Labor Party's weekly newspaper. In 1879, he won the SLP's nomination for president, an honor he was forced to refuse because he was not old enough.

And in 1882, when a more radical—some might even say sinister—strain of social revolution arrived on American shores, Parsons would be among those most intrigued.

——

Heavily bundled against freezing temperatures, a score of people gathered around Pier 38 at the foot of King Street in New York the morning of December 18, 1882. They had come to greet the *Wisconsin*, which had docked in the wee hours of the morning after a perilous Atlantic crossing. Four days overdue, the ship had endured two weeks of high seas, sleet and snow, and even a collision with another ship. The waiting group, wearing scarlet ribbons in their lapels and clutching blood-red flags, mixed with reporters from the city's major newspapers as their eyes scanned the deck, hoping to spot Johann Most at the rails. Known in Europe for the inflammatory writing that extolled anarchy and had recently landed him in jail, Most had attained a sort of cult status even before leaving England for the New World. Here he hoped to introduce his ideology to what promised to be a willing population.

Finally recognizing the sandy beard, blue eyes, and fair complexion of the *Wisconsin*'s infamous passenger, the crowd surged toward the gangway. Reporters readied their notepads, eager to find out whether the time spent behind bars had dampened his ardor. For those looking for a snappy quote, Most did not disappoint. "Violence is justified against tyranny and tyrants," he told the journalists. "I am more radical than ever."[14]

The illegitimate son of a clerk and a governess who were too poor to pay for a marriage license, most had suffered through a nightmarish childhood of unfulfilled dreams and social rejection. At age twelve, he was expelled from school for organizing a strike against a teacher. That same year, both his mother and sister died, and before long he was at the mercy of a stepmother whom he detested. Then at age thirteen, Most suffered the defining event of his early life. A painful inflammation had developed in his jaw that required surgery. The procedure was well within the abilities of doctors of the time, and his ailment should have been readily dealt with. But Most's family selected a physician that history books describe simply as a quack. He ended up with a nasty disfiguring scar that ran across half his face.[15]

For a young teenager, the ugly and permanent wound changed everything. He was condemned to spend the rest of his school days as a social pariah, noticed only when bullies chose to make fun of him. It was a childhood that had left him "deeply embittered."

Most would not feel socially at ease until 1868 when, able to hide his deformity with a beard, he fell in with a group of Swiss socialists who fired his imagination with their views of justice. "From then on," he later wrote, "I began to feel like a real human being. . . . I began to live in the realm of ideals. . . . The cause of humanity became my cause."

Most made a name for himself over the next ten years by following the traditional path of a social revolutionary—delivering speeches, writing radical pamphlets and songs, editing socialist newspapers, and serving several prison sentences. His only dabble with a respectable profession came when he was elected to the German Reichstag, and he might have remained in German politics had Otto von Bismarck not expelled political undesirables under the country's new antisocialism laws. Fleeing to London, he began publishing a fiery revolutionary newspaper, *Freiheit,* and became a champion of a chilling new approach to dealing with social injustice that radical anarchists came to call the "propaganda of the deed," or, in more modern parlance, terrorism.

Terrorism neatly fit the philosophy of radical anarchy. A bomb or an assassin's bullet, so the thinking went, could destabilize society in a flash and lead to revolution. What's more, governments had used violence first, through police, prison sentences, and capital punishment. With their main adversary resorting to such extreme measures, anarchists felt entitled to respond in kind.

So compelling was the idea of "propaganda of the deed" that forty-five anarchists from around the world codified the concept in 1881 at a pub on Euston Road in London. Despite the best efforts of a French spy to infiltrate the highly combustible gathering, the meeting concluded that legal action would have to be abandoned and illegal measures made "the sole path leading to the revolution," whether through illicit publications or individual acts of violence.[16] For a radical thinker, here was a way to get the world's attention.

———

Most did not go so far as to personally practice the "propaganda of the deed," but he did his part to make it easy for others. Adopting a false name, he got a job at a dynamite factory in New Jersey to learn the fine points of making explosives.[17] He resurrected his newspaper, *Freiheit,* introducing Americans to his brand of no-holds-barred social revolution. And he published a pamphlet, *The Science of Revolutionary Warfare: A Handbook of Instruction in the Use and Manufacture of Nitroglycerine, Dynamite, Gun-Cotton, Fulminating Mercury, Bombs, Arsons, Poisons, Etc.,* which, as the name promised, explained how to make explosives and use them against the rich.

Most's talents, however, extended well beyond bomb making. He toured the United States and was, by all accounts, a mesmerizing speaker. Future disciple Emma Goldman described his manner in front of a crowd: "The rapid current of his speech, the music of his voice, and his sparkling wit, all combined to produce an effect almost overwhelming. He stirred me to my depths."[18]

Less than a year after he first disembarked in New York, Most was able to rally varied and often cantankerous social revolutionary groups to a congress in Pittsburgh on October 14, 1883, with the hopes of convincing them to work together, or at least spend less time fighting among themselves. Speaking to more than four hundred would-be revolutionaries and their hangers-on at a red-flag-draped Turner Hall, Most laid out ideas that were as sweeping as they were provocative. The whole establishment—the church, the state, and the educational system—he said, had to be destroyed "by all means." Political reform alone was pointless.

In the crowd, representing a contingent from Chicago, was Albert Parsons.

Parsons was by this time on his way toward fully embracing radical, even violent, visions of social revolution. Long gone was his belief that simply playing by the rules could achieve social justice. His faith in the ballot box was shaken by clear evidence of authorities tampering with votes to keep his comrades out of office. And with every upturn in the economy, supporters fled the SLP for more traditional alternatives that seemed more likely to actually wield power.

The radical ideas of Most, Parsons concluded, were the only hope the country had of ever throwing off its oppressive capitalist-dominated government, and he wasted no time in offering his backing to the charismatic German. Before leaving Pittsburgh, the two, along with several others, wrote a manifesto that would become a classic of the genre. Ridiculing capitalism as unjust, inane, and murderous, the manifesto flatly said the "struggle of the proletariat with the bourgeoisie will be of a violent revolutionary character." Political reform was futile, it went on, because the wealthy would never give up without a fight. "There remains but one resource—FORCE!"

Fired by Most's rousing rhetoric, Parsons returned to Chicago, where he took over as editor of the radical newspaper *Alarm* and went about thrusting himself into the center of the city's social revolutionary subculture. With Parsons playing a leading role, Chicago anarchists formed orchestras, choirs, and theatrical groups, debating clubs, literary societies, and even gymnastic and shooting clubs.[19] Saloons and beer gardens such as Greif's Hall, Zepf's Hall, Steinmueller's Hall, and Neff's Hall became favorite watering holes. Parades were frequently held through the middle of Chicago in which three to four thousand people might march, wearing red ribbons and carrying red or black flags. Their banners read POVERTY IS A CRIME and EXPLOITATION IS LEGALIZED THEFT, as well as GOVERNMENT IS FOR SLAVES—FREE MEN GOVERN THEMSELVES. The marches, often accompanied by brass bands playing "La Marseillaise" (the French tune had become an unofficial anthem of anarchists) and important figures on horseback, usually ended in a park such as Ogden's Grove for a picnic and speeches.

Anarchists even had their own Thanksgiving parade, which became almost as much an institution in Chicago as a turkey dinner. The gathering on November 27, 1884, was typical. Nearly three thousand people assembled in Market Square at 2 P.M., bracing themselves against a mixture of rain and sleet. Parsons led the crowd down Market Street, with a band playing martial music and marchers hoisting banners that blared DOWN WITH WAGE-SLAVERY! First stop was the Palmer House on State Street, a haunt of businessmen and politicians, where the band struck up "La Marseillaise." At a businessman's club on Dearborn, finely tailored diners crowded around the windows and rolled their eyes as the demonstrators hissed and booed. Winding its way through

Chicago's best neighborhoods, the crowd kept up its taunts, pausing at the home of Elihu Washburne, a former ambassador to France, and finally concluding at 107 Fifth Avenue, headquarters of *The Alarm* and the *Chicagoer Arbeiter-Zeitung,* where Parsons delivered another speech from his second-floor window.[20]

The Alarm held the community together with constant attacks on capitalism and violent undertones. In a June 1885 issue, a Professor Mezzeroff of New York, said to be the inspiration for an anarchist professor in Joseph Conrad's novel *The Secret Agent,* instructed readers to carry a bomb in their pocket just as he did.[21] Another writer, Gerhard Lizius, spoke effusively of explosives: "Dynamite! Of all the good stuff, this is the stuff. . . . In giving dynamite to the downtrodden millions of the globe, science has done its best work."[22]

Parsons might later regret allowing the articles to appear in his newspaper. A Chicago court would soon produce them as evidence that Parsons had incited murder.

"THE *MAINE* BLOWN UP!"

The air hung heavy and humid over Havana the evening of February 15, 1898, making an uncomfortable night for the crew of the *Maine,* now in port for three weeks. A flood tide had swung the ship around buoy number four[1] so that her bow pointed toward the mouth of the harbor. Voices and laughter drifted across the bay from nearby vessels, including the American steamer *City of Washington,* which was tied up off the *Maine's* stern. Except for the sentries and watch officers, the rest of the ship's crew relaxed. Enlisted men, wearing as little clothing as naval decorum would allow, danced in the starboard gangway to accordion music. The soft notes of a mandolin, played by a gunner's mate, echoed in the aft turret. Several of the officers had already gone to sleep in keeping with the ship's practice of turning in early.[2]

When her keel was laid in the New York Navy Yard on October 17, 1888, the *Maine* was meant to be an example of America's growing naval ambitions. At 319 feet and capable of seventeen knots, she carried four ten-inch guns and six six-inch guns in her main battery that were designed to penetrate the armor of an enemy ship. Seven six-pound guns were meant to sweep an enemy's decks. But she had suffered a star-crossed record even before her hull touched water. American naval expertise had disintegrated to such a point that it took nearly seven years to complete work. Her design was by then outdated. Unlike most modern naval vessels, which had guns built on the centerline, the *Maine's* ten-inch turrets were offset, the forward turret on the starboard side and the after turret on the port, an unwieldy configuration in battle that was based on a centuries-old idea that the ship might be called on to ram other vessels.[3]

With a white hull, and cabins and superstructure painted a dusty brown, she was commissioned on September 17, 1895, to an equally problematic life at sea. In February the following year the *Maine* ran aground, and a year after that five men were washed overboard off Cape Hatteras; only two were recovered. Two days later, two men were injured when a piece of ammunition exploded.[4]

Charles D. Sigsbee took over the ship on April 10, 1897, only a few weeks after being promoted to captain. A graduate of the Naval Academy and veteran of the Civil War, the studious-looking officer with a handlebar mustache and round glasses had, like most American sailors, spent little of his career engaged in real fighting. With the country at peace since the Civil War, he had focused on technical projects and in 1880 published a highly regarded but impossibly technical book called *Deep-Sea Sounding and Dredging.* As captain, he made his own contributions to the *Maine's* inglorious history. While attempting to enter New York Harbor without a pilot through the treacherous Hell Gates, he was forced to smash into Pier 46 to avoid colliding with a crowded excursion steamer.[5]

There had been no such excitement in the weeks since the *Maine* arrived in Havana. Fearful that his enlisted men might get into trouble ashore, Sigsbee restricted them to the ship. Their only taste of Havana was the view from the harbor, where it was possible to look up the cobbled streets into the center of the city and see its dilapidated white and pastel buildings. Sigsbee also took precautions to protect the ship itself. He had beefed up the number of men on watch from the time of entering port, moved ammunition to places where it could quickly be fired, and kept an extra boiler on line at all times to power the hydraulic turrets.[6] Yet in keeping with the stated friendly purpose of his trip, the captain had allowed officers to go ashore and had joined them many times himself.

Twice he attended bullfights, once to see Mazzantini, the famous gentleman bullfighter from Spain. He found it a depressing affair. "To comprehend the Spanish bull fight, it should be considered a savage sport passed down from generation to generation from a remote period when human nature was far more cruel than present." The sight of several horses being killed by bulls was "shocking to the American mind."[7] On another occasion, Sigsbee had lunched at the Havana Yacht Club. They were treated, American officers said, with correct politeness, but resentment clearly bubbled just below the surface. One flyer making the rounds of Havana described "these Yankee pigs who muddle in our affairs, humiliating us to the last degree, and . . . order to us a man-of-war of their rotten squadron." Enough copies of the flyer had been stuffed inside the consulate gates, Lee told Sigsbee, to plaster its walls.[8]

Tensions had grown perceptibly since February 9, 1898, when William Randolph Hearst's *New York Journal* splashed a private letter across its front page, written by the Spanish ambassador Dupuy de Lôme to a friend in Cuba. In it he mocked McKinley as "weak" and a "bidder for the admiration of the crowd."[9] Stolen by a member of the junta and supplied to reporters, the letter enraged Americans, who took any criticism of their president as a personal insult. Fully aware of the letter's combustible force, both the United States and Spain tried to paper over the incident. The Spanish recalled Dupuy de Lôme, and McKinley refused to make a big deal of it. But there was no assuaging America's wounded pride. Congress put forward three different resolutions demanding recognition for the rebels.

On the evening of the fifteenth, Sigsbee sat in the admiral's rooms aboard the *Maine* quietly writing at a polished wood table, wearing a lightweight civilian "office jacket" rather than his heavier uniform. He had just finished a letter to Theodore Roosevelt, advising him against employing torpedo tubes on battleships and cruisers, and was working on a letter home when, a little past the hour, he heard the ship's bugler play "Taps."

Putting his pen down to listen, the captain flinched at what sounded like a rifle shot. A few moments later, he recoiled from a tremendous "bursting, rending, and crashing sound or roar," followed quickly by "heavy, ominous, metallic sounds" as the ship lurched and began to list toward port.[10] Smoke billowed into his cabin.

Sigsbee would later admit that his first reaction was fear that the ship would sink with him trapped in it. But he quickly regained his composure and the "habit of command." He felt his way down the dark passageway where he collided with Private William Anthony. Despite the pitch darkness and smoke, the cabin orderly saluted and delivered the obvious news: There had been an explosion and the ship was sinking.

There had, in fact, been two explosions, the first on the port side, near two six-inch gun magazines, the second farther back, near the ten-inch magazine that contained between eight and nine tons of black powder. The sheer force of the explosions buckled the ship in half. Flames incinerated men in their bunks. Those near the blasts were killed instantly, their limbs and chunks of flesh part of a soaring plume of debris that would fall up to half a mile away. Other sailors were trapped belowdecks, doomed to suck at air pockets that shrank to nothing as the ship went down.

While members of the crew fought their individual battles of survival, Sigsbee made his way to the main deck and tried to survey the damage, though his eyes, still unaccustomed to the dark, could not take in the full extent of the carnage. In fact, his first instinct was to post sentries to protect the *Maine* from further attack. That there was little left to guard occurred to him only after a few moments of thought.[11]

Ashore, Havana had been alive with "happy and grotesque masqueraders" roaming the streets as carnival celebrations entered their second night. Those near the water first noticed a searing bright light from the direction of the moored ships. One group of American newspaper reporters recalled sitting at a brightly lit outdoor café when they saw the sky over the bay shine "with an intense light and above it all could be seen innumerable colored lights resembling rockets."[12] Then, rumbling across the water's smooth surface came the thunderous report, so loud that it shook buildings and shattered windows.

Lee had seen the explosion as well, "a great column of fire," and hurried to the waterfront, pushing his way through a large crowd for a view of the destruction. He could hardly comprehend the scene that greeted him. Flames still roared aboard the ship, which had nearly totally sunk. Only a tangle of wreckage and the ship's mast remained above the surface. Spotlights carried by small boats darted across the water's surface, illuminating debris and bodies.[13]

McKinley turned in early on February 14, 1898, climbing into one of two brass beds in his sparsely decorated sleeping quarters. About three in the morning, an aide gently woke him. Secretary Long was on the telephone with urgent news. Clad in a nightgown, McKinley groggily slipped out of bed and padded the few steps down the hall to his office.[14] He listened quietly as Long relayed Sigsbee's note. Pacing back and forth, the president muttered: "The *Maine* blown up! The *Maine* blown up." Details were as yet sketchy, but it was clear there had been an astonishing number of fatalities.

Aboard clanging streetcars, around farmhouse breakfast tables, and on factory floors, there was only one topic of conversation the morning of February 15. Not since the Civil War had the United States known such a military calamity. Of the 354 officers and men aboard the ship, 266 either lost their lives or died shortly thereafter.[15] Wives, mothers, and girlfriends of the sailors streamed toward the White House that first morning seeking the latest information; a surprisingly large number were ushered directly to the president's second-floor office. Not even Pulitzer and Hearst were able to come to grips with it all. The explosion, coming in the evening as it did, sent page one editors at both newspapers scrambling to rework their layouts for the next day's editions. In the *New York Journal*'s greater New York edition, a story on the explosion had to share space with a piece on the long-running gold versus silver debate, the headline an uncharacteristically sober CRUISER

MAINE BLOWN UP IN HAVANA HARBOR.[16] For once, the paper underplayed the facts, reporting that more than one hundred had been killed, less than half the actual figure.

As the magnitude of the event sank in, the media began to awaken to the wider implications. It was impossible to believe it had been an accident. The place and timing were too much of a coincidence. But if not happenstance, who had done it? It didn't take long for the newspapers to decide.

DESTRUCTION OF THE WARSHIP MAINE WAS THE WORK OF THE ENEMY, ran the *Journal*'s headline on the seventeenth, promising a $50,000 reward for anyone who could help convict the culprit.[17] On the eighteenth, the front page screamed: THE WHOLE COUNTRY THRILLS WITH WAR FEVER. Like its rival, the *World* didn't find its voice until the seventeenth. Ignoring the possibility of an accident, the paper speculated in a banner headline whether the explosion was caused by a bomb or a torpedo.[18] A dramatic illustration of the blast showing men tossed into the air consumed half a page. Two days later, the newspaper depicted how the Spanish ship *Vizcaya,* then due in New York as part of the original agreement to send the *Maine* to Havana, could easily bombard much of Manhattan and parts of Brooklyn.[19] That nobody possessed a shred of evidence as to the actual cause didn't slow down the *World*'s editors, who announced the paper was sending divers to perform their own investigation. Just as their owners hoped, the stories sent circulation of both newspapers soaring—in the case of the *Journal*'s, more than doubling to over a million.[20]

Americans mourned the *Maine* as if she were a martyred saint. Sober businessmen pinned REMEMBER THE MAINE buttons to their lapels. Families decorated living rooms with models of the ship. Music halls advertised patriotic productions depicting the *Maine* and her crew.

Their grief transcended the loss of one ship. The alleged bombing felt like an attack on the nation itself, and no country in the 1890s was as much in love with loving itself as the United States. Many of the patriotic songs and traditions of today date from this period. In 1893, Wellesley College professor Katharine Lee Bates, inspired by a visit to Pikes Peak, wrote the words to "America the Beautiful" with poetic images of "purple mountain majesties" and the "fruited plain." It was not just a line but a statement of fact for many: "God shed his grace on thee."

Three years later, aboard the British steamship *Teutonic* bound for New York from Europe, John Philip Sousa wrote one of the most stirring patriotic tunes the country has ever produced. As he strolled the deck with fellow passengers, bundled against the damp air, he heard a strange tune playing in his head, as if his brain had suddenly turned into a radio, ceaselessly "playing, playing, playing" over and over for the rest of the voyage.[21] Writing the notes down once back in New York, Sousa thought the powerful tune of blaring horns was an impressive melody. It was to become the anthem of the age: "The Stars and Stripes Forever":

> Hurrah for the flag of the free!
> May it wave as our standard forever,
> The gem of the land and the sea,
> The banner of the right.
> Let despots remember the day,
> When our fathers with mighty endeavor,
> Proclaimed as they marched to the fray,
> That by their might and by their right,
> It waves forever.[22]

Displaying the flag had become a matter of course at parades and public events and inside private homes. Civic groups and charitable organizations raised money to buy flags for schools. The largest weekly magazine, *The Youth's Companion,* made distributing flags one of its main promotional activities, selling twelve-by-eighteen-inch silk flags for thirty cents each, and planning a nationwide flag day for schoolchildren.[23] Almost as an afterthought, the magazine's editors hit upon the idea of creating a salute that young students could recite and assigned the job of writing one to a member of its promotions department. Francis Bellamy, a thirty-five-year-old ex–Baptist minister, locked himself in a room for two hours after dinner one night to produce the following: "I pledge allegiance to my flag and to the republic for which it stands—one nation indivisible—with liberty and justice for all." A few tweaks and it was done the next day. What we now know as "The Pledge of Allegiance" first appeared in print in the September 1892 edition of *The Youth's Companion*.[24]

McKinley had never been one to subscribe to knee-jerk reactions and would not break form now. As was routine for major accidents, the navy announced immediately that it would investigate the explosion. Over the course of three weeks, nearly eighty witnesses and survivors would be interviewed, naval experts would be consulted, and—importantly as it would turn out—the wreckage of the ship would be studied. The president would take action only after this considered review. And with good reason.

There were perfectly plausible explanations for the disaster that had nothing to do with the Spanish. Spontaneous combustion of coal, which could easily have caused such a massive explosion, was an all-too-common occurrence aboard U.S. naval ships. Since 1895, three coal bunker fires had been reported on the *Olympia*, four on the *Wilmington*, and at least one each on the *Petrel*, the *Lancaster*, and the *Indiana*. Coal fires on the *Cincinnati* and the *New York* had nearly caused their magazines to explode. And the *Maine*, like several other ships, suffered from a design flaw that made it especially vulnerable: The coal bunkers and the magazines shared a bulkhead through which heat might pass and ignite the ammunition.[25]

Meeting Senator Charles W. Fairbanks, a Republican from Indiana and a leading conservative, on February 17, 1898, McKinley promised to keep a level head. "I don't propose to be swept off my feet by the catastrophe," he said. "My duty is plain. We must learn the truth and endeavor, if possible, to fix responsibility. The country can afford to withhold its judgment and not strike an avenging blow until the truth is known. The Administration will go on preparing for war, but still hoping to avert it. It will not be plunged into war until it is ready for it."[26]

While combat sounded like a grand adventure and a welcome test of manhood to hotheads like Roosevelt, it was a waste of humanity for men who had been there, even veterans like McKinley who had seen plenty of glory. When Leonard Wood, an army officer and friend of Roosevelt, met McKinley at the White House one morning, the president snapped, "Well, have you and Theodore declared war yet?" Wood replied no, but that he still thought war was coming. McKinley fired back, "I shall never get into a war, until I am sure that God and man approve. I have been through one war; I have seen the dead piled up; and I do not want to see another."[27] It was a noble commitment, but one that would exact a severe price from the president.

McKinley's attempts in the coming weeks to resolve the conflicting pressures of the Cuban crisis cemented his image as one of the most enigmatic of American presidents. He would be criticized, in Roosevelt's words, as having the backbone of a chocolate éclair.[28] Yet he would display iron fortitude in pursuing his goals. He opposed war, despite enormous public pressure, as a matter of principle. Yet he quietly undertook steps that would extend military action to the Pacific. He would literally worry himself sick over the public's thirst for Spanish blood, yet made little effort to bring the national mood off the boil.

For many observers it was the résumé of a weak and ineffectual president, a rudderless leader swept away in the current of events, a peace-at-all-costs administration. Many had long thought of him in these terms anyway. It fit the image the Democrats had tried to fashion of him during the campaign—a puppet of Mark Hanna, the man who slavishly bowed to public opinion by keeping his ear so close to the ground that it was "full of grasshoppers." As Secretary of the Treasury Lyman G. Gage wrote in his memoirs, "By many he was misjudged as complacent and weak, subject to undue influence from the more powerful among those responsible for his action."[29]

That McKinley had never articulated a coherent foreign policy, other than the faint reference to dignity in his inaugural address, only made him harder to understand. When events were thrust upon him, McKinley's reaction was to deal with each crisis individually and as an extension of his domestic agenda to aid the economy. Pragmatism and opportunism rather than ideology would govern his thinking in foreign affairs. The results might appear inconsistent, but he was proud of this quality. "We cannot always do what is best," he once told a gathering in Canton, "but we can do what is practical at the time."[30]

McKinley's personal style didn't help to shed light on the workings of his mind, either. Thundering speeches with colorful images of national glory were not part of his biological makeup. Loud public pronouncements seemed to limit room for maneuver, a vital advantage for a dealmaker such as himself. Instead, McKinley preferred to manage from behind the scenes, steering people by baby steps in the direction he wanted. McKinley, for example, often conducted cabinet meetings by the Socratic method. Even when he held a firm view on an issue, he would lead gatherings of his advisers without expressing an opinion, gently steering the group toward decisions he had already reached. During these critical weeks, he made only one major public appearance, a February 22, 1898, speech at the University of Pennsylvania celebrating George Washington's birthday. He hardly touched on anything remotely relating to Cuba, other than to remind his audience that Washington had emphasized "sober and dispassionate public judgment," adding, "Such judgment, my fellow-citizens, is the best safeguard in the calm of tranquil events, and raises superior and triumphant above the storms of woe and peril."[31] Yet McKinley was now, in his own quiet way, proving that there was much more to him than his critics understood.

Until now, most Americans had assumed the country stood before two distinct alternatives where foreign affairs were concerned. The first was to avoid foreign dealings altogether, save in the rare case of a Cuba. The second was to acquire colonies that could be controlled politically by Washington and possibly become part of the Union. Benjamin Tracy, secretary of the navy from 1889 to 1893, underscored how many Americans perceived the concept of empire when he had told *The New York World* in 1891, "The sea will be the future seat of Empire. And we shall rule it as certainly as the sun doth rise. To a preeminent rank among nations, colonies are of the greatest help."[32]

McKinley, more out of intuition than calculation, began pursuing a third alternative. The United States would extend its influence abroad, but it would be neither political nor territorial. Rather, the country would aim to establish a commercial hegemony.

What has variously come to be known as "informal empire," "the new imperialism," or "commercial empire" was, in fact, not a new concept as McKinley entered the White House. The British, as early as the 1840s, had moved away from the classical notion of colonial empire to one based on free trade. The repeal in 1846 of Britain's infamous Corn Laws, originally enacted to protect domestic farmers from foreign competition, was a major step in this direction. In the decades that followed, the British found their industries prospered just as well in free markets as they had in the heyday of colonial expansion.[33]

The concept of a commercial hegemony instinctively appealed to McKinley and the nation's business leaders. On the one hand, there need not necessarily be any soul-searching domination of foreign countries. For an "informal empire," all that was needed abroad were reliable and protected trading routes—as well as political and economic stability within America's trading partners. Bringing such conditions to attractive markets was the sort of global role that ordinary folks could also feel good about as they sat in church on Sunday mornings. What backward nation would not relish America's civilizing patronage?

Moreover, this was a vision of empire that ideally suited American industry. With their massive economies of scale and hyper-competitiveness, U.S. companies could not lose in a truly open global marketplace. The *Iron Age* wrote in December 1897 that the United States is "slowly realizing that we hold the key of the position, since there are no indications that European manufacturers will ever displace us in the van of progress."[34] As businessman and leading proponent of the "trade, not territory" school of foreign affairs Edward Atkinson put it, "commerce is today the prime factor in the world's work. Its development is the chief object of nations."[35]

Such thinking had driven McKinley's approach to Cuba from the start. Though genuinely anxious to aid sick and starving peasants there, his primary objective was to establish political stability. This he aimed to achieve as practically and peaceably as possible. First, he had hoped that with American help, the Spanish might restore order on their own. He would continue to pursue that option as long as possible while exploring other peaceful solutions. He even offered to buy Cuba; both Spain and key U.S. senators quickly rejected that idea. But with the sinking of the *Maine,* and continued Spanish intransigence,

McKinley began to accept the idea that only American arms could bring order to Cuba.

As McKinley quietly prepared for war, he demonstrated a clear understanding of what war with Spain would really entail, as well as America's place in the world once the shooting stopped.

On Friday afternoon, February 25, 1898, Secretary of the Navy Long decided to take the afternoon off for "mechanical massage," a device in which the patient was strapped into an electric chair that caressed his stomach and legs. Something of hypochondriac, he had suffered mightily under the strain of the sinking of the *Maine* and the public outcry that followed. Aware that Roosevelt, his deputy, was prone to hyperactivity, Long left written directions not to touch anything while he was away. He should have known better. Like a mischievous child, Roosevelt churned out an orgy of orders while the adult was out of the room. Among other things, he asked the House Naval Affairs Committee to authorize the enlistment of "an unlimited number of seamen," and had guns sent from Washington to the Brooklyn Navy Yard to be mounted on cruisers.

Whatever benefit Long received from his treatment was surely lost by Saturday morning when he discovered what his subordinate had been up to. Long wrote in his diary: "The very devil seemed to possess him yesterday afternoon. . . . He has gone about things like a bull in a china shop. . . . It shows how the best fellow in the world, and one with splendid capacities, is worse than useless if he lacks a cool head and careful direction."[36]

There was one order, however, that Long heartily approved. Roosevelt had told Commodore George Dewey, commander of the American fleet in Asia, to move the bulk of that fleet from Nagasaki in Japan to the British colony of Hong Kong. The American vessels were to be ready for "offensive operations" in the Spanish colony of the Philippine Islands.[37] Long added his stamp of approval the next day with his own message: "Keep full of coal, the very best that can be had."[38]

When McKinley sifted through ship-deployment orders and studied the maps, he was struck by the meager size of the U.S. armed forces. There was almost no army to speak of, a grand total of twenty-five thousand or so troops, well short of what the job ahead seemed to demand. In Cuba alone, the Spanish had as many as two hundred thousand soldiers, depending on how many were out sick. The navy was no better. Despite a recent building spree, the U.S. fleet still resembled a bathtub flotilla. There were but four first-class battleships, only one second-class battleship, and a pair of armored cruisers. The rest of the fleet was a collection of monitors and protected cruisers.[39]

The Spanish, on the other hand, possessed an extensive collection of torpedo gunboats and torpedo-boat destroyers—classes of vessels that the United States lacked entirely. And Spanish crews were thought vastly superior to the tattered collection of American sailors, many of whom didn't even speak English. The conventional wisdom in Europe, and among more than a few Americans, was that the Spanish could put a superior force to sea.[40]

With these worries in mind, on Sunday evening, March 6, 1898, McKinley summoned "Uncle" Joe Cannon, the profane and blunt-speaking chairman of the House Appropriations Committee, to the executive mansion. Escorted to the president's library, Cannon found McKinley waiting for him at the door. Without offering a chair or hardly a hello, McKinley dove in: "Cannon, I must have money to get ready for war. I am doing everything possible to prevent war, but it must come, and we are not prepared for war. Who knows where this war will lead us; it may be more than war with Spain. How can I get money for these extraordinary expenditures?"

Taken aback at the president's unusual abruptness, Cannon noticed the tension in his face. "His manner was grave; his face showed the lines of care." As the two talked, McKinley still did not sit, nervously striding back and forth.

While the president paced, Cannon explained that he had already reviewed the Treasury's reports and was sure there was $50 million or so that could be raised "without embarrassment or without having to provide for a bond issue or new taxation." After briefly discussing the details, McKinley walked to his desk to provide Cannon the written documentation of his request for funds. On a blank sheet of telegraph paper, he wrote a single sentence: "For national defense, fifty million dollars." Cannon put the scrap in his pocket, returned to his hotel, and drafted legislation.[41] Three days later, on March 9, 1898, the House passed the bill with a vote of 311 to 0. The Senate likewise passed the legislation without a hint of opposition, 76 to 0. Joe Wheeler, a representative from Alabama, greeted the vote with a rebel yell.[42]

If the president's financing request was meant to shock and awe the Spanish, as some historians believe, the gambit succeeded. The size of the American war chest staggered Sagasta's government. It was unthinkable to the nearly destitute Spanish that any nation could summon such funds so quickly. From Spain, Woodford wrote to McKinley: "To appropriate fifty millions out of money in the Treasury, without borrowing a cent, demonstrates wealth and power. Even Spain can see this. . . . The ministry and the press are simply stunned."[43]

Late on the evening of March 24, 1898, four naval officers stepped off the train from Key West at Pennsylvania Station to a waiting crowd. For three days, they had carried the naval board of inquiry's report into the sinking of the *Maine.* Wrapped in sailcloth and heavily sealed, the report was kept under constant guard. They elbowed their way past reporters and curious bystanders. Lieutenant John Hood, a *Maine* survivor, hugged the report with one hand and fingered a revolver under his coat with the other.[44]

The navy had turned to numerous sources in its investigation, but the work of its own divers provided the most compelling explanation for what had happened. Descending to the bottom of Havana harbor in primitive dive suits with large metal helmets and air tubes connected to a pump on the surface, the divers discovered evidence that an external explosion had sunk the ship. After probing in the muck and darkness, they reported that the plating on the bottom of the *Maine* had been shoved inward, forming an inverted V about fifty-nine feet from the bow. Divers also found a large hole in the muddy sea bottom directly underneath, measuring fifteen feet in diameter and seven feet deep.[45]

Naval experts such as Commander George Converse, skipper of the *Montgomery,* concluded the damage was caused by a low-grade underwater mine, probably filled with nothing more than gunpowder, that had been placed on the harbor bottom. Yet the board of inquiry stopped there. Determining the identity of the alleged bombers was not their job.

So began the darkest hour of McKinley's presidency. For the public, there was little doubt that Spain was responsible for the *Maine* tragedy, even if the board of inquiry had not provided a smoking gun linking the country to the crime. Yet McKinley, ever sober, ever pragmatic, stood fast against the war cries. Evidence that the Spanish were responsible for the *Maine* was circumstantial at best. Without an overwhelming reason to go to war, he would remain fixated on the North Star that guided him all along: to preserve Cuba's commercial value as cheaply as possible—without shedding American blood. Maybe now, he told himself, the Spanish would finally be shaken out of their stupor and get down to some serious negotiating. Quietly, he prepared a fresh ultimatum for Woodford to present to the Spanish. Rather than announce a call to arms, as so many hoped and expected he would, McKinley now told Congress that he would keep them advised of the progress in renewed peace talks and that "in the meantime deliberate consideration is invoked."

From coast to coast, incredulous Americans let out audible cries of outrage when the president's plans began seeping into headlines. The shock transcended economic and political lines. Newspaper editors, laborers, industrialists, and even members of his own party turned on McKinley with venom that the gentle president had never imagined possible.

"If the occasion goes past and we allow this Cuban struggle to run on indefinitely, the American people will have lost several degrees of self respect and will certainly not have gained anything in the opinion of mankind," *The Washington Post* wrote on March 29.[46]

Biting personal attacks began to surface. In Virginia, a raging mob burned effigies of McKinley and Hanna and fired revolvers into the dummies.[47] McKinley's picture was hissed at in theaters and torn from walls. Congressmen descended on the executive mansion and State Department, demanding action. Jokes made the rounds, such as "How is McKinley's mind like a bed? It has to be made for him." Fifty Republican members of the House, calling themselves the "reconcentrados," asserted the right of Congress to declare war. A delegation of "war" Republicans demanded an immediate war message.

Roosevelt, who had been angling for a war—any war—since before joining the administration, now nearly burst with enthusiasm. With characteristic abandon, he dispatched naval attachés around the world to scour shipyards for vessels that were battle ready or could quickly be made so, anything from private yachts to spanking new ships. When Spain's Ministry of Marine tried to buy two Brazilian navy cruisers under construction in the United Kingdom—the *Amazonas* and the *Almirante Abreu*—he snatched them away with bids that the cash-strapped Spanish couldn't match. He also purchased the *Diogenes,* a new cruiser built in Germany for another country. Ships in Key West and Hampton Roads were stripped and made ready for war. Part-time arms dealer Charles R. Flint was stunned at Roosevelt's haste. When Flint told Roosevelt that the Brazilian warship *Nictheroy* might be available for half a million dollars, Roosevelt jumped so fast he didn't even waste time drawing up a written contract. All told, the navy purchased or leased more than one hundred ships.[48]

At times, Roosevelt's passion turned against McKinley's advisers. On Saturday night, March 26, 1898, Roosevelt delivered a rousing call to arms at Washington's Gridiron Club. "We will have this war of freedom," he said in an after-dinner speech, punching a clenched fist into an open palm. And then he turned to speak directly at Hanna, in his eyes the living embodiment of spineless economic interests, and added: "The interests of the business world and of financiers might be paramount in the Senate," but not with the public. Anyone who wanted to stand in the way of popular opinion was "welcome to experiment." The Ohio senator's face flushed and he gripped the arms of his chair.[49]

Roosevelt might have done a bit more homework before making the accusation. Republican Senator Redfield Proctor of Vermont, a former secretary of war and wealthy businessman, had already gone a long way toward winning business leaders over to the idea of going to war with an electrifying speech about the horrors he had witnessed firsthand in Cuba during a recent trip. Cuba, he said, was condemned to misery as long as the Spanish remained in charge. Captains of industry, including John Jacob Astor, Thomas Fortune Ryan, William Rockefeller, and Stuyvesant Fish, soon came around to the conclusion that it was time for the United States to fight. According to a special emissary sent by McKinley to gauge their mood, they were now "feeling militant." From Boston on March 21, 1898, Senator Henry Cabot Lodge reported that economic leaders now believed that "one shock and then an end was better than a succession of spasms such as we must have if this war in Cuba went on." Four days after the Lodge update, a New York newspaper correspondent sent a telegram to Washington that likely was shown to the president: BIG CORPORATIONS HERE NOW BELIEVE WE WILL HAVE WAR. BELIEVE ALL WOULD WELCOME IT AS A RELIEF TO SUSPENSE.[50]

Even small children were caught up in the militant mood. On one of his customary carriage rides in late March, McKinley happened across a group of young children playing at military drill. On the order of their eight-year-old commander, a glittering toy pistol hanging around his neck, the group dropped to the ground and fired off rounds from their cap guns in a mock volley just as the president passed. A *Washington Post* reporter later asked the stern-faced little commander for a comment. "If our mamma would let us, we could go wight [*sic*] down now and blow up Spain easy."[51]

The criticism and the strain of holding the frothing-at-the-mouth country to leash took a terrible toll on the president. McKinley's secretary George Cortelyou wrote in his diary that the president "did not look well, and his eyes had a far-away, deep-set expression in them. For lack of sleep and worry, the president looked exhausted and dark circles ringed his eyes. His voice shook when he spoke." He jumped at the slightest sound and began taking narcotics to help him sleep.

McKinley's old friend H. H. Kohlsaat, on one visit to the White House before the board of inquiry report, found him in a fragile mood. Sitting on a large crimson brocade lounge in the White House Red Room, the president held his head on his hands with elbows on his knees. "I have been through a trying period," he said, noting that his wife's health was worse than usual. "It seems to me I have not slept over three hours a night for over two weeks. Congress is trying to drive us into war with Spain. The Spanish fleet is in Cuban waters, and we haven't enough ammunition on the Atlantic seacoast to fire a salute."

According to Kohlsaat, the president then broke down and cried like a "boy of thirteen." Together the pair sat there, Kohlsaat consoling McKinley by putting a hand on his shoulder until McKinley gathered himself. He finally said, "Are my eyes very red, do they look as if I had been crying?"

"Yes," Kohlsaat replied.

"But I must return to Mrs. McKinley at once. She is among strangers," the president said. The First Lady was then in the Blue Room, attending a piano recital.

Kohlsaat suggested a plan. "When you open the door to enter the room, blow your nose very hard and very loud. It will force tears into your eyes and they will think that is what makes your eyes red." According to Kohlsaat, the president carried out the scheme with "no small blast."[52]

While newspaper editors and headline-seeking politicians poured out their scorn on the president's measured response to the board of inquiry report on the *Maine*, his ambassador in Madrid, Stewart Woodford, shuttled back and forth between the U.S. mission and Spain's foreign ministry. The door to a peace deal still remained open, if only just a crack. McKinley directed Woodford to tell the Spanish on March 29, 1898, that they could avert U.S. intervention if Spain would agree to a plan that included ending the reconcentration program, distributing supplies to the needy, and agreeing to an immediate armistice that would last until October 1, during which time McKinley would, if desired, help mediate a peace settlement.[53] If peace terms could not be decided by that deadline, the president was to be the final arbiter of the dispute. He gave the Spanish until March 31 to reply.[54]

The answer, when it arrived late that evening in Washington, revealed that pride—combined with fear for what capitulation would mean for the brittle Spanish monarchy—made an agreement impossible.[55] The Spanish had acceded to some of McKinley's conditions, ending the concentration camps and providing relief to the needy. They also suggested submitting the *Maine* disaster to an international arbitrator. But Spain would agree to an armistice only if the rebels asked for it first. Madrid could under no circumstances look like it was surrendering. War now seemed all but assured. McKinley promised an anxious Congress that he would present a "war message" in early April 1898.

In the remaining days, a flurry of eleventh-hour diplomatic activity emanated from corners that heretofore had shown little interest in getting between Madrid and Washington. The major European powers, many friendly to Spain, dispatched their ambassadors to the White House to plead for a peaceful solution. There were suggestions that the pope, hoping to help Catholic Spain save face, might mediate a resolution. All were politely rebuffed. Nor had McKinley given up on bringing the Cubans around to an autonomy plan.

Horatio Rubens, the junta spokesman, described a dramatic interaction with McKinley, who had summoned him to the White House. Looking like "an eagle" under "shaggy heavy brows," the president strode around his office with such force that the tails of his frock coat "seemed to swing with a warrior determination." McKinley, Rubens said, barked at him: "You must accept an immediate armistice with Spain." When Rubens asked if Spain was now ready to grant Cuba its independence, the president answered with a rising voice: "That isn't the question now. We may discuss that later. The thing for the moment is the armistice."

Rubens refused to back down: "But, Mr. President, we can talk here, while they continue to fight down there."

McKinley answered sharply. "No, no. That cannot be thought of. The loss of life and property must stop at once."[56]

Finally, on April 10, 1898, the day before McKinley was to send his "war message" to Congress, Spain performed one final act in the theater of negotiation. In Madrid, Woodford was told that Spain was now prepared to suspend hostilities, thereby fulfilling the last of McKinley's demands from March 29. Assistant Secretary of State Day was so excited by the Spanish response that he snatched the paper directly from the operator and scurried across the White House lawn where McKinley was meeting with the cabinet.

The room fell quiet as the president read Woodford's report and laid it on the table. There were caveats to the Spanish proposal. The Spanish commander in Cuba was to decide how long and under what conditions fighting would stop. And there was no mention of America's role as a mediator between Spain and the rebels.[57]

Several members of his cabinet, perhaps the last peaceniks in the country, seized on the concession. As debate moved around the table, they argued that the president should inform Congress that a delay was needed. McKinley, however, would not change course, not at this late hour. With little explanation, he simply appended the dispatch to the papers he had already prepared to send to Congress.

McKinley's long-awaited war message generated the same anticipation as the latest Charles Hale Hoyt Broadway production. Congressmen, journalists, visitors—anybody who could get in—packed into the House of Representatives on April 11, 1898, eager to hear the call to arms. The audience listened "with intense interest and profound silence"[58] as House pages took turns reading the seven-thousand-word message. Hastily written and the product of too many cooks, it was dejectedly described by Long as "the best that McKinley could do" given the strain the president had suffered under.[59] The message began slowly, with a laborious recitation of the history of the dispute and a clinical explanation of the justification for American intervention— namely to address the humanitarian crisis and protect American commercial interests. Far from the clarion trumpet sounding a charge into war that many had hoped for, McKinley's message simply asked lawmakers to "authorize and empower the President to take measure to secure full and final termination of hostilities between the government of Spain and the people of Cuba."

To the surprise and dismay of many, McKinley did not call for Cuban independence. In fact, he said, it was not "wise or prudent for this government to recognize at the present time the independence of the so-called Cuban Republic." What's more, when the Spanish were evicted, the United States would hand Cuba over to the Cubans only when Washington decided they were ready. "When it shall appear hereafter that there is within the island a government capable of performing the duties and discharging the functions of a separate nation, and having, as a matter of fact, the proper forms and attributes of nationality, such a government can be promptly and readily recognized."[60]

This is precisely the view that McKinley had held all along, yet newspapers and congressmen recoiled in bitter disgust. THE PRESIDENT'S CUBAN MESSAGE DISAPPOINTING TO THOSE WHO WANT CUBA FREED was *The New York Times'* headline on April 12, 1898, the paper adding that it had caused "great discontent in Congress."[61] Telegrams and letters poured into the capital from ordinary citizens demanding the United States help Cuba attain its freedom. *The Washington Post* reported that McKinley's real ambitions had been unmasked. "The foremost ground of criticism and the one which was paramount was the absolute silence of the president [in his message] as to the independence of Cuba. This omission took Congress by surprise and created the utmost feeling of dissatisfaction and disappointment. Whatever else might have been in the President's mind, it was supposed that the ultimate aim of his policy was the freeing of Cuba, but the message gave no corroboration of this fact." Senator Marion Butler of North Carolina expressed the view of many when he complained, "If I can understand the message, it means that the president is opposed to Cuban independence now and forever."[62]

For Butler and others, it was unthinkable that the United States could enter into a war with Spain until McKinley had been convinced to speedily grant Cuba's independence. For over a week—a painfully long period for Congress and a nation that had been counting the days until war would commence—the president sparred with an odd coalition of jingoists, populists, and political rivals who wanted to reword the resolution to authorize military action in a way that also compelled the president to recognize Cuba's independence. McKinley's friends, especially in the House, rallied to his cause. Speaker of the House Thomas Reed turned his rooms in the Shoreham Hotel into what one newspaper reporter described as "the headquarters of a commander-in-chief."[63] Time and again, McKinley's congressional opponents and supporters debated semantics and linguistic nuances until Senator Henry Moore Teller, a Republican from Colorado, stepped forward with a carefully scripted compromise that was acceptable to the president and a nearly exhausted Congress. In the wording of what would become known as the "Teller Amendment," the United States acknowledged that "the people of the island of Cuba are, and of the right to be, free and independent." But it went on: "The United States hereby disclaims any disposition or intention to exercise sovereignty, jurisdiction, or control over said Island except for the pacification thereof, and asserts its determination, when that is accomplished, to leave the government and control of the Island to its people."

"Except for the pacification thereof"—it was a loaded phrase, the importance of which would soon become clear.

The Spanish now realized, maybe for the first time, that they were actually going to war. The government broke off relations with Washington, and American diplomats were ordered out of the country in a flight that nearly produced the first shooting of the war. Angry Spanish mobs were waiting for the legation's special train as it pulled out of Madrid station, pelting the cars with rocks as it built up speed. As stones bounced off the train's roof, an equally enraged Woodford sprang from his bed in a skimpy nightshirt and, mustache bristling, cocked a six-shooter and prepared to fight his way out of the country if he had to.[64]

In Washington the president was doing a little bristling of his own. McKinley ordered a naval blockade of stretches of the Cuban coast and published a call for 125,000 volunteer soldiers.

Almost lost in the rush to arms was the conflict's victim. Angry at being cut out of the diplomatic loop and opposed to the war, Secretary of State Sherman resigned on April 25, 1898—a departure that must rank as one of the least noticed in American diplomatic history. William Day, who had essentially been doing the job since McKinley moved into the White House, replaced him.

On the rainy morning of April 25, 1898, the president finally sent a formal declaration of war to Congress. It was the end of an excruciating process that had sapped his strength.

As Congress went about the formalities of declaring war, McKinley tried to take advantage of a rare moment when attention was focused elsewhere and lay down on his bed to nap. Ida happened to be spending a weekend away, visiting friends in New York, and the president couldn't stand the solitude. Desperate for company, he asked a visiting friend to stay in his room. Still, he couldn't relax. Getting out of bed, he wandered down the hall before finally collapsing on a sofa. As he stretched out, he asked a group nearby to keep up their chatter to help him sleep.[65] At about 4 P.M., the doorkeeper brought the resolution for the president to sign.

It had been a trying time for McKinley, one in which he was caught between two powerful historic forces: the rise of one empire and the decline of another. Such realignments seldom happen peacefully. Now, with war inevitable, McKinley cast his gaze beyond the immediate events in Cuba. It was strange in many ways. He had spoken with heartfelt emotion about the horrors of war, yet now that fighting was at hand, he was ready to expand it.

The United States was about to learn an important lesson of foreign relations: Once overseas adventure has been launched, it is difficult to row back. McKinley fully appreciated the risk he had taken. "I am not anxious about the result of the war. There can be one result and it will not be long delayed," he told a friend. "What I have in mind is what will come after war—the problems we do not see now but that are sure to come in some way. And they will not be easy problems. Other nations have had that experience, and we shall not escape it."[66]

11

"FIRE AND KILL ALL YOU CAN!"

Chicago's rank-and-file workers in the 1880s reviled few industrialists as intensely as they did Cyrus McCormick, Jr. With a finely clipped beard and a steady gaze, he had taken over the McCormick Reaper Works from his father at the age of twenty and ruthlessly began cutting costs. Employing economics lessons freshly learned at Princeton, he ordered a company accountant to calculate labor costs per unit of output. He was presented with a finding that he believed showed shocking inefficiencies. Wages would have to be cut.[1]

McCormick's response to the inevitable strikes and worker protests was textbook for the times. Pinkerton men—the private army of choice for captains of industry—were hired to protect replacement workers, smash heads, and generally lend an air of authority to the area around his factory. Appealing directly to Chicago's mayor, McCormick also made sure the police were ready to lend a hand, including the most notorious labor buster in a police uniform, Captain John Bonfield, who led a detachment of burly police known as "Bonfield's Bully

Boys." So harsh were McCormick's tactics that in one round of wage cuts, in April 1885, even the city's other industrialists felt he was going too far. Meatpacking king Philip Armour pleaded with him to treat his workers better.[2] McCormick summed up his philosophy to a journalist that spring: "The right to hire any man, white or black, union or non-union, Protestant or Catholic, is something I will not surrender."[3]

Few were surprised that it was outside the gates of a McCormick plant that blood was eventually shed. At midafternoon on Monday, May 3, 1886, some two hundred strikers gathered at the entrance of McCormick's reaper factory. Tensions were running high on both sides. On May Day, hundreds of thousands of workers around the nation had walked off the job and joined massive parades in support of an eight-hour workday, two hours shorter than the average.[4] In Chicago alone, sixty thousand marched down Michigan Boulevard and brought the city's business to a standstill.

As the bell signaled the end of the shift, replacement workers who had taken up the vacant jobs began to file out. Angry words were exchanged, and strikers threw rocks at the scabs, who retreated back inside the factory compound. Summoned by watchmen, scores of police on foot and in clattering paddy wagons raced to the scene. Much confusion remains about what happened next, but when calls to disperse were met with taunts and jeers, the police unholstered their pistols and began firing into the mass of strikers. A number were wounded and two were likely killed, though the number could never be confirmed.[5]

Anarchists, conditioned to interpret any whiff of violence as a sign that revolution was finally at hand, sprang to life. Radical newspaper editors hastily penned scathing attacks on the police, inflating, perhaps intentionally, the number of dead. They circulated some 2,500 copies of the *Chicagoer Arbeiter-Zeitung* carrying the headline REVENGE! WORKINGMEN! TO ARMS! Some editions carried the code word *Ruhe*—German for "rest"—in an upper corner as a signal to workingmen to make ready to bomb police stations. Still other pamphlets were hastily handed out around the front gates of the McCormick Reaper Works.[6] A demonstration was planned for the evening of May 4, 1886, near Haymarket Square, not far from McCormick's.

———

Located near Chicago's meatpacking and lumber districts, the Haymarket Square was the sort of earthy venue that appealed to anarchists. Produce was sold from pushcarts during the day, and the rank odor of rotting vegetables and horse manure hung in the air at night. The rally on the fourth would not take place in the square proper, rather in an alley just off it, behind the brick wall of Crane Brothers metal products factory. A wooden wagon pulled to one side would serve as the speakers' platform, dimly illuminated by a single gaslight. By around eight o'clock, some two to three thousand people had arrived. They were eager to hear Parsons, the main draw of the evening.

The mood around Haymarket that night was tense, so much so that Chicago's mayor, Carter H. Harrison, decided to swing by on his way home from city hall. He made his presence known by repeatedly striking a match, as if to light a cigar, illuminating his bearded visage. Although undeniably one of the city's power brokers—the former real estate magnate wore silk underwear and smoked fine Havana cigars—Harrison sympathized with the plight of the workingman, or at least found it politically advantageous to do so, and had appointed socialists to important city posts. That he could circulate in this crowd was a testament to the respect he had earned. "I want the people to know that their Mayor is here," he said.[7]

Possibly because the mayor was on hand, or just as likely because he lacked the energy for a fiery speech after a long day, Parsons struck a moderate tone, sticking to well-trod calls for workers' rights. Addressing the crowd for almost an hour, he championed a shorter working day and described the miners he had recently met in Pennsylvania and Ohio. "Do you know that the military are under arms, and a Gatling gun is ready to mow you down?" he asked. "Is this Germany or Russia or Spain?" One voice called out from the crowd: "It looks like it." Yet Parsons also spoke against murdering those whom the crowd blamed for their problems. "To kill an individual millionaire or capitalist would be like killing a flea upon a dog," he said, because others would simply take the dead man's place.[8]

Harrison, relieved to hear there would be little new from Parsons this night, concluded that the evening would pass without incident and walked to the Desplaines Street police station. He met old blood-and-guts Bonfield and told him that he didn't have anything to worry about. From there, the mayor swung his large frame into the creaking saddle of his white horse and left for dinner at his mansion on Ashland Avenue.

Parsons finished up around ten o'clock. Hopping down from the wagon, he took a seat with his wife and two children, Albert and Lulu, on the back of another cart and waited for his friend Samuel Fielden to finish the evening program. Strong gusts of wind swirled scraps of paper in the air and violently rattled street signs. Lifting his eyes upward, Parsons could see a large dark cloud, pregnant with moisture, blowing in from the north. Hurrying to escape what looked like a downpour, Parsons gathered up his family and walked half a block north toward Zepf's Hall, a tavern he knew well at the corner of Lake and Desplaines streets. It was one of the last carefree moments the family would spend together.

With Parsons gone, Fielden rushed through the end of his address, taking on an edgier tone. Newspaper artists would later depict him wearing a long beard and heavy coat, leaning forward, pumping his fist in the air. He exhorted the remaining die-hard listeners, "You have nothing more to do with the law except to lay hands on it and throttle it until it makes its last kick. . . . Keep your eye upon it, throttle it, kill it, stab it, do everything you can to wound it—to impede its progress."[9]

Two plainclothes officers who had decided to brave the weather scowled at such talk. They had stayed precisely to ensure that violence and lawbreaking were not championed. Slipping from the crowd, they rushed along the cobblestone street to the police station and reported to Bonfield that an inflammatory speech was under way.[10]

Orders were barked out in the halls of the station. Captain William Ward and seven lieutenants gathered 176 police officers, laid on that night from around the city, and formed them into ranks. Not knowing what to expect, the men tugged caps down on their foreheads, pulled their blue jackets over their shoulders, affixed double rows of brass buttons and assembled in an alley next to the station. In double time, they moved down Desplaines Street toward the rally, filling the street from side to side.

By now the gathering had melted away to only a few hundred people, and Fielden was wrapping up, literally saying "In conclusion" when someone shouted that the police were coming. Receding to either side of the street, the crowd allowed Captain Ward to lead his men close enough to Fielden's wagon to touch it with his club.

The rain now started to fall. The wind whipped stinging drops against the faces of the officers and soaked into Fielden's beard. Captain Ward bellowed, "In the name of the people of the State of Illinois, I command this meeting immediately and peaceably to disperse."

Fielden answered, "Why, captain, this is a peaceable meeting." An awkward moment of silence passed before Ward repeated his command and ordered his men forward. "All right, we will go," Fielden said, and climbed down from the wagon.[11]

Then someone, history will never know who, struck a match and lit the wick on a round, lead object a bit larger than a baseball. As the flame sparked to life, the man cocked his arm. Witnesses would later say they could see red sparks twinkling in the dark night and that it made a "spluttering" sound as it arched toward the second row of police officers. Lieutenant J. P. Stanton, a Civil War veteran, recognized immediately what was happening. "Look out!" he shouted. "Boys, for God's sake, there is a shell."[12]

Mayor Harrison had just undressed and was about to slip between the covers when the faint thump of something that sounded like an explosion reverberated through the house. He first thought it might have been a thunderclap. But then he heard fainter rattling, what sounded like shooting. He quickly threw his clothes back on and got his horse ready.

Comfortable in the warmth of Zepf's Hall, Parsons was holding a schooner of beer and looking out the window when he saw the explosion, a "white sheet of light" followed immediately by a booming roar. "What is it?" cried his friend Lizzie Holmes.

"I don't know," Parsons replied. "Maybe the Illinois regiments have brought up their Gatling guns." An instant later, bullets whistled past the bar's open door and anguished men rushed inside.[13]

Made from dynamite packed with metal projectiles, what the newspapers called an "infernal machine," the bomb created an explosion strong enough to shatter windows and leave a small crater in the street. Whether from the concussion of the blast or the shrapnel itself, several officers were knocked to the pavement. Patrolman Mathias J. Degan, a widower and member of the force for just a year and a half, fell hard on the wet cobblestones. A piece of shrapnel had severed an artery in his left leg, and thick blood soaked his uniform, hardly visible in the darkness but sticky to his touch. Other officers staggered about, groping at wounds and crying for help.[14]

The policemen still standing responded with blind rage. Unholstering their Colt revolvers, they fired madly into the darkness in a scene of "wild carnage" as *The Chicago Herald* would call it. "Fire and kill all you can!" shouted Lieutenant James Bowler, who emptied his revolver and then reloaded and began shooting again. Police fired as rapidly as their fingers could squeeze the triggers. Inspector Bonfield seized a second revolver from the hand of a fallen officer and fired with both hands into the darkness.[15] Shadowy figures collapsed on the sidewalks and street, blood streaming from their wounds. The crack of pistol fire nearly drowned out cries for help. "Oh God, I'm shot," "Please take me home," "Take me to the hospital." "Oh, God! Oh, God! Save us." Bleeding workers crawled on all fours to escape the line of fire; others who could walk limped into shops for help. Some fled into bars, barricading themselves with overturned tables or hiding behind counters.

Whether anyone in the crowd fired back at the police is a matter of conjecture. Almost surely, some carried pistols. Yet eyewitnesses would later say they didn't see anyone other than the police actually firing their weapons. In the space of only a few minutes, around one hundred people were hit. The exact toll of civilian casualties remains unknown, but historian Paul Avrich estimates that seven or eight were killed, and thirty to forty were wounded.[16]

The police casualties were just as serious. Although Degan was the only one killed that night, six other officers would die of their wounds in the coming weeks. Some sixty policemen were injured, many apparently the result of their own fire.[17] The next day, pools of dried blood still caked the street for an entire block.

———

At Zepf's, Parsons's first thoughts were for his family. With shooting still echoing in the street, he hurried his wife and children, as well as a group of friends, into a back room where they huddled in darkness for a quarter of an hour, straining their ears for sounds from outside. Whatever had happened, Parsons's instincts told him that he would likely be blamed. With considerable trepidation, he led his family out into the rain-slickened streets. Going home was unthinkable. In a matter of hours the police would come pounding at his door. Instead, Parsons would go home with Holmes to her house in Geneva, a suburb of Chicago, not likely to be investigated for a few days at least. All knew that the situation was grave. Parsons turned to his wife with a "sad, almost prophetic, tone" and tenderly whispered, "Kiss me, Lucy. We do not know when we will meet again."[18]

======= ·=· =======

DEWEY AT MANILA

Turned out smartly in their white uniforms, American naval officers swapped stories and toasts with their British counterparts at the bar of the Hong Kong Club, an ornate building at the foot of the imposing 1,810-foot Victoria Peak. Between sips of gin and tonic on the club's veranda, the Americans could gaze out on sampans and junks, and—with a certain level of pride—point out their own ships to their British hosts. The U.S. vessels, having arrived from Nagasaki in early March 1898, had recently been repainted, their peacetime white hulls and buff decks and cabins brushed over in the dull gray color of war, an admission to what was by now obvious. It was April, and everyone down to the club's laundry boy knew that the Americans would soon be weighing anchor for a showdown with the Spanish in Manila.

Optimistic and probably more than a touch naïve, the Americans endured incessant skepticism about their endeavor. The Spanish fleet, the Hong Kong newspapers reported, had fortified Manila into an impregnable fortress with shore batteries and mines. What ships did enter the harbor would be cut to pieces. British officers, normally up for a friendly wager, were so convinced of doom that they wouldn't place a bet on the Americans' return, not even at the heaviest odds. At one club dinner, the universal observation was that the Americans were "a fine set of fellows, but unhappily we shall never see them again."[1]

It was hard to refute such pessimism when the Americans had only the haziest idea of what awaited them in Manila. The strength of Spanish forces and their positions were largely blank spots in the U.S. battle plan. Commodore George Dewey had so little information about the Philippines that he dispatched his officers to scour Hong Kong to buy maps and to find locals who knew anything of the archipelago. One of these was a slightly built Filipino with a pockmarked face and a George Washington complex.

Emilio Aguinaldo, a member of a well-to-do family of mixed Chinese and Tagalog heritage, had worked as a businessman and mayor of the town of Kawit, not far from Manila, when a rebellion against the Spanish began in 1896. Yearning for excitement and burning to achieve great things, he seized the moment and became an overnight military legend. Leading guerrillas armed with knives and homemade rifles, Aguinaldo repeatedly sprang upon Spanish troops and monks from the dense jungles and swamps not far from his home. So successful were his tactics and so large was his ego that by October 1896 he felt confident enough to announce plans to form a government similar to that of the United States. Paraphrasing the French Revolution, he, too, promised to provide "liberty, equality, and fraternity."

Aguinaldo's bold ambitions were not necessarily the best thing to declare so publicly. Though not the power it had once been, the Spanish military still had centuries of experience in the Philippines and could field a capable fighting force when provided with the right provocation. Spain replaced commanders, redeployed troops, and encouraged harsher tactics. By the winter of 1897, the Spanish had nearly snuffed out the uprising and forced Aguinaldo deeper and deeper into the jungle, along with thousands of supporters and their families, finally cornering him in an old iron mine in the mountains about sixty miles from Manila.

In exchange for a promise to quit his revolutionary activity and never return home, Aguinaldo and twenty-seven of his men were granted safe passage to Hong Kong and awarded a series of payments totaling 800,000 Mexican pesos.[2]

Yet Aguinaldo had no intention of giving up.

From his ramshackle accommodation—frugality left more money for bullets—he quietly cheered as the U.S. fleet assembled in Hong Kong, convinced that in these Americans, the means of his repatriation was at hand. The United States, he knew, was a rich nation on the rise. As a former colony, it provided a blueprint of sorts for his own country.

Yet Aguinaldo remained suspicious. Would they really leave the Philippines once the war with Spain was over? Time and again, he asked some version of the question to every American of any authority he met, and each time received the same answer: Don't worry.

When Aguinaldo later grilled Edward Wood, captain of the USS *Petrel,* Wood replied, "The United States, my general, is a great and rich nation and neither needs nor desires colonies."[3] Further reassurance came a few weeks later, in the form of an explicit offer of an American deal. Then visiting Singapore, Aguinaldo was summoned to a late-night meeting with the ranking American diplomat on the outskirts of town. In what Aguinaldo later described as a "cloak-and-dagger" atmosphere, E. Spencer Pratt urged him to relaunch his war against the Spanish. "Ally yourselves with America and you will surely defeat the Spaniards!" Aguinaldo quoted Pratt as saying. "America will give you much greater liberty and much more material benefits than the Spaniards ever promised you." Pratt then encouraged Aguinaldo to return to Hong Kong and join Dewey for the attack on the Spanish fleet.[4]

With visions of a glorious return to the Philippines dancing in his head, Aguinaldo hurried to Hong Kong where he would again hear, or so he claimed, that once America defeated the Spanish, the entire archipelago would be returned to its rightful owner—him.

What he didn't know was that furious notes had been flying back and forth between Washington and its diplomats in Asia: "AVOID UNAU-THORIZED NEGOTIATIONS WITH PHILIPPINE INSURGENTS."[5]

In the weeks before Dewey's attack on Manila, McKinley revealed an inclination for realpolitik. The Philippines presented a new economic opportunity, an American toehold that fit neatly into the visions of Alfred Thayer Mahan and his Pacific stepping-stones. Even before the end of 1897, McKinley's advisers were whispering that if the United States went to war with Spain, he should consider retaining an outpost on the islands. Roosevelt, to no one's surprise, urged McKinley in November to "take and retain the Philippines." And the same month, Senator Orville Platt and a House member visited McKinley and argued that Manila was the linchpin to America's presence in Asia.[6]

McKinley initially didn't put much stock in such suggestions. They smacked of just the kind of "jingo nonsense" that he had promised would not be part of his presidency. And like most Americans, he knew next to nothing of the Philippines. He would later admit that he "could not have told where those darned islands were within 2,000 miles!"[7]

Yet gradually McKinley convinced himself that taking a piece of property such as the port of Manila, where American ships could take on coal and make repairs, was not a violation of his commitment to the integrity of other nations. McKinley calculated the risks and rewards and the changing international landscape. The real risk presented by the Philippines would be in doing nothing.

Just as Africa had been carved up by the European powers over the previous three decades, a race to lay stakes in China was under way in the spring of 1898, and the U.S. government had not even entered.

It began in 1894 when Japan, still new to the international stage and regarded as little more than a nation of sandal-wearing carp tenders, destroyed the numerically superior Chinese in an almost farcical war over control of the Korean Peninsula. There was something admirable about these plucky Japanese, Americans felt, and few questioned Emperor Meiji when he, like European powers in the past, demanded and won slices of China as war reparations. Japan secured parts of mineral-rich eastern Manchuria and what is now Taiwan.

Japan's victory, however, said more about Chinese weakness than Japanese strength, a message that was not missed by the other great powers.

Within months of the signing of the Sino-Japanese peace treaty, Russia brazenly occupied the entire Liaodong Peninsula and fortified territory at Port Arthur that it had already acquired, ignoring Chinese pleas to at least pay for some of it. Soon, others were lining up. London, not to be outdone, demanded and won wider access for British traders on the Yangtze.[8]

Charles Denby, secretary of the U.S. legation in China, considered the Sino-Japanese War and its aftermath the most important event in the history of the East. "It did more to startle, more to develop, China than any experience in her past," he wrote in an article in the influential *North American Review*. "This war has done more to open this vast field to western commerce and civilization than five hundred years of foreign trade and one hundred years of missionary teaching."[9]

Yet the American government had largely failed to grasp the importance of what was happening. Caught up in events in Cuba, and averse to any whiff of imperial displays, the United States had taken scant notice of events in the Middle Kingdom. As one frustrated American diplomat explained, "All these powers recognize the fact that trade follows the flag. . . . They recognize that the present is a critical period in the history of China; that when the breaking up and the inevitable partition come, those who have established themselves will obtain recognition of their interests, those who have failed to do so must see their trade go to the masters of the soil."

Business leaders were determined that McKinley recognize the stakes, and launched a publicity blitz to make sure that no part of the problem escaped him. On January 6, 1898, half a dozen executives led by James McGee of Standard Oil formed the so-called Committee on American Interests in China. Together they organized chambers of commerce throughout the nation to agree to a resolution calling on McKinley to make a "prompt and energetic defense" of existing treaty rights, and for the "preservation and protection of their important commercial interests." Warned by its Shanghai office of the "critical" situation, the China and Japan Trading Company wrote Secretary of the Interior Cornelius Bliss begging for help, as did other cotton exporters. The New England Shoe and Leather Association wrote McKinley directly asking him to work with Britain on preserving open markets in China. The New York *Journal of Commerce and Commercial Bulletin,* in whose pages southern textile firms placed many large ads, assumed the key role of spokesman for the China lobby and asserted that Washington was failing its duties. The newspaper wrote in an editorial on January 5, 1898, of the coming "extinction of China [as a market]" and warned that "no great productive interest in the country" would be left untouched by aggressive European commercial policies. If Washington did nothing, the paper went on, it would be "perpetrating the most colossal blunder in the history of the foreign policy of the United States."[10]

Trial balloons soon began to take flight from the White House. Someone leaked to the *New-York Tribune,* a paper friendly to the president, that part of the Philippines could be retained by the United States. Discussing the future of the islands, McKinley was purported to have said he would wait until after the war to make up his mind, there being "time enough to discuss the sale, barter, or retention of the islands when Spain has been driven to abandon Cuba and sue for conditions of general peace."[11] And in the first week of May 1898, the president left a telling clue to his thinking. In an unaddressed note, he wrote, "While we are conducting war and until its conclusion, we must keep all we can get. When the war is over, we must keep what we want."[12]

"Keep what we want." The phrase signaled a meaningful change to American military strategy in the Pacific. Simply sinking or bottling up the Spanish fleet in Manila was not going to give the United States much leverage to keep anything. Troops would have to be sent. Territory, not just water, would have to be conquered and held.

McKinley arrived at these conclusions much earlier than he would publicly admit, his generals would later say, indicating his forward thinking and ambition. In his autobiography, Secretary of War Russell

Alger said the president had decided to send an army to occupy the Philippines before a single shot had been fired against the Spanish.[13] And as far back as late April 1898, while Dewey was still in Hong Kong, McKinley had instructed Major General Nelson A. Miles to prepare recommendations for a full Philippine invasion.[14] The stage was set for something much grander, something much more dangerous, than simply dealing with a Cuban revolution.

On Sunday afternoon, April 24, 1898, Arent Schuyler Crowninshield, the chief of the U.S. Bureau of Navigation, was enjoying himself at an Arlington golf course. Relaxing amid the velvety lawns and leafy trees that lined the fairways, as well as the occasional anguished expletives of frustrated golfers, he noticed a carriage carrying Navy Secretary Long and his daughter approaching. After brief hellos, Long explained that they were on their way to the country to spend a quiet afternoon together.

After finishing at the links, Crowninshield went to the Navy Department and happened upon a message from George Dewey. With the United States and Spain formally at war, the U.S. fleet had been ordered out of Hong Kong, a step the British governor reluctantly took in keeping with Britain's neutrality. Dewey would take the American ships thirty miles up the China coast to a small protected area called Mirs Bay and await direction. Crowninshield rushed the message to the president.[15]

The evening of Monday, April 25, 1898, George Dewey was seated at a green felt–covered table in his cabin aboard the *Olympia* studying charts of the Philippines when there was a knock at the door. Into his cabin stepped Ensign Harry Caldwell who had just arrived aboard the fast boat *Fame* from Hong Kong, where he had remained to relay orders after the fleet left. "Here is a cable from the Secretary, sir," he said, and laid an envelope next to the maps. There was little doubt about what it would say. WAR HAS COMMENCED BETWEEN THE UNITED STATES AND SPAIN. PROCEED AT ONCE TO PHILIPPINE ISLANDS. COMMENCE OPERA-

TIONS PARTICULARLY AGAINST THE SPANISH FLEET. YOU MUST CAPTURE VES-
SELS OR DESTROY. USE UTMOST ENDEAVORS.[16]

Dewey was about to realize a dream he thought had passed him by.
Back in the United States he had lamented what seemed to be a disappointing career, telling a friend, "I do not want war, but without it
there is little opportunity for a naval man to distinguish himself. There
will be no war before I retire from the Navy, and I will simply join the
great majority of naval men, and be known in history only by consul-
tation of the records of the Navy Department as 'George Dewey who
entered the navy at a certain date and retired as rear admiral at the age
limit.' "[17]

The son of a Vermont physician, Dewey had squeaked into the U.S.
Naval Academy and served during the Civil War under legendary officer David Farragut, famous for quipping "Damn the torpedoes" during the Battle of Mobile Bay in 1864. In the decades that followed,
however, Dewey spent the bulk of his career in less exciting pursuits—
a succession of desk jobs such as lighthouse inspector, chief of the Bureau of Equipment and Recruiting, and supervisor of the naval
observatory. It was hardly the career that young naval cadets aspired to.

A desk-bound life, however, did give the bachelor plenty of time for
the Washington social circuit, where he was known with some admiration as "gentleman George Dewey."[18] Standing five feet seven inches
tall with a neat white beard and dark eyes, Dewey was a regular at the
Metropolitan Club and a sought-after dinner companion with a taste
for fine food. In the evenings, he displayed a talent for whist and poker
and was not bad at billiards.

Washington was not such a bad place for networking, either. By
throwing himself into a heavy leather chair at one of his clubs, or
making a reservation for dinner at one of the city's fashionable restaurants, Dewey found himself in the company of powerful men. It
wasn't long before the frustrated officer met and impressed Roosevelt,
first with his determination to cut through red tape and later with his
imperialist leanings. "You are the man who will be equal to the emergency if one arises," Roosevelt praised Dewey. And when the opportu-

nity to take charge of the Asiatic Squadron opened in October 1897, Roosevelt launched a full-court press on Long to ensure Dewey got the job.

The seven ships of Dewey's fleet were closer in size and technology to those Lord Nelson used to defeat the French and Spanish at the Battle of Trafalgar in 1805 than they were to modern warships.[19] Dewey's flagship, the *Olympia*, although one of the largest in the U.S. Navy at the time, could today easily be stored on the flight deck of an aircraft carrier such as the *John F. Kennedy* without preventing planes from landing.[20] Range finders were still in their infancy and the latest version, developed by Lieutenant Bradley Fiske of the *Petrel*, had never been tested in battle. Communications aboard ship had hardly advanced at all. The captain's orders to his gunnery crews were delivered by a messenger who had to shout above the firing to be heard. Orders between ships were limited to hoisting signal flags.

The sailors, however, were well trained. A strict disciplinarian, Dewey drilled his men without letup during the voyage to Manila. And when not rushing to their guns in a simulated call to battle stations, crews were kept busy stripping the ship of any excess wood trim and decoration that might catch fire or splinter during combat.

Dewey and his men first saw the Philippine capital on May 1 around 5 A.M., its lights twinkling on the horizon just as the faint glow of the sun was rising over green hills behind. Whether Dewey could appreciate the beauty of the scene is doubtful. With the most decisive moment of his entire career only minutes away, the commodore was doing all he could to keep his breakfast down, the victim of an unhealthy mix of green tea, coffee, and hardtack that a Chinese servant had supplied overnight. In the words of one witness, Dewey entered the theater of combat as sick as "a youngster just going out of port into heavy sea on his first cruise."[21]

His stomach churning, Dewey surveyed the harbor around Manila and discovered the Spanish had adopted a perplexing strategy. The

Spanish admiral Patricio Montojo y Pasarón had opted to group his ships at Cavite, a curving wisp of land not far from the city that provided a natural breakwater, instead of in the open water of the bay. The admiral aimed to spare Manila any destruction caused by errant shells; and the shallow waters around Cavite would also make it easier to beach damaged ships in defeat. Whatever the Spanish thought, their ships resembled the static targets of a training exercise.

Shortly before five thirty, Spanish shore batteries fired their first salvos, their shells sailing overhead with terrifying whistles that cast spray on the American sailors when they hit the water. Refusing to reply, Dewey kept his fleet on course until he reached a range of 5,500 yards, the distance he had decided was best to begin his attack. The command, delivered in a coolheaded, businesslike style, would soon become something of a national catchphrase. Speaking to the captain of the *Olympia*, Dewey deadpanned, "You may fire when you are ready, Gridley."[22] The scene unfolded with Wagnerian bombast. Cannons erupted. Crews cheered. And thick black smoke filled the air. So powerful was the fire that gunners could scarcely remain on their feet as the decks shook and quaked.

The American plan was straightforward. With the Spanish ships remaining close to shore, Dewey would lead his fleet on a series of stately two-mile runs back and forth parallel to the coast, firing broadside as quickly as his men could load, closing their range on the Spanish with each pass.

As simple and well organized as the battle plans were, confusion seemed to reign. The entire area became shrouded in thick smoke, and desperate American officers thumbed the focus on their binoculars looking for a hole through which they could sight the enemy, yet saw little. Dewey, for one, assumed the worst. No matter how many shells the Americans poured on the Spanish, they kept firing back.

Dewey's concerns about whether he was actually hitting anything, however, were mollified by the fact that the Spanish could not hit his ships, either. In fact, the American fleet was nearly unscathed, protected as though by an invisible shield. Spanish shells fell all around, just short, just long, exploding overhead, but few found their marks. In the words of one officer, the Americans operated in a "charmed circle" where a hundred shells fell within a ship's length during the first two hours of the battle without inflicting any serious damage. The Spanish gunners were not very accurate, but the law of averages seemed to suggest that with so many shells raining down, at least a few would have caused serious damage. Even when one did strike home, the Americans' luck held. Aboard the *Boston*, paymaster John Martin watched in stunned terror as a Spanish shell slammed into the wardroom five feet from his head and failed to explode.[23]

Although they didn't know it, the Americans were, in fact, inflicting tremendous damage. Aboard the old wooden cruiser *Castilla*, the 4.5-inch forward gun was quickly knocked out, and soon thereafter the secondary battery was as well.[24] Admiral Montojo's flagship, the *Reina Cristina*, was hit repeatedly when he tried to make a run on the American line. One shell tore through the *Cristina*'s forward turret, killing all the gunners. Within minutes of Montojo's attack, nearly half of his crew of 353 men had been killed or wounded. Fearing that the entire ship would soon go up if its magazines caught fire, Montojo ordered it to make for shore, where she quickly sank to the level of her main deck. When she was raised from the muddy bottom five years later, eighty skeletons were found in the sick bay.

The entire Spanish harbor became a scene of naval Armageddon. Fires raged on all the Spanish ships save the *Isla de Cuba;* some were slowly sinking. Men cried in agony from burns and shrapnel wounds. The *Isla de Luzon* blazed fore and aft, and the *Marques de Duero* was making a desperate run to shore behind the cover of the Cavite arsenal before she sank.[25]

By seven thirty Dewey had closed the range to as little as a mile and was about to begin another barrage when the captain of the *Olympia* announced shocking news. Ammunition was running low. All that remained for the five-inch battery were fifteen rounds per gun, enough for only five more minutes of firing. The report was as "startling as it was unexpected," as ammunition was a constant worry. According to one report, when the fleet left Hong Kong, they had only 60 percent of their allotted wartime munitions.[26] Dewey was seven thousand miles from home, and it would take at least a month to resupply.

Signal flags were hoisted on the *Olympia* ordering the fleet to stand off out of range of the Spanish to take store of the supply of shells; "the gloom on the bridge of the *Olympia* was thicker than a London fog in November."[27] As the men recounted their ammunition, they discovered there had been a mistake. Dewey had asked how many rounds remained for five-inch guns and was told fifteen. But his question had been misunderstood, and, in fact, fifteen rounds had been *fired*. There were ample supplies of ammunition.

The pause in the action was fortuitous. While the sailors, many stripped to the waist and glistening with sweat, nibbled on crackers and gulped water, their officers took the opportunity to study the Spanish fleet now that the smoke was clearing. Through holes in the haze they could see what they had accomplished—the Spanish fleet had very nearly been completely destroyed. Only the gunboat *Don Antonio de Ulloa* was in a position to offer any resistance. Two of the three ships afloat, the *Isla de Cuba* and the *Marques del Duero,* had withdrawn to behind the breakwater of the Cavite arsenal. Only a light mop-up was needed.

Dewey had wiped out the entire Spanish presence, all in a morning's work. While nearly four hundred Spaniards had been killed or wounded, the lone American death was due to heat exhaustion, and not a single ship required repairs that could not be carried out at sea.

Such a resounding victory was almost too amazing to comprehend. The United States had sunk the entire Pacific fleet of a European power, albeit a fading one, with the loss of but a single sailor. The country had, in the space of a single morning, become a power that every nation on earth would have to reckon with.

Overnight, Dewey became one of America's first superstars. Babies were named in his honor, as were streets, yachts, and racehorses. Torchlight parades, festivals, and ceremonies were held. State legislatures voted their appreciation. Proud homeowners displayed his picture. Souvenir dishes, silver spoons, paperweights, shaving mugs, and even teething rings were decorated with his name. Girls would soon wear Dewey blouses and sailor hats while men dressed in the morning with Dewey neckties, stickpins, and cuff links. A new brand of chewing gum, "Dewey Chewies," appeared on store shelves. Congress approved $10,000 to be spent on a gift for Dewey, a gold-studded sword custom-made by Tiffany & Co., and promoted the commodore to rear admiral.[28]

The terms of the war had now changed. Before Manila, the desire to help Cuba was couched in humanitarian arguments. Now, suddenly, there seemed no reason to hide imperialist ambitions. American naval officer French Ensor Chadwick noted, "The victory at once gave a new aspect to the whole subject of the war."[29] Speaking at a celebration at the Manhattan Club, James B. Eustis, a former senator, declared, "From the foundation of our government it has been a question debated by the ablest of statesmen whether the acquisition of territory would be beneficial to this country. But Dewey has settled the question. He has conquered foreign territory, and I am afraid that he has given Uncle Sam a damn big appetite for the particular article of food."[30]

The *Rocky Mountain News* printed a cartoon of Uncle Sam sticking American flags into Spanish possessions on a miniature globe, saying "By gum, I rather like your looks." And *The Providence News* wrote, "We do not know much about our new possession in the far Pacific, but what little we do know indicates that they are of great value. . . . They are certainly well worth keeping."[31]

Almost forgotten in the delirium was that very few people, other than a handful of business leaders and strategists, knew anything about the Philippines or had wanted to have anything to do with them in the first place. With a perspective that many others had lost, the *Philadelphia Ledger* asked "Why was Uncle Sam like a lady throwing a stone? Because he had aimed at Cuba and hit the Philippines."[32]

Of course, the aim of Uncle Sam had been perfect. The real riddle was this: What would McKinley do with his target now that he had hit it?

With the Spanish fleet still smoldering in Manila Bay, on May 2, 1898, McKinley began his day pondering a map of the Philippines. The exercise was fairly frustrating, as the map had been torn from a schoolbook that was no larger than his hand.[33] Manila Bay was the size of a pea. Stunned that the commander in chief had no better lay of the land, Henry Pritchett, superintendent of the U.S. Coast and Geodetic Survey, rushed more detailed maps—produced by the British Admiralty— to the grateful president. Clearly he was going to need them.

In the days and weeks ahead, with most of the country still celebrating too much to notice, McKinley began to tilt his war effort to the Pacific. Men who had enlisted believing they were headed to the Caribbean found their transport trains heading to the West Coast instead. Under the command of Major General Wesley Merritt, troops assembled at the windswept Presidio military installation near San Francisco—ironically, a facility originally built by the Spanish in the late eighteenth century—for an attack on Manila itself.[34] In what would be the subject of considerable internal debate, McKinley soon decided that twenty thousand sailors and troops should get ready to sail to the Philippines, more than the United States would initially dispatch to Cuba and quadruple the number that Dewey estimated were needed to take Manila.[35]

The role of the troops in the Philippines seemed also to be growing, too, although McKinley had not clearly stated his intentions. On the fifteenth, Merritt tried to nail down the president, writing him: "I do not yet know whether it is your desire to subdue and hold all the Spanish territory in the islands, or merely to seize and hold the capital. It seems more than probable that we will have the so-called insurgents to fight as well as the Spaniards."[36] McKinley answered four days later. The United States, he wrote, had two goals: the "reduction of Spanish power in that quarter" and the introduction of "order and security" to the islands while they were held by the United States.[37] He intended to create "a new political power." One can easily imagine Merritt pounding his head on his desk wondering what exactly McKinley meant.

In the weeks that followed, three different flotillas departed for Manila. The first, commanded by Thomas H. Anderson, steamed out on May 25, 1898, a second under Brigadier General Francis V. Greene followed, and the final departed under Arthur MacArthur, Jr., the father of World War II general Douglas MacArthur, whose own biography would become intertwined with the islands.

With little appreciation for what he had gotten the nation into or where it would ultimately lead, McKinley had dramatically changed the framework of the war. This sideshow in the Pacific was now bidding for equal billing with the main attraction in the Caribbean. The United States had taken the first step toward becoming a global power. And not a shot had yet been fired in Cuba, the source of it all.

13

A RESPECTABLE TRAMP

Chicago awoke on May 5, 1886, the morning after the Haymarket bombing, gripped in hysteria and paranoia. Behind every lamppost, in every saloon where immigrants congregated, in every darkened room, lurked a shifty-eyed anarchist clutching a dagger dripping with the blood of his latest victim, a bomb in his pocket ready to be thrown. Rumors ran wild: Radicals planned to kill all the police, blow up public buildings, and take over city hall. What had happened the night before was seen as not just a crime, but an attack on the nation itself. Where the national security was concerned, any measure of defense was warranted.

David Swing, a liberal pastor of the Central Church, typified the sense of alarm. "We need a careful definition of what freedom is. If it means the license to proclaim the gospel of disorder, to preach destruction, and scatter the seeds of anarchy and death, the sooner we exchange the Republic for an iron-handed monarchy the better it will be for all of us."[1] Brand Whitlock, the future mayor of Toledo, described the climate as "one of the strangest frenzies of fear that ever distracted a whole community."[2]

The zeitgeist dictated that retribution for the Haymarket bombing must come swiftly and without mercy. Theodore Roosevelt, still years away from joining the McKinley administration, wrote from his ranch in the Dakota Territory that his cowboys knew how to deal with anarchists. "I believe nothing would give them greater pleasure than a chance with rifles at one of the mobs," he wrote.[3] In Michigan, the state assembly voted to condemn "anarchy and revolutionary schemes" and to recognize the American flag as "the only emblem of American working men."[4] The city's leading industrialists, including Marshall Field, Philip Armour, and George Pullman, secretly committed $100,000 to battle revolutionaries, much of it given to support the police in the upcoming trial. Similar amounts of money would be raised every year through 1891.

Newspapers screamed for revenge, referring to the attackers as "Bloody Brutes," "Red Ruffians," "Bloody Monsters," "cutthroats," "thieves," "assassins," "fiends," and, perhaps most cleverly, as "Dynamarchists."[5] Long before it could be determined who shot whom, the *New-York Tribune* wrote that "The mob [at Haymarket] appeared crazy with a frantic desire for blood and, holding its ground, poured volley after volley into the midst of the officers." The normally sober *New York Times* added, "No disturbance of the peace that has occurred in the United States since the war of rebellion has excited public sentiment throughout the Union as it is excited by the anarchists' murder of policemen in Chicago on Tuesday night." The *St. Louis Globe-Democrat* proclaimed, "There are no good anarchists except dead anarchists."

This, people nodded in agreement, was no time for civil liberties. The very fabric of their society was at risk. In the coming days and weeks, the police searched for suspects with little regard for decency or the law. Mail was intercepted and opened, anarchist newspapers were shut down, and editors were arrested. Dozens of bars, clubs, and homes were ransacked. Hundreds of people were arrested on the thinnest of suspicion, thrown in jail, and frequently roughed up.

Yet Parsons, the one person the police really wanted to find, had disappeared.

The thin Texan's whereabouts quickly became a national obsession. A $5,000 reward was offered for his capture. Newspapers around the country carried stories claiming that he had been spotted in points as distant as Ohio, Pennsylvania, Missouri, Kansas, Arkansas, Florida, and even in Cuba.

As weeks passed, the police turned their fury on his wife, Lucy, determined to force her to reveal her husband's whereabouts. Investigators shadowed her as she went about her daily affairs and arrested her several times. Police ransacked her home and smashed furniture. On one raid, they tore open mattresses and threatened her six-year-old son by wrapping him in a carpet and spinning him around. "Where's your daddy?" they demanded. "We're going to string him up when we get him."[6] Lucy remained defiant throughout, wearing a red handkerchief around her neck and refusing to give the police the slightest clue.

Parsons was, in fact, readying the final phase of his escape. Hiding at the Holmes house, he began by shaving off his mustache, a simple procedure that "altered his appearance amazingly."[7] Then, tucking his pants into his boots and removing his collar and neck scarf, he looked for all the world like a "respectable tramp." He briefly considered taking a pistol with which he might make a final stand if confronted by the police but thought better of it.

On May 8, 1886, Parsons thanked his friends and started off down a dusty road for the train station. He had an idea of where he might hide but wasn't sure how he would be welcomed. Still, anything was better than staying put. The next day, the county sheriff knocked on the Holmeses' front door looking for him.

Two days later, Parsons walked into the workshop of Daniel Hoan, the owner of a small pump factory in Waukesha, Wisconsin. A spa town, Waukesha was noted for its lovely green hills and the natural springs that had attracted visitors for years, among them Mary Todd Lincoln. Parsons knew Hoan was a socialist and a subscriber to *The Alarm*, yet Hoan didn't know him and would not have recognized him in his disguise. Testing Hoan's leanings, Parsons began a casual conversation, gently steering the chat to Haymarket. As Hoan spoke, it rapidly became apparent that Parsons had found a man who would help hide him.

For the next six weeks, Parsons enjoyed an idyll in Waukesha. Introduced around town as Mr. Jackson, a somewhat destitute and avuncular man, Parsons quickly became a fixture in the community. During the day, he helped out at Hoan's factory with carpentry work and did chores around his home, repairing latticework and the porch.[8] The townspeople quickly came to accept Mr. Jackson as one of their own and even invited him to lecture at the local church. One lady in the village remarked, "What a nice man Mr. Jackson seems to be. What a pity he cannot dress better."[9] It was surely not a comment the sartorially proud Parsons had heard before. Only once did anyone suspect his real identity, but bullied by Hoan, the sharp-eyed local was quickly convinced otherwise. The fugitive might have remained there as long as he wanted.

Yet Parsons's hatred of capitalism and the landed class still burned intensely. On May 22, 1886, he wrote Lizzie an angry letter, posted through a circuitous route so he couldn't be traced. "The property beast is in the last days of its power, its bloodthirstiness, its cruelty. Private capital with its pack of bloodhounds—the police and militia—will ere long be powerless in the presence of an aroused and fearless people."[10] In the same package, Parsons included a letter to his wife with an important question: Should he return to stand trial?

During Parsons's flight, seven of his friends had been arrested and charged with murder. They faced the very real possibility that they would not only be found guilty, but given the death penalty as well. Terrified at that prospect, family members and supporters had held picnics and dances to raise money for their legal defense. Donors as far away as Bombay and Tokyo had chipped in. Although finding an attorney to represent anarchists had been a challenge, they had secured the services of one of Chicago's most well-known corporate lawyers,

William Perkins Black, to lead their defense, over the objections of Black's wife, who feared for the family's social standing.[11]

Confident in the legal system, Black felt sure that Parsons would be acquitted if he turned himself in. Surrender could also be seen as evidence that he and the others had done nothing wrong, helping them all. Yet other members of the legal team were not so sure. There was no telling what might unfold in a city that still hungered for revenge.[12] The decision would have to be made by Parsons. He later wrote, "I felt that it was my duty to take my chances with the rest of my comrades. I sought a fair and impartial trial before a jury of my peers, and knew that before any fair-minded jury I could with little difficulty be cleared. I preferred to be tried and take the chances of an acquittal with my friends to being hunted as a felon."[13]

On the afternoon of June 21, 1886, Parsons arrived back in Chicago and quickly went about assuming his old identity. That very day, he shaved off his shaggy beard, put on neat clothes, and dyed his white hair black. Around two o'clock, he climbed into a cab and made his way to Cook County Criminal Court where Black was pacing on the sidewalk waiting for him. As the two entered the three-story Romanesque building and ascended the first landing to join the other defendants, they happened to pass a journalist speaking with none other than Detective Bonfield, who had been pulling his hair out over his failure to find Parsons. The reporter stared agape, muttering, "I'll bet a dollar to a nickel that that little man is A. R. Parsons."

One detective scoffed, "Nonsense, not in a thousand years. Why, man, don't you suppose I know Parsons when I see him? He isn't within five hundred miles of Chicago."

But a stunned Bonfield knew otherwise. "I'll be d——d, if it ain't" and took off after him.[14]

With a group of anarchists now in court, the entire city looked forward to revenge, none more so than the judge. With white sideburns running the length of his jaw, Joseph E. Gary was a respected jurist. But the anarchist trial and the publicity it generated seemed to bring out the worst in him. As the proceedings unfolded, he made little attempt at objectivity, harshly refusing objections raised by the defense and granting considerable latitude to the prosecution. In court, he surrounded himself with head-turning young women who whispered, giggled, and ate candy. On some occasions they even sat on the bench with him, smiling and doing puzzles while the lawyers made their arguments.

The composition of the jury was likewise stacked against the defendants. A special bailiff who was appointed to summon jurors made sure of it. He boasted to friends, "I am managing this case and I know what I am about. These fellows are going to be hanged as certain as Death. I am calling such men as the defendants will have to challenge peremptorily and waste their time and challenges. Then they will have to take such men as the prosecution wants."[15]

The trial, when it began on June 21, 1886, hinged on a single question: Who had murdered Officer Degan? Although seven other police officers had died, it was quietly established that they had perished from friendly fire, and so it was impossible to charge any of the defendants for their deaths.

State's attorney Julius Grinnell, a politically ambitious prosecutor with short-cropped hair and a bushy mustache, produced several witnesses who claimed to have seen one or another of the defendants commit the deed. One of his star witnesses, Harry Gilmer, claimed he saw the whole thing and that one of the accused, August Spies, actually lit the bomb while another man whom he didn't know had thrown it. But as would happen repeatedly throughout the trial, the prosecution's claims suffered mightily under cross-examination. It turned out that Gilmer was not only a habitual liar but that he had received money from Detective Bonfield, almost surely for his testimony. Judge Gary put a stop to the questioning before the full measure of Gilmer's fabrications could be shared.[16]

As the trial progressed, Black provided irrefutable evidence that six of the defendants were not even at Haymarket when the bomb went off. The other two were on the speakers' wagon in full view of the police and the crowd and could not possibly have lobbed a bomb without hundreds of witnesses. Nothing directly linked anyone to the bombing itself.

Grinnell then attempted to establish the next best thing: The defendants were responsible for motivating the bomb thrower, whoever he was. Days passed in the courtroom as the prosecution read articles from *The Alarm* and the *Chicagoer Arbeiter-Zeitung.* Excerpts were also read from Most's inflammatory pamphlets, the *Pittsburgh Manifesto,* and other publications that, especially in light of the public mood, cast the men in a damning light.

By the closing arguments, Grinnell had zeroed in on the crux of his argument. It didn't matter if any of the defendants had thrown the bomb or what support they may have provided. They were anarchists and that was a good enough reason for any court to hand down a conviction. These men, he told the jury, wished to destroy the American government, and for nothing less than the security of the nation they must return a guilty verdict. "In this country, above all countries in the world, anarchy is possible," he argued. "There is but one step from republicanism to anarchy." To free the defendants would be to invite other anarchists to "flock out again like a lot of rats and vermin."[17]

Shortly before three o'clock on August 19, 1886, the jury retired to the Revere House Hotel to deliberate. Anxious for any indication about their progress, crowds gathered outside to peer in the open windows. Inside, plainly visible, were jury members relaxing in shirtsleeves, smoking, and enjoying themselves.[18]

In the noisy saloons of the German quarter as well as on front porches near the lake, Chicago buzzed with rumors. The Haymarket jury had taken just a few hours to reach a verdict. And now, on the morning of August 20, 1886, the criminal court building was surrounded by a stout police cordon. Putting two and two together, many people believed it added up to not only a guilty verdict, but death sentences. By ten o'clock some one thousand people had assembled outside the courthouse hoping to get a seat inside, or at least to celebrate the moment when the anarchists would learn they would go to the gallows.

All grew quiet as the jury filed in. In a clear voice, the foreman read out the verdict: "We the jury find the defendants, August Spies, Michael Schwab, Samuel Fielden, Albert R. Parsons, Adolph Fischer, George Engel, and Louis Lingg guilty of murder in manner and form as charged in the indictment, and fix the penalty of death." Another defendant, Oscar Neebe, was also found guilty but spared the death penalty. He was given fifteen years of hard labor.

Death. The penalty had always been possible, but now that seven executions had been handed down, it seemed inconceivable. The news floored Black. "I was never so shocked in all my experience as I was this morning. I should not have been more horrified had I myself received the death sentence." He continued: "I had expected a conviction . . . but seven men convicted to hang!"[19] The defendants' families were staggered. Maria Schwab, the wife of Michael, a "tall and graceful woman of pure pink-and-white complexion," fainted into the arms of Lucy Parsons. Quickly revived, she became hysterical, "sharp, shrill, agonizing screams rent the air of the court room," wrote a reporter. Christine Spies, mother of August, began to cry. Lucy Parsons sobbed quietly.

The defendants tried with varying degrees of success to accept the decision stoically. Parsons stood and tied the string of a window shade into the form of a noose and displayed it to the crowd outside, which roared its approval. Others were not so cavalier. Spies and Fischer looked pale. Fielden shuffled as he walked out of the courtroom and had to be helped. Schwab looked like he might at any moment need to be supported. Neebe, for whom evidence was so lacking that even Grinnell thought conviction unlikely, had fully expected to be found innocent and now looked deeply shaken.[20] Hangings were set for December 3, 1886, pending appeal.

The Cook County Jail, where the condemned were held, rapidly assumed an odd air—part penitentiary, part backstage at a Broadway hit. Each prisoner was confined in a six-by-eight-foot stone cell, received limited exercise, and was never allowed outside. Yet they also gave interviews, wrote memoirs, and entertained a steady stream of fawning visitors. *The New York World* dispatched one of its top reporters, Charles Edward Russell, who filed daily reports.[21] Twice a day, at 10 A.M.

and 4 P.M., well-wishers lined up to bring the men creature comforts—wurst, ham, smoked beef, herring, cheese, and cigars. Most visitors could not get closer to the defendants than a wire mesh barrier, but children were often allowed to sit and play with their fathers. In between, they played cards, wrote, and in Parsons's case, carved tiny toy boats.

Other than Parsons, the two biggest stars were the bachelors, Spies and Lingg, the latter described by one newspaper as a "devil masked in the form of a Grecian god."[22] Both attracted numerous female visitors—women who favored the ultimate bad boys. Spies, for one, developed a relationship with a well-tailored, well-bred Vassar graduate by the name of Nina Van Zandt. The heiress to a small fortune earned by her father who manufactured medicines, Van Zandt visited Spies daily, and in a delightful twist for newspaper editors, the two announced plans to wed. Unable to attend the nuptials himself, Spies arranged for his brother to act as stand-in groom during the ceremony at the Van Zandt family home on January 29, 1887.[23]

Despite the death sentences, it did not seem far-fetched to think the seven would yet escape the noose. With all of the bizarre behavior in the courtroom during their trial, a not insignificant number of legal experts around Chicago figured there was a good chance that an appeal—Black quickly filed one with the Illinois Supreme Court—would lead to a retrial. Indeed, in November 1886, the court ordered a temporary stay of execution while it studied the case.

At the same time, the prisoners' friends and supporters established an amnesty association, hoping to generate so much support that Illinois governor Richard Oglesby would commute their death penalties to life sentences. Something of a softy and sympathetic to the working class, Oglesby watched closely as petitions streamed in from around the country. So well organized was the amnesty group that by November 7, 1886, some one hundred thousand Americans had added their names to the lists, as did a number of foreigners, including such celebrities as Oscar Wilde and George Bernard Shaw.[24]

The prisoners would soon learn that their best chances to live lay with the governor. On September 14, 1887, the Illinois Supreme Court ruled that yes, Gray could have conducted a better trial. But it also decided that the ultimate decision had not been affected and upheld the decision of the lower court. An attempt to seek a higher authority also failed. The U.S. Supreme Court looked at the case and punted, declaring that it lacked proper jurisdiction to render a judgment. A new execution date of November 11, 1887, was set.

The fate of the condemned now rested solely in the hands of Oglesby. The three-term governor, a popular general during the Civil War when he was simply known as "Uncle Dick," decided to give the anarchists a chance to have their sentences commuted to life in prison, as long as they submitted a formal appeal for clemency. It seemed like a small price to pay for one's life.

Yet for most of the defendants, such a statement constituted a violation of their principles. Only three—Fielden, Schwab, and Spies— would take the governor up on his offer. And Spies quickly withdrew his request, shamed by howls of protest from his German friends. Parsons would remain bitterly defiant. Writing from prison on the prospect of dying, Parsons said, "We are ready to meet it like men— like anarchists. If by our death at the hands of the executioner, 'liberty, fraternity, and equality' can be made to triumph, then we welcome death in such a cause."[25]

Amid all the reporters, girlfriends, and activist fellow travelers who called on the prisoners, an innocent-looking gentleman with a long, pointed mustache and thinning hair by the name of Dyer Lum escaped notice. Though a well-known anarchist, Lum won the confidence of the prison guards and even received a pass from the sheriff to, under some circumstances, go directly to the cells. So porous was the security that Lum managed to sneak in a pair of one-pound dumbbells to Parsons, who wanted to exercise.

Sometime before November 6, 1887, Lum smuggled in something more sinister. During a visit to Lingg, probably the most dangerous of the convicts, Lum carried small pipe bombs hidden under his coat. The twenty-two-year-old Lingg had arrived in the United States from Germany less than a year before and was a well-known anarchist and disciple of the "propaganda of the deed." Never holding a regular job in the United States, Lingg had spent considerable time tinkering with bombs and was well versed in their use.[26] What exactly Lum's nefarious gift was to be used for—suicide, a breakout—would never be learned. In the bare confines of a jail cell, guards soon found the dynamite sticks hidden under Lingg's cot in a wooden box. With considerable relief and shock, they assumed they had foiled an anarchist plot. They were wrong.

At 9 A.M. on November 10, 1887, a sharp explosion echoed throughout the jail. Rushing to Lingg's cell, the source of the noise, guards were confronted with a gruesome sight. Lingg had placed dynamite cartridges, somehow missed by the guards earlier, in his mouth and lit the fuse. The force of the blast was strong enough to blow off half his face. His tongue, upper lip, and nose were shredded. Bits of flesh and bone were splashed on the walls and furniture. Yet Lingg would survive for six agonizing hours as doctors did what they could to ease his pain, a job complicated by the fact that their patient—lacking a mouth—could not speak.

The security lapse of Lingg in mind, the city took no chances on November 11 as the execution hour approached. Three hundred policemen armed with rifles, shotguns, and pistols guarded Cook County Jail and the surrounding area. Ropes were stretched across nearby streets and traffic was diverted. Several regiments of militia waited near city hall with Gatling guns and cannons. The homes of Judge Gary, the jurors, and others were placed under guard. Factories closed, and shopkeepers boarded up their stores. Cordons of police surrounded the courthouse and a policeman was stationed at every window, weapon in hand. The roof, one observer noted, was "black with policemen."

Lucy and her two children arose on what anarchists would come to call Black Friday, steeling themselves for an agonizing final hug and tender words from their father and husband. Yet as the small family, along with Lizzie, made their way to the prison, they became entangled in the police cordon. Racing up and down the sidewalk and street, shivering in the cold, their eyes puffing with tears, they desperately searched for a way through.

Hoping to force the issue with the police, Lucy finally led Lizzie and the children through the barriers and into the area sealed off around the prison. Rather than receiving a sympathetic hearing, however, they were promptly arrested. Ignoring Lucy's frantic pleas that the family be reunited one last time, the police briskly escorted the two women and the children to the Chicago Avenue Police Station where, with the clock counting down, they were strip-searched and thrown into a basement cell.[27]

Inside the prison, Parsons remained well composed, drinking coffee. He had had a good night's sleep, despite the faint hammering and sawing of men working on the scaffolding of the gallows. He eagerly ate fried oysters for breakfast and could be heard reciting poetry. After reading the newspapers one last time, he told his guard, "Now I feel all right. Let's finish the business."[28]

Each man—Spies, Fischer, Engel, and Parsons—was quietly dressed for his execution. Carefully, they were covered with white shrouds that stretched from their necks to their feet. A thick leather belt was placed around their arms, their hands handcuffed behind them.

Inside the execution room, some 170 witnesses, including more than 50 reporters, were already seated on benches before the gallows as the four men were led inside in single file. Engel looked happy; his eyes twinkled. Parsons, some thought, appeared to be distracted. None resisted as they were lined up in a row, face-to-face with the spectators. Guards bound their ankles and placed the ropes around their necks, knots fixed under their left ears. White hoods, each with a string at the neck, were slipped over their heads. Parsons, witnesses said, lifted his eyes as the hood was arranged so as to catch once last glimpse of the sun as it shone through a grated window.

As the executioners made their final preparations, Spies boomed out, "There will be a time when our silence will be more powerful than the voices you strangle to-day! Hurrah for anarchy!" Fischer shouted next, "Hurrah for anarchy," then Engel, "Hurrah for anarchy" yet more loudly.

"This is the happiest moment of my life," Fischer yelled.

Then Parsons spoke. "Will I be allowed to speak, O men of America? Let me speak, Sheriff Matson. Let the voice of the people be heard! O—." But before he could finish, the ax man swung his blade down on a rope that held the trapdoors on which the men stood. The four plunged earthward.[29]

It was not a clean drop. Spies writhed, his chest heaved, and his legs drew up and straightened in sickening convulsions. Fischer, too, twitched and jerked. Parsons flinched under his shroud. The autopsy would later show that the fall had failed to break any of their necks. All had died from strangulation that, from the time of the drop to the time the last man was pronounced dead, took seven minutes and forty-five seconds.

14

THE "LEAST DANGEROUS EXPERIMENT"

In the spring of 1898, Americans treated the prospect of war in Cuba like a cross between a debutante's ball and "Buffalo Bill" Cody's Wild West Show. No red-blooded man, regardless of training, wealth, or aptitude for firing a weapon, dared to be left out. It was simply the most rowdy, chaotic, even slapstick conflict that the United States has fought before or since. Only through a truly remarkable run of Yankee good luck and Spanish ineptitude did the United States manage to avert a national catastrophe.

For many the prospect of adventure in the Caribbean was simply too much fun to be left to the government. Frank James, brother of the notorious outlaw Jesse, offered to lead a company of cowboys into battle. Sioux Indians were said to be ready to go to Cuba to collect scalps. One enterprising engineer, John P. Holland, claimed to have developed a "submarine torpedo boat" and offered to demonstrate his craft by using it to transport a bomb to Havana's Morro Castle, provided the navy would promise to purchase one afterward. The offer was rejected.[1] Even William Jennings Bryan joined the fray, serving as a colonel in a Nebraska regiment, though he never got any farther than Florida.

McKinley and senior cabinet members had to fight off crowds of men seeking impressive-sounding commissions. "Everyone who has ever carried a musket . . . seems bent on getting a high command," the *Army and Navy Journal* wrote. One general reported a stack of applications that reached nearly to the ceiling. Secretary of War Alger felt so much political pressure to grant a personal hearing to well-connected applicants that he received more than a hundred visitors a day, forcing war planning to be conducted in the evenings and on Sundays.[2]

There were so many commissions to sign that McKinley and his aides formed a small assembly line to speed things up. Seated at a table, McKinley would take each piece of paper from a tall stack and sign it, and as he was reaching for the next one, an aide would whisk the signed order away and lay it on the floor while the ink dried. Grumbling, McKinley wondered aloud why he had to be the one to sign all the orders.

Throughout the heartland, eager young men flocked to enlist, lining up at makeshift booths or abandoned stores taken over by army recruiters while backslapping neighbors congratulated them on their patriotic spirit. They paraded together to train stations, crowds cheering, bands playing such hits as "Marching Through Georgia" and "Maryland." Young girls rode to city squares in their Sunday best to wave flags and beg for cartridges as souvenirs.

On New York's Fifth Avenue, the society set were more inclined to pay for their contributions than risk their own patrician necks. John Jacob Astor purchased a complete battery of artillery, including guns and ammunition, and donated them to the effort. The Armour Company promised a scarce refrigerator ship to transport food to the troops.[3] Heiress Helen M. Gould donated $100,000 of her private estate to the navy. Newspaper publisher Hearst made plans to buy "some big English steamer" and have her sailed to the Suez Canal and sunk to prevent the Spanish from reinforcing their fleet in the Pacific.[4]

The normally reserved *Atlantic Monthly* published an American flag on its cover.[5] The rival New York papers, the *Journal* and the *World*, scrambled to assemble fleets of boats to transport reporters, artists, and even printing presses to Cuba. Hearst, ever the patriot, was awarded the honorary rank of naval ensign for donating his yacht—the *Bucentaur*—to the war effort and would later lead a fleet of twenty tug-boats to Cuba. To his readers' delight, he would manage to personally help capture twenty Spanish soldiers and force them to kneel and kiss the American flag while his photographers captured the moment.[6]

For all of the delirious flag-waving, no group snared the public's attention like the First United States Volunteer Cavalry, owners of that most critical qualification for success in America: a catchy nickname. The Rough Riders were a publicist's dream, filled with larger-than-life characters of the sort that only the United States could produce. No persona, of course, was bigger than the second-in-command, Theodore Roosevelt. By rights, Roosevelt should have remained at his post as assistant secretary of the navy, where his skills were needed now more than ever. Long was incensed when he heard of Roosevelt's plan to fight. "He has lost his head. . . . He means well, but it is one of those cases of aberration—desertion—vain-glory; of which he is entirely unaware."[7] Yet Roosevelt, who had been dreaming and bragging to friends about leading men into combat for years, was no more likely to remain in Washington than Ida McKinley was to lead a combat division.

Within days of the announcement that the regiment was being formed, Roosevelt's mailbox filled to overflowing with some twenty-three thousand applications from a collection of candidates as diverse as the nation itself.[8] Many came from his rarefied social circles. From his alma mater there was the outstanding quarterback Dudley Dean and tennis champion Bob Wrenn. Other athletes included Craig Wadsworth, the steeplechase rider; Joe Stevens, a crack polo player; and Hamilton Fish, a former captain of the Columbia crew.[9]

Yet the man who had spent many a happy night under the stars of the Dakotas on hunting expeditions was no snob. The Rough Riders included cowboys, four New York City policemen, famed Indian hunters, and Native American Indians as well. One trooper who had never seen a body of water larger than the headwaters of the Rio Grande displayed the limited worldview that more than a few Rough Riders possessed. When his hat blew off aboard a transport ship miles from shore, the man shouted to a friend, "Oh-oh-Jim! Ma hat blew into the creek."[10]

Poor planning, bungled leadership, and interservice rivalries complicated the war's planning at every turn. Decisions as basic as the size of the American expeditionary force and its objectives changed almost by the day. The choice of a staging area caused no small headaches. At one point, the invasion force was ordered to assemble in Dry Tortugas, Florida. The command was rescinded when it was pointed out that there was "absolutely no water" there.[11] The eventual choice of Tampa Bay was a triumph of bureaucratic myopia over common sense. The first troops arrived to discover that only one rail line served the port itself, after crossing nine miles of sandy and swampy terrain. What's more, the military was forced to share the line with railroad companies that sold tickets to tourists.

Charged with getting the embarkation organized was William Rufus Shafter, a crusty old Indian fighter more famous for his portly frame than his management skills. The Tampa gossip mill estimated that he weighed at least three hundred pounds and could walk no faster than two miles an hour—"just beastly obese," as one observer put it.[12] Skillful strategist though he may have been on the frontier, Shafter lacked any background for leading such a large number of men. Tasks as basic as locating equipment and food were reduced to a hopeless muddle. Bills of lading and invoices on newly arrived trains were frequently forgotten or went missing, forcing officers to open each car to see what was inside. Many cargoes were simply lost. Some fifteen cars full of uniforms were marooned on side tracks around the city at the same time that militia troops were desperate for clothing.[13] Logistics grew so convoluted that at one point, supplies were backed up as far as Columbia, South Carolina, five hundred miles away.[14]

Most disappointing of all was that the army was desperately short of the latest rifles—the new Krag-Jorgensons that fired a smokeless powder. Most soldiers would have to make do with their old Springfields, single-shot rifles that emitted a black puff of smoke when fired, signaling their location to the enemy. In certain quarters, even a Springfield was a luxury. Some of the National Guard troops arrived with rusty weapons unfit for field service; others had no weapons of any kind. Arms were in such short supply that sentries at the Chickamauga Battlefield Park in Georgia marched with broomsticks.[15]

Yet as far as the senior officer class was concerned, whoever had picked Tampa had gotten one thing right: their accommodations. The palatial Tampa Bay Hotel might have been the entire area's only redeeming quality. While troops made the best of mildewed canvas tents, officers at the hotel relaxed in wicker chairs on porches "as wide and as long as a village street." Busy waiters kept the guests cooled with a constant supply of iced tea,[16] whisking through the luxurious lobby that blazed with flowers. On the hotel's round, stuffed sofas, American officers mixed with foreign military attachés in crisp dress uniforms. Evenings were spent dancing under colored electric lights and palm trees in the ballroom with female guests that included family members of soldiers and at least a couple of journalists. One panting Chicago correspondent described Kathleen Blake Watkins, a reporter for the *Toronto Mail and Express,* thus: "By gosh, for a five-card draw she's hot stuff. There's steam comes out of her boots all the time, and the whole Chicago fire brigade couldn't put her out."[17] One general summed up the feelings of many: "Only God knows why [Morton F.] Plant built a hotel here, but thank God he did."[18]

The fumbling mob of would-be soldiers might have stumbled along for weeks were it not for an astonishing discovery. On May 1, 1898, from the far-off Cape Verde Islands, a desolate few specks on the map four hundred miles off the west coast of Africa, a *New York Herald* correspondent reported that he had seen Spain's Atlantic fleet set sail in the direction of the United States. In fact, he had followed the fleet in a small steamer until it disappeared heading west and calculated it would be heading for Puerto Rico, a journey of 2,480 miles that would take twelve to fourteen days.[19] The *Herald* story, when it landed on American doorsteps, gave rise to a terrified manhunt for Pascual Cervera y Topete and his ships. A Spanish fleet consisting of four armored cruisers and three destroyers was heading in the direction of the East Coast with evil intent.[20] And nobody knew exactly where it was. With most of the American navy blockading Havana, the Spanish could in theory simply lay anchor off any number of American cities such as Baltimore, New York, or Boston and pound private homes and businesses into rubble.[21]

With panic spreading up and down the eastern seaboard, American naval ships chased down one ghostly report after another. A telegraph operator in Newfoundland claimed that he had heard gunfire at sea. Strange ships were spotted off Fire Island. New naval ships under construction near Norfolk were thought to be the target of Spanish torpedo boats. Commanders in the Caribbean guessed at the Spanish route, some taking up positions near Puerto Rico, where they waited for the enemy to arrive on the horizon. Fast scout ships were dispatched as far south as Venezuela to check one report. But the Spanish were nowhere to be seen.

While easterners moved inland and out of range of seaborne guns, and the American navy burned tons of coal in its wild-goose chase, a telegraph operator at the governor-general's palace in Havana, Domingo Villaverde, listened quietly as messages between the island and Madrid streamed back and forth. Villaverde had worked for the Western Union telegraph company and now eagerly shared intelligence tidbits with the U.S. government.[22] Among the many messages that now passed across his desk were notes suggesting that the Spanish fleet had laid anchor at Cuba's second city, Santiago de Cuba, on the southeast coast.

His report, when it landed in Washington, initially failed to win much credibility. It seemed such an unlikely place for the Spanish to be hiding, so far from Havana. It would take weeks before an incredulous and embarrassed naval commander would even check it out, but finally on May 29, 1898, Commodore Winfield Scott Schley sailed close enough to the harbor mouth for one of his men to take a good look inside. There, as they had been all along, were the Spanish ships, low on coal and praying for resupply.[23] He would not be able to attack them, well protected as they were in the harbor, but neither could they escape. Schley now triumphantly announced to a reporter from the Associated Press, "We've got them now, Graham, and they'll never go home."[24]

McKinley, too, in these early hours of the war, seemed to have realized that the Spanish fleet would never go home. Though American troops hadn't even left for Cuba yet, his ever-evolving thinking had already turned to what the economic and political landscape of the Caribbean and the Pacific would look like when Spain surrendered.

The first hint of how far he had let his imagination run came on June 6, 1898, in the form of a message that Secretary of State Day sent to John Hay, the American ambassador to the Court of St. James's in England, outlining the peace terms the United States intended to demand from the Spanish. Madrid, the president had decided, would have to evacuate and surrender Cuba. That was hardly a surprise. But now McKinley also required the Spanish to surrender a port in the Philippines. And he would not stop there. The president wanted the Spanish to cede Puerto Rico and at least one other Spanish possession in the Pacific.

The man with no overseas ambitions just a year ago now spoke of extending America's footprint from the Caribbean to the farthest reaches of the Pacific. Back in Canton, before the election, he would have scoffed at the absurdity. Yet much of what he had known and believed back then had changed. He knew he needed to find an outlet for excess production, but he had assumed that it could only be accomplished through painstaking trade negotiations. The conflict with Spain, however, presented him with a chance to open more territory to American commerce than he had ever dreamed of. Spain's entire empire, perfectly positioned for building a bridge across the Pacific, was there for the taking. He had even been presented with a legal fig leaf for taking it all over, as he could claim the territory as war reparations in the peace talks that would follow the end of the fighting. Perhaps most surreal of all was how enthusiastically the American public seemed to bless an expansionist agenda.

Time was also running out. Just as the United States was sensing a new role for itself in global affairs, so, too, were other powers. Japan, eager to be thought the equal of the Europeans, hoped to carve a place of importance for itself in Asia. Germany, united only two decades previously, was anxious to catch up to England as the world's dominant empire. In the fast-changing international landscape of the 1890s, just sitting still would have been a decision with important implications. If McKinley did not move quickly to safeguard the stepping-stones he needed to achieve his objectives, rival nations would. In a frank chat a year later with Henry Pritchett, superintendent of the U.S. Coast and Geodetic Survey, McKinley claimed he had initially opposed bringing additional territory under U.S. control. That began to change, he said, as he realized the public's willingness to accept expansion. Ultimately, the president continued, "alternatives had to be faced which rejection of those countries would involve." Taking Hawaii and Puerto Rico, McKinley said, was the "least dangerous experiment." He felt the same way about the Philippines.[25] Whitelaw Reid, a Republican newspaper editor and diplomat who knew McKinley well, described the president's predicament best. Without mentioning McKinley by name, Reid wrote, "The candid conclusion seems inevitable that, not as a matter of policy, but as a necessity of the position in which we find ourselves and as a matter of national duty, we must hold Cuba, at least for a time and till a permanent government is well established for which we can afford to be responsible; we must hold Puerto Rico; and we may have to hold the Philippines."[26]

Aboard the USS *Charleston,* one day out of Honolulu with the first American troops bound for Manila, Captain Henry Glass summoned his crew. The ship, he told them, had received fresh secret orders while in the Hawaiian Islands that he had been instructed not to open until now. Carefully ripping open the envelope that contained his papers, he began to read. With crew members exchanging puzzled glances, he announced that the small American flotilla would not go directly to the Philippines after all. They would be making a small detour to a dot of land none of them had heard of before—the Spanish colony of Guam.

Guam was ideally suited to America's new needs as McKinley saw them. Home to only ten thousand people and located halfway between Hawaii and the Philippines, it was a perfect stopping off point for American ships on their way west. None other than the great naval strategist Alfred Thayer Mahan had the island, or something like it, in mind when he referred to the importance of acquiring "other deep water ports" in the area.[27]

Glass and the American ships arrived off the coast of Guam on June 20, 1898, their ships shrouded by a driving downpour that engulfed them one minute, then passed just as quickly to reveal views of the lush island. Oscar King Davis, a correspondent with the *New York Sun* traveling on a troopship, waxed about the beauty of the place: "We could see that it was very green with heavy foliage and thick growth of trees. Along the shore was a line of sheer cliffs with a narrow sand beach in front of them. The beach was fringed with palms and heavy tropical growth which sometimes climbed the face of the cliffs."[28] The only thing missing was the Spanish military.

At the harbor of San Luis d'Apra, where Glass figured to find at least one Spanish gunboat, the scene was one of tropical tranquillity. Not only were there no ships, there were no soldiers either. Unopposed and not sure what to expect, Glass ordered the *Charleston* to enter the harbor, directly under the nose of Fort Santa Cruz. Puzzled by the silence, the Americans fired a handful of shells into the fort to see if they could wake anybody up. There was no response.

While Glass pondered what to do, his men spotted two small boats flying Spanish flags rowing in their direction. Aboard were the island's Spanish military leader, Lieutenant Garcia Guiterrez; an army health officer, Surgeon Romero; and a native, Francis Portusac, who claimed to have become a naturalized American citizen in Chicago in 1888.[29] Fearing little from the strange group, Glass saw to it that the men were welcomed aboard with crisp military salutes and ushered to his cabin—neither the Americans nor the Spanish knowing why the other was there.

The Spanish officer began: "You will pardon our not immediately replying to your salute, Captain, but we are unaccustomed to receiving salutes here and are not supplied with proper guns for returning them."

Perplexed, Glass answered, "What salute?"

Looking at each other with puzzled expressions, one of the

Spaniards replied, "The salute you fired. We should like to return it, and shall do so as soon as we can get a battery."

As the misunderstanding dawned on Glass, he explained with a wry smile: "Make no mistake, gentlemen. I fired no salute. We came here on a hostile errand. Our country is at war with yours."[30]

For a few moments, the Spanish sat silently as the news sank in. The isolated garrison on Guam had received no word that their country was at war. The mail boat, which visited every two months from Manila, was late this time, they explained, and they had just assumed there was some minor problem. Just when they had regained their composure, Glass gave them another piece of bad news. "You understand, of course, gentlemen, that you are my prisoners?" For a second time, shock and disbelief spread across their faces. The men had no choice but to give themselves up, and indeed offered to return to land to deliver Glass's surrender demand to the governor, who was four miles away in Agana. With nowhere to run, the rest of the Spanish garrison in Guam, as well as the irritated governor, surrendered the next day.[31] The United States had acquired its first possession of the war.

15

"THE CHILD HAS GONE CRAZY"

Emma Goldman, an eighteen-year-old Russian Jew living in Rochester, New York, had followed the Haymarket trial of 1886 with fascination. A comely teenager with blue eyes, fine blond hair, full lips, and what one referred to as a "saucy" upturned nose, she formed a sympathetic bond with the eight defendants, later writing of "their heroic stand while on trial and their marvelous defense." In this she might have been no different from the legions of impressionable young girls smitten with the rebels of Chicago. But hers was more than simple infatuation. She saw, she later wrote, "a new world opening" before her as she learned more of the defendants' exploits.[1]

Execution day—November 11, 1887—left Goldman on edge as she tried to pass time in her father's house. Goldman found herself in a "stupor" and feeling numb. It was "something too horrible even for tears." When the topic of the executions inevitably came up that evening—the whole country was talking about it—Goldman could not believe her ears when one shrilled-voiced woman visiting the house expressed approval of the punishment. With a sudden leap, Goldman lunged at the women's throat. "The child has gone crazy," someone shrieked in the background. Family members quickly succeeded in separating the two, but unable to control her rage, Goldman grabbed a pitcher of water from a table and heaved it with all her might at the woman's face. "Out, out!" she cried. "Or I will kill you."

The next morning the fiery young woman awoke feeling that "something new and wonderful had been born in my soul. A great ideal, a burning faith, a determination to dedicate myself to the memory of my martyred comrades, to make their cause my own, to make known to the world their beautiful lives and heroic deaths."[2]

Goldman was born on June 27, 1869, in the Russian province of Kovno, in what is today Lithuania, to "a petit bourgeois Orthodox Jewish family of declining fortunes."[3] Hers was an unhappy childhood full of complex issues. Her father's failed professional dreams, due in Goldman's mind to anti-Semitism, had turned him into a gloomy, hotheaded, abusive tyrant. Her mother, the widow of a physician with two daughters from her first marriage, was a powerful woman. Goldman would say that "no statesman or diplomat excelled her in wit, shrewdness or force of character."[4] Yet prone to imperiousness (she was nicknamed "the duchess"), the woman played the role of mother badly and left Goldman feeling uncared for.

As Goldman grew, she and her father, Abraham, fell into a bitter cycle of disobedience and punishment. According to her memoirs, Abraham once hit her for so long and so hard that he grew dizzy and passed out. On other occasions, she was forced to stand in the corner for hours or to pace back and forth with a glass of water in her hands, threatened with a beating if she spilled.[5] She wrote of her father, "I loved him even while I was afraid of him. I wanted him to love me, but I never knew how to reach his heart. His hardness served only to make me more contrary."[6]

By the time she was a teenager, Goldman seemed destined to spend her life in the menial pursuits that women of her age and means performed to get by. Moving to St. Petersburg, where her father was unsuccessfully attempting to manage a dry-goods shop, she stayed at home knitting shawls, a job she detested. She later worked in a glove factory and a corset shop in the Hermitage Arcade. All the while she wanted "to study, to know life, to travel." They were ambitions that only heightened tensions with her father, who saw no reason for Goldman to learn anything more than basic household duties. "All a Jewish daughter needs to know is how to prepare gefüllte fish, cut noodles fine, and give the man plenty of children," he said.[7]

When her sister Helene, twenty-five, decided to join another sister, Lena, in Rochester, New York, Goldman leaped at the chance to restart a life in the New World. With customary drama she secured her father's grudging permission by threatening to throw herself in the Neva River if forced to stay. In December 1885, she set off.

Goldman was quickly disabused of any romantic dreams about life in the United States. Rochester had been a popular destination for German Jews in the 1870s but now offered a cool reception to fresh immigrants. Working hours were long, the pay was minuscule, and opportunities for advancement were even smaller. Goldman's first job, sewing overcoats, kept her at work for ten and a half hours a day.

Lacking any other form of excitement and probably hoping to be rescued from her miserable state, Goldman married one of the first men she met, a fellow immigrant named Jacob Kershner, a young man from an aristocratic Russian Jewish family. The union, however, was doomed from the start. Goldman quickly discovered that neither his intellect, nor his abilities in the bedroom, measured up to her expectations. The marriage quickly ended in divorce. Compounding her error, she remarried him, only to sue for a second divorce. Bored, rebellious, and resentful of the society of her adopted home, Goldman searched for an emotional and intellectual outlet for her pent-up feelings. She found it in radical political theory. Like the experience of many of her generation, it was not a fascination born of the great thinkers such as Godwin, but something she simply felt in her gut. "Just mere theories do not move me," she would say. "It is not enough to grasp our ideas. It is necessary to feel them in every fiber like a flame, a consuming fever, an elemental passion."[8]

Leon Czolgosz

Buffalo and Erie County Historical Society, used by permission

President McKinley standing at the cabinet table

Library of Congress

Albert Parsons
Chicago History Museum

The Haymarket bombing
Library of Congress

McKinley at age nineteen
Library of Congress

McKinley home
from the Civil War
*Used by permission from
the McKinley Presidential
Library and Museum,
Canton, Ohio*

The "Front Porch Campaign" at the McKinley home, 1896

Used by permission from the McKinley Presidential Library
and Museum, Canton, Ohio

A sickly but still youthful-looking First Lady
Used by permission from the McKinley Presidential Library and Museum, Canton, Ohio

The McKinleys pose at a dinner party.
Used by permission from the McKinley Presidential Library and Museum, Canton, Ohio

Dewey aboard the *Olympia* in Manila Bay
Library of Congress

Troops departing for Cuba from Tampa
Library of Congress

Roosevelt and Rough Riders on the San Juan Heights
Library of Congress

A young Emma Goldman
*Collection International Institute of
Social History, Amsterdam*

McKinley and cabinet, with Hay opposite McKinley

Library of Congress

"Mosquitoes seem to be worse here in the Philippines than they were in Cuba."

Library of Congress

The 1900 McKinley campaign asks if voters want a man who will "cut down Old Glory."

Library of Congress

A Gatling gun crew sights Filipino positions near Manila.

Library of Congress

American troops head to Peking.

Library of Congress

McKinley's last speech, September 5, 1901

Library of Congress

McKinley at Niagara Falls hours before the shooting

Used by permission from the McKinley Presidential Library and Museum, Canton, Ohio

The shooting

Library of Congress

Emma Goldman, 1901

Library of Congress

LESLIE'S WEEKLY

McKINLEY EXTRA

Vol. XCIII—EXTRA NUMBER   *New York, September 9, 1901*   PRICE 10 CENTS

LEON F. CZOLGOSZ, THE ASSASSIN.

FIRST PHOTOGRAPH OF THE WRETCHED ANARCHIST WHO SHOT THE PRESIDENT AT FOUR P. M., SEPTEMBER 6th, 1901, AT THE PAN-AMERICAN EXPOSITION.—COPYRIGHTED BY JUDGE COMPANY, 1901.

A photo purported to be of Czolgosz behind bars

Library of Congress

Hanna and Roosevelt near the Milburn House, September 1901

Library of Congress

Like so many before her and so many since, Goldman sought a new life in the big city. In August 1889, she packed up her sewing machine, five dollars, a few belongings, and a couple of addresses—including that of Johann Most—and caught the train for New York. There, she said, she would "do what I like, live as I like, without asking anyone's advice, without feeling the need of it."[9]

Finding the company of those who shared her radical political views became her major mission in New York. That very night, she headed directly for one of Most's favorite haunts, Sachs café on Suffolk Street on the Lower East Side. Suffering under the humidity of a New York evening, she sat at her table and listened to the animated conversations of those around her. One, more than the others, caught her attention. Above the chatter of the dining room, she heard a voice call out "Extra-large steak! Extra cup of coffee." Wondering, she later confessed, who the glutton was, she turned to confront Alexander Berkman, the man who would change the direction of her life.[10]

A pleasant-looking young man with a strong jaw, high forehead, thick lips, and eyes that looked intelligent behind steel-rim glasses, Berkman had arrived in the United States from Russia in 1888 and immediately threw himself into New York's tightly knit anarchist community. Like Goldman, Berkman seemed to have been born to the role. As a boy he had shocked his teachers when he announced to his class "There is no God," a transgression for which he was punished by being demoted one grade. Orphaned at age eighteen, Berkman eventually made his way to New York, where he found various jobs including working as a cigar maker, a cloak maker, and a printer.

When he had time, Berkman also helped out at the *Freiheit*'s offices on William Street, and it was here that he once took Goldman, climbing "two dark and creaking flights" to introduce her to Most. Struck by a fawning young woman with a nice figure, Most immediately agreed to a second meeting to discuss anarchism and, no doubt, whatever else she wished. Goldman, displaying an incredible amount of naïveté or self-deception, could not understand his interest. She asked herself: "What could I give this man—I, a factory girl, uneducated, and he, the famous Johann Most, the leader of the masses, the man of the magic tongue and powerful pen?" One can only imagine the blood rising in Berkman's face as he realized the folly of his plan to introduce the two. In so doing, he had presented Goldman to a promising rival and thrust himself into a fiery love triangle in which he seemed to hold the weakest hand. Goldman would soon write, "Most became my idol. I worshiped him."

Predictably, Berkman and Most soon grew to detest each other. The German, Berkman felt, put his own ambitions above the cause of anarchy, spending money on himself that could have been put to better use promoting his political views. That Most was generous in pursuit of Goldman surely did not help. Once, seeing flowers that Most had given Goldman, Berkman roared, "Violets at the height of winter, with thousands out of work and hungry!" Most, for his part, held little sympathy for Berkman and no doubt enjoyed using his position to provide the young Goldman with opportunities that Berkman could not, such as organizing a speaking tour for her.

Still, Most found the competition daunting. For all his eloquence in front of enthusiastic crowds, he displayed a real talent for placing his foot squarely in his mouth. During one argument with Goldman, Most called love nothing more than "sentimental nonsense," arguing "There is only sex!"—an ill-advised way to impress any woman. On another occasion, when Goldman rebuffed his amorous advances, he launched into a tirade against Berkman, calling him "that Russian Jew." Goldman recoiled bitterly, reminding Most that she, too, was a Russian Jew. Cursing his ineptitude, Most fell to the ground, clenching his fists and "lay like a child before me, crying," Goldman wrote in her memoirs. "Was he, Most, the anarchist, an anti-Semite? And how dare he say that he wanted me all to himself? Was I an object, to be taken and owned?"[11]

Despite the distractions and dramas of her love life, Goldman found time to develop her own interpretation of anarchy. She read widely and quickly displayed a fine intellect, despite her limited education. The pursuit of personal liberty, in all its forms, would become a passion and govern everything about her vision of anarchism. Rebellion became a favored theme as she avidly studied Max Stirner's *The Ego and*

His Own, which attacked every form of social convention, including religion and obedience to family and state. She dallied with the labor movement, helping to organize a strike as early as 1890, but ultimately found such work to be an unwelcome infringement upon her pursuit of individual freedom because of the need to make deals and compromises. "I bow to nothing except my idea of right," she once said.

Goldman's vision of anarchy and personal liberty inevitably led her to espouse greater women's rights, though she recoiled at being labeled a feminist. Women, Goldman argued, had been enslaved by the institution of marriage. "The woman, instead of being the household queen, told about in storybooks, is the servant, the mistress and the slave of both husband and children. She loses her own individuality entirely, even her name she is not allowed to keep." Anarchism, which included principles such as free love—or the right of two people who loved each other to remain partners only as long as they wanted or to have multiple lovers—promised to liberate women from the chains of the family. Anarchism "holds everything for women—freedom, equality—everything that woman has not now," she told one journalist.[12]

She found the life of a professional agitator—in which she would be free to say what she wanted no matter the consequences—most appealing.[13] All she needed was a public identity that would convince people to pay attention.

16

SAN JUAN HILL

McKinley spent most evenings during May and June 1898 in the "war room" that had been fashioned just off his office. A top-secret facility that he himself had helped outfit, the chamber served as the command-and-control center from which McKinley, significantly more than any president to date, could view the progress of the war in a primitive version of real time. Technicians had installed a switchboard with twenty telegraph lines connecting him with officers in the field, the navy, and other locations in the Caribbean. Some fifteen telephone lines ran directly to the eight executive departments, as well as to the House and Senate.

After kissing Ida good night and tucking her in, McKinley would often linger in the room until well after 1 A.M., puffing on a cigar and amiably chatting with the telegraph operators who staffed the room around the clock. He would study huge maps hanging from the walls that had been procured by Henry Pritchett. Each was studded with the latest positions of American troops and ships—red pins depicting locations of Spanish forces, white pins showing the Americans. When ideas occurred to him, and they often did, he would leave messages for his secretary on the newly invented Dictaphone.

The first of the white pins on the Cuba map was placed on Guantánamo Bay around June 10, 1898. Some 648 marines had easily taken the harbor, the best on the southeast stretch of the Cuban coast.

Yet the point on the map that most fixated McKinley and his team was the area around Santiago. Here, with the Spanish fleet trapped in the harbor, the United States possessed an opportunity to deliver what might be a fatal strike to the Spanish. Sink the fleet there and Spain would have almost no means of resupplying its troops in Cuba. Even the stubborn generals of the Spanish army would then have to consider suing for peace.

The navy could not maintain a blockade outside Santiago forever, nor root the Spanish ships out on its own, so protected was the harbor's ocean-facing defense. The army, on the other hand, might be able to wipe Spanish troops off the hills behind the port and attack Santiago from the rear. The Spanish were so vulnerable to a ground attack that Rear Admiral William Thomas Sampson reported that if Washington could send ten thousand men, the city and the fleet could be in American hands within forty-eight hours.[1]

Getting the army to Cuba was easier said than done. The circus in Tampa was still tripping over itself and unready to put a force to sea. Pressured by the navy, which took a perverse delight in the army's misfortunes, as well as his own sense that victory was in his grasp, McKinley fired off a series of messages asking when William Rufus Shafter would be ready to sail. Polite inquiries at first, the presidential correspondence grew increasingly hard edged until he ordered his general to get moving. Even when the portly commander did get his men aboard invasion ships, there were further delays—they lost a week when the navy mistook its own vessels for the enemy.

Not until June 14, 1898, more than three weeks after the Spanish had been spotted in Santiago de Cuba, was the United States finally ready to mount an invasion.[2] Some 32 troop transports, 2 water tenders, 3 lighters, and 12 naval escorts containing 819 officers, 15,058 enlisted men, 30 civilian clerks, 89 newspaper reporters, 11 foreign military observers, 272 teamsters and packers, 2,295 horses and mules,

200 wagons, 7 ambulances, and 1 observation balloon set off for a rendezvous with the navy off Santiago. They still had no idea when, where, or how they would launch their attack. They would work that out when they got there.

On June 20, 1898, the American commanders Sampson and Shafter, surrounded by foreign military attachés and journalists, clambered into four small boats alongside the USS *Gloucester* and headed for a secluded stretch of Cuban coastline at Aserraderos, about twenty miles west of Santiago. The American flotilla had arrived off the southeast coast earlier that morning, greeted enthusiastically by Sampson, who had provided a tour of sorts by steaming slowly back and forth near the mouth of the harbor while Shafter studied the coastal defenses. Now they were heading ashore to meet the commander of the revolutionary forces in eastern Cuba, Calixto García e Iñiguez, for a firsthand assessment of the situation.

As their boats glided over the turquoise water, the Americans were struck by the beauty of the place they had come to liberate, a soft beach backed by craggy, steep hills bursting with lush vegetation. In the distance, they saw their welcoming party, rebels who had waded into the surf. Water glistening over their dark skin, the men waved excitedly at the approaching Americans. As each craft softly ground into the shallow bottom, the Cubans ran into the surf and hoisted the boats aloft, Americans still sitting in their seats, and carried them through the remaining stretch of water to the dry beach where mules were already waiting for them.[3]

Up a steep, rugged, twisting trail the group went, horses nervously placing each hoof so as not to slip, no animal more uncomfortable than the one assigned to the rotund Shafter, which gave "profound groans of anguish during its ascent."[4] The heat was hard to bear, especially for Shafter, who not only carried at least a hundred pounds he didn't need, but was also clad in a dark blue army uniform. All were relieved when their group arrived at a clearing, in the middle of which stood the thatched hut of the rebel commander García.

Tall and almost majestic with his high riding boots, white mustache, and balding head, García had dreamed of this moment for decades. He had fought in three uprisings against the Spanish dating back to 1868 and bore the scars to prove it. Once, to avoid capture as a young man, he had tried to kill himself by firing a heavy revolver under his chin. The bullet traveled through his mouth and exited the center of his forehead, but miraculously García survived, aided by two Spanish surgeons who took a "professional interest" in his case.[5] Well traveled—he had visited Paris and New York and could speak English well—García fancied himself a loyal and valuable ally for the Americans.

Spreading maps out on a rough table, the Cuban pointed with a strong finger at the place where he thought the Americans should land, settling a disagreement between Shafter and Sampson. The Spanish, García said, had only lightly defended the eastern shore around Daiquirí, a small village with a rickety old dock on a shallow indentation on the coastline. It would, he said, make a serviceable landing area. García also suggested attempting a second site, about five miles to the west at the village of Siboney. After an hour of suffering in the heat, the men shook hands and the newcomers made their way back down the trail to the ship.[6]

As the Americans thanked their rebel escorts and climbed into their boats, the two groups parted with vastly different ideas of their respective roles in the coming battle. The misunderstanding would prove disastrous for the Cubans.

The American landing on June 22, 1898, was carried out with all the good-hearted bumbling that characterized the war effort back home. Waiting aboard the "prison hulks," as the cramped transports were called, the soldiers sang songs and called out to passing boats, begging to be taken ashore. Wearing heavy blue flannel shirts and wide-brimmed hats, their long bedrolls tightly tied and slung over their left shoulders, the men were carried to the beach in rows of small boats pulled by a slow-moving steam launch and would have been easy pickings for a crack shot. Yet to everyone's relief, no Spaniards were to be found, likely scared off by an early morning naval bombardment or the presence of 1,500 rebels nearby. "The country would have offered very great difficulties to an attacking force," Roosevelt said. "It was little but a mass of rugged and precipitous hills, covered for the most part by dense jungle. Five hundred resolute men could have prevented the disembarkation at very little cost to themselves."[7]

Faulty logistics planning made the risk even greater. The ship that transported the Rough Riders from Havana promptly sailed away after unloading the men, leaving Roosevelt with only a yellow mackintosh, a toothbrush, and the extra pairs of glasses he had sewn into the linings of his tunic and hat. No provision had been made for transporting animals ashore, and dozens were simply herded off the transport ships for a swim of several hundred yards to the beach. Several of the first horses to disembark immediately became confused and began swimming out to sea, among them Roosevelt's own horse, Rain-in-the-Face, which drowned. A quick-thinking bugler helped prevent further losses when he guided the horses back to land by playing familiar tunes such as "Stables," "Boots and Saddles," "Four Right," and "Charge."

Among the rifles, rations, and gear that American troops waded ashore with that morning were Spanish phrase books that their officers had distributed in the hopes of fostering happy relations with the Cuban rebels they would soon meet. The men earnestly practiced simple greetings and basic questions that, even if delivered in an incomprehensibly thick American accent, would show their hearts were in the right places. Yet no sooner did they lay eyes on their new allies than their optimistic faces dropped.

The rebels on the beach were not at all what the U.S. soldiers expected. Oddly believing they were rescuing people just like themselves, many found the rebels' skin a few shades too dark for their liking. The men of the junta, the public face of the revolutionary movement in the United States, were largely of Spanish origin, a suntanned pigment. But here in the east of Cuba, most were ex-slaves from Africa, just like the ones the men knew in the Deep South.

The Americans might have eventually gotten over their initial prejudices, but they quickly decided that the rebels' conduct also left much to be desired. Clothed in rags that suggested little more than the "outline of a jacket or trousers," few seemed to bathe regularly, and their hair was dirty and ragged. Over and over, American troops would complain that the rebels looked "disgusting." One member of the Massachusetts Volunteers later wrote, "They are a filthy, indolent, thievish, immoral set, and it is a burning shame."[8]

Nor did the Cubans endear themselves with the way they interacted with their "liberators." British journalist John Black Atkins noted: "The Cuban insurgent regarded every American as a kind of charitable institution, and expected him to disgorge on every occasion. The Cuban was continually pointing to the American's shirt, coat, or trousers, and then pointing to himself, meaning that he desired a transfer of the property."[9]

One clash in particular irked the Americans, accounts of which quickly spread around their campfires. Several U.S. soldiers had happened upon a bull in Siboney and were about to humanely shoot it for food. But before they could, a handful of Cubans arrived and "stabbed and stabbed" it with their knives till it fell. " 'Why,' they [the Americans] asked in effect, 'should we fight for men like these? They are no better than the Spaniards.' "[10]

Such sentiments spread right up the chain of command. Roosevelt, upon meeting the insurgents, decided immediately they would be of no help in the actual fighting, describing them as "a crew of utter tatterdemalions as human eyes ever looked on, armed with every kind of rifle in all stages of dilapidation."[11] A major in the Ninth Cavalry said, "The Cubans in my opinion are not worth fighting for."

The harshest blow to proud García was Shafter's plan for integrating the rebels in battle. Having assumed that his men would fight shoulder to shoulder with the Americans, García was devastated to learn that Shafter planned nothing more glorious for his men than carrying supplies and digging trenches.[12] For an army, however ragged, that had been fighting for years, it was a humiliating affront, especially when delivered by greenhorns who, if entrusted with a machete, might have been a greater danger to themselves than to the Spanish. His temper up, García fired off a note to Shafter stating that his men would not be used as "pack animals" and were too weak from months of fighting to be reduced to carrying heavy loads.

Understandable sentiments though they were, the rebuff marked the first misstep in what became a public relations disaster for the Cubans. American newspaper reporters, no doubt with American officers whispering in their ears, interpreted García's complaints as a sign of laziness and ingratitude. From that moment on, nearly every effort by the revolutionaries to help with the invasion was spun in the worst terms or simply ignored.

Viewing each other with suspicion and derision, the two "allies" prepared for the march to the city of Santiago de Cuba.

On the afternoon of June 30, 1898, Lieutenant Colonel Joseph E. Maxfield gave the order for his small support team to twist the valves on tubes of hydrogen gas and watched his silk balloon gradually take shape. The pilot of the army's sole observation balloon, Maxfield would soon ascend to one thousand feet, a vantage point from which he could reconnoiter the San Juan Heights, the sloping hills where the Spanish and Americans would settle their dispute.

From Maxfield's balloon, the coming battlefield was a postcard of tropical beauty. To the left were the glistening swells of the turquoise Caribbean, ships of the blockading American fleet plainly visible. Ahead he could see San Juan Heights, principally consisting of San Juan Hill, a 125-foot summit crowned with a Spanish blockhouse, a small valley to the right with a pond at the base, and another rise that would become known as Kettle Hill for the sugar-making equipment that stood at its top. Both hills were well suited for defense, their flanks largely brown and barren, a scene that reminded some of the summer orchards of Orange County, California. Along each hill, the Spanish had prepared reinforced trenches, in places two or three rows of them, most fringed with strings of barbed wire.

Everywhere else, however, the jungle was thickly grown over. General Adna Chaffee, a veteran of the Indian wars, described it as a "sea of brush that was thicker, more dense, more difficult to penetrate than any place I had ever seen in my life. This brush is high and so thick as to exclude the circulation of air."[13] Dividing the jungle from the more barren slopes of the hills was the steeply banked, waist-deep San Juan River.

Gazing further to his right, Maxfield could see the red roofs and yellow walls of the tiny village of El Caney, where the sixteenth-century explorer Hernán Cortés was supposed to have prayed the night before he sailed for Mexico, but now was guarded by half a dozen block-houses and trenches. Atop a nearby hill stood the sturdy stone church that the Spanish had turned into a formidable fort called El Viso.

Shafter's plan of attack was remarkable only for its optimism. One division led by Brigadier General Henry Ware Lawton was to charge on El Caney, securing the Americans' right flank. Then, after what was assumed would be no more than two hours, Lawton was to wheel his men around to join the main assault on the heights, where two divisions under the command of Brigadier General Jacob Kent and Major General Joseph Wheeler's Cavalry Division would have launched attacks of their own. García and the rebels were to block roads leading to the battlefield, preventing nearby Spanish reinforcements from joining the attack. By the afternoon the Americans would be looking down on Cervera's ships and the city of Santiago, demanding the Spanish surrender.

Shafter, gravely ill since coming ashore, believed that his overwhelming numbers and his artillery could carry the day. Indeed, in one skirmish on the road to the heights, the Spanish had fled when they saw superior American forces. Some 5,400 Americans would attack the El Caney fortification, held by just 520 Spaniards under General Joaquín Vara del Rey y Rubio. On the San Juan Heights, the numbers were even more heavily stacked in Shafter's favor, some 10,000 of the Fifth Corps against a mere 521 Spanish soldiers and two pieces of light artillery.[14] Seeing little reason to wait for more men and equipment to be brought up the El Camino from the landing beaches, Shafter gave the order for his men to get ready to attack at shortly after dawn on July 1, 1898.

On June 8, 1898, McKinley took a break from his war planning to celebrate Ida's birthday. The weight of war notwithstanding, these were happy days for the president. A tremendous mental and physical burden had been lifted now that the suspense was over. Despite the endless days, the pressure, and the undeniable fact that, deprived of exercise, he was hopelessly out of shape, he wrote his sister Helen that he was "standing the hard work better than I ought to have any right to expect."

Most evenings McKinley would try to make time to walk for an hour or so around the White House grounds. Forced to host only a handful of obligatory social events during the spring and summer, he was able to spend evenings much as he liked, with Ida and in the company of close friends. Though the fighting in Cuba was just about to start, the glow of Dewey's victory still shone brightly over the White House. Congratulations still echoed, and the threat of a protracted and bloody battle with the Spanish seemed to be subsiding.

In the newspapers that he read each day and from friends in Congress, it was becoming evident that the country was coming over to his way of thinking. His earlier reluctance to declare war was forgiven, in fact even admired as the work of a skilled statesman. As *The Chicago Times-Herald* wrote, "We find that we want the Philippines. . . . The commercial and industrial interests of America, learning that the islands lie in the gates of the vast and underdeveloped markets of the Orient, say 'Keep the Philippines. We also want Porto Rico. . . . We want Hawaii now. . . . We want the Carolines, the Ladrones, the Pelew, the Mariana groups.' . . . Much as we may deplore the necessity for territorial acquisition, the people now believe that the United States owes it to civilization to accept the responsibilities imposed upon it by the fortunes of war."[15]

Indeed, McKinley now moved closer to scoring another long-sought victory, this one not on some distant shore, but on the floors of Congress. The campaign to annex Hawaii, repulsed in its first attempt and driven into hiatus in the run-up to war, had suddenly come back to life and was gaining a certain sense of inevitability. Arguments that the United States needed Hawaii as a way station in the Pacific—once theoretical—were gaining a fresh urgency now that an American fleet was anchored in Manila Harbor and American boys were on their way there. The first U.S. ships bound for the Philippines had stopped in Honolulu for several days, a logistical necessity that Hawaiian president Sanford Dole had used to curry American favor by throwing luaus and lavish dinners for the soldiers. And that was to say nothing of the territorial ambition that had infected every corner of American society. Even McKinley was adopting the slogan of the day: "We need Hawaii just as much and a good deal more than we did California. It is Manifest Density."[16] When the Hawaiian annexation bill was brought before the House in mid-June, it was approved by a wide margin, 209 to 9. The Senate passed it 42 to 21 and on July 7, 1898, McKinley signed Hawaiian annexation into law.

A low mist clung to the San Juan Heights in the early hours of July 1, 1898, slowly burning off as the sun rose over the hills to the east. The sounds of the jungle filled the morning air—loud complaining birds and the rustle of broad-leafed plants that had been soaked by rain.

During the night, American troops had wheeled artillery into position and amid the peaceful scene made final preparations to begin their attack. At six thirty the first of Captain Allyn Capron's men jerked on their firing lanyards and in an instant the still morning was shattered by the roar of cannons, their throaty reports reverberating throughout the valley. At El Pozo, the other main U.S. battery, Captain George Grimes, "who had the bespectacled air of a professor," opened fire on San Juan Hill shortly thereafter, thick black smoke belching from each cannon as the shells were launched toward their targets. Shafter had hoped this opening barrage would soften up the Spanish and clear the way for the Americans to make their advance, uphill and across open terrain. It was to be the first of many miscalculations this day.

Capron's guns, positioned more than a mile away, failed even to startle the Spanish. The old stone fort he targeted was hardly damaged at all,[17] and the surrounding forms of Spanish soldiers crouching in trenches were so unmoved by the firing that American soldiers joked they must have been dummies. Grimes's cannons were, if anything, less effective. The smoke they emitted only made it easier for Spanish gunners to zero in on them with their own, more advanced, smokeless cannons. Peering toward the Spanish lines, it appeared to American reporters and artillerymen to be all too easy for the enemy. First they noticed a "tiny ring of bluish smoke" and an instant later, the "vicious scream of shrapnel" as a shell burst over their heads, fragments striking the Cubans and Rough Riders who had unwisely gathered nearby.[18] After less than an hour, Grimes halted fire. And so, with an inauspicious start, the battle for Cuba began.

According to plan, Major General Lawton and his men had maneuvered around El Caney the night before and now surrounded the area on three sides. He had a scant 120 minutes to lead his force uphill and take four wooden blockhouses, a church in the village—the sturdy El Viso—as well as numerous trenches. Undisturbed by the artillery, however, the Spanish easily cut down the first troops who emerged into the open with their accurate Mausers, a smoke-free weapon that made it nearly impossible for the Americans to determine the exact location of the Spanish marksmen. There was little Lawton's troops could do but throw themselves to the ground and attempt to slither up the hill in the tall grass, hardly the banzai charge that Shafter had hoped would send the Spanish fleeing.

At the main point of attack, opposite the San Juan Heights, the Americans still had to make a tortuous one-mile trek through the jungle, cross the San Juan River, and then somehow spread out on the fringe of the exposed banks of San Juan and Kettle hills, where they were to wait for the order to advance. It would have been hard enough, but Maxfield's observation balloon, floated aloft along the same trail, provided an unmistakable guide to the Americans' position. "Why it was ever taken to such a position nobody knows, but there it was— huge, fat, yellow, quivering—being dragged straight into a zone of fire that would surely ruin it," one journalist wrote.[19]

When the Americans emerged from the jungle and tried to fan out at the foot of the hills, they were hit hardest, try though they would to conceal themselves in folds in the ground or in the tall grass. More men would die here, trying to hide in the brush and wondering what was going on with their commanders, than in any other place during the war.

The brigade led by Colonel Charles Wikoff suffered the most. Crossing the San Juan a little past noon, Wikoff was trying to position his men along the riverbank when he was shot through the chest. He died within fifteen minutes. Lieutenant Colonel William Worth did his best to take over, but he, too, was gravely wounded, as was Lieutenant Colonel Emerson Liscum when he assumed command.[20]

To the right, things were no better for Roosevelt and the Rough Riders, who had taken up positions in a sunken lane in front of Kettle Hill. Smartly attired in his custom-made khaki Brooks Brothers uniform trimmed with a blue polka-dot scarf, Roosevelt was much impressed by the Spanish fire. "The Mauser bullets drove in sheets through the trees and tall jungle grass, making a peculiar whirring or rustling sounds; some of the bullets seemed to pop in the air," he later wrote.[21]

Among Roosevelt's Rough Riders was Captain Bucky O'Neil, who believed officers should never display fear. Paying scant regard to the enemy, he calmly moved among the troops casually smoking a cigarette. As O'Neil strutted back and forth, his men implored him to take cover. Addressing one plea, O'Neil removed his cigarette long enough to blow a puff of smoke and laugh. "Sergeant, the Spanish bullet isn't made that will kill me." Several minutes later, however, exactly one such round tore into his mouth and exited the back of his head, "so that even before he fell his wild and gallant soul had gone out into the darkness."[22]

By 2 P.M., Shafter, still very much sick and attempting to manage the battle from a cot, had grown so frustrated with the attack at El Caney, where troops had just taken a two-hour break, that he ordered Lawton to withdraw and support the main attack on San Juan Heights. Lawton ignored the command, fearing a blow to morale and yet more casualties. The entire battle teetered on disaster.

Throughout the afternoon, however, the Americans repositioned themselves for a fresh assault. Capron and his men, who had earlier failed in their bombardment, were wrestling their cannons over the rough terrain to better positions from which to fire on El Viso. At about the same time, American sharpshooters worked their way close enough to Spanish trenches to finally hit the riflemen.

The combined effect would sow panic into the Spanish lines. Shells from Capron's booming cannons devastated the walls of El Viso, blowing off heavy chunks of rock and masonry. It was finally the break the

Americans needed. Sergeants called on their men to fire faster, and "Remember the *Maine!*" echoed above the din of battle. Troops moved closer still until General Adna Chaffee ordered the Twelfth Infantry to get to their feet and charge the Spanish position. Jumping over wire fences and leaping trenches "like a hive of angry bees," the Americans swarmed up the hill toward El Viso.[23]

A gruesome scene awaited them. A dozen Spaniards lay dead on the floor, their blood splattered on the walls. Outside, body parts littered the ground. Along one trench, a string of men lay with bullet holes in their heads, their brains leaking out "like white paint from a color tube."[24]

With the remainder of the Spanish force running for their lives, the Americans cavorted "like school boys, cheering and waving their hats." Now occupying the high ground, the Americans could pour down fire on the blockhouses and village, one round shattering the skull of wounded Spanish general Vara de Rey as his men tried to pull him to cover. By 3:45 the fighting at El Caney was over. Of the original 514 Spaniards at El Caney, only 103 made it back to Santiago, the rest killed or taken prisoner. The Americans lost 441 men—81 killed and 360 wounded.[25] It was a terrible price for a sideshow to the real attack.

The final charge up San Juan and Kettle hills, one of the most celebrated events in American military history, is depicted in drawings as a heroic rush of unified lines, swords drawn, a flag carrier leading a solid mass of men. Nothing could be further from the truth. Journalist Richard Harding Davis watched the charge. "I think the thing which impressed one the most, when our men started from cover, was they were so few. It seemed as if someone had made an awful and terrible mistake. One's instinct was to call them to come back," he wrote. The men moved forward laboriously, "slipping and scrambling in the smooth grass, moving forward with difficulty, as though they were wading waist high through water, moving slowly, carefully, with strenuous effort."[26]

Foreign attachés, observing from behind American lines, were aghast. "It is very gallant, but very foolish," one said. "Why, they can't take it you know!" But on they came. "It was a miracle of self-sacrifice, a triumph of bull-dog courage, which one watched breathless with wonder. The fire of the Spanish riflemen, who still stuck bravely to their posts, doubled and trebled in fierceness, the crests of the hills crackled and burst in amazed roars, and rippled with waves of tiny flame. But the blue line crept steadily up and on."27

The next few moments defined the reputation of the young Colonel Roosevelt. Displaying a level of bravery that bordered on foolishness, he led his men from the saddle of his horse, Texas, up the slopes of Kettle Hill. Clearly an officer and a prized target, Roosevelt ignored the whizzing Mauser bullets that struck the earth around him and exhorted his men to speed their charge. One bullet grazed his elbow, and Texas was hit several times. Proximity to Roosevelt could prove fatal. Coming across one soldier sheltering behind a small bush, Roosevelt shouted, "Are you afraid to stand up when I am on horseback?" Before Roosevelt could finish bawling him out, the man pitched forward, felled by a round likely intended for the colonel.

The Spanish, holding the crest of Kettle Hill all morning, might have been able to repulse the American rush. But whether intimidated by the charge or intending to clear the way for an artillery barrage, they decided to make a run for it. By the time the Rough Riders and members of the Ninth Cavalry, an African American unit, reached the summit, the Spanish trenches were empty.

The simultaneous battle on San Juan Hill also now tilted in the American favor, thanks in large part to Lieutenant John Parker, a free-thinking West Pointer who arrived at the front with a new weapon that even his commanders did not fully appreciate how to employ in combat. Parker realized that the long-range modern rifles forced cannons to remain too far off their targets, greatly reducing their accuracy and effectiveness. Gatling guns, however, could be used in close support of the infantry, providing them with the covering fire they needed to make their rush on the hilltops of the San Juan Heights. "Machine guns, with a fire equivalent each to a regiment of sharpshooters, were a decisive and controlling factor, completely taking the now impossible function of artillery and performing it better than artillery ever did in history," Parker later boasted.28 From a range of six hundred to eight hundred yards, Parker's Gatlings raked the rim of the Spanish trenches for eight minutes. One Spanish officer later said, "It was terrible when your guns opened—always. They went b-r-r-r, like a lawn mower cutting the grass over our trenches. We could not stick a finger up when you fired without getting it cut off."[29]

At around the same time, Roosevelt, standing atop Kettle Hill, joined the attack on San Juan Hill, crossing the small valley that connected the two rises. Stepping over a wire fence, Roosevelt called on his men to advance and set off at a run, fully expecting to lead a swarm of yelling soldiers into the Spanish flank. Yet after one hundred yards he turned around to find only five men with him. Scampering back to Kettle Hill, ready to curse his cowardly troops, he learned his command had been drowned out by battle. Trying a second time, Roosevelt led the group helter-skelter up the side of San Juan Hill, arriving at its summit to find that most of the Spanish had already fled.

By late afternoon, the Americans held all of the San Juan Heights. In the entire battle, they lost 225 dead and 1,384 wounded, 10 percent of their force. The officer corps was especially hard hit, with 22 dead and 94 wounded. Far from invigorated, the Americans were physically spent. Only three-quarters of a mile from Santiago, they didn't have the strength to finish the job. Indeed, Shafter doubted his men could even hold the hilltops for which they had just so dearly paid.

LUNCHROOM

Emma Goldman found herself in an unlikely place for an aspiring anarchist the summer of 1892—behind the counter of a lunchroom in Worcester, Massachusetts, preparing sandwiches and grilling pancakes. With Alexander Berkman and their friend Modest "Fedya" Stein, a photographer and onetime love interest, Goldman had transformed a ramshackle store into an attractive restaurant that bustled from breakfast until well into the evening.

Running a business didn't exactly belong in the anarchist handbook, but Goldman longed to be liberated from the sewing machines she labored over in New York. With any luck, they would earn enough money to leave the United States, where, in Berkman's view, even the typical farmer was a "small capitalist," and return to Russia. With surprising pride for someone who disdained the American economic system, Goldman would later write about how their lunch parlor prospered, enough to quickly repay a $150 loan taken to get the restaurant started and to invest in a soda-water fountain and what Goldman found to be "lovely colored dishes."[1]

One day in early July 1892, Goldman brought an ice cream to a customer who was relaxing with a newspaper. As she set the dish on the table, she sneaked a peek over his shoulder at the day's headlines. Her eyes fixing on one, her face hardened. "Are you sick, young lady, can I do anything for you?" asked the customer as she leaned in to read. "Yes," Goldman answered. "You can let me have your paper. You won't have to pay me for the ice-cream. But I must ask you to leave. I must close the store."[2] In a place called Homestead, Pennsylvania, the revolution that she, Most, Berkman, and other radicals had long dreamed of seemed about to begin.

Perched on a bend in the Monongahela River seven miles upstream from Pittsburgh, dingy Homestead was home to Carnegie Steel Company's most important and technologically efficient plant. Clanking and hissing day and night, every day of the year save Christmas and the Fourth of July, the works consumed a massive six hundred acres. When shifts changed each afternoon, some 3,800 exhausted people would pass through its gates, many confident that they were reasonably well paid by the standards of other plants. Yet few here knew anything other than misery and squalor.

The muddy river that flowed swiftly around the town was so full of pollutants, including sulfuric acid, that "no respectable microbe would live in it," muttered one resident.[3] Hundreds of smokestacks at Homestead and other nearby factories belched so much filth into the sky that the sun rarely penetrated what was a nearly permanent yellow haze hanging in the trees. In the meager town, as "squalid as could well be imagined,"[4] which sprawled out up the hill from the factory gates, there were no paved streets nor a sewage system; most of the town's eleven thousand residents had to relieve themselves at outdoor privies.[5]

Carnegie himself rarely visited the site, and with good reason. It didn't fit the image he worked hard to create and maintain. Spending months each year in his native Scotland, he enjoyed the company of prime ministers and royalty, artfully portraying himself as an enlightened industrialist—the kind who founded libraries and championed worker rights. But Carnegie was by some accounts the "cruelest taskmaster" in American industrial history. At Homestead, Carnegie expected his employees to clock twelve hours a day of muscle-breaking, dangerous labor. In the summer, the heat of the molten iron was so intense that the men had to stop from time to time to pour the sweat out of their rubber boots. Ghastly accidents were a regular occurrence.

What's more, Carnegie hated the union that represented his men. The Amalgamated Association of Iron and Steel Workers, the strongest trade union in the country, claimed twenty thousand members, and, in the view of the factory's managers, had gained considerably more power than any labor organization should. Factory practices as basic as shift schedules and details of how employees carried out their responsibilities had, at times, to be approved by union leaders. It was impossible to do much of anything without some "busybody" interfering, the managers complained.[6] Hoping to scrape up higher profits, Carnegie had tried to break the union in 1889 and failed. Now, three years later, he was determined not to lose again.

Making sure to stay well clear of any unpleasantness, Carnegie and his wife sailed for Europe as wage talks grew testy in the spring of 1892, leaving the dirty work to his trusted hatchet man Henry Clay Frick. Their strategy was simple: Make an unreasonable demand on workers—in this case pay cuts of 18 to 26 percent[7]—wait for the union to reject them and go on strike, lock the workers out, secure the plant with Pinkerton men, and reopen under armed protection, inviting striking workers to apply for work individually and hiring new ones from outside the area. It was a tried and tested formula that, Carnegie and Frick reasoned, was bound to succeed.[8] Also expected was the very real risk of violence, and Frick was prepared. He ordered construction of a sturdy fence to protect the site, a three-mile-long barrier that was twelve feet high and topped with eighteen inches of barbed wire. Rifle ports were cut at regular intervals at shoulder height. Workers christened the plant "Fort Frick."[9]

Frick's carefully laid scheme, however, failed to accurately assess the visceral hatred of the workforce and their determination to oppose him. When word of his plan broke, workers crowded into meeting halls around Homestead and planned a counterattack. With military precision, men were dispatched to surround the plant; others were placed as sentries along the main roads into town, and some went down to the river and organized a small fleet of boats to guard against a waterborne invasion of scabs and Pinkertons. A system of alarms and whistles was arranged to alert the town to any sign of trouble.

At the apartment Goldman shared with Berkman and Stein, the two men were resting for the evening shift when Goldman burst breathlessly through the door, having run the three blocks from the lunch counter as fast as her short legs would carry her. Waving a half-opened newspaper, Goldman cried in the bitter voice of a "wounded animal"[10] and thrust the headlines forward: LATEST DEVELOPMENTS IN HOMESTEAD— FAMILIES OF STRIKERS EVICTED FROM COMPANY HOUSES—WOMAN IN CON- FINEMENT CARRIED OUT INTO STREET BY SHERIFFS.[11] Berkman leaped to his feet as he read the story, pausing for a moment to let the magnitude of the story sink in. "Homestead," he yelled. "I must go to Homestead!" Goldman flung her arms around him and shouted his name. "The great moment has come at last!" Selling everything at the store that afternoon, the couple left first thing the next morning.[12]

As the train sped southward, Berkman's blood boiled with rage against Frick. "The toilers of Homestead had defied the oppressor. They were awakening," he thought. "But as yet the steel-workers were only blindly rebellious. The vision of Anarchism alone could imbue discontent with conscious revolutionary purpose; it alone could lend wings to the aspirations of labor."[13]

A COUNTRY "FULL OF SWAGGER"

The rising sun burned off a light fog outside Santiago de Cuba on the morning of July 3, 1898—what surely looked to be just another boring Sunday for the sailors of the American fleet.[1] For more than a month the officers and their men, including those aboard four new battleships, had suffered in the tropical heat with nothing to do but keep a close eye on the mouth of the harbor where the Spanish sheltered. Some men began the day attending religious services, others went about routine chores, such as setting up an awning on the quarterdeck of the *Brooklyn* to protect officers from the harsh sun. At shortly after nine thirty aboard that same ship, navigator A. C. Hodgson and quartermaster Neils Anderson peered through a long glass at the harbor as they had so many times before. On this occasion, however, they noticed something new. "That smoke is moving, sir," Anderson said. Asking to take a look himself, Hodgson found the dark plume and brought it into focus. Without saying a word, he let the long glass fall, Anderson quickly snatching it before it hit the deck. Lifting a megaphone,

Hodgson barked, "After bridge there! Report to the Commodore and the Captain that the enemy's ships are coming out."[2]

The Spanish naval commander, Pascual Cervera y Topete, unaware how tenuous a hold the Americans had on the San Juan Heights, had rather rashly decided to make a run for it. Accepting that not all his ships, consisting of four armored cruisers and two torpedo boats, could possibly escape the American fleet, Cevera decided to power his flagship, the *Maria Teresa,* head-on toward the *Brooklyn* and ram her. After confusing the Americans, the armored cruiser *Vizcaya* could lead the rest of the Spanish fleet in an escape along the coast to the east.

Racing toward their battle stations, American sailors could not help but sneak a look into the harbor and admire the majesty of the Spanish ships gliding out into the smooth Caribbean, colorful flags flying from every mast. It was a fleet of the old school, and it seemed a shame to try to do them harm. This studied approval turned to alarm, however, when it became clear what the *Maria Teresa* was up to. The ship was charging straight for them.

Quickly weighing his response, Commodore Winfield Scott Schley barked to Captain Francis Cook to turn hard to port. The maneuver succeeded in avoiding a collision with the Spanish. But it threw the *Brooklyn* directly into the oncoming *Texas.* For a brief instant it appeared that Cervera's plan would disable not one but two U.S. ships. Only the quick thinking of *Texas* captain John Philip, who slammed his engines into reverse, prevented a disastrous collision. As the *Brooklyn* "glided past, all of us on the bridge gave a sigh of relief," Philip said.[3] Schley's maneuver, he later said, caused him "more alarm than anything Cervera did that day."[4]

Surviving the initial close call, the Americans quickly gathered themselves, gave chase to the fleeing ships, and found their range. Within minutes, the *Maria Teresa* was hit repeatedly, one American eight-inch shell exploding in the admiral's cabin. With many of his senior officers seriously wounded or dead, Admiral Cervera intentionally beached the ship six miles from the mouth of the harbor. As the hull ground ashore, internal explosions ripped through the vessel, and sailors threw themselves into the water.

The American vessels—bigger, newer, and in better condition— were too fast for the fleeing Spanish. One by one, smoking and burning, the Spanish lowered their colors and turned toward the shore. The *Almirante Oquendo*, with multiple fires burning and trailing black smoke, was the next to beach herself, followed by the *Pluton*, the *Colon*, and the *Vizcaya*.[5] Despite the best efforts of their officers to save lives, their casualty lists were horrific: 323 were killed and 151 seriously wounded, some 22 percent of the Spanish sailors who had sailed out of Santiago de Cuba.

On Sunday, July 17, 1898, the notes of a most American melody, "Hail to Columbia," filled the square in front of Santiago's city hall. Artillery officer Capron directed the firing of a twenty-one-gun salute, and the Stars and Stripes was smartly hoisted up the flagpole, replacing the red and yellow Spanish standard that had flown there every day since the building was made. It had taken two weeks of surprisingly difficult negotiations, but the city now belonged to the Americans and more victories seemed assured. Milling about the square in knots of conversation, men and officers in dusty blue uniforms speculated as to how long Spanish troops in Havana would hold on. There would be no resupply from Spain—not with the fleet smoldering on the beaches not far away.

The mood among the Spanish locals was surprisingly festive and welcoming. Thousands turned out for the handover ceremonies, including the mayor and archbishop. American soldiers found shopkeepers and restaurant waiters friendly and eager to take their orders. Even Spanish troops, whom they had been trying to kill only a few weeks earlier, turned out to be all right. Former adversaries now broke out phrase books and tried with mixed results to exchange war stories. Beers were purchased for one another, and souvenirs were swapped.[6]

The rebels themselves, however, were nowhere to be seen.

The Cubans, to their utter astonishment, had not been invited to the ceremonies, nor even allowed into Santiago city limits. Shafter, in a galling affront, had told García as well as the world's newspapermen that the rebels could not be trusted to enter the city because they were likely to loot and terrorize Spanish civilians. Worse insults would soon follow. The Americans, the Cubans soon learned, planned to keep in place much of the Spanish legal and administrative system that they so hated. For the time being, Spanish officials could remain in their current jobs if they chose. Spanish law would prevail. Spanish judges would continue to sit on their benches; the Spanish police force would be retained.[7] All would report to an American commander, but for the Cuban rebels it was a shocking blow.

García was unable to contain his rage. "We are not savages ignoring the rules of the civilized warfare. We are a poor, ragged army as ragged and poor as was the army of your forefathers in their noble war of independence, but like the heroes of Saratoga and Yorktown, we respect our cause too deeply to disgrace it with barbarism and cowardice."[8] Few American commanders cared when the rebel leader resigned in protest. In fact, they thought their jobs might well be easier with him out of the way.

On a late July day the president and his cabinet gathered on a dock on the Potomac River and boarded a converted lighthouse tender for a gentle cruise and some relief from the summer heat. Tinkling ice hinted at the promise of cold drinks that stewards would soon serve; cigars were lit and the men gazed out into the channel in hopes of a cooling breeze upon the water. Having seen to their physical needs, the president asked the group to deliberate the question they had been called upon to answer. What, he wanted to know, should the United States demand of Spain once the war was over?

Since the middle of the month, Madrid had been flirting with how to end the war diplomatically and with a minimum loss of her empire and asked the French ambassador in Washington, Jules Cambon, to act as a go-between. Carrying a letter from the queen regnant, the veteran diplomat met McKinley and John Hay in the White House library on July 26, 1898, and offered a proposal for an armistice. If the Americans agreed, he said, fighting could soon stop and Spanish and American diplomats could later meet to arrange a formal peace treaty. Studying the letter and listening to Cambon, McKinley learned that the Spanish were ready to make a single concession: They would grant Cuba its independence or allow Washington to make it a protectorate or even annex the island. To the Spanish, it was a perfectly reasonable request. Wasn't this what McKinley had wanted all along?

The president, however, by this juncture, possessed much grander visions. It went without saying that Spain would hand over Cuba. In fact, U.S. forces were likely to remain on the island for some time. But new conditions were tossed in. As an indemnity, Washington wanted Puerto Rico. Any country that lost a war in the nineteenth century could figure on paying some sort of restitution to the winner for having taken the trouble to defeat them. As Spain was broke, and the United States wasn't cash-poor, McKinley reasoned that Puerto Rico fit the bill perfectly. The Frenchman was told the United States would also require an unnamed island in the Ladrone Islands, presumably Guam, which it already held.

There was to be another American demand. The president, as far back as June, had expressed an interest in taking a port in the Philippines and polled his cabinet for their views. Two, Agriculture Secretary James Wilson and Interior Secretary Cornelius Bliss, favored the extreme position of annexing the entire archipelago, Bliss for one fascinated by the commercial opportunities the Philippines presented. Others, including Secretary of State William Day and Secretary of the Navy John Long, favored placing a more moderate demand upon the Spanish—a naval base and a cable station, or, at most, the entire island of Luzon. Others did not express an opinion. McKinley, as was his habit of putting things off as long as possible, decided for the moment in favor of taking just Manila, but left his options open. The Spanish were told that the United States was "entitled to occupy" the city, bay, and harbor of Manila until formal peace talks were held that would decide once and for all the control, disposition, and government of the entire archipelago.

In the ornate government offices in central Madrid, Práxedes Mateo Sagasta and his ministers read of McKinley's demands with fist-pounding, vein-popping Latin fury. These were no indemnities: What McKinley was demanding was nothing short of theft. Bitter orders were cut to the French ambassador to tell the Americans so, a mission he happily accepted. Just because the "fortune of arms has permitted an American soldier to put his foot" on a Spanish possession, the Frenchman told U.S. negotiators, did not make it conquered territory.

Even the United States recognized this, he said, pointing out that the country had in 1847 declined to take all the land its troops conquered during the invasion of Mexico.[9] And if it was an indemnity the United States wanted, wasn't American control of the rich island of Cuba plenty?

McKinley, however, was not interested in diplomatic swordplay. Cambon was told that articles concerning Cuba, Puerto Rico, and Guam "do not admit of discussion." Negotiations were to be limited to the future of the Philippines. And if Spain continued to balk at the American offer, McKinley informed Cambon, the terms would become only more strident.[10] If the Spanish doubted McKinley's resolve, they need only look at what was happening on battlefields in the Pacific and the Caribbean.

Lounging aboard the canopied deck of the *Olympia* in his favorite wicker chair, George Dewey spent the days after sinking the Spanish fleet in Manila Harbor like an Ottoman pasha. He testily asserted his authority over the bay when German naval officers arrived and failed to show the Americans due respect. He received Filipino visitors on board, but with limited patience. When one shipboard guest proved irksome, Dewey had the poor man thrown over the side. Not even his masters in Washington could rapidly give him orders, thanks to his decision to cut the only telegraph cable running out of Manila. Yet his power had its limits. His beloved dog, Bob, a pampered Chinese Chow, was so hated by his crew that they formed a secret society made up of members brave enough to kick it.[11]

There were other restraints on Dewey's authority. Inland, beyond the small sliver of land near the port that Dewey's blue jackets could secure, people quaked with uncertainty. Some twenty thousand Spanish civilians and soldiers had barricaded themselves in Manila—not for protection from the Americans but from Filipino rebels who sensed that independence was at last at hand.

Filipino rebel leader Emilio Aguinaldo arrived in Manila from Hong Kong aboard a U.S. ship on May 19, 1898, and wasted no time introducing himself to Dewey, rushing that very day to the *Olympia*. Meeting in Dewey's stateroom, the newly minted rear admiral looked resplendent in his stripes, and Aguinaldo attempted to cut a similarly impressive military silhouette, carrying with him a captured Spanish sword. What exactly the two said to each other remains a controversy to this day, but the meeting launched weeks of misunderstanding, mutual suspicion, and haughty exchanges between two of the biggest egos in the Pacific.

What does seem clear is that Aguinaldo pressed Dewey on whether the United States would indeed grant the Philippines independence when the Spanish were defeated. Dewey, who would later write that Aguinaldo struck him as an "unimpressive little man," claimed he made no such promise. "My policy was to avoid any entangling alliance with the insurgents," he later wrote.[12]

Aguinaldo recalled otherwise. Dewey, Aguinaldo later said, promised him on his honor that the United States, "rich in territory and money," didn't need colonies, and that he should "have no doubt whatsoever" about American intentions.[13] So cordial was their visit, Aguinaldo claimed, that he was invited to spend the night aboard the flagship, and the next morning Dewey sent him off saying "Go ashore and start your army," even supplying him with a number of Mauser rifles and ammunition to get started.[14]

Regardless of what actually transpired, Aguinaldo wasted no time in announcing a "provisional dictatorship" of the Philippines with himself as head. Like the school outcast who had somehow managed to befriend one of the popular kids, he bragged about his relationship with the United States and how Dewey would help him and the revolution. The Americans, "my friends," had "promised me all that I have asked for, more than we had ever hoped to obtain, and are going to aid me in all things."[15]

How much conviction Aguinaldo placed in the claim is open to question, for he was also watching with considerable agitation as the first shiploads of American troops waded ashore. He felt the men were wholly unnecessary, given that his troops were more than sufficient to take Manila. The Americans seemed to enjoy toying with him. When General Thomas Anderson, guided by Dewey in a rare foray off his ship, met Aguinaldo for the first time, the two came with studied casualness—no sidearms, no ceremony, and as Dewey said, giving "no indication to Aguinaldo that we take his government seriously."[16]

Insults, real and imagined, rankled Aguinaldo's vainglorious side. Offended by an invitation to an American Fourth of July celebration that had been addressed to him as "general" rather than "president," Aguinaldo refused to attend. He grew increasingly unwilling to provide supplies to the Americans, and detained a couple of American officers who had wandered into an area occupied by his men.[17] Greatly overestimating his power, he warned Anderson against landing any more American troops without his permission. Aguinaldo should have realized by now that the United States was well beyond worrying about his tender feelings.

Throughout early August, messengers carried a series of secret notes between American commanders and their Spanish counterparts inside Manila that most decidedly were not shared with the Filipino rebel. General Fermin Jaudenes, who had just been appointed governor of Manila, was anxious to surrender the Philippine capital. Spaniards from around the country were huddled in the city to escape Aguinaldo and his men, quickly depleting the city's stores of food, water, and medicines. Already, Manila's inhabitants had been reduced to eating their own horses and setting up makeshift hospitals in churches. Water was running out. Disease was spreading at an alarming rate.

Yet Jaudenes was in a pickle. Spanish gentlemen simply didn't surrender. His predecessor, General Basilio Augustin y Dávila, had recently been demoted for proposing just that.

Using the Belgian consul to Manila, Edouard C. André, as a go-between, Jaudenes now offered the Americans a proposal that must have made their eyes twinkle with amusement. Would the U.S. Navy and Army be willing to stage a carefully scripted battle for the city? His own men, he promised, were willing to participate and if all went according to plan, the farce would be over by midafternoon and nobody would get hurt. This way, the Spaniard could report gallant resistance to the bitter end. The United States could score an easy victory. And, most important, at least from the Spanish view, such theater could be performed in a way as to keep the rebels safely offstage. Overcoming their incredulity, the Americans agreed.

As any experienced actor on Broadway can attest, opening-night performances rarely come off without a hitch, and so it was with the "battle" of Manila. Members of the Colorado Volunteers, who as the American ground troops were not privy to the charade, easily advanced from their trenches, their chubby regimental band leader lustily playing "There'll Be a Hot Time in the Old Town Tonight." Out to the right, American troops advancing down a narrow road stumbled on the rebels who, realizing an attack was on, hastily joined in, firing on Spanish positions. General Francis V. Greene, upon hearing the noise, snarled to a reporter as if to say "Those idiots of insurgents will spoil the whole game with their foolishness."[18] Before American commanders could pull aside husky young soldiers from Nebraska and forcibly block the gobsmacked Filipinos from entering the capital, six Americans and forty-nine Spaniards had died in the needless skirmish.[19]

Despite the glitches, by early afternoon mud-splashed American officers had made their way peacefully through the city gates where they were guided to city hall. There, waiting for them, were generals Augustin and Jaudenes and Admiral Montojo, well turned out in "handsome, fresh uniforms" complete with broad red sashes, ornamental swords, and impressive-looking decorations.[20]

As American troops were preparing for the faux attack on Manila, their compatriots in the Caribbean were racing to grab Puerto Rico.

Under the enthusiastic command of General Nelson Miles, for whom Puerto Rico had been a pet project, the Americans launched their "invasion" at dawn on July 25, 1898, at Guánica, a pretty little town perched before high cliffs. A single street, lined by pastel-colored houses, ran inland under shade trees.

After firing a couple of shells at the Spanish blockhouse, an advance team of American soldiers was sent ashore to reconnoiter. The astonished Spanish defenders put up a show of defending the town, but when the Americans began firing their Colt machine gun at a group of cavalry, they fled for their lives.[21] Townspeople, frightened by the unexpected sight of American troops in their little village, were not far behind and took cover in the hills. There they nervously remained for about an hour until, concluding the Americans were not dangerous after all, they returned and did a brisk business selling food and trinkets to the new arrivals.

The most dangerous moment of the whole attack came that night when outposts manned by the Sixth Illinois, hearing strange noises, fired blindly into the darkness. Their attackers turned out to be nothing more than a couple of badly frightened mules. The incident might have ended with a few embarrassed chuckles except that stray bullets whistled out over the bay and pinged off a Red Cross ship carrying excitable American nurses, and—even worse—a grumpy General Miles who was trying to get some sleep.[22]

The rest of the invasion passed smoothly. General Miles, whose overriding goal was to acquire the island with a minimum loss of American life, had made sure the countryside was well scouted in advance and that his plans could come off like clockwork. In an oft-repeated pattern, the Americans advanced down major roads, encountered pockets of Spanish resistance, regrouped, attacked in force, and sent the Spanish to their heels. None would qualify as major land battles; they were, rather, a series of small-scale skirmishes with minimal injury to either side. The Americans, in fact, would never conquer more than half the island. They didn't need to.

On August 12, the Spanish agreed to an armistice.

McKinley had forced the Spanish to accept nearly all of his objectives. They would cede Puerto Rico, grant the United States the Pacific island it wanted, and discuss the future of the Philippines. Only on the small matter of the location of the final peace talks did they extract a concession. The meeting would take place in Paris no later than October 1, 1898, not in the American capital as the president had hoped.

The United States had, overnight, become a global power. For four months, squeaky military bands and grimy soldiers had, proud tears in their eyes, hauled the Stars and Stripes over places that many Americans had hardly heard of before. American territory now stretched from the Caribbean to the farthest reaches of the Pacific. Henry Adams said, "I find America so cheerful, and so full of swagger and self-satisfaction, that I hardly know it."[23] U.S. companies were gaining access to foreign markets, which helped recharge the economy and ease social pressures at home. *McClure's Magazine* wrote that the new territories under American control—Cuba, Puerto Rico, and the Philippines—were equal to "nine good states," so rich were they in resources such as tobacco, coffee, hemp, and sugar. Luzon, the island containing Manila, equaled the size of the state of New York.[24] At the same time, foreign countries were being introduced to America's self-described superior economic and political traditions. *The Times* of London wrote: "In the future America will play a part in the general affairs of the world such as she has never played before." McKinley would soon find playing that part a risky proposition.

19

BLOODY HOMESTEAD

Much of America was preparing to go back to work after the long Independence Day weekend the first Tuesday of July in 1892. Men still chatted about the fireworks displays they had witnessed the night before and bragged about victories in sack races and pie-eating contests. Women tossed out watermelon rinds and washed homemade ice cream makers.

There had been little time for such frivolity for Alexander Berkman and Emma Goldman. On the train to New York, they excitedly planned their response to the Homestead strike. Pausing the conversation occasionally as the train's whistle blew at crossings, they contrived to head straight to the apartment of an Austrian anarchist when they arrived in New York. Though the man known as "Mollock" had a wife and two children who might hesitate to share their flat with unannounced strangers, Goldman and Berkman were sure he would put them up for a while. He had to. They had neither the money nor the time to spend any effort looking for another place. Berkman was already mulling plans to write a fiery manifesto denouncing Carnegie, and Goldman hoped that speaking engagements for her might be arranged in Pittsburgh. It was exhilarating.

Late in the evening of July 5, 1892, two heavily armored barges, the *Iron Mountain* and the *Monongahela,* set off upriver for Homestead, crowded with three hundred Pinkerton men charged with the job of securing Carnegie's plant. Mostly rookies, the men included a number of roughneck down-and-outers, criminals running from the law, and nervous university students looking to make a few bucks for tuition. The men had been told little about the job that awaited them and were unusually green by Pinkerton standards. Some were plainly uncomfortable with what they had gotten themselves into. With more than a little trepidation they put on uniforms that gave them the look of a paramilitary unit—slouch hats, blouses with metal buttons, and dark blue trousers with light blue stripes running along the leg.[1] Even more unsettling was the cargo that they noticed had been stored on board: crates of Winchester rifles.[2]

Pulled by side-wheel steam tugs, the barges moved slowly against the current during the night. A few men tried to sleep, but many peered into the gloomy darkness out of firing holes cut in the side of their vessels, wondering if anybody had noticed them. In fact, they had been first spotted not long after pulling away from shore by strikers manning the Smithfield Street Bridge. Men on the riverbanks monitored their progress, while the town of Homestead erupted as strike leaders ran from house to house, barking orders to repel the Pinkertons when they tried to land.[3] With grave faces, men armed themselves with whatever was available—some with old-fashioned Civil War rifles, others with shotguns and revolvers. Still others carried little more than spiked clubs they had fashioned by pounding nails through wood torn from fences.

By the time the barges arrived around dawn, some ten thousand men, women, and children were crowded along the river near the factory to taunt the newcomers and possibly do battle. Inside, the Pinkerton officers checked their weapons and steeled themselves for what promised to be a tricky situation. One thing they had learned in past confrontations, however, was to always exude an air of authority. Brimming with bravado, Pinkerton captain Frederick Heinde strode out on a gangway linking the barges with the shore and bellowed to the crowd, "We were sent here to take possession of this property and to guard it for this company. . . . We don't wish to shed blood, but we are determined to go up there and shall do so. If you men don't withdraw, we will mow every one of you down and enter in spite of you."

Angry words were exchanged. There was the crack of rifle shot and then, before anyone could react, the bank and the barges erupted with smoky gunfire. Heinde was hit twice. Another strikebreaker was shot through the head and fell dead, and four others were wounded. Among the steelworkers, three were killed and dozens more wounded.[4]

Over the next twelve hours, an orgy of bloodshed and terror unfolded. Both sides poured down rifle fire on each other, the Pinkertons crouching in their barges and the union men hiding behind scraps of iron that littered the area. Strikers unsuccessfully attempted to roast the Pinkertons alive, first floating a flaming oil-soaked raft downriver and into the barges and later rolling a burning railroad flatcar down a track and onto the dock. Trapped and with no chance of escape because their tugs had fled, the Pinkerton rookies panicked. Some hid under mattresses; others threw themselves into the river.

In Pittsburgh, news of the violence stunned leaders of the Amalgamated Association of Iron and Steel Workers. Standing up to management was one thing; killing had to be stopped. Senior union men led by William Weihe rushed to Homestead, arriving by midafternoon just as strikers were preparing a fresh attack. Shouting to be heard over howls of "burn them" and "kill them," the union officials argued that the strikers had killed plenty of Pinkertons already. To murder them all would only damage public support of the union and invite the military to intervene. It was time to declare victory and go home. Only grudgingly and in the face of overwhelming logic did the men agree.[5]

Yet the company, not the strikers, ultimately prevailed. On July 10, 1892, Pennsylvania governor Robert Pattison ordered all 8,470 members of the state militia to Homestead. They quickly drove off the strikers and surrounded the plant.[6] Days later, Frick would restart the factory with scabs collected from around the country who were housed in a specially constructed dormitory on the factory grounds. It didn't take long before the men of Homestead with hungry children at home began crossing their own picket line.

For Berkman, the bloodshed changed the rules of the game. This was no longer a contest to be waged by speeches and protests but by violence, starting with the top. Convinced that the more "radical the treatment . . . the quicker the cure," Berkman decided that the best way to rally workers and to call attention to anarchism was an act of self-sacrifice. He must kill Frick. Murder, he believed, was a fully justifiable act. "The killing of a tyrant, of an enemy of the People, is in no way to be considered as the taking of a life," he wrote. "To remove a tyrant is an act of liberation, the giving of life and opportunity to an oppressed people."[7] And this would be no cowardly attack. Berkman would blow Frick up and give his own life in the process.

As was so often the case with anarchists, there existed a sizable gap between vision and reality. Neither Berkman nor Goldman knew anything about explosives and would have to teach themselves the fine and dangerous art of bomb making. Using instructions printed in Most's *Science of Revolutionary Warfare,* they set up a crude lab in Mollock's apartment, well aware that with any slip they might blow up half the building, including the children of their hosts. Goldman justified an obscene calculus. "It was for them that we were going to give our lives. What if a few should have to perish?—The many would be made free and could live in beauty and comfort. Yes, the end in this case justified the means."[8]

Ultimately, the children and others in the building had nothing to fear. Berkman proved to be such an incompetent bomb maker that he could not get one to detonate even when he wanted to during tests on Staten Island. Clearly out of his depth as an explosives expert, Berkman hit upon a reliable but less spectacular plan. He would dispose of Frick the old-fashioned way: by shooting him. Then he would blow himself up with a nitroglycerin cartridge, thereby exiting this world just as his Haymarket hero Louis Lingg had done in his prison cell.

———

Knowing that Frick was looking for strikebreakers, Berkman decided to disguise himself as an employment agency executive and had business cards printed to that effect. With little difficulty he secured an appointment with his target at 2 P.M. on July 23, 1892, at his offices at the Chronicle-Telegraph Building overlooking Fifth Avenue in Pittsburgh. All he needed now was a respectable-looking suit, and of course, a gun. Broke, the couple could afford neither.

In an era when daily wages were measured in cents, Goldman turned to the only way she could think of to raise money quickly. The night of July 16, 1892, she shoehorned herself into high heels and what she considered to be seductive clothing and wobbled up and down New York's Fourteenth Street, decidedly uneasy about what lay ahead. The inexperienced streetwalker fled from her first potential customer and might have abandoned the whole idea were it not for one kindly white-haired gentleman. Seeing that Goldman was a rookie, the man gave her ten dollars for nothing more than sharing a beer. With that, Goldman declared her career as a lady of the night over and returned home. Combining her take with a loan from a friend, Goldman and Berkman had all they needed to carry out the attack.

Arriving at Frick's building on July 23, 1892, a little before two o'clock, Berkman climbed the stairs to the second-floor offices of the chairman and presented himself to a messenger boy. He watched anxiously as the door to Frick's office was opened and he was announced. Peeking through the door, he could see there were not one but two men at the far end of the office, about twenty-five feet away. One was Frick sitting sideways in his chair, legs thrown over one arm. The other was John G. A. Leishman, vice chairman of the Carnegie Steel Company, with whom Frick had just finished lunch at the Duquesne Club. "Frick is engaged. He can't see you now," the receptionist told Berkman. As if to leave, Berkman took a few steps toward the outer door, then turned on his heel, brushed aside the startled receptionist, and burst into Frick's office. With his right hand, he reached for his .38-caliber bull-nose revolver.

For a frozen moment, Berkman, Frick, and Leishman stared at one another in stunned silence. Berkman was having trouble seeing his target, blinded by unexpectedly bright sunlight pouring through the office windows. And his shot could not waver. Convinced that Frick would be wearing body armor, he had decided to aim for the industrialist's face, not easy for a rookie marksman firing a pistol at twenty-five feet. Steadying his extended hand, Berkman squeezed the trigger. The room shook with the report and Frick cried out in pain as he fell to the floor, bleeding from his neck. Berkman again aimed at Frick's head, this shot hitting the other side of his neck. He was sighting for a third shot when Leishman reached him with a powerful tackle, knocking him to the floor and forcing the round to fire wildly into the ceiling. Again, Berkman attempted to shoot. This time, the weapon only lamely clicked without firing.

Outside the office window, passersby stopped in horror as they heard the gunshots and wondered what was happening in the important-looking office. Incredibly, despite taking two bullets to the neck, Frick remained very much alive—and strong enough to throw himself on Berkman. In a bizarre wrestling match, the three men struggled on the floor of Frick's office, tearing at one another's suits and fighting for control of the gun.[9] Pulling one hand free, Berkman was able to reach into a pocket where he had hidden a dagger, which he thrust into the already gravely wounded executive's back and legs.

The shots, the screams, and the fighting were easily heard down the hall where a carpenter was working in a nearby office. Taking a tool with him, the handyman burst into Frick's office and he, too, threw himself on Berkman. Someone shouted, "Where is the hammer? Hit him, carpenter!" The first blow caught Berkman on the back of the head. Searing pain pulsed through his eyes. The carpenter was about to deliver a second blow when Frick shouted at him to stop. He wanted his attacker taken alive.

The men lay on the floor, gasping for breath, trying to process what had just happened. Frick was seriously hurt. Two gunshots and several stab wounds had left him weak and bleeding. But it wasn't over yet. As Frick studied the face of his attacker, he noticed that he remained conscious and strangely appeared to be teething something. "What's in his mouth, see what he's chewing," Frick shouted. Again, the men threw themselves on Berkman and pried his lips apart. Carefully slipping their fingers inside his mouth, they felt a strange object, a capsule of fulminate of mercury, an explosive strong enough to blow up everybody in the room.[10]

Frick had survived the initial attack, but it was far from clear how long he would last as several doctors carried him to a nearby office, including his personal physician Dr. Litchfield, who had also been lunching at the popular Duquesne Club. Despite tremendous pain, Frick refused anesthesia for two hours so he could assist doctors as they probed his body for the bullets. "There, that feels like it, Doctor," Frick said, as one hunk of lead was pulled from his flesh.

While doctors cleaned his wounds, he dictated messages to Carnegie and his mother. When they were done, he demanded to be propped up at his desk so he could finish work from earlier in the day, completing a loan application and a press statement among other things. "This incident will not change the attitude of the Carnegie Steel Company toward the Amalgamated Association. I do not think I shall die, but whether I do or not the Company will pursue the same policy and it will win," he wrote.[11] He would live for twenty-seven more years.

If Berkman had hoped to inspire others to anarchism in the way that the Haymarket attacks had captured his imagination, he utterly failed. Anarchist newspapers around the country were unrelenting in their abuse, heaping scorn on Berkman for smearing the cause with a murder attempt. Nobody took more delight, nor concocted more outlandish attacks, than Johann Most. In *Freiheit,* Most disingenuously spoke against the "propaganda of the deed" and suggested that Berkman may have used only a toy pistol in his attack on Frick.[12] In Goldman's words, "hardly a week passed without some slur in the *Freiheit*" against her lover.[13]

Most's charges enraged Goldman. Of all people, she would later say, none should have approved of a violent attack more than Most. She demanded proof of his charges. When Most ignored her, Goldman plotted to call her former lover out. At a speech Most gave during the height of his accusations, Goldman made sure to arrive in time to secure a seat in the front row, her hand resting on something under her long gray cloak. As Most took the podium, Goldman rose from her place in the audience and shouted, "I come to demand proof of your insinuations against Alexander Berkman." Most mumbled something about a "hysterical woman." With that, Goldman rushed to the stage and produced a whip, lashing his face and neck. As astonished as his audience at the sudden attack, Most fled, no doubt resolving not to cross Goldman again.[14]

Berkman's attack may have failed on a number of levels, but it did succeed in one respect: It launched Goldman into the big leagues of radical agitators. During Berkman's trial, the fiery young woman received almost as much publicity as the attacker himself as prosecutors correctly tried to implicate her as a coconspirator. They were unsuccessful, but all the attention helped create an intriguing new public personality that combined good looks with a hint of danger.

Goldman would soon tour the country, speaking at halls packed with supporters. She served a year at New York's Blackwell Island Penitentiary for inciting a riot—though one never took place. And she would captivate the press. In one interview, she deftly charmed *The New York World*'s Nelly Bly—the intrepid reporter who won fame for herself and her paper by circumnavigating the globe in fewer than the eighty days it took the fictional Phileas Fogg. In a flattering portrayal, Bly wrote that Goldman, who arrived for the interview in a modest blue serge Eton suit, was an attractive woman who "did not show her 120 pounds."[15] Goldman told Bly: "I am satisfied to agitate, to teach, and I only ask for justice and freedom of speech." Goldman was, Bly concluded, "a little Joan of Arc."

Through it all, Goldman grew ever more passionate. Emerging from prison, she announced she was "determined to use every means in my power to spread my doctrine among the people."[16]

20

SPOILS OF WAR

McKinley's train hissed to a gentle stop at eight forty-five the morning of September 3, 1898, at the Montauk, New York, station. There to greet him under a brilliant blue sky was an enthusiastic crowd "as motley a one as can well be imagined"—some two thousand soldiers, sailors, railroad employees, teamsters, and a few farmers from the surrounding countryside. Even Theodore Roosevelt was there, just back from Cuba. Determined to personally congratulate the president for winning the war, they surged toward McKinley, shouting their approval.

A short carriage ride away, nestled in the sand dunes, lay a hastily constructed hospital and convalescence center for returning soldiers named Camp Wikoff. In neatly laid out white tents, some eighteen thousand men, including a bedridden General Shafter, had assembled in an oddly impressive sight. "This is beautiful," McKinley said as his carriage paused for a moment at the crest of a hill. "I think I never saw a handsomer camp."[1]

McKinley, still every bit the former army officer, grilled nurses and doctors, toured kitchens, and examined horses brought there to give men exercise. The presidential visit hadn't been widely advertised, and soldiers were stunned to hear from outside the flap of a tent that a surprise guest was about to enter. "Boys, the president has come to see you," an officer would announce. Weak and gaunt with such tropical diseases as malaria and yellow fever in addition to their battle wounds, they propped themselves up in their cots as best they could to exchange a polite word with the commander in chief, offering as upbeat a prognosis on their conditions as possible, and mumbling platitudes such as, "I'm getting along, sir."

It was a hot day with only a faint breeze wafting in from the ocean and, as usual, McKinley was overdressed for the occasion. Under his frock coat and waistcoat, he perspired profusely. His straw hat provided scant protection from the sun's burning rays. Genuinely moved by the desperate condition of the most gravely ill and wounded, he brushed aside doctors' warnings and entered wards containing contagious men. Reporters noticed that, emerging from the tent of one mortally ill soldier, McKinley's eyes were moist and downcast.[2] Time and again, *The New York Times* reported, the president could be heard commenting, "How sorry I am to see these brave fellows in such condition."

The visit was a sobering reminder of what McKinley had to do next. As *The New York World* editorialized in July, "We are not spending our blood and treasure in putting down one anarchy in Cuba for the sake of setting up another."[3]

American soldiers don't normally set the tone of the national psyche, but they were on the cutting edge in their conviction that handing the island over to the insurgents was lunacy. General William Ludlow, whom McKinley quickly appointed military governor of Havana, believed it would take at least a full generation before the Cubans would be fit for self-rule. "They are not as we are," he wrote to McKinley. "They are Latins, and belong to a dying race, which seems not capable of reconstruction as a stable people as is the Anglo-Saxon."[4] The irascible General Shafter expressed his doubts in the colorful language of a former frontier solider. Responding to a reporter's question, Shafter blurted out. "Self-government! Why those people are no more fit for self-government than gunpowder is for hell."[5]

Comments like Shafter's, which circulated widely, fueled an abrupt shift in the national mood regarding the whole Cuban problem. Arguments that had been overlooked or ignored before now suddenly seemed persuasive. It was pointed out, for example, that it would not be democratic for the United States to hand the island over to the insurgents when no more than 30,000 out of a population of 1.5 million had ever taken up arms.[6] *The New York Times* summed it up in August when it wrote that the "higher classes" feared a "long reign of terror in which all who opposed the insurrection will suffer greatly." The island's business class feared a "government by machete."[7]

The most egregious example of mob amnesia was how quickly lawmakers and pundits flip-flopped on the Teller Amendment, U.S. legislation to ensure Cuban independence. Written just a few months earlier, it was intended to provide moral cover for the war by declaring its noble purpose. Now Americans had second thoughts. It would be wrong to walk away from such a chaotic situation, given that the United States had unleashed it.

Congressmen conveniently discovered a rather large loophole they could use to escape their self-imposed straitjacket. The United States, the Teller Amendment read, "hereby disclaims any disposition of intention to exercise sovereignty, jurisdiction, or control over said island except for pacification thereof, and asserts its determination, when that is accomplished, to leave the government and control of the island to its people."

The New York Times in mid-August found plenty of wiggle room in what became known simply as the "pacification clause." The pledge "by no means binds us to withdraw at once, nor does full and faithful compliance with its spirit and letter forbid us to become permanent possessors of Cuba if the Cubans prove to be altogether incapable of self government."[8] Senator John T. Morgan, a member of the Senate Foreign Relations Committee, bluntly told a Cuban delegation that the Teller Amendment would require withdrawal of U.S. troops only "in such a manner and at such time as the competent authority in the United States shall provide."[9]

For the Cubans, it was a horrific turn of events. They had struggled for decades to cut themselves free from the Spanish, and suddenly a new foreign power was seamlessly stepping in. And this time, the colonial experience would be unlike anything they had witnessed before.

While Spain had devoted neither resources nor vision to Cuba, the Americans descended with the energy and enthusiasm of a nation new to the colonial game and eager to show how it's done. They distributed emergency food supplies to starving people in the countryside[10] and dispatched doctors. In Havana, American officials led a house-by-house inspection of medical and sanitary conditions. They began cleaning streets, overhauled the water supply, and set up a native police force. New schools were opened and the educational system was reorganized to combat what had been widespread illiteracy.[11] And it was all carried out under tight security. By March 1899, the United States had nearly forty-five thousand troops in Cuba, more than double the number it had sent to take Santiago.[12]

Benevolent though such work may have been, the Cubans had a more cynical view of the relationship. At times the humanitarian projects felt like the work of a SWAT team sent ahead to soften up the country for the real mission.

By the boatload, American businessmen began arriving in Havana almost as soon as the shooting had stopped—real estate tycoons, sugar and tobacco magnates, mineral company executives, and railroad engineers. Contracts for utilities and streetcar lines were handed out. Massive mineral deposits were opened to mining. Rich agricultural lands were put to the plow. All over the island, one could look up and see a sunburned American with a stack of papers under one arm, directing Cuban workers with the other.

Mining expert Charles M. Dobson, commissioned by the U.S. government to examine metal deposits, discovered enough manganese to meet 40 percent of American demand, as well as deposits of lead, copper, and zinc.[13] As his report spread wildly, American money poured in, so much so that by the end of the occupation, over 80 percent of Cuba's mineral exports were in American hands, most of those under the control of the Bethlehem Steel Company.

R. B. Hawley, another investor and former congressman from Texas, purchased sixty-six thousand acres of land near Puerto Padre, a harbor on the north coast, for himself and a group of Wall Street investors to build the largest sugar mill on the island. His farm alone could produce two hundred thousand bags of sugar, or about 10 percent of the entire Cuban crop.[14] In 1899, the Havana Commercial Company, organized in New York City, scooped up twelve cigar factories and one cigarette factory in Havana and then took control of an important leaf-importing business. Altogether, by 1903, Americans would own thirty-seven different agricultural settlements in Cuba, accounting for between 7 and 10 percent of the entire island.[15]

As the American historian John Clark Redpath commented in the summer of 1899, "The idea that we are in Cuba on a philanthropic and humane mission has gone to join the other misplaced, absurd, and hypocritical pretexts which history has flung with a lavish hand into limbo near the moon."[16]

——=:=——

HUNTING RABBITS

Warrensville, Ohio, on the outskirts of Cleveland, was pastoral middle America at its best, with rolling green hills that were home to rabbits and other game, leafy forests that turned wonderful hues of orange and yellow in the fall, and sparkling streams from which anglers might easily catch dinner. It was here in 1897, on a fifty-five-acre spread with a large house, a barn with cows, and a small pond, that Paul Czolgosz finally achieved his dream to own land, purchased when the extended family pooled its money and moved in together. Here, too, his son Leon would spend much of the rest of his brief life.

The closing years of the nineteenth century had not been kind to the younger Czolgosz. Around 1897, while going about his daily business in Cleveland, he first noticed that his breathing was unusually labored. He was also having strange palpitations. In an era when little was known about respiratory diseases other than their deadliness, the symptoms were alarming, and he visited doctors four times in the following months. What exactly Czolgosz suffered from was unclear; the only surviving medical report offers little more than a recounting of his symptoms. Nonetheless, doctors prescribed flasks of medicine and Czolgosz was soon frequently seen carrying a box of tablets.

One historian has postulated that Czolgosz may have convinced himself that he had contracted syphilis.[1] His medical records show treatments that many doctors of the era believed would help with the disease, including an herbal remedy and potassium iodide. There was also no shortage of unethical or incompetent doctors who may have willfully diagnosed syphilis in order to sell him medicines, some of which, as a side effect, produced exactly the type of symptoms that a person with syphilis would exhibit.

How Czolgosz thought he might have contracted the disease is another matter. There was, of course, the traditional method. Czolgosz would later claim that he had slept with a woman who then betrayed him. Yet the shy young man had rarely been seen in the company of the fairer sex, let alone striking up a relationship, and his father discounted such claims.[2] Another, more unusual, explanation is that Czolgosz possibly believed he had been exposed to syphilis during a previous job. Many who worked in glass factories thought syphilis could be passed between workers who shared blowing rods.

Whatever the cause, the treatments failed to heal him and, on the orders of one of his doctors, Czolgosz decided that he needed to rest. In August 1898 he marched up to his foreman, Mr. Page, and tendered his resignation.[3] He was, he explained, not feeling well and planned to go live in the country. No one at the factory had noticed anything about Czolgosz's health, especially something so severe that he would leave his job. Such was the secret life of Leon Czolgosz.

Arriving at the family farm with his suitcase and a small collection of belongings, Czolgosz moved into a room with his brother Joseph and began to reestablish the close family ties from his childhood. After years of factory work that had led to a simmering hatred of industrialists, it was a refreshing chance to start anew. The work would be hard, yet he was no stranger to long days of labor, and at least he was surrounded by plenty of the fresh air he needed.

Czolgosz, however, avoided joining his family in their chores around the farm. While they rose in the early morning darkness to feed the animals, he would roll over in his bed, pull the blankets up, and drift blissfully back to sleep. As time went on, his brothers and sisters began to suspect that he never intended to work. He seemed well enough, yet continued to laze about. Having tasted a life of leisure, Czolgosz discovered that he wanted more. In the summer, he would pass his days sleeping under a favorite shade tree. In the winter, he would read inside, frequently falling asleep in a comfortable chair. Normally fastidious about his appearance, he now looked "all ragged out."[4] Only once did Czolgosz apply for a real job, as a conductor on the electric railroad, the Stanley Company.[5]

Yet when presented with a challenge that interested him, Czolgosz could spring to activity. He once took apart a clock and successfully reassembled it. He also repaired a shattered pitcher, using wire to bind it tightly enough to hold milk. His brother would later say that Czolgosz "could do anything in the way of fixing up." When he was in the right mood, he would play with the young children at the house. He also developed an interest, and skill, in hunting and fishing, pursuing rabbits on the property with a pistol or breech-loading shotgun or starting a fire near a warren of rabbits and driving them into a sack. Other times, he brought a fish back to the house, caught in a nearby pond.

Despite the comforts of country life, he missed one element of his old existence. He still harbored an interest in radical social ideology that could not be satisfied among the cows and chickens of the Ohio countryside.

====== == ======

"IT IS ALWAYS THE UNEXPECTED THAT HAPPENS, AT LEAST IN MY CASE"

In September 1898, the president could comfort himself with a genuine sense of satisfaction. In relaxed dinners at the White House with close friends such as Mark Hanna, where white-gloved waiters delivered the simple meat-and-potatoes fare that he and Ida favored, McKinley could boast about how well things were going in Cuba and how Americans had come around to his way of thinking. He could take credit for personal efforts to help American business leaders acquire railroad contracts in Cuba and note how the infrastructure would open the backcountry to commerce—good for the Cubans as well as the Americans. Yet after his guests had stepped out into the cool Washington evening for the carriage ride home, he would lie in his own bed and toss and turn. Often unable to sleep, he would walk the quiet, empty halls and at times drop to his knees and pray for guidance.

Asia weighed heaviest on his mind. McKinley's efforts to secure new markets for American business were beginning to provoke challenges he had never envisioned in 1896. Together with his compatriots, he learned one of the fundamental tenets of international relations: One seemingly innocent step abroad often leads to another and another. National prestige, prospective economic and security gains, and—not to be underestimated—public opinion can propel a country's foreign policy to destinations that had never been intended. As he once noted, "The march of events rules and overrules human action."[1]

McKinley's thinking about the Philippines had steadily evolved since he took office, leading to the decision to take Manila, and he was again toying with making a momentous shift. He now began to wonder whether he needed to control the whole archipelago to achieve his objective. He didn't relish acquiring more territory, yet he feared he might have no choice. With Aguinaldo back in the islands, courtesy of U.S. diplomats, the prospect of a protracted war between the Spanish and the insurgents was highly likely. It would be difficult for the United States to hold a small enclave in Manila if the rest of the islands were at war. And there were no assurances that the Spanish would keep control of the rest of the country. Spain could turn around and sell it to the Germans, who were aggressively trying to build an empire in Asia.

The chief of the Bureau of Equipment, Commander R. B. Bradford, visited Manila three times to study the situation and sketched out a domino theory. If Washington wanted to hold Manila, it would probably need to possess all of Luzon. Yet holding Luzon would require a massive defense force, given the close proximity of other islands that could well fall into hostile hands. "The harbor of Manila without the island of Luzon would be a source of weakness rather than strength," he told the American Peace Commission in Paris in October. Yet taking and holding Luzon or other islands without their neighbors would be equally problematic because "a cannon shot can be fired from one island to another in many instances."[2]

It was late in the game for McKinley to ratchet up his demands. The peace protocol had already been signed with Spain in August, and formal peace talks were slated for Paris in October. Then in February 1899, whatever was agreed to in Paris would have to be put before the U.S. Senate, which held constitutional power to approve treaties. Even a quick head count revealed that McKinley faced an uphill, if not impossible, battle to convince the Senate to approve full annexation.

Still burning from his poor handling of public opinion in the run-up to declaring war on Spain, McKinley proceeded carefully. This time he would engage the public rather than wall himself off from it. He called members of Congress to the White House for meetings, and made sure to scan through the letters that piled up in the mail room, often more than one thousand per day. In October, he used a ten-day speaking tour of the Midwest, stumping for Republican candidates in the forthcoming election, to gain a firsthand feel for the mood in the heartland. In Hastings, Iowa, the president told a cheering crowd, "We have good money, we have ample revenues, we have unquestioned national credit; but what we want [are] new markets, and as trade follows the flag, it looks very much as if we were going to have new markets."[3] Speaking at the Trans-Mississippi and International Exposition in Omaha on October 12, 1898, he ratcheted up his imperial tone. "Shall we deny to ourselves what the rest of the world so freely and so justly accords to us?"

"No!" the audience shouted.[4]

Not only was there a compelling logic for annexing the Philippines, McKinley came to believe, but a significant share of the people wanted it. As one aide put it, the president "seemed to fear" the wrath of the nation if he settled for anything less than taking over the islands in full.[5]

Yet for every voice clamoring for empire, another wailed against it. A group of prominent politicians and business leaders formed what they called the Anti-Imperialist League, spearheading a movement that quickly built support.

The list of those opposed to annexing the archipelago read like a who's who of American politics, commerce, and the arts. Former president Grover Cleveland referred to the idea as the "dangerous perversions" of conquest.[6] Mark Twain was moved to write "To the Person Sitting in Darkness," a stinging satire of imperialism aimed at McKinley and others with similar ambitions. And, rather surprisingly, Andrew Carnegie chimed in, too.

In fact, Carnegie was among the most ardent anti-imperialist campaigners, penning magazine and newspaper editorials, working the halls of Congress, and even meeting with the president. John Hay could hardly believe Carnegie's manic devotion to the cause. "Andrew

Carnegie really seems to be off his head," he wrote. "He writes me frantic letters, signing them 'Your Bitterest Opponent.' "7

The arguments were as varied as they were passionate. Some opposed taking the islands purely for reasons of race. Admitting ten million Asians, most of whom were Catholic and didn't speak English, was not an idea that many Americans cared to contemplate. Others cited the U.S. Constitution, which made no mention of colonies or boundaries when it said government derived its power from the "consent of the governed." Still others complained that an imperial policy would damage the American psyche and tarnish its ideals of freedom and democracy.

There was also the very real prospect that Aguinaldo and his men, who had already fiercely defended themselves against one foreign conqueror, might be ready to do battle with another. Henry Adams weighed in with his usual biting style: "I turn green in bed at midnight if I think of the horror of a year's warfare in the Philippines . . . where . . . we must slaughter a million or two foolish Malays in order to give them the comforts of flannel petticoats and electric railways."8

Good arguments could be made for both options: grant the Philippines their independence and freedom, or shoulder the burden of "civilizing" them. McKinley agonized over the conflict until a hint of divine intervention helped crystallize the answer.

He explained his final decision to the General Missionary Committee of the Methodist Episcopal Church: "One night late it came to me this way—I don't know how it was, but it came . . . that there was nothing left for us to do but to take them all, and to educate the Filipinos, and uplift them and civilize and Christianize them, and by God's grace do the very best we could by them, as our fellow-men for whom Christ also died. And then I went to bed, and went to sleep, and slept soundly, and the next morning I sent for the chief engineer of the War Department and I told him to put the Philippines on the map of the United States, and there they are, and there they will stay while I am President."9

His mind made up, McKinley needed to intercept the peace talks in Paris, which William Day was leading. On October 26, 1898, Secretary

of State Hay cabled Day: THE CESSION MUST BE OF THE WHOLE ARCHIPEL-
AGO OR NONE. THE LATTER IS WHOLLY INADMISSIBLE. AND THE FORMER MUST
THEREFORE BE REQUIRED. The message also noted that McKinley believed controlling the whole country would ultimately entail less trouble than taking on just a portion.[10] For the chain-smoking head of the
Spanish delegation, Don Eugenio Montero Rios, the decision must
have triggered a coughing attack. The United States had conquered
nothing more than a small sliver of land around Manila, yet now was
demanding the entire country? French newspapers, which reflected
the views of the Spanish, were aghast. *Le Matin* speculated that the entire peace talks would collapse. On November 5, Hay sheepishly con-
soled his team in Paris, cabling that the president appreciates the
"difficulties and the embarrassments" that he had caused. But he offered little advice, leaving it up to Day to interpret his boss to the Spanish.[11]

McKinley, who hated nasty arguments, would not have wanted to
do the job he assigned to Day. But separated by an ocean from Spanish
scorn, the president played his powerful hand for all that it was worth.
He knew that Spain, thoroughly whipped on the battlefield and on the
high seas, lacked the resources to restart the war even if it wanted to.
With hardly a thought he dismissed its pleas to turn the Philippine
question over to an international arbitrator and rebuffed demands for
$100 million in compensation. Instead, he offered Spain $20 million
and declared the proceedings over.[12] The Spanish negotiators in Paris
bitterly packed their bags and went home, thankful at least that they
would not have to deal with these strong-armed Yankees again.

While the Americans were gutting the Spanish in Paris that autumn,
Aguinaldo had spent his time trying to establish himself as the legitimate leader of the Philippines. Never one to sell himself short,
Aguinaldo set up a provisional capital in a beautiful monastery in the
town of Malolos, about twenty miles from Manila, with all the trap-
pings of the power he hoped to obtain. Furnishings and decorations
removed from Spanish homes were installed, uniformed guards kept
watch at the doors, and elaborate plans were made for a meeting of
the national assembly on September 15, 1898. Self-important dele-

gates, clad in top hats and cutaway coats, arrived that morning to a fanfare of music and flags. Mimicking the French, members of the body addressed each other as "citizen" and enjoyed a magnificent banquet of more than a dozen courses that included salmon hollandaise, *coquilles de crabes vol-au-vent,* and *dinde truffée,* all washed down with fine wines.[13] Amid the pomp, the body voted Aguinaldo as president and Apolinario Mabini y Maranan as prime minister. A well-to-do attorney drafted a constitution with power centered in a legislature to be dominated by the upper classes.

Aguinaldo's delusions were dangerously disconnected from the negotiations in Paris. When word of the treaty reached Manila in December, he said decades later, the news hit him like an atomic bomb.[14] Relations between Filipinos and U.S. troops, never good, deteriorated to a tense mutual hatred. They began taunting one another from their positions around Manila. Americans could not walk the streets alone, and most local men took to carrying a knife or a bolo hidden in their clothing. U.S. soldiers ransacked homes to search for weapons and were quick to brandish their rifles at the slightest sign of protest. American sentries shot and killed one insurgent who didn't remove his sidearm while walking near their outpost. The Filipinos, for their part, arrested and imprisoned a group of American mapmakers who were scouring an area near the small village of Santa Ana, east of Manila.

On the evening of February 4, 1899, the tinderbox ignited. Private William Walter Grayson, a thin former innkeeper from Nebraska, and a buddy, Orville Miller, began a routine patrol outside a U.S. military camp at Santa Mesa, an eastern suburb of Manila. The area of their patrol was sensitive, located near the meeting of the Pasig and San Juan rivers in territories the insurgents claimed as their own. On this particular night, Grayson and Miller trod through scrub brush, slapping at persistent mosquitoes and suffering in the humidity that soaked their clothes. At a bridge over the San Juan, they heard low whistles and saw a red lantern waved from a Filipino barracks. They made out the silhouettes of four men in the gloom. Raising his Springfield, Grayson shouted "Halt!" Back came a mocking echo *"Alto!"* The exchange was repeated. Grayson, refusing to take any guff, fired. A shadowy figure fell. Miller squeezed off a round and another figure dropped. Then Grayson dropped a third. In a panic, the two Americans sprinted back to their camp shouting "Line up, fellows, the niggers are in here all through the lines!"[15] Within minutes, rifle fire cracked up and down the ten-mile line that separated the two sides.

Months of sitting around, getting sick, and trading insults with the rebels had left the Americans itching for the shooting to start. When it did, nobody wanted to be left out. A California regiment captured an ammunition dump at Santa Ana and then pressed ahead to San Pedro Makati, two miles outside Manila. The Utah artillery covered a rush by the Nebraskans, who took San Juan Bridge. Troops from Idaho and Washington State forced Filipino soldiers out of their positions near the Pasig, and many of them, skilled shots from their civilian days, calmly stood on the bank as if in an arcade game and picked off rebels as they clumsily tried to swim the river. "More fun than a turkey shoot," one said.

Inside Manila itself, American troops ruthlessly hunted down saboteurs. They torched buildings where rebels were believed to be hiding and shot suspects on the spot, including six who were caught cutting fire hoses. One local church was destroyed by big guns in an effort to root out partisans. In the entire engagement, some 59 Americans were killed and 278 were wounded. Filipino numbers were more difficult to establish, but reports circulated that around 3,000 were killed.[16]

At eleven thirty on a Saturday night, McKinley was working on a speech he hoped would celebrate a successful Senate vote, now just two days away, ratifying the Treaty of Paris. A telegraph clerk slipped in and handed him a message containing the *New York Sun*'s coverage of the firestorm in Manila. He read the dispatch several times, laid it down, and leaned back in his chair, letting the significance sink in. "It is always the unexpected that happens, at least in my case," he said. "How foolish these people are. This means the ratification of the treaty; the people will insist on its ratification."[17] He was right—at least partially so. Few votes appeared to have swung in McKinley's direction when the next head count was taken. But as the day of February 6 wore on, the president's supporters worked on the fence sitters who could not have ignored the fact that American boys were dying in the Philippines—nor that rejecting the treaty would mean a major embarrassment for the country. Support began to gradually build. At two thirty, one senator turned, then a bit before three another, and finally one more shortly thereafter. When the roll call was taken, fifty-seven of the eighty-four senators who voted gave a "yea," one more than the required two-thirds majority.[18] Lodge wrote to Roosevelt that it had been "the closest, hardest fight I have ever known."[19]

The president was still glowing with his narrow victory when he and a small group of advisers boarded a train headed for Boston on the cold night of February 15, 1899. Peering out frosted windows at the effects of a three-day snowstorm, McKinley contemplated an address he would give the next evening at the Home Market Club. It would become a landmark of his presidency.

The New York Times called it the largest banquet ever held in the country. An army of waiters operated with military precision, directed by silent hand signals, serving nearly 1,900 diners. In galleries decorated with bunting and shields, another 3,800 people crowded in. Above the speakers' table, large portraits of Washington, Lincoln, and McKinley hung, along with more bunting and electric lights and the word "Liberators" printed in giant lettering.

When he was finally introduced to enthusiastic applause and cheering, the president took the podium and explained his colonial ambitions in the high-sounding, moralistic code that the country most liked to hear. Providence, he said, had entrusted the Philippines to the United States as an unavoidable outcome of the war with Spain. Until they were fit to govern themselves, the natives of the Philippines must be made to understand that "their welfare is our welfare, that neither their aspirations nor ours can be realized until our authority is acknowledged and unquestioned." Rejecting the anti-expansionist argument that the United States had no right to govern others, he said it was not "a good time for the liberator to submit important questions concerning liberty and government to the liberated while they are engaged in shooting down their rescuers."

It was a triumphant speech, the audience leaping to its feet in applause every time he mentioned the flag. Even McKinley's critics were filled with admiration. *The Nation* wrote, "McKinley is one of the rare public speakers who are able to talk humbug in such a way as to make their average hearers think it excellent sense, and exactly their idea."[20]

"Humbug." Aguinaldo and his men might not recognize the American slang, but they certainly would have agreed with the definition. They had no intention of laying down before their self-described "rescuers." The skirmish between U.S. soldiers and Aguinaldo's rebels was now a war.

Northern Luzon, the area around Manila, was a smooth, rolling basin made up of fertile farmland framed by high mountains. From afar, and through a blurry lens, it might have looked like any number of forested areas in the United States, but the terrain was, in fact, a dense, putrid jungle unlike anything the Americans had fought in before.

The weather alone was enough to make most generals want to hide under their cots. During the rainy season, clouds dumped some seventy inches of rain, washing out rail lines, bridges, and roads. Any kind of sustained offensive was almost impossible, and soldiers were reduced to hunkering down in sopping tents, waiting for the seasons to change, and trying not to contract any number of fatal afflictions that could ravage the ranks—cholera, malaria, and venereal disease.[21] During the dry season, the Americans could and did use superior technology and numbers to overrun hundreds of square miles of enemy territory. Yet it was ground they could not long hold; they were too short of men and it was too difficult to get supplies once the rains started. Albert Robinson of the New York *Evening Post* wrote, "There are towns here which have been 'captured' again and again, each time with a 'glorious victory.' Today it is unsafe for an American to go even ten miles from the city of Manila."[22]

Many American commanders were also surprised by the hostility of the general population. As early as March 1899, the brutally frank Arthur MacArthur, Jr., acknowledged that the American occupation faced widespread opposition. "When I first started against these rebels, I believed that Aguinaldo's troops represented only a faction. I did not believe that the whole population of Luzon was opposed to us; but I have been reluctantly compelled to believe that the Filipinos are loyal to Aguinaldo and the government which he represents."[23]

——

Back home, Americans were still celebrating the victory over the Spanish and didn't want to hear anything about troubles in Asia. In October 1899, George Dewey, the hero of Manila Bay, finally arrived in the United States to a joyous reception. In New York, he and his sailors delighted women and envious men with tales of battle. A monument was planned for Madison Square. A vibrant parade of marching bands and members of the armed forces snaked through Washington, which Dewey and McKinley watched from a replica of the bow of the *Olympia*.[24] If McKinley had any doubts about what he was up against in the Pacific, he wouldn't share them with the public. "The first blow was struck by the insurgents," the president said in a Pittsburgh speech, ignoring that it had been American sentries who had fired blindly into the night. "They assailed our sovereignty, and there will be no useless parley, no pause, until the insurrection is suppressed and American authority acknowledged and established."[25]

The man the U.S. military now hoped would establish American authority in the Philippines came with the perfect résumé for the job. Major General Henry Ware Lawton, a rugged six foot four inches tall and immaculately groomed, had led the hunt for Chief Geronimo, driving his men for thousands of miles through every manner of hardship before capturing the elusive Apache. Who better, American journalists and the public asked, to lead a fresh effort to end the insurgent uprising by chasing down and killing Aguinaldo?

With the same energy and resolve he had used on the American frontier, Lawton and his men quickly picked up Aguinaldo's trail and pursued him deep into the mountains. Several times, success was excruciatingly close. At one point the Americans captured his mother and son, and on another occasion his wife. Yet Aguinaldo would time and again slip through their fingers. Finally, on December 2, 1899, he disappeared for good, fleeing through a narrow mountain pass.[26]

The escape marked a turning point for the war. Isolated from his troops and constantly on the move between mountain hideaways, Aguinaldo realized he could no longer direct classic military battles and dissolved his "Army of Liberation." Instead, he would lead—or at least try to lead—a guerrilla campaign. American supply columns were jumped, lonely guards on duty were hacked down by bolo-wielding rebels, and booby traps were set. The pace of the attacks was unrelenting. In the first four months of 1900, guerrillas launched 442 attacks on American forces, killing 130 and wounding 322.[27] Hideous contraptions that American soldiers in Southeast Asia would come to know well decades later were employed—concealed pits with sharpened bamboo stakes, or trip wires that unleashed spears and arrows. Any U.S. soldier who had the misfortune to be captured could count on a gruesome end. In June 1900, one patrol happened upon the remains of an American who had been buried up to his neck with his mouth propped open with a stick. A trail of sugar had led an army of ants to eat the poor man inside out. Other times, American soldiers discovered the remains of their comrades who, taken prisoner, had been shot execution style, their bodies mutilated.

Confronted with ruthless tactics and a remorseless enemy, American soldiers responded in kind. "No prisoners" soon became their motto, and soldiers wrote home boasting they would kill any Filipino even remotely suspected of being an insurgent. Entire towns were burned to the ground as revenge for harboring rebels. Artilleryman Anthony Michael described going into one village near where Americans had been hacked to death. "We went in and killed every native we met, men, women and children. It was a dreadful sight, the killing of the poor creatures." Colonel Arthur Lockwood later acknowledged that innocent people were killed when entire towns were leveled but noted the Bible justified mass killings. "The Almighty destroyed Sodom," he said.[28] Even torture could be justified. According to Private Evan Wyatt of the Eighth Infantry, soldiers held a prisoner's mouth open while funneling the contents of a full water tank down his throat until he looked like a "pregnant woman." Every few minutes, soldiers would kneel on his stomach to force the water back out. This "water cure" was repeated until they extracted the information they wanted, or the victim died.[29]

RED EMMA

Emma Goldman was a rising star on the lecture circuit by the late 1890s. Her audiences, while mostly consisting of leftists, increasingly included ordinary folks eager to see the famous young anarchist known as "Red Emma." Her podium manners were legendary. Blunt, powerful, a "sledgehammer" in the words of one, she was the "very embodiment of the doctrine she preaches."[1] Skilled at employing sarcasm and humor, she belittled business leaders, political figures, and the police alike. Run-ins with the law in whatever town she was speaking in had become so routine that Goldman took to keeping a good book with her to provide entertainment while serving her frequent brief spells behind bars.

Goldman embarked on her grandest tour, an eight-month odyssey, in 1898 with—as she liked to boast—nothing more than two dollars in her pocket and a train ticket. The tour would take her to the West Coast, including San Jose, Los Angeles, and Portland, and throughout the Midwest. Before it was over, she would give 210 lectures, visit 60 cities, and address 50,000 to 60,000 people.[2]

The nation's newfound passion for foreign conquests provided an especially juicy target. Patriotism, so key to providing the public support for aggression, was a sad excuse for killing, she complained. "To be patriotic," she told a Pittsburgh audience, "one must wade ankle-deep in the blood of his fellow men. He must kill, slay, destroy, in every conceivable manner and form, else he is not living up to the sacred meaning of that sacred word."[3] Continuing her tour abroad, Goldman mocked the Spanish-American War to a London audience. The noble sentiment that had drawn the United States into the war—saving Cubans from Spanish brutality—only "served the American governors as a good pretext for fighting Spain in order to get Cuba into their clutches."[4] In the end, she went on, the Cubans were hardly better off. "I say that all the blood spilt, all the lives lost, all the money spent has been in vain; the Cubans have been freed from the atrocious government of Spain but only to fall into the hands of another almost as unscrupulous."[5]

The haranguing, shouting, and thumping of podiums all made for good theater. Who could doubt Goldman's considerable oratory skills? And even a few of her opponents had to acknowledge the merits of her arguments. Yet there was something lacking about the message she delivered with such passion. Anarchy proved a consistently hard sell in the New World. At most, there were ten thousand practicing anarchists out of a total population of sixty-two million, and probably many fewer.[6] Many of the anarchists' difficulties were self-inflicted. Deep divisions split the movement. Issues such as cooperating with labor unions and whether to vote were as hotly debated as their hatred of industrialists. The use of violence was likewise a source of bitter rancor. Though hard-core radicals tried to justify it, the majority of anarchists remained firmly opposed to killing, believing bombings and assassinations only soured the public's view of the movement and, more important, were fundamentally at odds with the idealistic hope that anarchism offered.

More than any other reason, however, anarchism suffered simply because the American dream still remained a very real beacon for the overwhelming majority. The shiploads of immigrants that landed on

American docks every day were coming to the United States to improve themselves, not to plot against the government. At best, anarchists were viewed as a collection of intellectual crackpots, almost exclusively foreign born, and maladjusted. At worst, they were a devious rabble bent on destroying American society through any means possible. Anyone who read the foreign section of the local newspaper knew that all too well.

Europe in the 1890s trembled from bombs. Anarchist attacks and threats of attacks terrified citizens in just about every major European city—London, Rome, and Barcelona. And then there was Paris, especially Paris, where for a two-year stretch in the early part of the decade, anarchists, the courts, and the police descended into a bloody cycle of bombing, executions, and revenge attacks that at times left the city's inhabitants fearful even of stepping outside.

French newspapers tallied one bloody encounter between police and anarchists after another. In the town of Fourmies north of Paris, the gendarmes gunned down nine demonstrators in 1891 when May Day events celebrating the Haymarket bombing spun out of control. One of those killed was the charismatic eighteen-year-old Maria Blondeau, who was decapitated by one bullet.[7] Later, François-Claudius Ravachol, an aspiring anarchist who raised money for the cause by grave robbing, was sentenced to death for attempting to blow up the homes of a judge and prosecutor who had meted out stiff sentences against anarchists. Ravachol never denied his guilt and at his sentencing boasted he had done what he had done for the "anarchist idea." Sent to the guillotine on July 11, 1893, he was unbowed. As he approached the device, he sang out "To be happy, god dammit, You have got to kill those who own property." His final cry of defiance, *"Vive la révolution!"* was cut short by the powerful slice of the blade.[8]

In early 1894, Parisians gasped at the story of Auguste Vaillant, a poor family man who decided to sacrifice his life, not out of revenge or hatred, but simply to call attention to the plight of the underclass. Unable to afford even food for his wife and daughter, and unwilling to return to the life of petty crime he had known as a child, Vaillant devised a plan that he hoped would "hasten the advent of a new era." Concealing a crude bomb made from a saucepan, nails, and a small explosive charge, Vaillant climbed the stairs to one of the balconies of the Chambre des députés shortly before 4 P.M. on December 9 and threw it to the floor below. Just as he calculated—not always the case with homemade bombs—the device erupted with a thunderous explosion, killing no one but causing the carnage he intended.

In court, Vaillant claimed that he had intentionally constructed the bomb so that no one would be killed. There was something appealing about his sincerity and devotion that struck a chord with the public. Displaying a large measure of sympathy for an anarchist who had made great efforts not to kill anyone, yet was willing to risk his own life, many people pleaded for the authorities to show leniency. Letters calling for his pardon poured into the office of French president Marie-François-Sadi Carnot, including from some of the victims. Yet the French leader would not be moved, and Vaillant was sent to the guillotine on February 5, 1894, his final words the familiar *"Vive l'anarchie."*

Paris soon thereafter seemed to crawl with terrorists. On February 12, 1894, a bomb exploded in the Café Terminus near the Gare St.-Lazare train station, in the midst of a crowd of working-class people who were listening to a band. The explosion injured twenty, one of whom later died. On the rue St.-Jacques, a bomb killed a passerby, another exploded in the Faubourg St.-Germain, and yet another, carried in the pocket of Belgian anarchist Jean Pauwels, exploded at the entrance of the Church of the Madeleine, killing Pauwels.

The repeated blasts and the apparent inability of the police to stop them reduced Paris to a collective fetal position. The upper classes shunned expensive restaurant and shops. Some were afraid to visit the Bois de Boulogne due to rumors that anarchists congregated there. Tourists stayed away; hotels were empty, as were theaters and museums. Troops were positioned in the outskirts of Paris to be deployed in case of another attack. During one theatrical performance, the audience ran screaming from the building shouting *"Les Anarchistes! Une bombe!"* when a piece of scenery fell over backstage, making a loud thump.[9]

What struck many about the anarchists was that they were so stubbornly unrepentant. When Emile Henry was arrested and charged with the Café Terminus attack, he admitted not only to the bombing,

but to the attack at the Paris office of the Société des Mines de Car-
maux that had killed five policemen in November 1892.[10] The terminus bombing, he told police, was to avenge Vaillant, and he had
intended to kill "as many as possible." Police later found in his apartment enough material to manufacture twelve to fifteen bombs.[11]

At his trial, Henry said anarchists were willing to kill women and
children. "Are not those children innocent victims who, in the slums,
die slowly of anemia because bread is scarce at home: or those women
who grow pale in your workshops and wear themselves out to earn
forty sous a day, and yet are lucky when poverty does not turn them
into prostitutes; those old people who you have turned into machines
for production all their lives, and whom you cast on the garbage dump
and the workhouse when their strength is exhausted. At least have the
courage of your crimes, gentlemen of the bourgeoisie, and agree that
our reprisals are fully legitimate!" Like those before him, Henry was
sentenced to death.[12]

No headline won more widespread attention in the United States
than the assassination of the president of France. On June 24, 1894,
Carnot was riding through Lyon in an open carriage waving at enthusiastic crowds when a young man approached. Twenty-year-old Italian
Sante Caserio, a baker's apprentice, stepped from the crowd with a
rolled-up newspaper that looked like it might contain flowers. Caserio
belonged to several anarchist groups and had been deeply angered by
Carnot's refusal to grant Valliant a pardon. When he read that the
French leader was coming to Lyon, he decided to commit some sort of
"great deed."[13] Approaching the president, Caserio pulled a knife from
the newspaper and plunged it six inches into Carnot's stomach. He
died within three hours.[14]

Taken together, the bombings and attacks fit a familiar pattern.
They were perpetrated by young men who often possessed only a hazy
understanding of anarchist theory, who usually felt they had nothing
to lose, who were motivated by revenge or the example of someone
else, and who were willing to die for their cause. Americans would
soon recognize the pattern in one of their own.

24

OPEN DOORS

On February 10, 1899, a government tug plowed through the waters of San Francisco Bay toward the Japanese liner *America Maru*, just arrived from the Orient. On deck, bags at his side, waited the tall, athletic Lord Charles William de la Poer Beresford. England's most celebrated living naval officer and the cream of British society—raised on a spread of one hundred thousand acres near Waterford—Lord Charles was accustomed to special treatment. But this time, an entire nation eagerly awaited the arrival of Britain's leading authority on China.[1]

For the next several weeks, Lord Charles traveled the width of America in a highly celebrated tour. He tirelessly granted newspaper interviews and delivered speeches to enthusiastic business groups. Addressing three hundred of Chicago's leading businessmen on February 18, 1899, he spoke of his recent visit to China in breathless wonder: "I found that the natural resources of the country are simply enormous. They are perfectly incalculable. The possibilities of trade in the future are limitless," he said, adding, "First and foremost, it is necessary for commercial enterprise and industry and investment that China should hold the open-door all through that empire."[2] By the time he reached the East Coast, all doors were open to him. John Hay hosted a luncheon in his honor for fourteen privileged guests.[3] President McKinley met with him privately.

Lord Charles's message was clear: The United States must thwart the attempts of France, Germany, and Russia to dismember China and instead preserve the vast wealth of the Middle Kingdom for all nations. London called this the "Open Door" policy, and had worked hard to enforce it for nearly half a century. But drained by the Boer War and its colonial obligations, it needed the United States to take the lead.

Washington could barely contain its delight that the British Empire was asking for help in opening up the markets of the Far East. What better evidence that the United States, by virtue of its economic might and defeat of the Spanish, had earned admittance to the club of nations that ruled the world.

Perhaps most tantalizing was the financial promise of the Open Door policy itself. The approach to China reflected precisely what McKinley had been striving to articulate since the Spanish-American War first started. He did not want to colonize nor rule far-flung corners of the globe. What he did want were open markets, combined with the means for U.S. ships to reach them and the navy to protect them. Britain had built an empire on which the sun never set. American greatness would instead be measured by its commercial hegemony.

This discussion of the Open Door policy also acknowledged the elephant in the room. The United States had acquired Hawaii, Guam, and a contested portion of the Philippines, all on the argument that those possessions were needed to ensure access to China. Yet no blueprint had so far been drafted for opening China itself.

There was one more reason for the president to take seriously the pleadings of Lord Charles: John Hay, the man who was now seated at his right hand at the cabinet room conference table. McKinley could for the first time look into the confident eyes of a secretary of state who was ready to take the initiative. If anybody could figure out how to prevent the world's most coveted market from slipping into the clutches of the Europeans, this was the man.

———

Hay, one of the most remarkable Americans of the nineteenth century, had already led several lives by the time McKinley appointed him top diplomat in September 1898. Aged sixty-one, handsome and dignified with a trim goatee, Hay had worked as an attorney and historian and served in U.S. diplomatic missions in Paris, Vienna, Madrid, and London. He wrote editorials for the *New-York Tribune*, published poems and novels, and collaborated on a popular ten-volume history of Lincoln's presidency. He knew a great deal of the topic, having served as the assassinated president's aide, and he was by Lincoln's side across the street from Ford's Theatre when he died.

Hay was in many ways the perfect partner for Lord Charles. For starters, he was an unrepentant Anglophile and had admired how the British managed their version of the Open Door during his years as ambassador in London.

Hay also firmly believed in a sense of moral entitlement in the battlefield of commerce, as people (and countries) pursued something greater than profits. Free markets, such as those the Open Door policy sought to achieve, were all part of God's great plan. Hay would say, "That you have property is proof of industry and foresight on your part or your father's; that you have nothing is judgment of your laziness and vice, or on your improvidence. The world is a moral world, which it would not be if virtue and vice received the same reward."[4]

Hay's background, impressive though it was, fell short in one respect. He knew nothing of the Orient. For all his travels in Europe, he had never been to Asia, nor even to the immigrant-heavy West Coast of the United States. Keenly aware of this shortcoming, and equally aware of Asia's growing importance, Hay turned to an old acquaintance to head up America's China policy. William W. Rockhill, then serving with considerable disgust in the diplomatic backwater of Athens as the U.S. minister for Greece, Romania, and Serbia,[5] could not have been happier to take the job.

Rockhill threw himself body and soul into the China problem. A Sinophile, his reasons for wanting to protect the nation from ravenous

Europeans were unique in the money-driven society of the day. China, he believed, with its culture and historical accomplishments, was simply too grand a country to be carved up. The language, the art, and the music had to be protected. Always anxious to spend time with someone who shared his cultivated views, in June 1899 Rockhill accepted an invitation for lunch with an old friend named Alfred Hippisley. Meeting at a Washington, D.C., restaurant, the two caught up on the years spent together when they were both stationed in Peking, Rockhill with the State Department and Hippisley as a member of the British foreign ministry.[6] Rockhill listened with fascination as his friend, just back from China, gushed with vivid descriptions of what was happening there. Most important, he was captivated by Hippisley's conviction that the United States could save it from being dismantled.

The McKinley administration, Hippisley argued, could do nothing to end the spheres of influence that already existed. European powers had expended considerable effort to carve them out and were unlikely to happily walk away. Yet there was a way to make them less of a threat to U.S. commerce. McKinley could demand that tariffs be uniform throughout the country and that ports be made open to all. No other power could orchestrate this Open Door policy, Hippisley said, because the Europeans and Japanese were too suspicious of each other's motives. The United States could still act as an honest broker.

Impressed, Rockhill arranged for Hippisley to meet Hay early that summer, who immediately understood the opportunity and urged Hippisley and Rockhill to get down to work. The pair produced a document called the Open Door notes that would serve as American policy in China for decades to come. The great powers could keep their spheres of influence, they agreed, but no nation should be allowed to use its possessions there to discriminate against the trade of others. So clearly did the document capture the feelings of Hay and McKinley that it sailed up the chain of command with only the smallest of changes.[7] That summer, the State Department sent it to Moscow, Tokyo, London, Berlin, and Paris, hoping they would agree.

Predictably, foreign ministers in each of the capitals read the proposals from the upstart Americans with icy consternation. Each complained about some portion of the plan, offering evasive and noncommittal replies. But as negotiations over the fine print continued, it emerged that no one was likely to reject the plan, either. Peer pressure played a useful role, as no government really wanted to reject an emerging consensus. What's more, none wanted to risk war in distant Asia. On March 20, 1900, Hay triumphantly announced that the overall feedback had been "favorable" and that he considered his policy "final and definitive."[8]

In giddy turn-of-the-century America, authorship of the Open Door policy was seen as yet more evidence that the country had become a force to be reckoned with. Hay had used his pen to boldly demonstrate Washington's growing power in the world. *The New York Times* declared the American initiative a "remarkable diplomatic achievement." *The Philadelphia Press* hailed the Open Door as a greater coup than winning the Spanish-American War.

In reality, however, the Open Door notes were as much the product of Washington's weakness as its strength. The other powers had offered grudging acceptance at best, and the United States was not in a position to police the agreement. Despite its recent buildup, the U.S. armed forces posed little threat to nations such as France and Russia. Hay described the American predicament in surprisingly honest terms: "The inherent weakness of our position is this: we do not want to rob China ourselves, and our public opinion will not permit us to interfere, with an army, to prevent others from robbing her. Besides, we have no army. The talk in the papers about our 'preeminent moral position giving us the authority to dictate to the world' is mere flapdoodle."[9]

Hay's fears would soon prove to be well founded. China, the one country that had not been consulted as part of the Open Door, still had something to say about foreign powers and their interfering decisions.

Calling themselves the "Fists of Righteous Harmony," members of a grassroots movement of Chinese peasants had swept through the north China countryside since the fall of 1898, gathering members attracted to their creed of superstition, religion, and xenophobia. Striding confidently into forlorn villages wearing their distinct red sashes, they claimed that their bodies had been taken over by spirits that made them impervious to bullets or blades, and they performed spectacular shooting and sword tricks to prove it. It was now their mission, the peasants said, to throw the foreigners out of China.

Dubbed the "Boxers" by Westerners amused by their martial arts, the peasant soldiers had legitimate reasons to resent the Europeans and Americans who lived among them. Foreign steamers plied their rivers, putting local boatmen out of work. Bible-thumping missionaries roamed throughout the country, condemning China as a backward society. Imperial powers were threatening to carve up their homeland. What's more, the Boxers saw a string of natural catastrophes as proof that they were being called upon to act. In 1898, the Yellow River had overflowed its banks, flooding 2,500 square miles and destroying 1,500 villages. Plagues of locusts and drought followed.[10] For the simple peasants, the reasons were clear: They were being punished for allowing the "foreign devils" to desecrate their land.

Displaying considerable imagination, the Boxers invented every manner of tale to build their following. Among the accusations was the claim that Chinese children taken into Christian orphanages were mutilated and their hearts were gouged out. Other stories told of Christians sending home entire ships full of human eyes, blood, and female nipples. Some said they needed the eyes, especially from children, for photography. Locomotives, believed to be dragons, were set on fire. Telegraph lines were torn down, because wind whistling through the wires sounded like tormented spirits.

Missionaries who had for decades made deeper and deeper inroads into China were the prime target of the Boxers. They made themselves unpopular by frequently banning converts from participating in local festivals and forbidding them to practice ancestor worship. As one Chinese scholar put it, "As soon as a man becomes a Christian, he really ceases to be a Chinaman." Dr. Robert Coltman, professor of surgery at the Imperial University in Peking and correspondent for *The Chicago Record,* reported that missionaries antagonized locals by blindly supporting Christian converts in legal proceedings. Many Chinese took advantage of religious loyalty to attack people they had personal grudges against, he wrote.[11] The empress didn't hide her disdain. "These Chinese Christians are the worst people in China. They rob the poor country people of their land and property, and the missionaries of course always protect them in order to get a share themselves."[12]

Worst of all, they were coming in greater and greater numbers. By 1900, some 850 nuns and priests, mostly French, looked over a flock of 700,000 Catholic Chinese. Representing the Protestant faiths were 2,800 American and British missionaries who had converted 85,000 Chinese.[13] Throughout the United States, churches and community centers echoed with impassioned speeches about the souls to be saved in China. The Student Volunteer Movement for Foreign Missions became part of the YMCA after 1887, and soon there were chapters on nearly every American campus. Yale sent three of the loudest evangelical voices who would ever go to China, including Henry Luce, father of the founder of *Time, Fortune,* and *Life* magazines.

By mid-May 1900, the uprising appeared to be spinning dangerously out of control. Reports reached the French legation that sixty Chinese Catholics had been murdered in Kaolo, a village ninety miles from Peking, and their bodies thrown down a well. Weeks later, the Boxers attacked Chinese Christians in Peking itself. Homes were burned and shops looted.[14]

For increasingly nervous foreigners, the only safe places for retreat were the diplomatic communities in Peking and Tientsin, where foreign troops were stationed to protect the compounds.

The diplomatic compound at Tientsin was strangely at odds with its surroundings, a quaint English town in the middle of China. Church steeples soared above leafy streets lined with handsome brick municipal buildings, hotels, and a well-stocked library. English tea, French champagne, American crackers, and month-old newspapers lined the store shelves. The British had even built a racecourse outside the city where expatriates in crisp suits and floor-length pleated dresses gathered on Saturday afternoons to place bets and sip drinks served by smartly dressed Chinese barmen. Fringed by the Pei Ho River and surrounded by a mud wall, it was a substantial village, covering an area somewhat less than five hundred acres and built a good mile away from the Chinese city to stay clear of the odor of human excrement, sweat, and strange food.

Yet as spring approached, the normally teeming streets quickly thinned as Chinese servants, shopkeepers, and nannies all vanished, hoping to melt into the general population and mask their association with the foreign community. Tales of Boxer atrocities against foreigners and anyone associated with them had spread rapidly. Rumors flew that they planned to lay siege to the compound where 800 civilians and 2,500 soldiers from Europe, the United States, and Japan huddled.

Among them was Herbert Hoover, a freshly minted Stanford University engineering graduate who would one day be the thirty-first president of the United States. He and his wife, Lou, had sailed for China the day after their wedding in Monterey, California, on February 10, 1899, for what they hoped would be an adventurous working honeymoon. Hoover, handsome and athletic, had accepted a job as the chief mining engineer at the Chinese Engineering and Mining Company, tasked with finding new deposits of iron and, the investors hoped, gold. He explored throughout northern China and Mongolia, riding a shaggy Manchurian pony and leading a team of mules that carried prospecting equipment. Yet by spring even Hoover had retreated to the relative safety of the city.[15]

He arrived none too soon. By June 1900, some twenty-five thousand Boxers, soon joined by another twenty-five thousand imperial troops, had completely surrounded Tientsin and begun firing on anything that moved. Chinese artillery crews would rain sixty thousand shells on the compound in the coming weeks, punching holes in some of the squat buildings and reducing others to rubble.[16] Peering over walls of the compound, Chinese sharpshooters picked off the unwary, screeching "sha, sha, sha," or "kill, kill, kill." The club where expatriates relaxed with a beer or gin and tonic had been transformed into a makeshift hospital, with a single doctor tending the wounded lining the floor. As the empress observed to her leading adviser, Prince Tuan, "The foreigners are like fish in a stew pan."[17]

The Boxer Rebellion was a horrifying turn of events for McKinley. Not only did he worry over the safety of Americans trapped in Peking and Tientsin, but America's economic and political standing in the Far East were at risk. Trade with China quickly nosedived. Cotton textile exports to China fell from $10.3 million in 1899 to $5.2 million in 1900. In no time, several American textile companies were on the verge of closing, and fears spread that the entire industry would slip back into recession.[18]

Most worrying for McKinley was that the Boxer uprising threatened to destroy the Open Door policy and all that it stood for. It was only a matter of time until American rivals—especially Russia—sent troops to the rescue, and they were sure to use any victory as a pretext to dismember China. Indeed, that June, he and the rest of the administration watched in alarm as Moscow dispatched 4,000 troops from Port Arthur to Peking. It was an appropriate number for a rescue mission, yet rumors circulated in Washington that the force was just the beginning of a deployment that could include a staggering 200,000 soldiers.[19] Speculation swirled that Japan, with the support of its ally England, would send 20,000 to 30,000 of its soldiers through north China to Peking. German blood was up, too, after their minister to Peking, Baron Ketteler, was dragged from his carriage and stabbed to death in the streets outside the foreign compound.

Should the United States intervene? American troops, shoulder to shoulder with the Europeans, killing Chinese—it wasn't how Americans saw themselves. Americans were special, above the colonial-style butchery that Europeans employed to keep their subjects in line. What's more, elections were looming in 1900. Hay could not realistically contemplate sending so much as a bugler to China, not with an election only months away. Eager to paint McKinley as a Midwestern Queen Victoria, William Jennings Bryan and his supporters watched the administration's unfolding dilemma with a measure of delight. The prospect of American troops sailing off to fight in yet another Asian country would be delicious campaign fodder.

There likewise were questions about whether the United States had the manpower for the job even if it wanted to get involved. MacArthur was already warning that Hay should not even think about taking troops from his command in the Philippines. No wonder Hay would confide to a friend, "I need not tell you the lunatic difficulties under which we labor. . . . If I looked at things as you do in the light of reason, history and mathematics, I should go off after lunch and die."[20] Henry Adams teased his friend Hay by writing, "Your open door is already off its hinges not six months old. What kind of door can you rig up?"[21]

Hay would rig up a second, more strenuous attempt to bind the global powers down with diplomacy. The Open Door notes of September 1899 had, he realized, conferred upon Washington at least a modest role in filling the leadership vacuum among the great powers in China. He would try to make use of that political capital to again bring order to the unfolding chaos, and with any luck, further solidify America's position in the Orient.

On July 3, 1900, Hay issued a circular to the other powers, warning against the temptation to use the Boxer Rebellion as a pretext to declare war on China itself. It was United States policy, he said, to "preserve Chinese territorial and administrative entity." He went on to affirm the "principle of equal and impartial trade in all parts of the Chinese Empire."[22] Hay didn't even expect or request that others reply. Yet, for many of the same reasons that the September 1899 Open Door notes had been a success—the great powers wanted to avoid a nasty confrontation in far-off China—Hay's second gambit worked. Russia pledged that it was opposed to dismembering China. German foreign minister Bernhard von Bülow similarly told a Bundesrat committee that the government sought to work in concert with other nations.[23] On July 14, a surprised Hay was able to write to journalist and diplomat Whitelaw Reid that "the attitude of all the powers is, on the surface at least, the same as ours."[24]

What lay beneath the surface of European intentions, however, remained a very real American obsession. The Yellow Sea along the China coast was starting to look like Britain's famous Cowes Week of yacht races, so many were the naval ships that were lying at anchor. Some had already moved up the Pei Ho River and bombarded Chinese forts. The Europeans may have made all the right noises about dealing with China after the Boxers were put down, but Hay and McKinley feared otherwise. Should one country even hint that it might like a few extra acres of Chinese territory, the others would dive in. Ultimately, there was only one way for the United States to save China and its markets and that was to secure a seat at the conference table when the Boxer Rebellion was over.

Despite considerable hand-wringing in the cabinet, and against the pleadings of MacArthur, a detachment of marines, some 104 officers and men, was ordered to sail from Manila to the China coast on June 14, 1900, the first of what were expected to be 2,000 American troops.[25]

———

Trusting in luck as much as their weapons, the marines landed at a rickety old dock on the Pei Ho River and set off immediately for their first objective—to rescue the foreigners trapped twenty-seven miles inland at Tientsin. It would take the marines, lacking even basic maps of the area, two attempts to liberate the foreign compound from thousands of Chinese. The first failed miserably when Boxers hiding in trenches outside the city walls sprung upon the disoriented troops. In a sight that the Chinese had seldom seen before or since, Americans and Russians ended the day side by side, running for their lives.[26] The second attempt, made several days later, was more like what foreign troops fighting in China expected. This time, joined by two thousand Germans, British, Japanese, and Italians, the marines were almost able to waltz into the compound, the Boxers having pulled back to defend the old part of town. Hoover rated their rescue as one of the happiest moments of his life. "We climbed on the roof of the highest warehouse to get a glimpse," he wrote in his memoirs. "We saw them coming over the plain. They were American marines and Welsh Fusiliers. I do not remember a more satisfying musical performance."[27]

Tientsin, however, was really only a warm-up for the main performance weeks later in Peking. Moving down the dusty road from Tientsin, a liberating force of twenty thousand troops, including two thousand Americans, looked like they had stepped off the pages of a military guidebook—the French in their traditional red and blue, blond Germans in pointed helmets, Italian Bersaglieri with tossing plumes, Bengal cavalry on Arabian stallions, turbaned Sikhs, and Royal Welsh Fusiliers wearing a threefold cascade of ribbon down the backs of their necks. The Americans, by contrast, took pride in their almost studied casualness. Few wore complete uniforms, and many wore articles of Chinese clothing. Officers of other countries snickered at such lack of discipline. One German officer was heard to remark, "That's an army? Why with the Berlin Fire Brigade I could conquer the whole of America."[28]

The morning of the attack on Peking began just as one would expect from such a collection of egos. While troops of the other nations slept, the Russians had tiptoed out of camp and rushed the last few miles toward the city, determined to be first. As soldiers of Japan, the United States, England, and France rubbed the sleep out of their eyes and put the coffee on, they realized what their supposed allies had done. In fact, they could hear faintly in the distance the Russian cannons. With much cursing and barking of orders, the Japanese hastily followed suit. The mad dash for the capital was on.

Scaling the thirty-foot stone walls that surrounded Peking, American troops were among the first to enter the capital, even beating the Russians, who waited for the gates to be opened. Still, to reach the foreign compound, they faced a bloody house-to-house battle through a warren of winding, unfamiliar streets. Behind every cart, in every window, atop every roof, a Boxer waited with a well-aimed shot, until the marines wheeled in powerful cannons that easily reduced the flimsy structures protecting the Boxers to tangles of shattered masonry and splinters. By that afternoon, the troops had secured the foreign compound and, with the joyous civilians who had been trapped there, set about consuming the last of the community's alcohol and hunting down Boxers. Only a few days later, hundreds of captured Chinese began what was a daily procession from a makeshift prison to a sword-wielding executioner who lopped off heads with assembly-line efficiency.

25

"*AVANTI!*"

On warm days in the spring of 1900, a thirty-one-year-old Italian-American immigrant named Gaetano Bresci would gather up his wife and three-year-old daughter and head out into the woods not far from his home in Paterson, New Jersey. The two girls delighted in the crisp country air and amused themselves picking flowers. As they clambered about, or relaxed on a fallen tree, they could hear the sharp regular crack of gunfire as Bresci worked on his marksmanship.[1]

Bresci had lived in the United States for six years, most recently in a boardinghouse with his family. When not at his job as a silk weaver, he was an avid reader of local anarchist newspapers, including *L'aurora*,[2] and regularly attended Wednesday evening meetings of the anarchist Gruppo Diritto all'Esistenza, or Group of the Right Existence. Among the many grievances that the community dwelled on during those meetings were the miserable conditions in the old country. And no villain was more sinister than Italian king Umberto I.

Umberto had long been an unpopular figure among radicals. In

1878, an anarchist by the name of Giovanni Passanante had attempted to murder the monarch during a parade in Naples. The attack failed, thanks to the king's own quick sword work, and Passanante was sentenced to solitary confinement for life, his cell four and a half feet high and lacking sanitation. Not surprisingly, he later died in a mental institution.

Public hatred of the king, especially among the working class, reached a boiling point in the spring of 1898 when Umberto brutally quashed riots over the rising price of bread by placing much of Italy under military control. Milan, under the command of General Fiorenzo Bava-Beccaris, saw the worst bloodshed. Faced with one violent protest, the general ordered his troops to lower their cannons to zero degrees declination and fire point-blank into a crowd, killing more than a hundred people. Rather than condemn the act, Umberto gave his general a medal for putting down the riot.

In far-off New Jersey, radicals among the thousands of recent Italian immigrants read of such events with rage. Those back home, they believed, had neither the will nor the means to stand up to the tyrant. The job had to be theirs. At one of their meetings that spring, the small collection of anarchists solemnly drew lots to determine who would carry out the attack, and Bresci won. After perfecting his skills with a gun, he bade his wife and daughter good-bye and set off for Italy in what all recognized was going to be a one-way trip.

On July 29, 1900, King Umberto had just seated himself in his royal carriage in Monza where he had been distributing athletic prizes when a tall, roughly dressed young man pushed his way through the crowd. Before anyone had time to react, Bresci drew the pistol that he had trained with in New Jersey and fired three shots into the stunned king at a range of not more than two yards. Umberto stared blankly at his attacker for a moment, slumped onto the shoulder of his aide-de-camp, and shouted *"Avanti!"* to the driver, who sped off.[3] He died forty-five minutes later.

Escape had never figured in Bresci's plan, and he was immediately apprehended. The result of the trial was likewise a foregone conclusion. He was sentenced to life in prison, the first seven years to be spent in solitary confinement. Alone in his cell, the isolation playing horribly on his mental state, Bresci used his thumbnail to carve the word "vengeance" in the wall. He also spent time contemplating ways to kill himself. Using a towel, he formed a noose and strung it through a ceiling grate. Guards later found his body hanging from it.

In New York, Emma Goldman read of the assassination with approval. "King Humbert was justly put to death by a brave man, who dared to act for the good of his fellow-men, among whom he considered himself but a unit in a universe," she told a meeting on East Fourth Street. And she said one more thing. She would hate to be in the shoes of a monarch, or of President McKinley, due to the "fickleness of the masses."[4]

From his easy chair on the farm in Ohio, Czolgosz also read of the assassination. He carefully clipped a newspaper account of the story and placed it in his wallet.

26

THE AMERICAN CENTURY

The president awoke on January 1, 1900, to find a fresh blanket of snow covering Washington. It was going to be a busy day. Inside the Blue Room, he and Ida would hold their customary New Year's greeting. Despite the cold, some two thousand people would queue around the White House, stomping their feet and blowing warm air on their hands, heartened as they drew nearer by the melodies of the Marine Corps band, resplendent in their red dress uniforms.

It had been a difficult holiday season for the president. At age fifty-seven, he was reminded of his mortality when Vice President Hobart grew progressively sicker with a heart ailment. Ever loyal, McKinley had visited Hobart often and received frequent notes on his condition until Hobart died in late November.

Ida also felt unwell again and the president seemed preoccupied with her, agonizing over the choice of a Christmas gift. The high-maintenance First Lady had always enjoyed expensive presents, but this year she protested against anything fancy. Realizing the president's

anxiety, his steward William Sinclair went out on his own to Galt's jewelry store and purchased a beautiful vase and a jewel-studded picture
frame in which Katie's photograph was placed. Ida loved them.[1]

Were it not for these emotional weights, McKinley's mood would
have been buoyant. The economy was firing on all cylinders, the primary goal of his presidency and a tremendous success. Many business
leaders had come to share the view of James T. Woodward, president
of the New York Clearing House Association, when he wrote in *The
New York Times* that the United States economy was the envy of the
world. "The year 1899 will stand marked in our national history as a
period of unprecedented commercial and financial prosperity. . . . All
trade reports show that our factories are taxed to the utmost capacity
in filling their orders; the railroads are unable to cope with the traffic
that is offered . . . on every hand we hear of a record breaking business
and at constantly increasing prices, while wages of employees are also
being increased."[2]

Relief washed over the Midwestern states as prices for farm
products—cotton, wheat, corn, beef, and pork—climbed to their highest levels in years as demand picked up. Farmers who had scrimped just
to survive began to acquire simple luxuries such as pianos, bicycles,
and lace curtains. Indeed, around the country, people were purchasing
items they never had imagined they could own, including Kodak cam-
eras, phonographs, Hoover vacuums, Detroit gas ranges, Whitman's
chocolates, and washing machines.[3]

Amazing new inventions were changing how people lived, starting
with the miracle of electricity. Electric streetcars were increasingly
common in big cities. Middle-class families stood in wonder as workmen installed electric lights in their homes, and electric automobiles
began to appear on city streets—at least the paved ones with a level
grade. Automobiles with internal combustion engines made their
noisy debut as well, much to the disgust of others on the road who
hated their noise and smoke. "Get a horse!" was a common curse
around the byways.

In the fields of commerce, medicine, and architecture, the United
States seemed to be outstripping the rest of the world. New York was
challenging London as the center of global finance. Dr. Walter Reed
proved that mosquitoes carried the yellow fever virus, a discovery that

eventually saved untold lives in the American South and the country's new colonial possessions. Visitors to New York streamed to lower Manhattan to see the Park Row Building, which, at twenty-nine stories, was the world's tallest structure.[4]

Leisure activities grew in popularity as well. Railroads offered residents of the North a chance to escape the snow and cold and travel to Florida and California—an astounding feat for people who never could have imagined feeling the warm sun on their faces in January. College football games attracted large crowds, first to Ivy League contests but increasingly to large state universities. In a shocking move, the University of Michigan lured away Princeton's coach Langdon Lea for the startling high salary of $3,500 a year. Professional golfers and baseball players became household names.[5]

Most important for the president, the expansionist foreign policy was finally paying off. Exports soared as hoped. The total value of American products sold abroad had climbed to $1.4 billion from $883 million in 1896.[6] The gains were especially impressive for machinery exports, which had surged to $78 million by 1900 from $29 million in 1896.[7] The total value of American agricultural implements advanced as well, more than doubling to more than $2.6 million in 1900 from $1.22 million in 1896.

The country would soon be able to recite these statistics almost by heart. McKinley's campaign staff would see to that. The numbers, the president could point to with pride, were reason alone that he should be reelected that November.

As in 1896, the 1900 national election boiled down to a test of wills over which subject would dominate the debate. For McKinley, the choice was obvious: the wealth creation of a recovering economy. Campaigning for "four more years of the full dinner pail," he touted an economic rebound that had started almost from the day he set foot in the White House. Campaign posters depicted the president astride a dollar coin the size of a manhole cover lifted aloft by happy workers under the slogan PROSPERITY AT HOME, AND PRESTIGE ABROAD.

Bryan, on the other hand, seemed unable to move beyond the last campaign. He remained bogged down in the gold versus silver debate—a puzzling fixation as most voters had forgotten about it once the economy was improving. And just as in 1896, Bryan attacked McKinley as a stooge of big business. This risked flopping as well, until the Democrats found two compelling arguments to help flesh out the unflattering portrait they attempted to paint.

McKinley, Bryan argued, had stood idly by while American businesses grew to fantastic proportions. Free competition had fueled the U.S. economy, yet giant trusts—corporate groupings that monopolize their markets—threatened competition in many industries. If somebody didn't act soon, he argued, companies might one day become so powerful that the government would never be able to rein them in.

Trusts were not invented during the McKinley administration—the Standard Oil Trust was established in 1882—but he made life easier for them. According to one estimate, four new major industrial combinations were created in 1895. That number rose to 16 in 1898 and jumped to 63 in 1899. Another 21 were created in 1900, and 19 in 1901.[8] And it wasn't just their number that grew, but their strength. Some of these new conglomerates could conquer 70 percent, 80 percent, and even 90 percent of their markets. Many companies became so powerful they remain household names to this day, giants such as DuPont, Eastman Kodak, International Harvester, and Otis Elevator. Others, overtaken by technological advances, did not—American Ice, for one.

McKinley was very much of two minds about what if anything should be done. In order to boost exports, the United States needed big companies capable of slugging it out overseas. What would be the point of creating a level playing field in global commerce if the American government benched its best players? What's more, large conglomerations seemed to be a natural creation of the market economy in which so many so fervently believed. And contrary to what the critics claimed, there was evidence that prices of products made by industrial combinations had actually come down, not gone up, as populist politicians said they would.

Yet for many Americans, there was something inherently wrong about so much power concentrated in the hands of so few. Competition was one of the founding principles of the country—the means by which companies and individuals were pushed to improve themselves. Government could not sit idly by and watch it be destroyed.

The two sides to the argument seemed to paralyze McKinley. After he met one evening with his friend Charles Dawes, then serving as comptroller of the currency, his secretary George Cortelyou recorded that "the president said he didn't know" but that "the great need in such matters was protection to the companies as well as to consult the interests of the people at large." In public, McKinley often as not side-stepped the trust issue, urging Congress or the states to take action but providing few ideas of his own.

Compelling though Bryan's attacks on the McKinley–big business axis were, he saved his heaviest criticism for McKinley's foreign adventures, the theme that had so dominated the country the last four years.

Democrats quickly made the Philippines Exhibit A in their argument that McKinley's imperial policies were un-American and driven by the needs of his corporate friends. In the June issue of the *North American Review,* Bryan wrote, "The doctrine that a people can be kept in a state of perpetual vassalage, owing allegiance to the flag, but having no voice in the government, is entirely at variance with the principles upon which this government has been founded. An imperial policy nullifies every principle set forth in the Declaration of Independence."[9]

McKinley's connections with Wall Street, Democrats fumed, was what drove the nation's unethical foreign policy. "The purpose behind the imperial policy is the extension of trade . . . The man who says that an imperial policy will pay must be prepared to place a pecuniary value upon the soldiers who have already lost their lives in the Philippines or have become insane from the effects of the climate, and upon the soldiers who will be sacrificed in future wars of conquest. The Republican Party . . . now coolly calculates the value of human life measured by the Oriental trade."[10]

In attempting to play the imperialism card, Bryan was taking a major risk. Americans still tingled with the thought of their flag flying over distant corners of the globe. The moral and even legal questions that the Democrats raised could still be answered by the belief that God had given his blessing to America's new place in the world. And running a close second behind the Almighty in the hearts of many

Americans was the man who seemed to be flirting with joining McKinley's ticket.

The hottest political question in the spring and summer of 1900 was whether Roosevelt, beloved hero of San Juan Hill, would join McKinley as vice president. McKinley, who might have been expected to show at least a casual interest in the selection of his number two, had rather bizarrely checked out of the decision-making process, largely leaving it up to delegates attending the Republican National Convention in Philadelphia in June. It was likewise far from clear if the mercurial Roosevelt even wanted the job.

Now serving as governor of New York, Roosevelt harbored complex views about the vice presidency. He went out of his way to claim the job didn't offer enough to a man of his ambition and energy. He could accomplish more, he said, remaining as governor of America's most populous state, whereas "in the Vice-presidency I could do nothing. I am a comparatively young man yet and I like to work. I do not like to be a figurehead."[11]

Roosevelt's protests became so frequent, and so unsolicited, that many began to wonder if he might have an ulterior motive. Could he, in a clumsy, pesky way, be trying to get himself drafted into the job? In May he traveled to Washington to announce that he didn't want to join the ticket—an odd journey as no one had asked him. Writing to a friend, John Hay could hardly contain his smirk: "Teddy has been here: have you heard of it? It was more fun than a goat. He came down with a somber resolution thrown on his strenuous brow to let McKinley and Hanna know once and for all that he would not be Vice-President, and he found to his stupefaction that nobody in Washington except Platt [Orville Platt, Republican from Connecticut] had ever dreamed of such a thing."[12]

Yet Roosevelt's non-campaign was on a roll. In his own flamboyant style, he attended the Republican convention, even though Henry Cabot Lodge had asked him not to do so unless he genuinely sought the nomination. While other delegates wore hard straw hats in keeping with summertime fashion, Roosevelt made a point of wandering through hotel lobbies crowded with delegates wearing a broad-brimmed black felt chapeau that looked like what the Rough Riders wore. Some Republicans dubbed it his "acceptance hat." Mark Hanna, no fan of Roosevelt, was appalled. "Don't any of you realize that there's only one life between this madman and the Presidency?"[13]

Despite his knack for irritating McKinley's senior staff, Roosevelt made sense for the ticket. He was from New York, a state the Republicans had long wrestled with. And he was popular in the West, a region considered crucial for the election. It was a combination that, like it or not, conventional delegates could not ignore. Many genuinely enthusiastic, a few holding their noses, they lent their votes to a "Draft Roosevelt" campaign that he demurely accepted.

McKinley could have found no better antidote to Bryan's charisma. Roosevelt told a New York reporter that he was "as strong as a bull moose" and set off on the campaign trail that McKinley refused to tread. Everywhere Bryan scored a good showing, Roosevelt would arrive with an even better one.

Of course, it didn't hurt that Bryan really didn't stand a chance. With the economy booming and the nation's global reputation rising, protests against McKinley's imperial polices or his equivocating over the trusts held zero appeal. Other than socialists and anarchists, who were themselves widely detested, most Americans looked up to the wealthy as hard workers who were living, breathing proof of the American dream. When ballots were cast on November 6, 1900, the Republicans scored their biggest victory since 1872. Out of 447 electoral votes, McKinley pulled down 292. It would be more than a decade before the Democrats would recover enough to put one of their own in the White House.

WORDS THAT BURN

Most afternoons on the family farm, Leon Czolgosz would take a break from his idling for a half-mile walk to the village store. There he would beat a direct path toward the newspaper rack and eagerly scan the headlines. Thumbing through the day's editions, he would read the optimistic articles proclaiming the resurrection of the robust American economy and praising the president's policies. Other headlines, too, would have caught his attention. As a student of social issues, Czolgosz possessed a natural interest in the election of 1900. Though he was hardly a McKinley man, he took advantage of discounted train transport to Canton, only a short distance to the south, and joined the crowds that were again marching up Market Avenue North to see the candidate in person.

Having spent an afternoon listening to McKinley, Czolgosz might have been itching to get out of Canton and get home. Yet, home was becoming a difficult place to be. The relaxing, lazy life that he had built there was coming under attack from the lady of the house, his father's second wife. Catarina had had enough of her stepson's malingering and wasn't afraid to tell him so. Against such accusations, Czolgosz oddly made no attempt to defend himself; rather, he simply ran. When she was in the house, he refused to eat with the family, sullenly dining alone upstairs in his room on meals that consisted of milk from the barn, bread, and cake. When his stepmother was gone, Czolgosz became more sociable and might even cook for the family. But as soon as she returned, he would bolt, once leaving a frying pan of sizzling fish to burn rather than spend one second with her in the kitchen.

Czolgosz's siblings agreed, at least in principle, with Catarina, convinced their brother's ailment was nothing more than a severe case of self-pity. To one sister-in-law, Czolgosz showed no outward signs of illness other than that he sometimes "would spit out great chunks"— apparently coughing up phlegm. "If you said anything to him about his sickness he would get mad."[1] She would later join the chorus that he was "a rather lazy but nice boy." Fueling the perception that he was a malingerer, Czolgosz developed the strange habit of falling asleep at odd times. His brothers and sisters taunted him with names like "old woman" or "grandmother." To these jabs, Czolgosz displayed little sense of humor and would bitterly snap back. His brother Waldek encouraged him to go to a hospital but Czolgosz refused: "There is no place in the hospital for poor people; if you have lots of money you will get well taken care of!"[2]

Feeling harassed at home, and still harboring an interest in the broader world, Czolgosz increasingly took perplexing and mysterious trips. For days at a time, he would disappear without providing any explanation of his travels. The family, who quickly became used to his oddball nature, stopped asking questions and the young man was allowed to come and go as he pleased. The trips were for "meetings,"[3] Czolgosz explained.

The afternoon of May 5, 1901, Emma Goldman prepared to give what seemed to be a routine speech at Cleveland's Memorial Hall, organizing her notes and surveying the usual police detail that tracked her engagements. From across the room, a young man made his way toward her and began leafing through some pamphlets and books that were on sale. Noticing Goldman, Leon Czolgosz walked over and asked, "Will you suggest something for me to read?" He was, he explained, working in Akron and had to leave the lecture before she would finish.

Goldman later remembered him as "very young, a mere youth, of medium height, well built and carrying himself very erect. But it was his face that held me, a most sensitive face, with a delicate pink complexion; a handsome face made doubly so by his curly golden hair. . . ." After chatting briefly, Goldman suggested a couple of books and the two parted.[4] "Strength," she said, "showed in his large blue eyes."

A few moments later, Goldman began her address in a strong resonant voice that hinted slightly of a German accent. She exhorted the crowd to note that alone among radical ideologies, anarchism promised to liberate downtrodden workers. "We do not favor the Socialist idea of converting men and women into mere producing machines under the eye of a paternal government. We go to the opposite extreme and demand the fullest and most complete liberty for each and every person to work out his own salvation upon any lines that he pleases so long as he does not interfere with the happiness of others."

Anarchists were opposed to bloodshed to achieve their ends, she told the crowd. "Some believe that we should first obtain the force and let the intelligence and education come afterwards. Nothing could be more fallacious. If we get the education and intelligence first among the people the power will come to us without a struggle."

But she next stated that it was understandable that some anarchists carried out violent attacks. Some men were so consumed with passion that they could not simply stand idly by and watch wrongs being committed.[5]

Goldman's remarks that evening overwhelmed Czolgosz. He had been interested in social revolution for years, and apparently had been introduced to the idea of the propaganda of the deed long ago. But the philosophy had never been presented like this. Her words had, he later said, burned in his head with such intensity that it made his skull hurt. Goldman's eloquence and stage manners surely had something to do with it. When she was on her game, few could hold an audience as well. But maybe more important was the state in which he now heard them.

Czolgosz had for years allowed himself to slip deeper and deeper into an emotional and psychological hole on the farm. It was a downward spiral that he was surely well aware of—he possessed a solid work ethic and was smart enough to realize what was happening. Yet he hadn't known how to pull himself out. He found in Goldman's remarks the inspiration and the method of escape. He hadn't worked out how exactly, and probably only vaguely understood what it meant, but Czolgosz seemed from this night on to have resolved to pursue the life of radical social revolutionary.

Among the publications that Czolgosz likely perused that evening—he would later speak of frequently reading it—was a small newspaper titled *Free Society*. The country's leading radical journal in the later part of the 1890s, *Free Society* was the brainchild of Abe Isaak and his wife, Mary, a pair of pacifist Mennonites who had fled czarist Russia in 1889. Together, they had first attempted to forge a simple agrarian life in distant Portland, Oregon. Halted by police for their paper's radical ideas, however, they began publishing in Chicago, that center of radical American thought.

Curled up on his bed back at home or outside under a shade tree, away from prying family eyes, Czolgosz might have flipped through pages that in any given issue offered a caustic commentary on the powers that ruled the country. One front-page contribution, for example, was written in the form of a poem noting that even monkeys had sense enough not to elect leaders who would inevitably rob and cheat the others.

Though less likely to be the object of a satirical poet—possibly for lack of suitable words that rhymed with "McKinley"—the president, too, was a popular subject for *Free Society*'s writers. He had become, in the imagery of one author, self-appointed royalty whose aim was the enrichment of members of his court. "Mr. McKinley is more an absolute monarch than King Edward," the paper said in its May 5, 1901, issue, stating that Mark Hanna was McKinley's Cardinal Richelieu, a reference to the minister of France's King Louis XIII. "The real rulers today are neither kings nor presidents, but capitalists and police."

Large concentrations of commercial power, readers of *Free Society* were told, lay behind McKinley's more sensational pursuit of a foreign empire. The president's ambitious plans for Cuba, his handling of the Boxer uprising, his efforts to thrust a foreign government upon native peoples, all were ready-made fodder for the paper. And then there was the deepening military quagmire in the Philippines. "More than 3,500 Americans have perished in the Philippines in order to carry out an after-thought of the emperor at Washington by subduing a race who innocently imagined they might set up their own brand of political authority," wrote one columnist in a front-page story in June 30, 1901. "The earth is for the strong. And so the government is backed by the majority in carrying out the doctrine that might is right."[6]

In Europe, heads of state had been killed for transgressions less egregious than these. Should the president of the United States suffer a similar fate? On this, *Free Society* was largely opposed, though for purely pragmatic reasons. Radicals, one article said, could do worse than what they were up against in the United States. "The anarchists are treated with sufficiently gross injustice even in this country. But they are at least allowed the right of conducting peaceful propaganda and the consequence is that McKinley, hated and despised though he is, needs no body guard to protect him from revolutionaries." The paper went on: "No anarchist wants McKinley assassinated. He is of more use to us right where he is, an object lesson of the worst results of representative government. Any fool who should kill the paltry Napoleon would be the deadliest enemy of anarchism."[7]

"SURRENDER OR BE KILLED"

Brigadier General Frederick Funston, a ruddy-faced, redheaded son of the Kansas plains, was attending to paperwork in his Manila office one evening in early February 1901 when a bedraggled insurgent who had just been captured was brought before him. Dressed in rags and a wide-brimmed straw hat, the rebel had been caught carrying letters from homesick fighters to friends and relatives around the islands. Among these Funston's staff had discovered a few intriguing names. Some of the correspondence he carried was signed by one "Colon de Magdalo," a false name known to have been used by Aguinaldo. Desperate to know more, Funston's men subjected the courier to what were later referred to as "forceful" means—likely the water cure—to flesh out the story.[1] In due time, the rebel revealed that Aguinaldo was holed up in a tiny isolated village in northeast Luzon called Palanan. Funston began to ponder the possibilities.

The intriguing clue about Aguinaldo was the latest piece of good news for the Americans in the Philippines. McKinley's reelection the previous autumn had delivered as devastating a blow to the insurgents as any they had suffered on the battlefield. Now, there appeared no hope that the United States would leave the islands anytime soon. Rebel troops either quit fighting or surrendered. In December, some two thousand insurgents gave up all at once, an unprecedentedly high figure. At the same time, the new American governor in the Philippines, a portly former judge from Ohio, William Howard Taft, was doing an admirable job of using a "Policy of Attraction" to make life with the Americans seem like a better alternative to remaining in the jungle and being shot at.[2] Spain's centuries-old legal system was replaced with one modeled on American jurisprudence. Infrastructure projects were begun. Soon shiploads of fresh-faced American college kids arrived, eager to start work as teachers and nurses. Like a proud father witnessing his baby's first steps, Taft watched on February 22, 1901— George Washington's birthday—when crowds gathered in Manila's big park, the Luneta, for the formal birth of an American-backed political party. As brass bands played and the American flag flew overhead, Pardo de Tavera, the founder of the Partido Federal, told crowds "I see the day near at hand . . . when it shall transpire that George Washington will not simply be the glory of the American continent, but also our glory, because he will be the father of the American world, in which we shall feel ourselves completely united and assimilated."[3]

Fortified with whiskey and coffee, Funston and two aides stayed up until the wee hours working to decipher coded letters confiscated from the courier that might corroborate his story. The pattern they discovered was simple, one that substituted numbers for the letters of the alphabet in reverse order. As they banged the correspondence out on a typewriter, their tired eyes brightened with the realization that not only did the story check out, but that Aguinaldo was in need of troops.[4] It was all Funston, who loved adventure and the notoriety that came with it, needed to know, and he set about devising an audacious plan to capture the rebel.

The problem that most vexed Funston was how to get enough men to carry out the raid without being detected. All trails leading to his hideout in Palanan would surely be monitored by Negrito and Ilongot tribesmen, who knew the territory and would swiftly alert the insurgents. American troops would not be able to travel a mile without being discovered. Turning it over in his mind, Funston was struck by Aguinaldo's call for four hundred men. If Aguinaldo needed troops, that's what he would give him.

The "troops" would be Macabebe scouts, indigenous people who, because of their uncertain historical origin, had always been considered outcasts in the islands and were loyal to the Americans since George Dewey first landed at Manila. Lazaro Segovia, who had fought on both sides of the insurrection before joining the Americans—as a Spanish officer and a member of the Army of Liberation—would play the role of a senior insurgent officer. Funston and four other Americans would pose as prisoners.

The plan was as dangerous as it was clever. The expedition would land near the village of Casiguran, twenty-seven miles from the nearest American-held territory at Baler. They would have to march more than one hundred miles through unknown terrain solidly loyal to Aguinaldo. The odds were clearly not in their favor. Upon hearing the plan, Arthur MacArthur, Jr., confessed he didn't think he would ever see Funston again.[5]

Put ashore in the stormy early morning darkness of March 14, 1901, the group of eighty-nine men began their march on Aguinaldo's lair.[6] For more than a week, they trudged along the beach and through rice paddies and traversed mountainsides under a canopy of rattan, bamboo, palms, and giant ferns. Carrying little food of their own, the men subsisted on dishes of moldy rice and stews of snail, limpets, and tiny fish—"a revolting mess" in the words of one.

Yet the group could so convincingly tell their story that they were without reservation treated as rebels. Villages loyal to Aguinaldo offered them lodging, and when word reached the insurgent leader that the group was looking for him, he dispatched scouts to guide them directly to his headquarters. There was but one complication. Aguinaldo's scouts insisted that the American "prisoners" remain behind.

Cut off from the Americans who were supposed to give the orders, Segovia and his men arrived at Aguinaldo's headquarters, a village of eighty or so thatched huts bounded by a river on one side and the jungle on all others, and prepared the final act of their charade. Marching into the town square, the men presented arms, paid their respects to the blue, red, and white Philippine flag hanging from a high pole, and did their best to appear friendly. Somewhat nervously, for he didn't know how his men would take to being left in close proximity to their enemy, Segovia climbed the steps of Aguinaldo's headquarters and was introduced to the most wanted man in the Philippines.

Dressed in a starched khaki uniform with Spanish riding boots, his dark hair in a pompadour over a high wide brow, Aguinaldo engaged Segovia and another spy, Hilario Tal Placido, in friendly conversation. Going through the motions of exchanging pleasantries, Segovia's mind remained fixated on his men in the square, where the slightest provocation might trigger a confrontation and kill his chances of nabbing Aguinaldo, now so close at hand.

When the meeting ended, Segovia made his way outside where his anxious men, their eyes pleading for permission to attack, watched for a signal. Segovia raised his hat and shouted, "Now is the time, Macabebes! Give it to them." Before the perplexed rebel honor guard realized they had been duped, the Macabebes delivered a fusillade at nearly point-blank range. Segovia, his pistol drawn, spun and ran back inside to find Aguinaldo, "You are our prisoner. We are not insurgents, we are Americans! Surrender or be killed." Aguinaldo, pale and with tears in his eyes, could only ask, "Is this not some joke?"

Funston, who by now had tricked his guards into bringing him to the village, arrived just as Segovia was springing his trap. Assuming command of the group, Funston led the troops and Aguinaldo down the mountain trail and to the beach where, according to plan, the USS *Vicksburg* waited. Using a white bedsheet as a semaphore, the landing party signaled WE HAVE HIM. SEND BOATS FOR ALL. After a brief pause the reply from the ship was signaled back: BULLY! A faint cheer echoed across the water from the ship's deck.[7]

After months on the run, Aguinaldo suddenly seemed drained of his fighting spirit. Back in Manila, MacArthur gave the prisoner a comfortable suite of rooms with a view of parade grounds, from which he watched in confusion as American soldiers played pickup football games.

His dreams of playing the role of George Washington of the Philippines now shattered, Aguinaldo would write he was relieved that, finally, it was all over. "I had known for some time that our resistance was doomed to failure. . . . Now, it was over and I was alive." He grew to grudgingly respect the Americans, concluding that the United States would prove better masters of the islands than the Spanish had. He would even develop an "undeniable admiration" for Funston.[8]

"HAVE YOU ANY SECRET SOCIETIES?"

The evening of May 19, 1901, about two weeks after he first heard Emma Goldman, Leon Czolgosz approached a modest home near a stand of thick woods about twelve miles outside Cleveland. Dressed in casual clothes, he had come to see Emil Schilling, a German radical well known in Ohio. Middle-aged with wide-set, small eyes, Schilling was an unsettling figure. People who met him noticed a tendency to fix his gaze for several moments "with great concentration." His expression could then change quickly, his face able to contort into an "ugly, almost malignant look" that gave him the appearance of a "dangerous looking person."[1]

Czolgosz introduced himself under his alias Fred Nieman as a friend of a fellow radical by the name of Howser.[2] He was, Czolgosz explained, interested in anarchism and wanted to learn more. Schilling was intrigued by the earnest young man and asked him about himself. Czolgosz described how he had been a member of Sila and other socialist groups but had grown weary of the constant infighting. Impressed, Schilling invited him to join the family for dinner. Czolgosz accepted but remained a quiet guest. "I thought he was all right this time when he called on me," Schilling said later. The two parted warmly, Czolgosz carrying with him a book Schilling provided about Albert Parsons and the Chicago anarchists.

By this time, Czolgosz had reached a sort of emotional and intellectual tipping point. Life on the farm, among his family, had become an unbearable grind. Yet he was trapped there, having contributed most of his savings—and he had earned nothing since—to the purchase and operation of the farm. Although he was hardly the most popular person around the house, none of his brothers or sisters, nor his father, wanted to refund his investment. Throughout the spring and into summer, Czolgosz's demands for his money became increasingly bitter.

Again, too, he seemed preoccupied with his health. Once, while standing on a street near a dying tree, his brother Waldek pressed him on why he wanted to leave. "Look," Leon said, "it is just the same as that tree that commences dying—you can see it isn't going to live long."[3] He would go west, he said, where the warmer climate would be good for him. He would search for employment that would not have appealed to someone who was truly sick—working as a conductor, binding wheat, or fixing machines. More likely was that Czolgosz felt that his spirit was being crushed on the farm. Tortured by his stepmother, intellectually starved, he craved the company of radicals. Waldek, who never could figure out what was driving his brother, once pressed him. Czolgosz simply answered, "I can't stand it any longer."[4]

In the meantime, Czolgosz continued to nurture his growing fascination with anarchist thought. One more time he turned up on the doorstep of Emil Schilling, on this occasion his interest more pointed than his earlier visit. The idea of joining the underground world of violent, dangerous radicals had captured his imagination, though probably more for the romance of it than anything else.[5] In quick and clumsy ways, Czolgosz asked questions about whether any subterfuge was then being considered by anarchists: "Say, have you any secret societies?" Czolgosz asked. "I hear the anarchists are plotting something like Bresci; the man was selected by the comrades to do the deed that was done."

Schilling disabused Czolgosz of any thought of joining a plot. "Well," Schilling said. "You did not read it in any anarchist newspaper."

Schilling now developed quite a different opinion of the man who called himself Nieman. "I think that Nieman wanted to be smart enough to find out something as a secret detective and I think he was not smart enough to do what he wanted. I think he was very ignorant." Schilling later said that Czolgosz appeared strange to him. "When I answered him he was always laughing at my answers as if he either felt superior or had formed a plan and was putting out a feeler." The relationship soured further when Czolgosz returned Schilling's book from the first visit, but said he hadn't had time to read it. "This made me mad and I was suspicious of him," Schilling said.

After dinner, the two went for a walk, during which Czolgosz's social ineptness was plainly evident. He repeatedly declined an invitation to have a beer, offering instead a cigar, which Schilling refused. Finally, the exasperated Schilling convinced him to stop for a drink, but even then Czolgosz would order nothing more powerful than a soda. So odd was his behavior that Schilling decided to look up Howser and ask him about the young man who used his name as a reference. Howser confirmed Czolgosz was a good and active member of the Polish Socialist Society of the Labor Party, but that his name wasn't Nieman; it was something else, though he couldn't remember exactly what.

A week later, Nieman returned to see Schilling yet again, this time dressed in his Sunday clothes. He now poured out his heart, saying that he was tired of life and that he was abused by his stepmother. His father, he said, was too dominated by the woman to protect him. Still, he looked good. His clothes were neat and clean. "He had a red complexion, was healthy looking," Schilling said.

Czolgosz also asked Schilling for a letter of introduction that would enable him to meet Emma Goldman. The speech he had heard in May had left a mark on him, he said, and he was anxious to tell her so. The suspicious Schilling refused to give a written letter but advised Czolgosz to catch up with Goldman when she was in Chicago. "I go to Chicago," Czolgosz announced.[6]

———

He was also around this time finally able to leave the farm for good. On July 11, 1901, sick of his complaining and idling, the family scraped seventy dollars together and told Czolgosz that he could leave.[7] So delighted was Czolgosz by the news that he left without saying when he would be back, nor even saying good-bye to his father.[8] In typical Czolgosz fashion, he offered several different versions of his intentions. He told a sister-in-law that he was going to Kansas. To his sister, Victoria, he said he was going to California for his health. After three days he wrote home a brief note from Fort Wayne, Indiana, explaining that he was heading west.[9]

On the afternoon of July 12, 1901, Goldman was just finishing up a small luncheon thrown on her behalf at the Chicago home of Abraham Isaak, the publisher of *Free Society*. Exhausted from her speaking engagements and the hot summer, Goldman had spent several weeks with the family, at one point taking their teenage daughter Mary on a short holiday. This afternoon she was to leave.

After saying good-bye to the last of her friends, Goldman went upstairs to finish packing when the doorbell rang. Mary answered and found on the porch a well-dressed young man who explained he urgently needed to see Goldman. The name he gave was Nieman. Running late for her train, Goldman shouted down to have the gentleman wait. Whoever it was, whatever he wanted, she could talk with him on the way to the station.

Descending the stairs a few minutes later, Goldman quickly recognized Nieman as the "handsome chap of the golden hair" who had spoken with her in Cleveland. Together the two chatted as they walked to the elevated train and boarded, carrying on their conversation while tightly gripping the straps as the train jerked and twisted through Chicago. Nieman told Goldman that he belonged to a socialist club in Cleveland but that he had grown frustrated because the members were unenthusiastic and lacked vision. He had now decided to leave Cleveland and was eager to make contact with anarchists in Chicago. The two continued to talk as they made their way to the Lake Shore station where they met a small knot of Goldman's anarchist friends.[10]

Goldman introduced Czolgosz to the others and asked them to look after him. He had apparently failed to ingratiate himself with her during their ride together. While Czolgosz spoke with Hippolyte Havel, a Czech radical, Goldman whispered to Isaak that the gentleman had "been following her around" and she didn't have time to devote to him. She asked Isaak to find out what Czolgosz wanted.[11]

As Goldman's train pulled away from the platform, Czolgosz tried clumsily to fit in with the men—just the sort he had been hoping to meet. He referred to Isaak as "comrade" and bluntly asked if there were any "secret meetings" that he might attend.[12] Again, he rehashed his background, explaining he had been a socialist for seven years but had grown weary of the constant quarreling. Curiously, according to Isaak's account, Czolgosz claimed he was not an anarchist and that he knew nothing of the ideology other than what he had heard Goldman describe in the one address he had attended.[13] Czolgosz handled himself in such a ham-fisted manner and, apparently, was so ill informed that Isaak began to wonder if he might be some sort of police spy. Indeed, two other "comrades" among the group on the platform were so suspicious of Czolgosz that they wanted to offer him overnight lodging just so they could rifle through his pockets while he slept for proof that he was a government agent.[14]

Still, as he studied Nieman's face, Isaak "could not help thinking that his eyes and words expressed sincerity." Arriving back at Isaak's house, the two chatted on his front porch and Czolgosz explained that he was tired of socialism and now sought something "more active." The McKinley administration, Czolgosz said, had disillusioned him. In particular, the "outrages committed by the American government in the Philippine Islands" seemed to trouble him. "It does not harmonize with the teachings in our public schools about our flag," Czolgosz said.[15]

Despite concerns about Czolgosz's intentions, Isaak was willing to give the strange young man the benefit of the doubt. He would not give Czolgosz money but took him to a rooming house owned by Esther Wolfson on Carroll Avenue and rented accommodations for him. It was the last Isaak saw of the mysterious young man. Sometime that night, Czolgosz slipped out without Wolfson knowing.[16]

———

At home on the edge of the forest outside Cleveland in August, Schilling received a letter from Isaak. He wrote that he had met a curious man a few days earlier who used the name of Nieman and was throwing Schilling's name around town. As his eyes made their way down the page, a knock came at the door. It was Czolgosz.

Schilling quickly folded the letter and put it in his pocket. The coincidence was too much to ignore and he suspected that his curious visitor may have intercepted the letter and read it.[17] Still, Schilling invited Czolgosz to have a seat and asked what he had been up to for the past two months. Czolgosz described working in a cheese factory in Akron, though as was his manner, he laughed when he said it. Things were getting worse and worse, Czolgosz said. "They were getting more brutal against the strikers and . . . something must be done."[18]

Schilling then invited his visitor to join him and a neighbor on a walk. Where was Czolgosz going next, Schilling asked as they strode in the summer warmth. "May-be Detroit, may-be Buffalo," Czolgosz answered, but added very little.[19] Like many who had spent time with Czolgosz, Schilling was puzzled. The evasiveness, the persistent questions, the social awkwardness. It all left the big German feeling wary. Anarchists were always on the lookout for government agents who they believed periodically attempted to penetrate anarchist circles, and maybe this was how they behaved.

Not long thereafter, Schilling wrote Isaak, suggesting that he publish a warning about Czolgosz in *Free Society*. On September 1, 1901, this notice appeared:

> ATTENTION! The attention of the comrades is called to another spy. He is well dressed, of medium height; rather narrow shouldered, blond and about 25 years of age. Up to the present he has made his appearance in Chicago and Cleveland. In the former place he remained a short time, while in Cleveland he disappeared when the comrades had confirmed themselves of his identity and were on the point of exposing him. His demeanor is of the usual sort, pretending to be greatly interested in the

cause, asking for names, or soliciting aid for acts of contemplated violence. If this individual makes his appearance elsewhere, the comrades are warned in advance and can act accordingly.

After summering with the Isaaks, Goldman made her way to Rochester where she was extending her vacation. There, as she often did, she purchased a copy of *Free Society*. As she flipped through the publication's few pages, she was astonished to find the warning about the man whom she had just encountered in Chicago.

Goldman hadn't been able to spend much time with him and found the man slightly annoying, but displaying deeper levels of perception than her colleagues in Chicago and Cleveland, she saw nothing in Czolgosz that suggested he was a spy. "I was very angry," she wrote later. "To make such a charge, on such flimsy grounds!" Her blood up, she penned a letter to Isaak asking for proof of his accusations. And when he hesitated, she fired off a second missive that finally prompted the publisher to publicly apologize for his accusation.[20] "It must have hurt him to the quick to be so cruelly misjudged by the very people to whom he had come for inspiration," she later wrote. "It was apparent that he had sought in anarchism a solution to the wrongs he saw everywhere about him. No doubt it was that which had induced him to call on me and later on the Isaaks. Instead of finding help, the poor youth saw himself attacked."[21]

30

GOING TO THE FAIR

McKinley began his second term grateful that the nasty pace of the previous four years seemed to be slowing down. Subjects such as trade agreements, trust regulation, and the practicalities of building a canal across the isthmus of Central America now tussled for his attention. They were important, but nothing like the geopolitics that had consumed him the past four years. His presidency became much more like what he had envisioned when he first moved into the White House. He even found time to read S. Weir Mitchell's *Hugh Wynne, Free Quaker,* a popular story of the American Revolution.

McKinley also began to plan the most extensive trip of his presidency, something of a victory lap celebrating his overseas achievements. Cuba was firmly under American control. Hawaii had been annexed. The Boxer Rebellion had been put down, America had established itself as a power in China, and it appeared that Taft was turning the Philippines into a peaceful colony.

McKinley's journey out west was one that Hannibal would have approved of. Just as the Carthaginian drove elephants over the St. Bernard pass in the Alps, McKinley proposed to transport his entire cabinet on a journey skirting the outer edge of the country, traveling to Louisiana, California, and through the Northwest, and concluding on June 13, 1901, with a visit to the Pan-American Exposition in Buffalo. Six weeks in all.

A number of cabinet ministers eventually managed to find excuses not to make the journey, yet it was still a spectacle when some forty-three officials, friends, and staff members settled into a special train on April 29, 1901, and pulled out of Washington.[1] Ida McKinley was feeling unwell but brought along plenty of people to look after her, body and soul—her maid Clara, a favorite niece, Mary Barber, as well as her personal physician, Dr. Rixey, who had studied her case and, to the president's approval, had cut down on the bromides that she had been receiving.

At each stop the entourage received an enthusiastic welcome, though none more lavish than the one provided in Los Angeles in the second week of May. There well-wishers threw a floral parade while McKinley's carriage was pulled by half a dozen white horses. On one receiving stand, rose petals piled up ankle deep.[2]

Ida, however, was suffering from a pain in her hand. Before arriving in Los Angeles, the First Lady had developed a bone felon—a pocket of pus caused by an infection—on her forefinger, which Dr. Rixey tried to lance. It still bothered her on Friday when McKinley left for San Francisco, so much so that the presidential train had to be stopped for an hour while Dr. Rixey again attempted to treat the finger. By the time the group arrived at the Del Monte Hotel, Ida was decidedly unwell.[3]

At first, she did her best to keep up with her husband and accompanied him on trips around the Bay Area for a couple of days, but she quickly weakened. On Sunday, McKinley broke his own rule against travel on the Sabbath and took her to the home of H. T. Scott, head of the Union Iron Works. Scott had built the battleship USS *Ohio*, named after McKinley's home state, and one of the planned highlights of the trip was to witness its maiden launch. Ida was given a comfortable bed and trained nurses. In an unintended comment on the quality of medical treatment at the time, a millionaire's guest room was seen to offer better care than a hospital.

Yet Ida's health continued to worsen, apparently from blood poisoning caused by one of the lancings, and she suffered at least one fit. For days she lived off beef broth and brandy and at times lost consciousness. On Wednesday, shortly before dawn, her pulse weakened and she fell into a stupor before heart stimulants were given. Those knowledgeable of her condition began to grow genuinely concerned, one telling *The New York Times*, "Mrs. McKinley is as sick as any woman I ever saw."[4] Across the street, in Lafayette Park, hushed crowds gathered to offer their support.[5]

Yet Ida once again managed to pull herself out of a dangerous condition, aided by heart stimulants and intravenous injections of salt. Although still considered critical, she began to speak and even smile. She was well enough, the president decided, for him to attend the launching of the *Ohio*.

Traveling to the shipyards in the tugboat *Slocum*, the president witnessed what *The Washington Post* called the most impressive seaborne event since the day George Dewey arrived on the Hudson River from the Philippines. Enthusiastic crowds gathered on wharves to watch the tug motor past. Sailors aboard warships in the harbor had decked out their vessels with signal flags from stem to stern. It was all framed by a view of the city of San Francisco, "a perfect mound of waving flags." Aboard one troop transport, just returned from the Philippines, soldiers crowded the rails shouting and waving their hats while the band struck up "The Star-Spangled Banner." Beaming, McKinley waved a handkerchief in reply.[6]

Ida, however, remained very much on the president's mind, despite the best efforts of his staff. Telephone connections were established at the dock and shipyards, enabling doctors to reach the president at any moment, other than when he was actually on the *Slocum*. He was so eager to return that, on the way back to the Scotts', he leaped from the transport tug to the dock and nearly ran to a carriage that would carry him back to Ida. Though his wife was looking better, McKinley cut the trip short, canceling all the remaining dates save one. He would merely postpone his visit to the Pan-American Expo. Plans were made for him to attend the fair in September.[7]

Ida was still looking ill—her face thin and pale—on the sultry evening of July 5, 1901, when she and her husband boarded their private car on the seven forty-five Western Express for Canton and the start of a three-month holiday in their hometown. She had made marked progress from the worst of the trip to the West Coast, and it was hoped that relaxing among friends and cooler air would fully restore her.[8]

It was ostensibly a working vacation for the couple. McKinley would continue to guide affairs of state from his home library, which had now been turned into a small Oval Office. He brought some of his top staff with him, and a steady stream of visitors soon followed. Still, the pace of events slowed to a leisurely cadence. As much work as possible was handled by staff in Washington, and only matters requiring McKinley's personal attention were sent to Canton.[9]

In Washington that summer, John Hay took on the heavy lifting, deep in the diplomacy needed to forge the missing link in McKinley's trade route with the Far East—a canal across the isthmus of Central America.

A waterway linking the Pacific and Atlantic oceans had been an American dream since the days of the California gold rush, when eastern prospectors had bolted west. Rather than crossing the continent or sailing a schooner all the way around South America, many found the fastest route was to hop on a ship heading south but then cut westward across Nicaragua or Colombia by train—or even on foot—before catching another ship headed north.

Neither American investors nor the U.S. government, however, showed much practical interest in constructing a waterway, and it had been a Frenchman, Ferdinand de Lesseps, who first attempted to construct a passage across what is now Panama in 1880. For thirteen years, the French, confident in their abilities after constructing the Suez Canal, dug and dynamited a sea-level route before they were defeated by lack of technical expertise and malaria-infested jungles. Abandoning the project in 1893, they left behind their equipment, disappointed investors, and one giant hole in the ground.

The publication of Mahan's classic *Influence of Sea Power*, however, revived U.S. interest in 1890. He described the construction of a canal as a catalyst for American expansion, and support had been building ever since. Of course, Theodore Roosevelt was keen for an American project as soon as he heard of it, and in 1897 wrote that the United States needed to get it started "at once." The challenging voyage of the USS *Oregon* demonstrated most dramatically what canal proponents sought. In the weeks before the United States declared war on Spain, the ship had been ordered from its home port in Bremerton, Washington, to the waters of the Caribbean. Desperately needed in the fight against the Spanish, the ship required an astonishing two months to make the twelve-thousand-mile journey. Had a canal existed at the time, it would have cut the trip eight thousand miles shorter, to say nothing of avoiding the dangers of sailing around Cape Horn.[10]

As daunting as the engineering and financial challenges were, the biggest roadblock to getting started had been a diplomatic one. Almost half a century earlier the United States and Britain had signed the Clayton-Bulwer Treaty committing the two nations to joint control of any canal built across the isthmus.[11] Though he would have preferred to spend the summer in cooler climes, Hay now was stuck in Washington, renegotiating a treaty acceptable to both the British and the Senate that would give the United States exclusive control over a canal.

Unencumbered with affairs of state for the first time since entering the White House, McKinley seemed determined to recapture his old life in Canton. He took great pride in his yard and enjoyed discussing it with the gardener. He also oversaw a remodeling project that included a pillared porte cochere that roofed the driveway on the north side and the construction of an octagonal gazebo that overlooked the lawn and garden. "I don't suppose you can possibly appreciate how much it means to me to have a home of my own," he proudly told one visitor.[12]

McKinley spent quiet evenings with Ida on the porch catching up with old friends, or simply shouting warm greetings at people passing by on the brick sidewalk that ran in front of his house. Ida, visitors said, hadn't looked so good in years.[13] In a first for the president—indeed the first for any president—McKinley rode in an automobile. He was out for a walk when an old friend, Zebulon Davis, happened by and offered to take him for a spin. After at first demurring, an uneasy McKinley climbed in and was seen gripping the door tightly as the machine wound through the streets of Canton. The president was wise to stay firmly in his seat as Davis, who manufactured cars, at one point was forced to quickly swerve to avoid a cyclist.[14]

As September approached, the White House finalized plans for the trip to the Pan-American Expo in Buffalo. There would be a relaxed train ride to Niagara Falls, a fireworks show on the evening of September 5, 1901, on the fairgrounds, a speech, and a brief meeting with the public. George Cortelyou, who had tried to remove a meet-and-greet on the sixth from the president's schedule for security reasons, again tried to persuade him to call off the event, arguing that it would inevitably disappoint thousands of people who would not get a chance to meet him. "Well, they'll know I tried, anyhow," the president replied.

Worried about McKinley's safety at the fair, Cortelyou telegrammed Buffalo to sort out security arrangements and received a reassuring update. The Buffalo chief of police had already been in touch with police in Washington. The normal Secret Service team was to be beefed up with city patrolmen, exposition guards, railroad detectives, and Pinkerton men, as well as with two extra Secret Service agents. Special police, some in uniform, some in plain clothes, would be stationed night and day at the Milburn House, where McKinley would be staying. The president's carriage was always to be protected by a phalanx of soldiers and police.[15] All seemed to be well in hand.

═══╪═══

"I DONE MY DUTY"

Czolgosz's meanderings that summer of 1901 took him to Buffalo, the very place that McKinley now made plans to visit. Why Czolgosz chose that city is unclear, but it was likely as good a destination as any for a loner with a few bucks in his pocket. That Buffalo possessed a large Polish population may have had something to do with his decision, but so could have the Pan-American Exposition, whose considerable attractions had received wide newspaper coverage.

There Czolgosz made the acquaintance of two Polish workers. Meeting them on a street corner, he incredibly struck up a conversation that even more remarkably led to a friendly beer in a nearby saloon. Over the cold drinks, Czolgosz explained that he was new in town and asked about lodging. One of his new friends, Antoine Kazmarek, a railroad worker, rented out rooms of his home in the rural area of West Seneca and said he could probably find him a bed. It wasn't much. The house contained only four rooms for Kazmarek, his wife, three children, and at least one more boarder. In fact, Czolgosz, who was still telling everyone his name was Nieman, ended up at various times sharing a bed with the other guest or with one of the children. But he couldn't complain about the price, three dollars a month, washing included.[1]

With unerring predictability, Czolgosz mimicked the time he had spent with his family in Ohio while with the Kazmareks. He largely refused to eat with others in the house, instead preferring a diet of milk and crackers, usually consumed in a corner of the front room by himself. In the mornings, he would take a brief walk down West Seneca's quiet roads and then spend much of the day on the piazza, sitting with his chair tipped back, reading pamphlets and newspapers. Three or four times a week, he would get dressed up and mysteriously disappear, explaining his absences by saying he had to attend "meetings." The only thing that had seemed to change with Czolgosz was that he was now taking greater care of his personal appearance and would for a few moments each morning stop and fiddle with his clothes in a mirror.[2]

One morning in late August, Kazmarek came downstairs around seven o'clock and discovered Czolgosz, his bags packed, admiring his reflection. When Kazmarek asked his boarder where he was going, the usual vague answer was provided: "Maybe Detroit, Toledo, Cleveland or Baltimore—maybe Pittsburgh." Unable to pay the balance of his bill, $1.75, Czolgosz offered a revolver and a promise to return for it when he had the cash. Strangely for a man who could not settle his bill, he then paid one of the Kazmareks' sons ten cents to carry his bag out for him.[3] Later that day, Czolgosz boarded a Lake Erie steamer bound for Cleveland.[4]

Again, Czolgosz kept his movements private. It would later be reported that he had returned to Cleveland to pick up anarchist material. He may have collected money as well, for he was later seen in possession of an impressive roll of bills. Czolgosz himself later evasively explained the purpose of his trip as to just "look around and buy a paper."[5] Whatever the reason, Czolgosz also made his way to Chicago, the last place he had seen Goldman. There his eye fell on an intriguing newspaper article. President McKinley was to arrive at the Pan-American Exposition about a week later. That same day he purchased a ticket back to Buffalo.[6]

At six twenty on the evening of September 4, 1901, the president's train eased to a stop at the Exposition's terminal station. With him, in addition to Ida and the omnipresent Dr. Rixey, was a full retinue of staffers as well as a number of local dignitaries who had wanted to be seen arriving with the president. Also aboard were three Secret Service operatives—George Foster, the president's cigar-chomping permanent bodyguard, Samuel Ireland, and Albert Gallagher.[7] As the party alighted on the station platform, Ida was still shaking from the greeting they had received at Buffalo's Terrace Station a few minutes earlier, where the concussion of cannons fired to salute their train had blown out several windows of one carriage. The enthusiastic greeting by a throng of anxious people who had to be restrained by police and uniformed soldiers did not calm her nerves.

In the preceding several days Czolgosz had been hit by a sort of epiphany. Since hearing Goldman in May, he would later explain, he had been looking for a way to demonstrate his commitment to anarchism. "Her doctrine that all rulers should be exterminated was what set me to thinking so that my head nearly split with the pain. Miss Goldman's words went right through me, and when I left the lecture I had made up my mind that I would have to do something heroic for the cause I loved," he later said. What form his heroism would take was something he could not decide upon despite months of reflection. Even when he read of McKinley's trip to Buffalo and decided to go there as well, he still didn't know what he would do. Czolgosz simply felt he should be near the man who seemed to symbolize the country's many injustices.

Czolgosz finally made up his mind the day before McKinley arrived. "It was in my heart; there was no escape for me. I could not have conquered it had my life been at stake. There were thousands of people in town on Tuesday. I heard it was President's Day. All those people seemed bowing to the great ruler. I made up my mind to kill that ruler."[8] That same day, Czolgosz went to Walbridge's Hardware Store on Main Street and purchased a .32-caliber Johnson revolver. He had, as yet, no clear plan for carrying out the attack other than to stalk the president during his three days in and around Buffalo and hope that an opportunity presented itself, as it had for Bresci in Italy, to fire at close range.

The revolver concealed in his pocket, Czolgosz neared the president, his wife, and others as they stepped down from the train. Before him, the McKinleys were guided to a carriage with John Milburn, the fair's president. Into the carriage behind stepped George Cortelyou. As the crowd cheered and waved, the procession made ready to rattle off for a quick pass through the fairgrounds on the way to Milburn's stately home on Delaware Avenue where the first couple would stay in Buffalo.

Pushing and shoving his way to the front of the crowd, Czolgosz drew no small amount of attention to himself, including that of a police officer who advanced toward him for a moment before being distracted by the president's procession. "I tried to get near him, but the police forced me back. They forced everybody back, so that the great ruler could pass. I was close to the President when he got into the grounds, but was afraid to attempt the assassination because there were so many men in the bodyguard that watched him. I was not afraid of them or that I should get hurt, but afraid I might be seized and that my chance would be gone forever."[9] He would, he told himself, have another opportunity tomorrow.

A brilliant sun quickly warmed the morning air on September 5, 1901, as thousands of people, the entire city of Buffalo it seemed, took to the streets to see the president. "Every street-car was loaded and passengers clung to the steps," noted one observer.[10] By nine o'clock, thousands had jammed the area around Milburn's house and along Lincoln Parkway to see the president travel to the fairgrounds to give a speech. Military bands filled the air with stirring martial music. Soldiers marched in dress uniforms, their swords gleaming in the sun.

Inside the fairgrounds, whose gates had been specially opened at 6 A.M., more than one hundred thousand people were expected, each of whom wanted a place next to the flag-draped presidential podium. The crowd murmured appreciatively as members of the diplomatic corps ascended the stage, the monocled Duke of Arcos, who now represented Spain, the Turkish minister in his red fez, and several Chinese diplomats in blue and gray silk robes.[11]

Everyone hushed when they noticed the president and his wife approaching in an open carriage, the clopping of the horses' hooves clearly audible. Dressed in an open frock coat, a neat black bow tie, and a tall silk hat, the president carefully helped Ida out of the carriage and guided her to the stage, one arm securely wrapped around her waist. Introduced by Milburn with the simple words, "Ladies and gentlemen, the President of the United States," McKinley stepped forward to thunderous cheers. Although he often tended to speak with flash cards, on this occasion he had written his speech out. As he reached into his pocket for his papers, the crowd fell silent.[12]

Commerce, as it had since he first entered the White House, dominated the president's message. "The quest for trade is an incentive to men of business to devise, invent, improve and economize in the cost of production. Business life, whether among ourselves, or with other peoples, is ever a sharp struggle for success. It will be none the less in the future," he told the massive gathering. "Our industrial enterprises, which have grown to such great proportions, affect the homes and occupations of the people and the welfare of the country. Our capacity to produce has developed so enormously and our products have so multiplied that the problem of more markets requires our urgent and immediate attention. Only a broad and enlightened policy will keep what we have."[13]

Among those standing closest to the president was Czolgosz. Awaking early that morning, he had secured a good spot "right under him" but one that was still at the outer range of his accuracy. Anxiously, Czolgosz argued with himself about whether he could hit the president at this distance and whether he might even be able to get the shot off with so many people jostling him. A half-dozen times, he thought of taking aim.[14]

The president, on this occasion, would make up Czolgosz's mind for him. As Czolgosz dithered, McKinley finished his remarks and disappeared into a phalanx of security men for a tour of the fair. There would soon be a luncheon and later that evening a boat ride on the fairgrounds to watch the Expo's spectacular lighting display and fireworks show. For Czolgosz, there would be no more opportunities to even consider getting close to the president for the rest of the day.

Foiled once again, Czolgosz gave up and returned to John Nowak's saloon, ordered a glass of whiskey, and went to his room to unwind. He would have one more day.

One part of the president's schedule that the papers, which Czolgosz used for his planning, did not report was McKinley's penchant for morning walks. September 6, 1901, was no exception. As the sun shone through the widows of the Milburn house, McKinley rose early, dressed himself as usual in full presidential splendor, and headed out into the beautiful neighborhood, almost slipping away unescorted by bodyguards or police who were caught unawares.

This deviation from the schedule would have been a golden opportunity for Czolgosz. He, too, woke early that morning, and then dressed in a somewhat less elegant suit, a dark one purchased in Chicago when he was visiting Goldman, which he accessorized with a string tie, a flannel shirt, a handkerchief folded into his breast pocket, and his revolver in a coat pocket.[15] But rather than visit the Milburn house, he skipped breakfast, bought a cigar, and left directly for the Exposition, arriving at eight thirty in time to see the president pass on his way to the train station.

This was to be a "restful day" for the first couple, built almost entirely around a pleasing trip to Niagara Falls. Departing by train at 9 A.M., the president and his wife watched a pastoral landscape of fruit trees and farms pass by their windows on the one-hour ride to Lewiston. Over the next several hours, a clearly thrilled McKinley savored the magnificence of the Niagara area—a giant whirlpool, the misty gorge below the falls, and a ride halfway across the international suspension bridge. At Goat Island, the president climbed like a schoolboy to the highest rock formation above the falls. Lunch had been arranged for the party in the ballroom of the International Hotel, with time built into the schedule for the president to enjoy a cigar and the fine view.

Czolgosz had vainly tried to keep up with the president and had also taken the train to Niagara. It quickly became obvious to him, however, that he would not get anywhere near his target, and he returned to Buffalo.[16] At 4 P.M., the papers reported, McKinley would meet members of the public at the Temple of Music, a cavernlike domed hall where concerts were performed. It was not an ideal place for an assassination attempt. There would be a long, slow-moving line, closely watched by police and a detachment of soldiers. But Czolgosz was running out of opportunities.

For a frozen instant, nobody moved. It was too fantastic to believe. From the dais where McKinley was shaking hands with the public the sound of a firecracker echoed. A second report soon followed. A slightly built young man, standing only a few feet from the president, was holding a gun covered in a white handkerchief. A small mushroom cloud of smoke wafted upward. The president clutched at his chest and was beginning to lean forward—his expression, not of pain, nor anger, but one of confusion.

As Czolgosz prepared to take a third shot, a crashing wave of bodies descended on his small frame. James Parker, a six-foot-four-inch African American from Georgia standing behind him in line, was the first to actually strike Czolgosz, leveling a blow to his neck with one hand and grasping for the revolver with his other.[17] In an instant, fists flew at Czolgosz from all sides. Francis O'Brien, a member of the Seventy-third Seacoast Artillery who had been assigned to help protect the president, and Detective John Geary threw themselves almost in unison on Czolgosz in a tangle of writhing limbs.[18] Angry shouts and curses filled the stage. Secret Service agent George Foster screamed to his colleague Albert Gallagher: "Get the gun, Al! Get the gun!"[19] Two privates from the army guard, Brooks and Neff, jumped on the pile. Amid the screaming, swearing, and punching was a brief remark from Czolgosz himself. To one of those who dragged him down, Czolgosz would simply say "I done my duty."[20]

A red mist of rage guided Czolgosz's attackers beyond the force needed to apprehend him. Guards beat his body with rifle butts and clubs, the severity of their blows limited only by the pushing and shoving of the pile on top of him. One witness said, "Parker, with his clenched fist, smashed the assassin three times squarely in the face, and was apparently wild to kill the creature, while all the crowd of artillerymen, policemen and others, also set upon the object of their wrath."[21] Foster hauled Czolgosz to his feet, shouting at him, and then punched him again, sending his light frame splaying to the ground.[22] It might have ended for Czolgosz right there were it not for the president himself.

McKinley, clutching his white waistcoat, was on the verge of falling when Detective Geary caught him and, along with George Cortelyou and John Milburn, dragged him over torn bunting toward a chair. The seriousness of the situation had not dawned on the president, and he at first tried to convince his secretary that he was not badly wounded.[23] Yet blood now had begun to ooze from his body, staining his white vest and his fingers as he tried to unbutton his garments to expose the wound. The pounding Czolgosz was taking nevertheless competed for the president's attention and his displeasure. "Don't let them hurt him," he said, an order that immediately brought an end to Czolgosz's beating. His clothes torn, blood streaming from his eyes and nose, hardly able to stand, Czolgosz was pulled to his feet and dragged to a small room in the northeast corner of the Temple.

Blood was by now steadily flowing from the president's abdomen, erasing any doubts that it was anything but a serious wound. McKinley also did not look well. His face had already lost color, and he seemed to be weakening. The president's mind raced to what word of the shooting would mean to his wife. He whispered to Cortelyou. "My wife—be careful, Cortelyou, how you tell her—oh, be careful!"[24]

Around the fair, news of the shooting spread rapidly. At the Indian Congress, where 2,500 spectators were waiting for the afternoon performance, the manager, Frederick Cummins, took the stage and announced "The President has been shot!" He offered to refund people's money, but no one took him up on it, and the crowd silently filed out. Word reached the Streets of Mexico exhibit just as a bullfight was about to start. "Ladies and gentlemen," an official announced, "It is my painful duty to tell you that our president has been shot by an assassin." One woman fainted. Another spectator, dressed in cowboy gear, ran to the door waving his Stetson, yelling "What are we going to do about it?" A group of Native American Indian performers, still in head-dresses, rode on horseback to the Temple door, one shouting "Big White Feather has been killed."[25] Rumors spread that a mail wagon was carrying the assassin and the frightened driver spurred his horses to flee the crowd before they could attack.

Shouts went up: "Don't let him get away." "Kill him." "Hang him." "Get the rope; kill the son of a bitch!" At the Temple's main entrance, where Czolgosz was first sequestered, marines made a show of loading their Lee-Metfords. Women began to cry, men struggled not to. Along the length of the Esplanade, thousands of people were out for blood.

"The roar of the crowd," said one, "was never to be forgotten by anyone who heard it."

In contrast to the bloodlust for those hunting the assassin on the grounds, a solemn silence spread throughout the crowd near the back door of the music hall. Fairgoers watched quietly as the president was carried out on a stretcher and placed in a small electric-powered ambulance. People shouted "Stand back" and "Move aside" as the vehicle navigated through the crowd on the short journey to the fair's hospital.

Looking down from the second floor of the police station, Czolgosz could see the enraged mob that had followed him from the fairgrounds. A cordon of police and mounted officers restrained angry men who chanted and yelled for revenge. Battered, bruised, and shaken by the mob, Czolgosz was in a sad physical and mental state. In the words of one correspondent, his body shook like "an aspen leaf."[26] He would in the immediate hours after his arrest offer police a tangled mixture of lies and truth about his identity and what had motivated him. To an Expo security officer, James Vallely, Czolgosz gave his name as Fred Nieman, going so far as to spell it out N-I-E-M-A-N and to say he was a blacksmith.[27]

Yet in a formal confession, made in the dim light of a sputtering gas lamp in a small police headquarters room, he offered a more introspective and correct account. He had been born in Detroit, he explained. His life had not gone the way he wanted. "I never had much luck at anything, and this preyed upon me. It made me morose and envious," he told police. For years he read books about socialism and associated with socialists and had grown more radical after hearing Goldman. "I am an Anarchist. I am a disciple of Emma Goldman. Her words set me on fire," he told police. "I don't regret my act, because I was doing what I could for the great cause."[28]

The next day, Czolgosz met with a medical expert and by now had fully found the voice of a social revolutionary. "I don't believe in the Republican form of government, and I don't believe we should have any rulers. It is right to kill them," he said. "I don't believe in voting; it is against my principles. I am an anarchist. I don't believe in marriage. I believe in free love. I fully understood what I was doing when I shot the President. I realized that I was sacrificing my life. I am willing to take the consequences." He went on: "I know what will happen to me,—if the President dies I will be hung. I want to say to be published—'I killed President McKinley because I done my duty. I don't believe in one man having so much service, and another man should have none.' "[29]

That the young man who idled about the farm and could not summon the ambition to perform even simple chores was capable of an act so bold flabbergasted his family back in Ohio. Yet there it was in black and white in the newspapers that Jacob had run out to get that morning: "My God! That is my brother!" Jacob cried. "How could he do it?" Jacob later spoke to the *Cleveland Plain Dealer*. "I don't know what to say—we have not seen Leon for several months. He always was a timid lad and we never would have suspected him of doing such a thing as this." Later asked if he thought his brother was mad, Jacob answered, "Oh no, he was no more than I am. He was peculiar in many ways, but he was not crazy."[30]

Czolgosz's stepmother, Catarina, who had feuded with him all those years, pounced on the opportunity to attack her stepson. "I can't believe Leon is the one. He was such a timid boy, so afraid of everything. Why, he was the biggest coward you ever saw in your life."[31] In fact, she seemed more concerned about the family welfare than Leon. "Now Paul will never get any work," she said. "People will point at him and say his son killed McKinley and no one will have anything to do with him. Oh! It is awful."[32] In an interview with *The New York Times,* she revealed how little she knew of her stepson. She told the paper he could not have been interested in Goldman's teachings as he was not intelligent enough to understand them. Indeed, she went on, the boy admired a brother who had been a member of the army during the Spanish-American War and liked his country.[33] To another she said, "He had no ill will against the rich or against the country's ruler." If such ideas came into his head, she insisted, it was after he left home. "I can't believe he ever became interested even in anarchists."[34]

Not even Czolgosz's father would speak a word in his son's defense. Paul said he wouldn't interfere with the legal process or a "proper punishment."

"In fact, none of us had a great liking for Leon," he said. "From the time he came to the farm, about three years ago, he would not work and was entirely worthless." Nor had he shown the slightest interest in politics. Like many others, Leon had received a free ticket to see McKinley in Canton during the 1900 campaign and had returned without saying a word against the man, his father said.[35] Leon's brother Joseph was no kinder: "If he has gone and done such a terrible thing he can suffer the penalty."[36] Jacob even dragged up childhood grievances, telling another reporter how Leon, who was older, used to beat him up and bullied him. None of the brothers got on with him, he said. "If Leon did it, I hope he swings for it."[37]

As police began their investigation, one question trumped all others: Had Czolgosz received any help? There were numerous reasons to suspect that he had. Bresci, the most famous anarchist assassin of the time, had been part of wider plot hatched in New Jersey. Surely, Czolgosz was just such a tool. There was his mysterious background. There was his less-than-perfect command of English, which seemed to suggest that he wasn't smart enough to act alone. There were his very open proclamations of admiration for Goldman. And there was some tantalizing circumstantial evidence.

Several witnesses claimed to have seen Czolgosz around the fair with other men. John F. von Muegge, a deputy U.S. marshal from Chillicothe, Ohio, happened to be visiting the fair and was only ten yards away from the president at the time of the shooting. He had noticed two men in line behind Czolgosz who he thought looked suspicious. Immediately after the shooting, he looked for the pair but they were nowhere to be found. R. I. Munn, who worked at the Liberal Arts Building, was certain that he recognized Czolgosz as one of three men he noticed the night before on the fairgrounds. The trio had caught his attention when a police officer briskly waved them along with his club. "Those fellows are up to some devilment," he thought at the time. "They have been in here for twenty minutes and whenever I come near them they stopped talking."[38] Adding at least some credence to theories of a plot was that one of the men Munn said was with Czolgosz that night fit the description that Secret Service agent Samuel Ireland gave of one man at the Temple of Music.

It was in Chicago, however, where police placed their greatest hope of establishing an anarchist plot. Within hours of the shooting, authorities telegrammed the Chicago police asking them to find out more about *Free Society*, the newspaper that had so seemed to inspire Czolgosz. Well aware of the publication, police there made a beeline for Isaak's house and were not disappointed. They found six men and three women in the midst of "an important meeting" and picked all of them up, Isaak included. Several of them, *The New York Times* reported, had already done prison time in "their native countries" for attempting to commit crimes inspired by anarchism. Three more anarchists were also arrested; among the incriminating evidence in their possession were pictures of Emma Goldman.[39] Indeed, more than anybody at *Free Society*, the infamous high priestess of anarchism was the one police most wanted to talk to.

On the day of the shooting, Goldman found herself in St. Louis engaging in the unlikely activity of selling stationery. She had first heard of the attack while riding a streetcar that evening, but saw no reason to think she could in any way be involved. Newspapers were reporting the assassin was a young man named Czolgosz, and she knew no one of that name. The next morning, Goldman went to a stationery store to close a $1,000 sale, the biggest of her brief career. While the shop-keeper finalized the paperwork, she glanced down at his desk where a blaring newspaper headline caught her eye: ASSASSIN OF PRESIDENT MCKINLEY ANARCHIST, CONFESSES TO HAVE BEEN INCITED BY EMMA GOLD-MAN. WOMAN ANARCHIST WANTED. Stunned, she managed to complete the transaction and hurry out of the store.

Outside, she raced to a newsstand, bought several papers, and slipped into a restaurant where she unfolded the papers on a table. Even for a woman who had lived her life very much in the public eye, she could not help but read these stories with amazement. Many of her close friends had already been rounded up, and some two hundred detectives had been dispatched around the country to look for her. Her friends, the papers said, would not be released until she was in custody. As she flipped through the pages, another surprise leaped off the page: a picture of McKinley's attacker. "Why, that's Nieman!" she gasped. Goldman decided her duty to her friends was clear. She must go to Chicago and surrender herself.

That night she boarded a train at Wabash Station and made her way to a sleeper cabin for the trip north. As the train clapped through the night she listened from behind her curtain with a wry smile to the voices of other passengers chatting in their bunks about her. "A beast, a bloodthirsty monster!" she heard one say.

"She should have been locked up long ago."

"Locked up, nothing!" another said. "She should be strung up to the first lamp-post."

Alone in the dark privacy of her bunk, Goldman wondered how her cabinmates would react if she were to step out and announce, "Here, ladies and gentlemen, true followers of the gentle Jesus, here is Emma Goldman!"

Around eight o'clock the next morning, Goldman descended from the train and strode out on the platform at Chicago's Polk Street Depot. She had decided against allowing herself to simply be arrested, and arranged a small sailor hat and blue veil over her face. Not knowing if the guise would work, she moved as confidently as possible along the hissing train and toward the station exit, nervously passing several men who she suspected were detectives looking for her. Yet no one noticed and, unmolested, the city's most wanted criminal suspect made her way out to the street and lost herself among the crowds of Chicago.

She chose not to go directly to the police, she later wrote, to see if Isaak and the others would be released on bail and to make preparations for their defense. Money for legal fees would be needed and, Goldman figured, she could raise some of it by selling her story to the newspapers.[40] In the meantime, she reveled in her fugitive status. That first day, Goldman walked around town, up and down State Street, brazenly past city hall several times. The following day she even made time to go shopping at Marshall Field's.

A friend, C. J. Norris, had learned that the *Chicago Tribune* was willing to pay her for an exclusive interview and offered to let her stay with him one night while final preparations for meeting a reporter were made. The apartment seemed a safe place to lie low, located as it was in an upscale neighborhood. And Norris himself was not a known anarchist. She accepted.[41]

The morning of September 10, 1901, Goldman woke and decided to begin her day with a relaxing soak in the bathtub. Who knew when she would next be able to enjoy such a treat? While she luxuriated in the warm water, Goldman heard a scratching sound at the window, which she at first ignored. Leisurely finishing her bath, Goldman was putting on a kimono when she heard the sound of splintering glass. Police had broken into the apartment and twelve men rushed in, led by a giant of a man named Captain Schuettler, who grabbed the still-damp Goldman by the arm: "Who are you?" he demanded.

Goldman didn't hesitate in answering. "I not speak English— Swedish servant girl."

The overbearing detective was completely taken in. "Stand back. We're looking for Emma Goldman," he said.

Even more astonishing is that, even after producing a photo, he still didn't realize that he stood face-to-face with Goldman. "This woman I not see here," Goldman replied. "This woman big." The men then proceeded to ransack the apartment and, finding nothing, were on the verge of leaving when one discovered a pen engraved with the name "Emma Goldman." Convinced she had been there and would likely return, two policemen were ordered to remain behind.

"I saw that the game was up," she wrote in her memoir. "It could serve no purpose to keep the farce up longer." To the astonishment of all in the room, Goldman revealed her real identity. For a moment the men looked at her "as if petrified" and then the captain exclaimed, "Well, I'll be damned! You're the shrewdest crook I ever met! Take her, quick!"[42] Still in her robe, Goldman convinced the police to give her a moment to change—as long as she left the bedroom door half open— and went off obediently to police headquarters.

Life grew dangerous for anyone with the thinnest connection to anarchism. In Pittsburgh, a mob dragged Goldman's friend Harry Gordon from his home in front of his screaming wife and two children. The vigilantes had already placed a rope around Gordon's neck and were seconds from lynching him when bystanders convinced them to stop.[43] On the evening of the assassination attempt, one man tried to enlist pedestrians on 125th Street in New York City to go with him to Paterson, New Jersey, one of the country's largest anarchist enclaves, to kill as many as they could find. Shouting to a quickly growing crowd, the would-be executioner said, "If President McKinley dies there will be 10,000 Anarchists killed in Paterson to avenge his death." It didn't take long to round up about one hundred men and boys to join him and head toward the train station, though their mass attack was never carried out.[44] On September 15, 1901, a group of about thirty armed men forced some twenty-five families belonging to a small anarchist village, Guffey Hollow, Pennsylvania, to flee the area. On the same night, a mob attacked the New York Yiddish-language paper *Freie Arbeiter Stimme* and wrecked its offices. Those inside ran for their lives.[45]

There were calls for expansion of the Secret Service, laws passed against carrying handguns, and a ban on anarchists entering the country. Senator Charles W. Fairbanks of Indiana said, "The anarchist stands as the personification of the destroyer. His hand is raised against law and order. He strikes at the institutions which are the foundation stones of our government, rather than at the individual whom he directly attracts. So it certainly is consistent with the spirit of our Constitution to protect ourselves against anarchism by Federal action of a drastic character."[46]

Johann Most, out on bail after his arrest for writing an article on political violence, was a natural target as well. Like other anarchists, he said he had never heard of Czolgosz and thought the assassination the work of a crank. "Every man who kills a President or a King is not an anarchist," he told *The New York Times*. His protests, however, rang hollow when it was discovered that his paper, *Freiheit*, had on the very day of the shooting called for the killing of "despots" and that it had savaged McKinley in another article. Most tried desperately to retrieve the paper, but copies soon found their way into the hands of the authorities. He was arrested on September 12, 1901, and would serve one year on Blackwell's Island for the inflammatory article.

Those who attempted to write Czolgosz off as a nut, however, knew little of the man now behind bars. Calm, cool, and collected, he consistently impressed his guards with his grasp of current events and his levelheadedness. "He is a remarkable man in some ways," Buffalo police chief William Bull said. "He is bright and shrewd and well versed in the political situation throughout the world."[47] He displayed a hearty appetite, receiving each day a portion of meat, a vegetable, bread and butter, and coffee. Other times he enjoyed a cigar or a glass of beer. His guards could not help being impressed. "Why he eats like a prize fighter training for battle," one said. "He talks as unconcernedly as one of the most sane men in Buffalo."[48]

So composed was Czolgosz that he disputed the amount of change that guards gave him after they purchased a new suit for him with money he had provided. At night he slept well and during the day easily conversed with experts sent to examine his mental state. Police captain Michael Regan added, "That man is by long odds the most unconcerned prisoner I have ever had behind bars. He will talk, no doubt of his crime, but I believe that he will never go to pieces physically. Why, there is a man about his age, who occupies a cell not far from Czolgosz's, and who was arrested for stealing a bicycle. That bicycle thief is all broken up over his crime, while the man who tried to murder the president is as unconcerned as possible."[49]

While the police continued their hunt for conspirators and attempted to learn what they could about Czolgosz's motives, they also waited for one rather awkward matter to resolve itself before he could go to trial. Was Czolgosz to be charged simply with attacking the president, or with killing him?

32

════╪════

THE OPERATING THEATER

Exactly eighteen minutes after the shooting, McKinley's electric ambulance rolled up the semicircular drive of the Exposition hospital. A small gray building in the old mission style, the hospital was better suited to dealing with skinned knees, heat exhaustion, and upset stomachs than assassination attempts. It did possess an operating theater, the shortcomings of which would soon become apparent.

The only medical personnel who happened to be at the hospital that afternoon were interns and half a dozen nurses serving one-month tours at the fair. Dr. Roswell Park, the best surgeon in the area for treating the president, was out of town. An expert on gunshot wounds who two weeks later would save a woman suffering a pistol shot almost identical to the president's, Park was at Niagara Falls performing a delicate operation on a man with a malignant neck tumor. Park learned of the attack on the president when someone burst into his operating theater shouting "Doctor, you are wanted at once in Buffalo."

Park cut him off. "Don't you see that I can't leave this case even if it were for the President of the United States?"

"Doctor," the intruder answered, "It *is* for the President of the United States."[1]

With Park unavailable, messengers were sent running through the fairgrounds in search of a surgeon. The first to arrive was Dr. Herman Mynter, an experienced physician who had served in the Danish army and navy before immigrating to the United States in the 1870s. He had actually met McKinley just the day before, and the president—who never forgot a face—now joked with the physician. "Doctor, when I met you yesterday, I did not imagine that today I should have to ask you for a favor."[2] As the staff prepared a hypodermic injection of morphine and strychnine that would numb the president's pain, others arrived, among them Dr. Matthew D. Mann, who had been in the middle of getting his hair cut when word of the emergency had reached him.

Once on the staff at Yale medical school, Mann now held a position at the University of Buffalo, where he was widely considered a leading authority on gynecology, having authored a renowned book on the subject. Considered a neat and clean surgeon, Mann unfortunately lacked any substantial experience with upper abdominal surgery or gunshot wounds.[3] He was, however, considered the best-qualified surgeon among those at hand, and Cortelyou, acting on the advice of Milburn, decided that he should attempt to locate and remove the bullets that had struck McKinley.

Repairing the damage done by abdominal gunshot wounds was at best a highly dangerous proposition. For hundreds of years doctors had done little more than offer comfort to those suffering such an injury until they died. It had been only seventeen years since the first successful surgery on such a bullet wound, a procedure performed by Swiss expert Dr. Emil Theodore Kocher. Pistol shot was especially dangerous because it tends to travel more slowly than rifle fire through the body, ripping and tearing tissue.

Indeed, nothing about the president's case was easy. The lighting in the operating theater was so poor that an assistant had to use a mirror to reflect sunlight onto the wound so the surgeon could see what he was doing. Simple surgical instruments such as retractors were not to be found among the hospital's equipment. Mann himself seemed overly excited and nervous and snapped at his assistants.[4] McKinley's weight made the search for the bullet considerably more complicated. "The greatest difficulty was the great size of President McKinley's abdomen and the amount of fat present," Mann wrote later. "This necessitated working at the bottom of a deep hole, especially when suturing the posterior wall of the stomach."[5]

Yet the president was by no means a lost cause. Even the most cursory examination revealed that only one of the bullets had caused a serious wound. One apparently had deflected off a button on McKinley's coat and struck his sternum, not penetrating deeply into his body. In fact, it simply fell out while medical staff was helping him undress.[6] The second bullet, which had sliced into his abdomen on the left side about five inches below the nipple, would prove more elusive.

Mann began the hunt by making an incision and squeezing his finger through the hole the bullet had carved. He encountered a shred of cloth just under the skin and removed it. Extending his finger farther, Mann traced the bullet's path through muscle and fat until he reached the president's stomach, where he clearly could feel a hole. The wound was immediately stitched. Partially removing the stomach, Mann examined the back side where he found a second hole, this one more ragged than the first. That, too, he sutured. Then, extending his hand still deeper, Mann probed behind the stomach. He was unable to find either the bullet or any signs of damage or bleeding.[7]

Mann might have turned to a primitive X-ray machine that was on display as part of the Exposition. He would decide, however, that using it would have disturbed the patient and might not have done much good anyway. There were also limits to how far Mann was willing to cut. Unable to find the bullet anywhere else, the surgeon concluded that it had probably lodged in McKinley's back muscles, an area from which it would be difficult to extract. To simply leave the bullet where it was, he believed, was a perfectly viable alternative to trying to dig it out. As Mann later wrote, "A bullet after it ceases to move does little harm."[8] The president was already in shock and there were worries about his pulse. Using black silk, Dr. Mann closed the incision and cleaned the area as well as he could.

———

While McKinley was at the fair, Ida had been resting at the Milburn house, recovering from the arduous trip to Niagara Falls and blissfully unaware of what had happened. Only when the surgery was complete did Dr. Rixey arrive to inform her of the shooting. Knowing full well how severely the deaths of her mother and daughters had shocked Ida, Rixey broke the news as gently as he could and provided scant detail about the procedure. Remarkably, she absorbed it with impressive self-control and calmly waited for the ambulance carrying McKinley to arrive at the house, where he would begin his recovery.

Overnight, the police turned the neighborhood around the Milburn house into a combination convalescence and communications center. For four blocks, heavy ropes and barricades were placed across streets guarded by the Fourteenth U.S. Army Regiment, which had just returned from overseas. A stable behind the house was made into a makeshift telegraph office, and a team of stenographers was installed in the house next door. Arrangements were made to receive the president's mail—thousands of cards and letters wishing him a speedy recovery, as well as a never-ending stream of medical advice urging doctors to try every manner of homespun remedy.

Newspaper reporters quickly descended en masse and set up an encampment across the street. They erected peaked canvas tents; unpacked typewriters, desks, and cots; and strung up telegraph lines, creating such a noisy scene that the president's doctors issued strict orders that "absolute quiet" be maintained. The press dutifully complied.

The house itself was likewise transformed. The ground floor would soon become a reception area for a steady stream of doctors, friends, and government figures. So many people hovered around that the president's personal chef was called upon to prepare as many as 140 meals a day.[9] The second floor, where McKinley rested, would become for practical purposes a hospital. McKinley's room was set up in the back where it was quieter. A large easy chair for Ida and doctors who would spend long nights by his side was brought in, and his bed was positioned such that he could gaze on beautiful trees outside and a portrait of George Washington that hung on the wall.

As far as the public was concerned, however, the epicenter of the entire operation was the Milburns' front porch. Here visitors and McKinley's doctors would update newspapermen about the president's condition in a busy stream of reports. Several such dispatches were issued during the first night.

To everyone's immense relief, it appeared that the president might actually be all right.[10] The reports stated that he had slept well and was free from pain. When Dr. Mann arrived early that morning, McKinley greeted him with a smile and even asked for a newspaper, not to read about the assassination but to gauge the reaction to his speech. Mann was confident enough in the president's condition that he went to the barber to finish the trim that had been interrupted by the shooting.[11] Over the course of the day, McKinley experienced occasional episodes of pain. But treated with small doses of morphine, he seemed all in all to be comfortable.

And so it continued for the next several days. Reporters heard shortly after 9 A.M. on the eighth that McKinley was looking better. Dr. Park, who became deeply involved in the president's treatment, reported "He is first rate."[12] On September 9, 1901, *The New York Times* wrote that there was GREAT HOPE FOR THE PRESIDENT and that all symptoms were favorable.[13]

The only blip in the impression of a steady recovery was the arrival of an X-ray machine on Monday, causing some excitement in the press tents. Thomas Edison sent it over, hoping it might be able to locate the missing bullet. Doctors attempted to try it out using a stand-in with an abdominal girth similar to the president's fifty-six inches, yet to Edison's embarrassment there seemed to be a part missing and the machine was never used.[14]

As the week progressed, there was no reason to think that McKinley would do anything but improve. Roosevelt told reporters, "You may say that I am absolutely sure the president will recover." On the tenth, McKinley's doctors put their names to a statement that read "If no complications arise, a rapid convalescence may be expected."[15] Some confident members of McKinley's staff and friends returned home. Roosevelt departed to join a family camping trip in the Adirondacks, twelve miles from the nearest phone or telegraph. Secretaries Lyman Gage and Philander C. Knox returned to Washington. On the twelfth, *The Cleveland Leader* reported that the president was in excellent spirits, feeling only lonesome as he was confined to his bed.[16]

33

———————

A PARK RANGER COMES RUNNING

On September 13, 1901, Roosevelt and a group of friends were hiking on the slopes of Mount Marcy, at over five thousand feet the highest peak in the Adirondacks and one of the most remote places in New York State. The weather was poor and a mist hung over the party as they prepared for lunch, unpacking their sandwiches near a little lake called Tear of the Clouds. At around one twenty-five, Roosevelt spotted a ranger running toward them through the trees below. In his hand, he clutched the yellow slip of a telegram.[1]

The president had suddenly taken a turn for the worse. Not long after lunch on the twelfth, doctors noticed that his pulse wasn't as strong as it had been. Although this was expected of anyone spending so much time in bed, doctors gave him an infusion of digitalis and strychnine. His pulse continued to weaken. At 3 P.M., the first bulletin was issued since the shooting that hinted he was not progressing. "The president's condition is very much the same as this morning. His only complaint is of fatigue."[2] His doctors now felt worried enough to call in a stomach specialist, Dr. Charles Stockton. Newspapers picked up on the unease. The next day's *Buffalo Courier* reported in a banner head-line PATIENT'S STOMACH FAILS TO ASSIMILATE SOLID FOOD.[3]

Lightning pierced the sky around Buffalo and a steady rain beat the windows of the Milburn house in the wee hours of Friday the thir-teenth. Through the morning and into the afternoon, McKinley's downward spiral continued. Cortelyou sent an urgent telegram to the White House: THE PRESIDENT IS CRITICALLY ILL. NOTIFY THE CABINET.[4] Newspapermen, noting the increasingly downbeat reports and the steady stream of worried politicians and family members entering the home, didn't take long to conclude that McKinley was worsening.

Doctors at the time did not know it, but the wounds left by the bul-let passing through McKinley's body had not healed. Gangrene had de-veloped on the walls of his stomach, and his blood was slowly being poisoned. Throughout the day, the president drifted in and out of con-sciousness. When awake, he remained, as always, the perfect patient. When nurses in the morning tried to adjust his bed to keep the light out of his eyes, he told them. "No, I want to see the trees. They are so beautiful," and remarked the weather seemed to be improving.[5] Around the nation, however, Americans read that the president's con-dition had taken a serious turn for the worse. Concerned citizens de-scended on the Milburn house to pray and offer advice. One old woman approached a guard asking that she be able to speak with Ida to give her a secret remedy of herbs and prayers.[6]

Events began to move with a surreal speed. The president's care-takers now had to admit to themselves that he might actually be dying. By late that afternoon, even McKinley realized that his condition was dire. He told doctors, "It is useless gentlemen; I think we ought to have a prayer."[7] With stunning speed, the president descended closer to the unthinkable. By 6 P.M., his doctors recognized they could not halt his decline. Members of the cabinet, old friends, and family members trudged upstairs, tears in their eyes, for what they were told would probably be a final visit.

Ida held up bravely during her husband's final hours. Sitting in an easy chair pulled close to his bed, she whispered to him, "I want to go, too. I want to go, too."

McKinley replied, "We are all going, we are all going." Looking around the room, he said, "God's will be done, not ours,"[8] and summoned enough strength to put an arm around his wife. Leaning close, she continued to whisper in his ear and once softly sang the words of his favorite hymn, "Nearer, My God, to Thee." The president continued to drift in and out of consciousness until, almost imperceptibly, he died. Doctors marked their books with the exact moment: 2:15 A.M., September 14, 1901.

THE CHAIR

The morning of September 23, 1901, detectives unlocked Czolgosz's cell and led him down a dark three-hundred-foot hallway known as the "tunnel of sobs." The "dank, reeking passage," six feet wide and nine feet high, had been dug under Delaware Avenue in 1878 to connect the Erie County Penitentiary and County and City Hall, where his trial would take place.[1] Czolgosz was, as he had been much of the time since his arrest, looking his best. Clean shaven with his hair neatly combed, he wore a new dark gray suit, a crisp white shirt, and a light blue bow tie. Handcuffed and flanked by a pair of detectives, Czolgosz seemed oblivious to all around him as he made his way to the New York Supreme Court, where he was to stand trial for murdering the president.

Czolgosz's behavior in the days immediately before his trial date only added to his mysterious public perception. When appearing before a grand jury and during his arraignment, he had completely refused to speak. He refused to answer the prosecutor when asked if he had a lawyer. He refused to enter a plea and refused to speak with his own lawyers, simply staring at the floor when anyone addressed him. Assistant Superintendent Patrick Cusack thought Czolgosz was smarter than people gave him credit for. "There are some of the people who think he is such an exceptionally queer prisoner, but I tell you he is a bad one, and a foxy one."[2] Assistant District Attorney Frederick Haller argued that Czolgosz was doing nothing more than aping the behavior of a prototypical anarchist. He predicted Czolgosz would remain silent until a death penalty was assigned, then he would shout "Long live anarchy!" and rant about the principles of that doctrine.[3]

Shortly after 10 A.M., Czolgosz was led past hissing spectators, and the doors to the courtroom were thrown open. The room itself was wholly unbecoming to such an important event. A small chamber on the second floor of County and City Hall, its high drab walls showed the "need of the scrubwoman's brush." The judge's bench and bar, placed near latticed windows, occupied more than half the floor space. The jury was seated on a six-inch-high stand with no bar or wall in front of them. The remainder of the room was given over to seats for about 150 spectators.[4]

It would be a remarkable trial, but for reasons that had little to do with the behavior of the defendant.

Perhaps most astonishing was the speed with which the proceedings were carried out, much to the delight of just about everybody involved, who simply wanted to get the affair over with.[5] The jury was selected in a scant two hours and twelve minutes, a working-class group of men, "not a smooth shaven" among them.[6] The trial itself began almost as soon as the final juror was named. By the following afternoon, it was over.

The pace was helped in no small part by the defense counsel, retired New York Supreme Court justices Loran Lewis and Robert Titus. Highly respected in their day, neither had worked as a trial lawyer in years and certainly didn't want to start now. Titus learned of his nomination while in Milwaukee. "I cannot understand why I have been selected for this unpleasant duty," he said. "I am very much depressed by the announcement. He should be defended by one of his own kind—an anarchist."[7] At Czolgosz's arraignment, Lewis made sure the public knew he shared Titus's view. Addressing the court, Lewis said, "I wish to say that I am accepting this assignment against my will and while it is more repugnant to me than my poor words can tell, I promise to present whatever defense the accused may have."[8]

Czolgosz himself also contributed to the trial's speed. The man who had impressed guards with his composure and confidence vanished the moment he first set foot in the courtroom. Perhaps it was coming face-to-face with the public, or his innate shyness, or simply the enormousness of what was now happening to him, but Czolgosz retreated deep into a shell from which he would rarely emerge. Throughout the trial he refused to cooperate with his legal counsel, stubbornly refusing to speak with them even in his cell. Journalists didn't know what to make of him. To some he looked proudly defiant, to others weak and shattered. "He walked through the aisle to his place before the judge's bench with as little concern as if he had been free and alone upon the street. . . . He looked as if he had just returned from an outing and was in the flush of health," noted one reporter.[9] Only rapid eye blinking suggested a deeper nervousness.

In the single remark he would utter before the end of the trial, he pleaded "guilty" when asked. Even that was wasted breath, however, when he was informed that in a trial of this magnitude he was not allowed to enter such a plea.

Much of the trial, limited though it was, focused on accounts of the assassination—where exactly all the important participants stood at the moment the president was shot and how they reacted. Nothing really contributed to the public's or the jury's understanding of the murder. The only time Czolgosz's defense showed any spark was over the issue of medical attention the president had received.

In fact, almost as soon as McKinley died, a very public debate erupted among surgeons and other experts over his medical care. The cause of death, according to the coroner's report, had been "gangrene of both walls of the stomach and pancreas following gunshot wounds."[10] For most experts, this was a far from satisfactory explanation. What had caused the gangrene? Dr. Park, who had followed the case closely, would later say he believed that injuries to the pancreas, which Mann had failed to recognize, were ultimately to blame.[11] Had the doctors discovered that, they might have been able to prevent the onset of toxemia by placing drains in the abdomen.[12] But there were other questions: Should the surgeons have carried out a more determined hunt for the bullet? What harm may it have caused resting in McKinley's back? Had his physicians done something during the operation to contribute to the onset of gangrene? And shouldn't they have known better than to issue such positive statements about the president's condition in the days after the attack?[13]

Drs. Mynter and Mann, both of whom would be called to testify, dismissed such questions as pointless. Dr. Mynter said there were a number of possible reasons for the onset of gangrene, but that none could have been prevented during the surgery. The president's condition, he said, was so delicate that they had been forced to conclude the operation as quickly as possible. That meant there was no time to look for the bullet or to hunt extensively behind the stomach for other damaged tissue. Finding the bullet, he said, would have entailed significantly enlarging the incision and removing all of the president's intestines, a process that would have killed him on the operating table. Mann said the autopsy proved they could not possibly have found it. The coroner, he pointed out, had labored over the president's body for four hours and never did find the bullet.

The most obvious means of sparing Czolgosz, the one everyone expected his defense to channel their energies into, was to establish that he was insane. It was clear from the very beginning, however, that that strategy was going to be a nonstarter.[14] Except for one brief episode of denial, Czolgosz had always been lucid, conversant, and more than willing to take responsibility for the murder. The only odd behavior they could name was his extreme fastidiousness about his clothing, which hardly qualified him as mentally deficient. Numerous experts paid visits to his cell almost from the day of his arrest to carry out tests and to study the assassin at close range, but found nothing that suggested he was mad. Probably the most noteworthy study was conducted just before the trial started.

Czolgosz was examined by Dr. Carlos F. MacDonald, a professor of mental diseases and medicinal jurisprudence at the University-Bellevue Medical College, and Dr. Arthur W. Hurd, both leading psychologists of the day. But Czolgosz refused to cooperate. Rather than answer their questions, he walked to the corner of his cell, turned his back on the pair, and gazed out the small window into the prison courtyard. When they refused to leave, he returned to his bed, lay down, and closed his eyes. During the entire interrogation, Czolgosz did not utter a single word. Having done all they could, the two doctors immediately conferred with others who had examined Czolgosz and pronounced him sane.[15]

With the only real means of defending Czolgosz eliminated, Lewis gave up on calling any witnesses. His twenty-seven-minute closing summation was the total of Czolgosz's "defense." In it, he praised the president as "one of the noblest men that God ever made . . . a man of irreproachable character . . . a loving husband, a grand man in every aspect that you could conceive of . . . and his death has been the saddest blow to me that has occurred in many years." He explained that he could not call any witness because Czolgosz had refused to cooperate with him. All he could do was feebly warn the jury against mob justice. All in all, it was a statement aimed more at defending his place in the community than an effort to spare his client the electric chair. As the judge discharged the jury and read them their instructions, Czolgosz, sweating, slunk down in his seat.

The jury would spend only thirty-three minutes in their quarters before returning with the verdict. And it didn't even take them that long to make up their minds. At least part of the discussion was on whether to kill some time before returning to court so that it would look like they had taken their job seriously.[16] At four twenty-four, the jury filed back in. Clerk Martin Fisher spoke first: "Gentlemen of the jury, have you agreed upon a verdict?"

"We have," replied foreman Henry Wendt.

"How do you find?"

"We find the prisoner guilty of murder in the first degree as charged in the indictment."[17] Sentencing was set for 2 P.M. on Thursday, September 26, 1901.

———

Shortly before eleven o'clock the next morning, Czolgosz was removed from his cell in "the dungeon" and escorted to a more hospitable room. Visitors were coming. It had been an uncharacteristically hard night, and the arrival of relatives was a welcome respite. He smiled when he saw who it was. Victoria, his baby sister, was the first to approach. "Leon," she sobbed as she buried her head in his shoulder. "Leon, what have you done? What have you done? Why did you do it Leon? Oh, God. Why did you do it?"

His lip quivering, he pushed her gently aside. "There is father. I must speak to him."

Paul took his son's hand but said nothing when Czolgosz addressed him in Polish. His brother Waldek spoke up. "I am sorry you have come to this, Leon."

Waldek then made a vain attempt to convince Czolgosz to provide the names of accomplices. Twisting the button on his coat and hanging his head, Czolgosz again insisted he had acted alone. Victoria sobbed so uncontrollably that Czolgosz asked her to stop. When it was time for them to go, Czolgosz held the hands of his father and brother as long as he could. Victoria kissed him good-bye.[18]

If Czolgosz ever intended to unleash a tongue-lashing on society and tout anarchism, it would have been at his sentencing. But now, with the spotlight on, the stage his alone, Czolgosz shrunk. It took the urging of the judge and the prosecutor to get him to say anything, and even those remarks were little more than clipped accounts of his life. There was no diatribe against government, the president, or the plight of the workingman—only a restatement that he had committed the act alone. As he clutched the back of a chair, Czolgosz whispered, "There was no one else but me. No one else told me to do it, and no one paid me to do it." So quietly did Czolgosz speak that Titus felt compelled to repeat his comments more loudly. Czolgosz went on: "I was not told anything about the crime and I never thought anything about murder until a couple of days before I committed the crime."[19]

"Anything further, Czolgosz?" White asked.

"No, sir," mumbled Czolgosz.

Judge White then read the judgment. "The sentence of the court is that in the week beginning October 28, 1901, at the place, manner, and by means prescribed by law, you suffer the punishment of death. Remove the prisoner." Detective Geary helped the weakening Czolgosz sit down and placed handcuffs around his wrists. Titus turned to his client. "Czolgosz, good-bye," he said, and the two shook hands. Solomon and Geary led Czolgosz back to his cell and watched as he took off his coat, sat down, and buried his head in his hands.[20]

At slightly after 3 A.M. on September 26, 1901, a train carrying Czolgosz, guards, and a collection of newspaper reporters screeched to a stop at the Auburn Prison, home to New York's electric chair—"the journey to the tombs" as one newspaper reporter called it. Rolling through the chill night, Czolgosz observed the crowds that had gathered at points along the tracks to shout insults. Those who had spent time with the prisoner noticed that he was now, however, as relaxed and comfortable as he had been at any time since his arrest, gorging himself on a large dinner before he left Buffalo, and then snacking continuously on sandwiches, pickles, and cheese.

He was also in a mood to open up to the newsmen traveling with him. As the train rattled and pitched through the night, Czolgosz expressed contrition for the first time. His exact words vary according to the report, but by one account he said, "It is awful to feel you killed somebody. I wish I had not done it. I would like to live, but I can't now. I made my mistake. I was all stirred up and felt I had to kill him." He went on to say he felt sorry for Ida and hoped she wouldn't die. And as a simple son of an immigrant, he had had no idea what the trial would be like. "It was all surprising to me," he said. "It was more than I expected. I thought I would be sentenced right off. What I heard there was more than I had heard before. I hated to hear about the wound and all that."[21]

Czolgosz's relaxed disposition swung violently when the train arrived at Auburn Prison. Built in 1817, the oldest prison in the state was located smack in the middle of town, and as luck would have it, right across the street from the train station. Several hundred people were there waiting for him, all apparently anxious to cheat the electric chair of its victim. Chanting and cursing, the mob was determined to grab

Czolgosz before the police could get him within the safety of the prison.

Surrounded by a phalanx of guards, Czolgosz was pushed, pulled, and dragged the fifty yards that separated the railway platform and the front gates of the prison. Ordering Czolgosz to remain close to him, his police escort absorbed repeated blows that were meant for the convict. Another guard tried unsuccessfully to restrain the crowd by brandishing his pistol. The mob was so rough that at one point it knocked Czolgosz to his knees. Picking up their charge "like a bag of salt," the guards carried him to the gates of the prison, where the crowd very nearly got its prey. One blow fell heavy on Czolgosz's neck. Someone managed to grab his shoulder. When the group finally reached the penitentiary gates, guard John Martin, a giant of a man, grabbed him and "with a mighty heave tossed him through."[22]

The experience terrified Czolgosz and reduced him to a stammering, helpless wreck. Martin had to pull him down the prison hall on his stomach and knees toward death row in the south wing, Czolgosz screaming, frothing at the mouth, and hysterically shouting "Save me! Save me," his voice echoing down the cell block and waking other prisoners. As one police officer put it, Czolgosz "shook and shivered and trembled and went all to pieces."[23]

The time Czolgosz would spend at Auburn was a torturous countdown for the emotionally empty prisoner. Where his guards at Buffalo had at least been able to respect him at some level for his cool head, here he was a universal object of derision. All were forbidden to speak with the prisoner, and extra guards were placed in his cell block because it was feared other inmates might try to escape just to murder him. Finding one guard who would talk, Czolgosz asked, "How does it feel?"

"How does what feel?" the guard asked.

"That in there," Czolgosz answered, jerking his thumb in the direction of the death chamber.

"Oh, you'll know," the guard replied.[24]

Other death row inmates enjoyed needling him. Clarence Egnor, who had killed a guard at the prison the year before and occupied the next cell, got a photo of McKinley, which he decorated in black crepe paper, hoping that Czolgosz would see it on his way to the chair.[25] Another prisoner, Fred Krist, taunted Czolgosz, "You will go through there and you'll never come back. . . . If you listen, you'll hear us cheer as you go."[26]

The repeated attempts of priests to console him offered Czolgosz no comfort. Asked if he wanted to see one, Czolgosz replied, "No, damn them. I don't want them and don't have them praying over me when I'm dead. I don't want any of their damned religion." Even when he did later relent, Czolgosz was unmoved. A Polish priest, the Reverend T. Szandinski, urged Czolgosz to give up anarchy and return to the church. Czolgosz refused.[27] Another priest, the Reverend Hyacinth Fudzinski, met with Czolgosz the night before the execution but was unable to connect with him and left frustrated. "It seems hopeless," he said. "I have tried in vain to bring Czolgosz to God. . . . He is the most heartless man I have ever saw. He has not the grace to love God. I think he is so without conscience that he will actually sleep tonight."[28]

In these final days of Czolgosz's life, Americans were gripped by a strange, pitiless fascination with what was about to take place. By the day of the execution, Auburn had received more than 1,200 requests to witness the event, even though there was room for only 26. Strangers submitted requests for Czolgosz's autograph, medical researchers had asked for portions of his brain. One museum curator offered $5,000 for either Czolgosz's body or his clothes. A kinetoscope owner offered $2,000 for permission to film him entering the death chamber. All were denied.[29]

Czolgosz was sleeping soundly at 5:30 A.M. on October 29, 1901, when Warden Mead unlocked his cell, stepped in, removed a piece of paper from his pocket, and began reading. It was the death warrant, the first step in a well-defined process that the state had prescribed for killing a man. Moments later a guard appeared with a stack of clothes—a pair of dark trousers with a slit in the left side for an electrode, a dark gray shirt, and a new pair of shoes. Czolgosz quietly got dressed. Though the journey to the execution room was only a few short steps, Czolgosz's knees had turned to rubber and were hardly strong enough to support his weight. Warden Mead would later say the guards "had virtually to carry him to the chair, he so nearly collapsed."[30]

The execution chair itself was made from simple rough wood and stood upon a rubber mat. Leather straps with heavy buckles had been prepared to bind the wrists and ankles. A headpiece, hanging from a wire about the width of a pencil, dangled from the ceiling. Czolgosz's lips quivered as uniformed guards fixed the straps around his body and placed a leather mask—with holes cut for the mouth and nose—across his face. He appeared to be searching the room for someone. As the guards finished their work, Czolgosz cried out: "I killed the President for the good of the laboring people, the good people. I am not sorry for my crime but I am sorry I can't see my father."[31]

Accounts of his final moments are remarkably varied. Some witnesses said he went to his death screaming, others that he was stoic. When Warden Mead gave the order to send 1,700 volts through his body, one witness said Czolgosz ground his teeth and cursed under his breath. *The New York Times* reported, "The rush of the immense current threw the body so hard against the straps that they creaked perceptibly. The hands clinched suddenly, and the whole attitude was one of extreme tension. For forty-five seconds, the full current was kept on, and then slowly, the electrician threw the switch back, reducing the current, volt by volt until it was cut off entirely."[32] Silently, the witnesses filed out of the observation room and into the morning.

Afterword

Midafternoon on September 14, 1901, a grave Theodore Roosevelt welcomed a small gathering of journalists and members of McKinley's cabinet to the Buffalo home of his longtime friend Ashley Wilcox. He looked exhausted. After a park ranger had delivered the news of McKinley's sudden decline, Roosevelt had raced through a rainy night and slept little. He now wore a frock coat, waistcoat, and striped trousers borrowed from Wilcox. A neighbor loaned a top hat big enough for Roosevelt's large head.

It was an incomprehensible moment for all present. What had begun as a working holiday for McKinley in Buffalo was now about to end with the swearing-in of a new president. Making their way to the home's library, many in the group fought back tears as Roosevelt repeated the oath of office and offered the first clues about the direction of his administration. Roosevelt assured them: "In this hour of deep and terrible national bereavement I wish to state that it shall be in my aim to continue absolutely unbroken the policy of President McKinley for the peace, prosperity and the honor of our beloved country."[1]

Following another's lead is not how the history books chronicle the life of the frenetic Roosevelt, hero of San Juan Hill, the president who walked softly and carried a big stick. Yet strangely there is much about the pledge he made that afternoon that would ring true for Roosevelt and indeed for presidents to follow. At home and abroad, McKinley was the first president of the twentieth century in more than chronology.

The physical empire that McKinley had created was not large—he had pulled in 138,187 square miles, nothing more than a forgotten back lot compared to the vast holdings of global rivals. By 1910, the American empire—counting Alaska—ranked seventh among the great powers and constituted only 6.4 percent of Britain's massive overseas holdings.[2] Yet it would be wrong to measure U.S. influence abroad solely by acreage. McKinley had sought to establish an American presence abroad that was based primarily on commerce, an approach that put a premium on establishing trading lanes, naval power, and stable, friendly markets.

All of this was still a work in progress at the time of McKinley's death. Most immediately, a decision still had to be made on the future of Cuba and the Philippines. Dreams of a great Asian market had yet to be realized. The navy was growing quickly, yet did not rule the waves. American sea power, standing twelfth in the world in 1890, had climbed only to a barely respectable sixth position a decade later.[3] Trade mirrored the navy. American exports had nearly doubled from $833 million in 1896 to $1.5 billion in 1901,[4] yet were nowhere near a level that could rescue the economy from future crises. The country was also discovering both new friends and new enemies abroad. While the United States and Britain forged a "special relationship" built on similar trade and strategic interests, Washington would find itself increasingly at odds with Germany and, later, Japan.

THE CANAL

No undertaking more excited Roosevelt in those early days in office than forging the last link of McKinley's trading empire—a canal that would join the Pacific and Atlantic oceans, the eastern seaboard with the riches of the Pacific. Here was an opportunity to advance American naval power and display the nation's industrial might and ingenuity, while—not coincidentally—leaving a monument to himself.

U.S. government commissions had studied the matter off and on since the 1870s, and it had long been assumed that Nicaragua, where the San Juan River and Lake Nicaragua seemed to form a blueprint, was the best place to build. Then Philippe Bunau-Varilla, the chief mining engineer during the failed French attempt, and William Cromwell, a New York lobbyist, stepped into the picture. The French company behind the effort, the Compagnie Universelle du Canal Interocéanique de Panama, still owned considerable assets in the Colombian province of Panama—a railroad, hundreds of buildings, digging equipment, and the partially completed excavation—and was looking for a buyer.[5] Together the pair worked the halls of Congress and plied newspaper editors with an intriguing argument. A canal through Panama would be only a third of the length of one through Nicaragua, with fewer curves and less digging, and therefore it would cost less.[6] They also claimed it would be safer, owing to the absence of the volcanoes that lined the Nicaraguan canal path. As if on cue, a volcano on the Caribbean island of Martinique erupted, and shortly thereafter one in Nicaragua began to rumble. Gleefully seizing on the timely acts of God, Bunau-Varilla secured a number of Nicaraguan stamps depicting volcanoes and placed them on desks during the Senate deliberation. In 1902, Congress agreed to buy out the French, and diplomatic preparations began for the "big dig" through Colombian territory.[7]

Negotiations with Tomás Herrán, Colombia's chargé d'affaires in Washington, quickly appeared to have settled the matter: The United States agreed to pay $10 million, plus another $250,000 a year for the rights to a six-mile-wide zone. To Roosevelt's utter disgust, however, the Colombian legislature rejected the deal, demanding more money for its depleted treasury.

Not to be put off by the "greedy little anthropoids"[8] running Colombia, Roosevelt cast his lot with Panamanian separatists who had long wanted to gain their independence from Colombia. How far Roosevelt actually went in promoting revolution, what he said, and to whom, is a matter of considerable debate. But when the uprising occurred in early November 1903, Roosevelt immediately recognized the new republic and dispatched troops to Panama City to prevent Colombian soldiers from intervening.

As soon as patriotic Panamanians raised their new flag, they struck a deal giving the United States rights to begin work, including the extraordinary provision that Washington would guarantee and maintain the independence of the Republic of Panama. With American doctors subduing the malaria and yellow fever that had killed so many workers on the French attempt, the Panama Canal was completed in 1914. Roosevelt later called the project "by far the most important action I took in foreign affairs."[9]

CUBA

American policy in Cuba had always aimed to help the "better classes"—landowners and businesspeople almost exclusively of Spanish descent—achieve power. During the September 1900 elections to select delegates to write a Cuban constitution, General Wood warned that the United States would not withdraw its army if the wrong kind of people were elected and campaigned hard against them. Voting rolls were even limited to landowners who Wood thought would elect the people he wanted.

When the "wrong" people were elected anyway, Washington took bolder steps to keep Cuba in line. Roosevelt's secretary of war, Elihu Root, wrote legislation to replace the Teller Amendment and demanded that a new Cuban constitution grant the United States extensive control over the island, including authority over any treaties, limits on how much debt the Cuban government took on, prohibitions against Cuba ceding territory, and deals providing naval bases for the

Americans. But, most important, Connecticut senator Orville Platt attached a rider to the Army Appropriations Act of 1901 stating "The government of Cuba consents that the United States may exercise the right to intervene for the preservation of Cuban independence, the maintenance of a government adequate for the protection of life, property, and individual liberty."[10] Faced with the choice of limited sovereignty or none at all, Cuba's constitutional convention adopted the Platt Amendment in June 1901 and on May 20, 1902, the United States formally ended its military occupation of the island.

Cuba quickly moved toward becoming an economic and military appendage of the United States. Under the Reciprocity Treaty of 1903, the United States slashed tariffs on Cuban agricultural imports by 20 percent in return for the Cubans making similar cuts in their own tariffs on vast swaths of goods. Armies of American farmers and colonists arrived, drawn by the cheap land producing a stunning variety of fruits and vegetables that could now be sold back home at favorable terms. By 1905, some 60 percent of all rural land was in the hands of foreigners.[11] By 1910, nearly seven thousand North Americans lived in Cuba earning a living in every manner of occupation—farmers, clerks, copyists, merchants, engineers, surveyors, mechanics, and teachers.[12]

The Americans, be they businessmen, colonial authorities, or the military, brought their culture with them. Soon clubs sprang up, a YMCA, the Women's Christian Temperance Union, Rotary and Lions, Knights of Columbus, and the American Legion. There was even a chapter of the Daughters of the American Revolution.[13] Cuba became a vacation destination; among the regulars were the du Pont family, which purchased a private home. American names began replacing Spanish ones: Charles replaced Carlos, Henry took the place of Enrique, and Frank edged out Francisco. New office buildings mirrored Manhattan.

Cubans looked on with a mixture of horror and admiration. In 1903, Cuban senator Manuel Sanguily observed, "Every day they leap ashore from the steamers coming from the North . . . these men of magnificent race, arrogant, their faces tanned by the cold north winds, with only a satchel but with wallets full of banknotes and their hearts aburst with impetuous blood, striding through our narrow streets with calculating eyes."[14]

The combination of growing U.S. investment on the island and a weak government almost guaranteed that it would not be long before the United States would again feel compelled to take political control. When, in 1906, rebels assembled an army of twenty-four thousand men and drove President Estrada Palma into resigning, Roosevelt established a second provisional government in Cuba under the leadership of Charles Magoon, a Nebraska lawyer. Though the U.S.-backed government would last only three years, marines would pay repeated visits to Cuba to make sure things went America's way—in 1912 to put down another revolt and again in 1917 to protect sugar interests, some staying through 1922.

PACIFIC COLONY

Despite Aguinaldo's call for surrender, guerrilla forces scattered on outlying islands in the Philippines remained determined to fight on. In no place would the resistance be more infamous than in Samar, the third largest island in the archipelago and one of the most wild. In September 1901, American troops were preparing to attend a church service commemorating McKinley's assassination when seventy-four American men and officers were ambushed in the village of Balangiga. The rebels, armed with bolos, caught the Americans unarmed and totally unprepared. They fought back with anything at hand, including baseball bats and, in the case of the doomed cook, by throwing cans of beans at the attackers. Only twenty of the seventy-four survived.

What the rebels hoped to accomplish is hard to understand as the United States clearly was not going to withdraw from the Philippines, and the horrific butchering only drove American generals to even greater displays of brutality. In early 1902 American forces would resolutely sweep through stretches of the countryside, razing villages and killing anybody they suspected of supporting the rebels. Orders were given to execute rebels older than ten on the spot. In an ironic commentary on what the war had done to American values, U.S. military forces under the command of Brigadier General J. Franklin Bell rounded up villagers and moved them to "protected zones" in an effort to cut rebels off from any means of support—exactly what the Spanish had done in Cuba.[15]

As bloody as the fighting had become, Filipino resistance was running out of gas. Deprived of their support among civilians in the field and losing out in the big cities where William Howard Taft was providing plenty of rewards in the form of jobs and government appointments to those who signed on to the American program, resistance steadily faded. On July 4, 1902, Roosevelt, anxious to end the fighting for political reasons, formally declared the war over. The cost to the United States had been 4,234 dead and 2,818 wounded. By American accounts, 16,000 native soldiers had been killed. Up to 200,000 civilians were thought to have died from famine and disease as well as by gunfire from both sides.[16]

As governor of the Philippines from 1901 to 1903, Taft began a period where America's better intentions began to reveal themselves. The portly Ohio lawyer negotiated a deal with the Vatican to acquire land that had once belonged to priests; he redistributed it to ordinary citizens. Dams were built, roads were laid, and a fair judiciary was established with native judges. Taxes were collected and spent on areas such as public health, dramatically slashing disease. An overhaul of the educational system, aided by thousands of American volunteer teachers, boosted the literacy rate to 50 percent from 20 percent within a generation.[17]

In the decades that followed, the United States would gradually ease the Philippines toward democracy. In 1907, the country was allowed to establish a national legislature, though the United States would maintain veto power. And to give the Filipinos a firsthand chance to see how a real democracy worked, two were allowed to join the House of Representatives, as observers. As in Cuba, the United States made no bones about taking sides in local elections, openly favoring the Federalistas party, which, in the words of a later governor, consisted of the "most conservative, best educated and talented Filipinos in the islands." To further tilt the political landscape toward the American view, voting was limited to taxpayers and landowners, a screening that reduced turnout to a scant 3 percent of the population.[18]

As in Cuba, the administration tried to create a reflection of America. English was taught as the primary language, and stretches of Manila were rebuilt according to the designs of an American architect in a Romanesque style reminiscent of Washington, D.C. As Finley Peter Dunne's "Mr. Dooley" quipped, "We'll larn ye our language, because tis easier to larn ye ours thin to larn ousilves ye'ers."[19] Products from the Philippines were given duty-free admission to the United States and, to the irritation of many Filipinos, American products were given similar access to the Filipinos, thereby giving the United States a virtual monopoly among foreign producers.

Just as American generals had forecast, however, the path toward independence would be a slow one. Despite steady pressure from the Filipinos, the movement did not gain serious attention in Washington until the early 1930s. Only in March 1934 did Congress pass a real timetable for Philippine independence, the Tydings-McDuffie Act, which offered the Filipinos their country back at the end of a ten-year period during which it would be given commonwealth status. That timetable would be delayed by World War II, but, finally, with the Treaty of Manila in 1946, the United States relinquished sovereignty over the islands.

CHINA TRADE

In the peace talks following the end of the Boxer Rebellion, McKinley largely secured the agreement among the allies that he had hoped for when he first committed troops in the summer of 1901. Under the leadership of William Rockhill, U.S. negotiators steered debate away from dismembering China (although McKinley bizarrely flirted with the idea of snatching a Chinese port) and toward reestablishing China as a market. The empress dowager was allowed to remain on her throne to help stabilize the country. And the United States won favorable concessions on Chinese tariffs, ones that allowed easy importation of its agricultural goods. Only on the issue of indemnities was Rockhill unable to enforce American thinking. The final peace protocol required China to make considerable payments to the allies for decades.

China, however, proved to be an elusive market. Exports climbed from seven million in 1896 to fifteen million in 1900[20]—but they never attained levels that had been hoped for and never made a difference in economic growth at home.

There were a number of reasons for the disappointing trade flows. With a few exceptions—such as Standard Oil, American cotton producers, and the British American Tobacco Company—companies failed to tailor products for the Chinese market. At the same time, American business leaders came to the startling realization that for all the eye-popping reports of China's vast size, the average consumer there actually could not consume. According to one 1898 estimate that few had taken notice of at the time, the average Chinese laborer made all of 5 to 7.5 cents a day. For such people, even a bar of soap was "an article of luxury."[21] And that was assuming that there existed roads and rail tracks to reach them. There weren't. What's more, many Chinese refused to buy American goods after they learned of insulting laws in California and other states that limited the number of immigrants from their country. Tremendously successful boycotts were launched. The British American Tobacco Company, which by 1902 was selling one billion cigarettes a year in China, was a popular target. Angry students fixed posters around major towns showing a dog smoking cigarettes with the slogan "Those who smoke American cigarettes are of my species."

Despite the setbacks, there was no shaking America's conviction that China offered a unique economic bonanza. As Roosevelt put it, the United States must "command the terminus of Asia—if we fail in this we shall break down." In 1903 he added, "We must do our best to prevent the shuttering to us of Asian markets. In order to keep the roads to these terminals we must see that they are managed primarily in the interest of the country."[22]

The persistent conviction that riches awaited in China, and that the Open Door was the best means to achieve them, would ultimately put the United States on a collision course with another Pacific empire in the making—Japan.

JAPAN AND THE OPEN DOOR

Few would have believed in the early years of the twentieth century that Japan would become America's greatest nemesis in the Pacific.

America and Japan seemed to be united by the common threat of Russia. Both nations looked on in horror when Russia, rather than withdrawing from Manchuria after the Boxer Rebellion as they had promised, built a railway through northern Manchuria to Vladivostok, their major port in the North Pacific. Equally alarming were Russian plans to build another railroad in the region and to fortify a harbor at Port Arthur.[23] They were advances the Japanese could not countenance. With U.S. blessing—and financing from American Jewish bankers who held little love for the anti-Semitic Russian nobility—Japan in 1904 attacked Russian forces in Manchuria and Korea and easily rolled over just about every Russian military unit they encountered in what would become a fairly one-sided, one-year war over control of northern Asia.

The war initially seemed to bring a measure of stability to China, and Roosevelt eagerly volunteered to oversee peace talks held in Portsmouth, New Hampshire, in the late summer of 1905. In the peace treaty that followed—Roosevelt won a Nobel Prize for brokering it—Japan and Russia agreed to leave Manchuria and respect Chinese territorial integrity.

But the deal also began what would become a long, slow drip of Japanese encroachments into China, often enabled by naïve and weak replies to Japanese aggressiveness. In lieu of indemnity, the Portsmouth peace pact awarded to the Japanese important Chinese ports that had belonged to Russia, including the main railway station in south Manchuria, half of Sakhalin Island, and a free hand in Korea. Still feeling undercompensated by the peace treaty, Japan went even further and soon made Korea a protectorate. Rather than coming to Korea's aid, Roosevelt struck a secret pact with the Japanese—the Taft-Katsura Agreement—whereby the United States recognized Japanese domination of Korea in exchange for Japan's promise not to interfere with the United States in the Philippines.[24]

Soon Tokyo closed Korea to American business and began expanding into Manchuria—directly challenging the Open Door. Roosevelt responded with as much bluster as a nation who refused to countenance a war would allow, assembling the entire fleet of sixteen battleships for a round-the-world tour. Painted in peacetime white, the force was quickly dubbed the Great White Fleet and made a high-profile stop in Yokohama, where it was hoped the Japanese would be so impressed they would leave China alone. The Japanese offered the visiting fleet all the politeness for which they are known and then quickly resumed their expansion plans.

As Roosevelt's handpicked successor, President Taft began his term with the full expectation that he would follow Roosevelt's policies—the press joked that Taft stood for "Takes Advice From Theodore." Under Taft, however, there would be less cozying up to the Japanese and a greater effort to put economic power to use in defending China. The result, however, was the same. Attempting to stem Russia and Japan, Taft proposed a consortium of English, French, German, and U.S. interests either to loan money to China to buy railroads owned by the Japanese and Russians or to build its own competing railways that could drive them out of business. The suggestion was roundly rejected by investors who feared for China's stability and only served to bring the Japanese and Russians into alliance against the United States.[25]

By the time World War I began in 1914, the Open Door and American willingness to defend it were rapidly crumbling. With the European powers busy fighting for their lives, Tokyo issued the secret Twenty-One Demands to the Chinese government. Taken in total, they would have reduced the Middle Kingdom to a Japanese protectorate. After the demands were quickly leaked to the United States, which sharply rebuked Tokyo's aggressiveness, the most heinous ones were eliminated. Yet two years later, with the United States fighting in Europe, Japan saw opportunity again, and made further inroads into China. Under an agreement signed by new secretary of state Robert Lansing, Washington acknowledged Japan's "special interests" in China in return for a Japanese pledge to support China's "territorial sovereignty"—a largely empty term by now.

In 1931, the United States watched almost helplessly as Japan, inventing several flimsy excuses, formally seized all of Manchuria, renamed it Manchukuo, and went on to invade and station troops in Shanghai, for decades the home to thousands of foreign residents. President Franklin Delano Roosevelt would continue to apply diplomatic and economic pressure on the Japanese but without effect. Japan would remain in China until forced to surrender to Allied powers in 1945.

CZOLGOSZ'S LEGACY

With the benefit of one hundred years of hindsight, it's hard to escape the conclusion that Czolgosz's attack accomplished little more than to waste his life and to set the cause of anarchism back for years. Rather than inspiring a new generation of social radicals, Czolgosz managed to turn much of the nation, other anarchists included, against him. Around the country, calls were made for new laws to purge anarchist thought from American society—some patently absurd. One suggestion, for instance, was that anarchists be shipped to a remote island in the Pacific.[26] Others were more realistic, if constitutionally dubious. New York State passed a law banning anarchist writings and speeches; New Jersey and Wisconsin enacted similar legislation.[27] In his December 3, 1901, State of the Union address, Theodore Roosevelt expressed the feelings of many: "Anarchy is a crime against the whole human race; and all mankind should band against the anarchist. His crime should be made an offense against the law of nations, like piracy and that form of man-stealing known as the slave trade; for it is of far blacker infamy than either."

In Washington, the Fifty-seventh Congress made defeating anarchism its main focus, pursuing essentially two avenues to deal with the menace: leveling especially harsh sentences against those convicted of attacks on elected officials, and barring immigrants with known anarchist backgrounds from entering the country. Although there was considerable support along both lines, petty differences between the House and the Senate in the closing hours of the congressional session limited what would finally be accomplished, and only legislation banning anarchists from entering the country was put into law. What became known as the Anarchist Exclusion Act was passed on the final day of the session, March 3, 1903.[28]

Further legislative steps would have to be taken, however, before the United States could rid itself of its most notorious anarchist— Emma Goldman.

GOLDMAN FIGHTS ON

In the weeks after her arrest in Chicago, Goldman was transferred from one jail to another, including the very one where Parsons and the other Chicago "martyrs" had spent their final weeks. Try as prosecutors might to build a case linking her with the assassination, nothing could be proven, other than that she had delivered an inflammatory speech attended by Czolgosz. She was released on the same day Czolgosz was convicted.

Rather than distance herself from Czolgosz, as nearly all other anarchists were busy doing, Goldman lionized McKinley's killer as a hero who had made the ultimate sacrifice for his beliefs. In an article published in the October 6, 1901, issue of *Free Society*, Goldman wrote of Czolgosz that his was a "soul in pain, a soul that could find no abode in this cruel world of ours, a soul 'impractical,' inexpedient, lacking in caution . . . but daring just the same, and I cannot help but bow in reverenced silence before the power of such a soul, that has broken the narrow walls of its prison, and taken a daring leap into the unknown."[29]

Goldman would pay a high price for her support of Czolgosz. Hounded by the media and hassled by the police, she came, as she put it, to feel "spiritually dead" and even adopted a false name, Miss E. G. Smith. For a time, she gave up speaking and turned to private nursing jobs, sharing a series of apartments with her brother, a medical student.[30]

Yet by 1903, Goldman seemed to have regained her old form and eagerly took up the cause of John Turner, a British trade unionist who had recently arrived in New York. Attracting the attention of police for his labor speeches, Turner was arrested when it was discovered he possessed a copy of *Free Society* and that he planned to give speeches commemorating Johann Most and the Haymarket Eight. While Turner was held on Ellis Island in a six-by-nine-foot cage normally used for insane immigrants, Goldman launched a spirited and very public effort to secure his release, albeit one that would ultimately fail. Turner was eventually deported.[31]

By 1906, Goldman had reclaimed her position at the center of a revived anarchist moment, founding *Mother Earth* magazine from her apartment in 210 East Thirteenth Street in New York, and had begun speaking again. From 1908 until 1917, and now putting on more than a few extra pounds, she lived like a vagabond, spending half the year on the road, staying with fellow anarchists or in lonesome hotel rooms. From Portland, Oregon, to Rochester, New York, she delivered a startlingly wide variety of lectures on topics such as "The Intermediate Sex," "Woman's Inhumanity to Man," and the "Psychology of War."[32] With the coming of World War I and the growing peace movement in the United States, her popularity surged and her lectures were routinely standing-room only. One night in New York in 1917 she drew eight thousand enthusiastic listeners.[33]

She was, however, walking an increasingly narrow line. Fears of leftist radicals were at an all-time high following the revolution in Russia in early 1917. In June that year, Goldman finally pushed the government too far and was arrested for speaking against the new selective service law. She would be sentenced to prison for twenty months and when released in September 1919 was quickly arrested again—this time for violating a new law giving the government the right to deport unnaturalized immigrants for transgressions such as belonging to organizations advocating revolution. Neither Berkman nor Goldman, as it turned out, had ever bothered to become American citizens despite their long years living in the United States.[34]

On December 21, 1919, Goldman, Berkman, and more than two hundred other immigrant radicals were loaded aboard a dilapidated U.S. army transport, the SS *Buford*. Under the watchful eyes of 250 armed guards, the "red ark"—as the newspapers called it—sailed into the icy North Atlantic for Russia. Goldman, who had written hopeful articles about the new government, was shocked to learn upon her arrival in Petrograd that civil liberties such as free speech, which she had depended on in the United States, were considered of little importance. She soon left, living for a time in Germany, London, and Canada, now not only preaching against capitalism but against the Bolshevik government as well. She would be allowed to reenter the United States only briefly on a lecture tour. She died May 14, 1940, in Toronto.

With or without Goldman, however, anarchists remained active in the United States, including those practicing violence.

ANARCHISM'S BLOODY COMEBACK

In the latter half of the 1910s, a series of bombing attacks rocked the United States, most in one way or another linked to an Italian immigrant by the name of Luigi Galleani, the spiritual heir of Johann Most who was committed to the propaganda of the deed. His genius, like Most's, lay more in inspiring others than in actually blowing anything up himself. Popularly known as Galleanists and almost exclusively Italian-American immigrants, his followers remained at their core very much committed to fighting what they considered an oppressive government. And now they had found new reasons for anger: the U.S. entry into World War I and draconian new laws meant to stifle radicals.

The first in a string of anarchist attacks occurred in New York in 1914 when bombs were placed in St. Patrick's Cathedral, the St. Alphonsus Church, and on November 11, the anniversary of the Haymarket executions, at the Bronx Courthouse. All failed to cause damage or were defused, but the city and the country had been put on notice that a violent strain of anarchists and radicals was on the loose.[35]

In 1916, Galleanist Nestor Dondoglio, a chef by profession, poisoned some two hundred guests at a banquet to honor Archbishop George Mundelein in Chicago. That attack failed when Dondoglio put too much arsenic in the food, causing the diners to throw up their meals—poison included—in what must have still been a gruesome event. A year later, in November 1917, Mario Buda, chief bomb maker of the Galleanists, was thought to have masterminded a deadly bombing in Milwaukee aimed at a rally hosted by Reverend Augusto Giuliani. Hoping to avenge several radicals who had been killed by police, Buda placed a bomb in the basement of Giuliani's church. Before it went off, the device was discovered and brought to a local police station. There, while police were studying it, the bomb exploded, killing ten officers and one civilian.[36]

In April 1919, Galleanists are thought to have sent thirty dynamite bombs through the regular mail to an eclectic assortment of judges, politicians, and financiers, John D. Rockefeller and Attorney General A. Mitchell Palmer among them. The ineptitude of the bombers, however, rendered the mass attack mostly harmless. Many of the packages lacked proper postage and were not delivered. Others were easily deemed suspicious because of their unusual markings—they were wrapped in brown paper and marked "Gimbel Brothers," "Novelty," and "Samples." The only casualty was a servant of Georgia senator Thomas Hardwick, whose hands were blown off when she tried to open one package.[37] Despite a painstaking investigation, police were never able to catch the bombers.[38]

A little more than a month later, on June 2, 1919, yet another wave of bombings shook the country. Within an hour of midnight, large explosive devices, each containing up to twenty pounds of dynamite, detonated in seven cities, all on the doorsteps of their targets—judges, businessmen, and immigration officials. Again, none of the intended victims were hurt, though a night watchman and a passerby were killed. At the site of each bombing, leaflets proclaiming the right of workers to defend themselves were found that were signed "The Anarchist Fighters." One of the bombers, Carlo Valdinoci, a former editor of the newspaper *Cronaca Sovversiva* and a close friend of Galleani, demonstrated how dangerous the bombings were—for the attackers more than the targets. Valdinoci had apparently been attempting to place his bomb on the front porch of U.S. attorney general A. Mitchell Palmer when he accidentally detonated the device. Police investigators collected bits and pieces of Valdinoci's body throughout the neighborhood.[39]

Police were largely unable to determine who was behind the attacks, but that didn't mean that those suspected went unpunished. Galleani was deported along with eight supporters. Andrea Salsedo, a typesetter who admitted to being an anarchist and who had printed a flyer found with many of the bombs, either jumped, was pushed, or fell from a fourteen-story window at the FBI office on Park Row in New York where he was being questioned.[40] And two avowed anarchists and known followers of Galleani, Nicola Sacco and Bartolomeo Vanzetti, were arrested in May 1920 for killing two men and stealing the payroll of the Slater & Morrill shoe company. In the highly charged trial and series of appeals that followed, the two were sentenced to death and executed in August 1927.[41]

Finally, radicals who some now believe were tied to Galleani undertook the most destructive attack on U.S. soil for the next eight decades.

Near noon on September 16, 1920, a horse-drawn wagon pulled to a stop at 23 Wall Street across the street from the headquarters of J. P. Morgan. The driver quickly alighted and disappeared into the thick lunchtime crowds, leaving behind a cargo that contained one hundred pounds of dynamite and some five hundred pounds of cast-iron sash weights. At slightly past noon, a delayed timer ignited the explosives, blowing the wagon and the horse to bits. The casting balls, strong enough to leave large divots in the stone walls of surrounding buildings that are still visible, ripped and tore into the flesh of the clerks, brokers, and messengers who were beginning their lunch breaks. Some thirty-eight people were killed. Despite a massive police investigation, no one was ever convicted of the crime.

CZOLGOSZ

One of the enduring controversies surrounding the assassination of William McKinley was the mental state of Leon Czolgosz. Anyone who kills a president, knowing that he will likely be executed for the deed, can't be seen as emotionally fit. Two alienists, Dr. Walter Channing and Dr. L. Vernon Briggs, came to this conclusion after Czolgosz was executed. Conducting a thorough examination of his life, the pair attempted to establish a pattern of mental instability, the crux of their argument centering on the mysterious sickness that led him to quit his job and to exhibit strange behavior thereafter.

Briggs and Channing had, however, never met Czolgosz, and their assessment runs against the conclusions of nearly every other study conducted by those who had. One group, Dr. Floyd Crego, Dr. Joseph Fowler, and Dr. James W. Putnam, met with Czolgosz no fewer than four times, on each occasion for two hours, applying every test of sanity known at the time. Two other experts called by Czolgosz's attorneys—Drs. Carlos F. MacDonald and Arthur Hurd—met with Czolgosz three times and, like the previous trio, concluded that Czolgosz was sane. Despite their repeated attempts to trip him up, Czolgosz consistently elaborated on his reasons for killing the president and likewise seemed to have a solid command of the current economic and political situation in the country. In their report to District Attorney Thomas Penny on November 2, 1901 (dated September 28, 1901), Crego, Fowler, and Putnam wrote, "The most careful questioning failed to discover any hallucinations of sight or hearing. He had received no special command; he did not believe he had been specially chosen to do the deed. He always spoke of his motive for the crime as duty; he always referred to the Anarchists' belief that the killing of rulers was a duty. . . . He is the product of anarchy, sane and responsible."[42]

A study of Czolgosz's brain, which was removed in the hours after he was executed, did not reveal any deformities that were associated with insanity.

IDA

It had been generally assumed that the shock of the president's death would be strong enough to kill Ida as well. The night before McKinley died, family friend Frank B. Baird had said as much, telling reporters that if the president passed away, they should be prepared for a double funeral.[43] Aides eased the First Lady into the news with sedatives and kept her away from the memorial services for the president that were held in Washington, believing that she needed to conserve all her energy for the funeral to be held in Canton. They were right. Arriving with her husband's body in Ohio, Ida practically had to be carried from the train to her carriage and later was unable to even attend a private service for the family held in her own home, instead listening at the door to the minister.[44] She would not visit the cemetery until September 20, 1901—after the funeral.

Yet predictions that she would soon follow her husband to the grave were incorrect. She would live on, her existence a melancholy ordeal dominated by a longing for her husband. At home she created something of a shrine to him, arranging a photo, a small bronze bust, and three vases upon an American flag that was draped over a small table. Visitors said the only topic on her mind was her lost spouse. The president's close friend Charles Dawes visited Ida in 1903: "Mrs. McKinley greeted us in tears and was depressed in spirits which is always the case with her now," he wrote.[45] She would idle away the time, waiting for death and to rejoin her husband in heaven, until she finally passed on May 26, 1907, at age fifty-nine.

THE *MAINE*

One of the greatest mysteries of American naval history is what actually sank the *Maine*. Despite the naval board of inquiry's finding that an external explosion had destroyed the ship, doubts immediately surfaced. It would have been extremely difficult, it was pointed out, for anybody to place a bomb the size of the one needed to sink the ship without being observed. Nor, in the short amount of time between when the *Maine* was ordered to Havana and when it arrived, could someone have prepared a waterproof bomb and placed it near the area where the *Maine* was tied up. Other skeptics pointed out that since the *Maine* had sunk, there had not even been the whiff of a rumor as to who had committed the deed. What's more, there were doubts that a Spanish mine could have blown up any ship so spectacularly. During the war itself, two American naval ships near Guantánamo had struck Spanish mines and neither had sunk.[46]

The debate gained fresh energy in 1910 when an opportunity arose to investigate the *Maine*. It was decided that for navigational reasons— the wreck still jutted above the surface and was creating an artificial shoal—the ship had to be refloated, dragged out to sea, and sunk in deeper waters. Raising the ship, it was obvious to all, would also provide valuable new insights into the explosion.

The extensive photographs and measurements taken when the *Maine* was exhumed led a second naval board, under the leadership of Rear Admiral Charles E. Vreeland, to two important findings. The first regarded the famous "inverted V" that the 1898 investigational group had assumed was the site of the external explosion. Now, the board found, there was no reason to believe that the blast had occurred there. But that didn't kill the external explosion theory, for the Vreeland board found that closer to the rear of the ship were signs of an explosion from outside the hull that, they believed, had ignited the contents of the six-inch reserve magazine and touched off the massive explosion. The details were different, but the result was the same as that of the 1898 naval board of inquiry. Somebody had deliberately blown up the *Maine*.

In the mid-1970s, however, probably the greatest challenge to the external explosion theory was advanced by a naval engineer, Ib S. Hansen, and an explosives expert, David W. Taylor. Working at the request of legendary admiral H. G. Rickover, the pair again pored over photos taken of the *Maine* in 1911, applying more modern analysis to the wreckage. They concluded that the original explosion occurred within the ship around the six-inch reserve magazine, which, in turn, caused partial detonation of the forward magazines. The inverted V, they concluded, had been caused by the twisting of the ship as compartments flooded, not as a result of a bomb. Although there did exist a small indentation and displacement of plating on the bottom of the ship under the six-inch reserve magazine, the two men concluded that the damage could have been caused by an internal explosion or as the ship sank. They found no scarring around that area that suggested there had actually been an explosion from outside the hull. The *Maine*, they concluded, had been sunk when its bituminous coal stores had spontaneously combusted, a not uncommon occurrence on ships of the day. Coal fires often smoldered for some time, creating no smoke nor raising temperatures that an alarm could have detected. The whole trigger for the Spanish-American War, and all that had happened in the years that followed, had been an accident.[47]

Acknowledgments

This book would never have been possible without the support at every level of my wife, Karen. First reader, sounding board, and inspiration, she was an invaluable partner. Our daughters, Elisabeth and Anna, cheerfully encouraged their often distracted father throughout the project.

My agent, Michael V. Carlisle, of Inkwell Management, deserves special thanks for taking on a first-time author. I would also like to thank my excellent editors at Random House—Jonathan Jao, Jessica Waters, Sam Nicholson—and copyeditor Michelle Daniel.

Karl Ash of the McKinley Presidential Library and Museum in Canton, Ohio, provided invaluable assistance with the library's collection of artifacts and newspaper articles. Gary Brown of the Canton Repository generously helped track down articles in his newspaper. Barry Pateman of the Emma Goldman Papers at the University of California provided copies of *Free Society* and helped find photos of Goldman. Elaine Grublin of the Massachusetts Historical Society helped me with the papers of Walter Channing. Bonnie O'Brian of the Bar Association of Erie County provided a transcript of the Czolgosz trial as well as a fascinating reenactment of the courtroom proceedings. The staff of the Library of Congress always delivered prompt and friendly help in acquiring photographs. I would also like to thank the many librarians of the University of Washington system who patiently aided my navigation of their vast collections.

Notes

CHAPTER 1: TEMPLE OF MUSIC

1. Gray, *Art Handbook: Official Handbook of Architecture and Sculpture*, 15.
2. See "Illuminations: Revisiting the Buffalo Pan-American Exposition of 1901," University of Buffalo Libraries, for an interactive account of the fair: http://ublib.buffalo.edu/libraries/exhibits/panam/index.html.
3. Goldman, *High Hopes*, 7.
4. Halstead, *Illustrious Life*, 429.
5. Stoddard, *As I Knew Them*, 231.
6. Johns, *Man Who Shot McKinley*, 19.
7. Goldman, *High Hopes*, 5.
8. Leech, *In the Days of McKinley*, 584.
9. Johns, *Man Who Shot McKinley*, 13.
10. Ibid., 13–14. Several different spellings of "Nieman" have been used. Some researchers have spelled it Niemann and on one occasion, Nieman himself spelled it Nimen.
11. Smalley, "William McKinley—A Study," 44.
12. Thayer, *Life and Letters of John Hay*, 2:266.

13. "President McKinley in War Times," 16.

14. Leech, *In the Days of McKinley*, 589.

15. Barry, *Historic Memento of the Nation's Loss*, 6.

16. Johns, *Man Who Shot McKinley*, 77.

17. Barry, *Historic Memento of the Nation's Loss*, 8.

18. "How He Saved the President's Life," *Leslie's Weekly*, September 21, 1901. This article describes part of Parker's story, though some details are at odds with other accounts.

19. Goldman, *High Hopes*, 9.

20. Barry, *Historic Memento of the Nation's Loss*, 12.

21. Johns, *Man Who Shot McKinley*, 91.

22. "I Hope He Dies. I Hope He Dies!" *The Cleveland Press*, September 8, 1901.

23. Everett, *Compete Life of William McKinley*, 34.

24. Garraty, *Labor and Capital in the Gilded Age*, viii–ix.

CHAPTER 2: "OH GOD, KEEP HIM HUMBLE"

1. Olcott, *Life of William McKinley*, 1:320.

2. "Making History in Canton," *The Sunday Repository*, October 25, 1896.

3. Ibid.

4. "He Stood Under a Crown," *The New York Times*, June 26, 1896.

5. Leech, *In the Days of McKinley*, 94.

6. Timmons, *Portrait of an American*, 60.

7. Morgan, *William McKinley and His America*, 233.

8. Storer, "How Theodore Roosevelt Was Appointed Assistant Secretary of the Navy," 9.

9. "McKinley to Stay at Canton," *The New York Times*, September 11, 1896.

10. Jones, *Presidential Election of 1896*, 277.

11. Phillips, *William McKinley*, 12.

12. Porter, *Life of William McKinley*, 42.

13. Phillips, *William McKinley*, 12.

14. Halstead, *Illustrious Life of William McKinley*, 109.

15. Armstrong, *Major McKinley*, 7.

16. Russell, *Lives of William McKinley and Garret A. Hobart*, 49.

17. Ibid., 55–57.

18. Armstrong, *Major McKinley*, 5.

19. Ibid., 5–6.

20. Morgan, *William McKinley and His America*, 18.

21. Armstrong, *Major McKinley*, 38–40.

22. Cashman, *America in the Gilded Age*, 23.

23. Smith, *Rise of Industrial America*, 114.

24. Bruce, *1877: Year of Violence*, 120.

25. United States Department of Commerce, *Historical Statistics of the United States*, 1:590.

26. Morris, *Tycoons*, 174.

27. United States Department of Commerce, *Historical Statistics of the United States*, 2:957.

28. David, *History of the Haymarket Affair*, 5.

29. Bogart, *Economic History of the American People*, 554.

30. Cashman, *America in the Gilded Age*, 178–79.

31. Ibid., 3.

32. Leech, *In the Days of McKinley*, 36.

33. Olcott, *Life of William McKinley*, 1:130.

34. McKinley, *Speeches and Addresses*, 1893, 19.

35. Stoddard, *As I Knew Them*, 245.

36. Croly, *Marcus Alonzo Hanna*, 70.

37. Based on the Economic History Association's CPI calculator, www.eh.net.

38. Morgan, *William McKinley and His America*, 174.

39. Alfred Henry Lewis, "McKinley's Political Manager and His War on Organized Labor," *New York Journal*, May 4, 1896.

40. Leech, *In the Days of McKinley*, 67.

41. Williams, *Tragedy of American Diplomacy*, 21.

42. Butterfield, *American Past*, 272.

43. Coletta, *William Jennings Bryan*, 137.

44. Glad, *McKinley, Bryan, and the People*, 176.

45. Ibid.

46. Coletta, *William Jennings Bryan*, 175.

47. Glad, *McKinley, Bryan, and the People*, 176.

48. Morgan, *William McKinley and His America*, 226.

49. Timmons, *Portrait of an American*, 56.

50. Ibid., 61.

51. Thayer, *Life and Letters of John Hay*, 2:151.

52. Beer, *Hanna* (1929), 155–56.

53. Marcus, *Grand Old Party*, 246–47.

54. Josephson, *Politicos*, 697–99.

55. Butterfield, *American Past*, 275.

56. Coletta, *William Jennings Bryan*, 199.

57. Dawes, *Journal of the McKinley Years*, 97.

58. 55th Cong., 1st sess., *Congressional Record* 30, pt. 3 (July 23, 1897): 2848.

59. Josephson, *Politicos*, 704.
60. Coletta, *William Jennings Bryan*, 168.
61. Josephson, *Politicos*, 702.
62. Marcus, *Grand Old Party*, 247.
63. Glad, *McKinley, Bryan, and the People*, 171.
64. Ibid., 172.
65. Ibid., 176.
66. Morgan, *William McKinley and His America*, 240.
67. Josephson, *Politicos*, 703.
68. Croly, *Marcus Alonzo Hanna*, 217.
69. "Greatest of Parades," *The New York Times*, November 1, 1896.
70. Jones, *Presidential Election of 1896*, 340.
71. Coletta, *William Jennings Bryan*, 190.
72. Dunn, *From Harrison to Harding*, 199.
73. Kohlsaat, *From McKinley to Harding*, 53–54.

CHAPTER 3: A QUIET MAN IN THE CORNER

1. Johns, *Man Who Shot McKinley*, 37.
2. Briggs, *Manner of Man*, 297. This scene is a compilation of the typical habits of Czolgosz.
3. Ibid., 229.
4. Ibid., 298.
5. Ibid.
6. Ibid., 300.
7. Smith, *Rise of Industrial America*, 214.
8. Reef, *Working in America*, 125.
9. Foner, *Great Labor Uprising of 1877*, 25.
10. Smith, *Rise of Industrial America*, 218.
11. Murolo and Chitty, *From the Folks Who Brought You the Weekend*, 110–11.
12. Reef, *Working in America*, 127.
13. Smith, *Rise of Industrial America*, 220.
14. Ibid.
15. Ibid.
16. Reef, *Working in America*, 130.
17. Anbinder, *Five Points*, 73.
18. Ibid., 80–81.
19. Bruce, *1877: Year of Violence*, 24.
20. Nicholson, *Labor's Story in the United States*, 105.
21. David, *History of the Haymarket Affair*, 10.

22. Francisco and Fast, *Conspiracy for Empire*, 34.

23. Briggs, *Manner of Man*, 289.

24. Hoerder and Rössler, *Distant Magnets*, 85.

25. Balch, *Our Slavic Fellow Citizens*, 220.

26. Briggs, *Manner of Man*, 281.

27. Ibid., 290. Throughout the Briggs notes, confusion arises from the spelling of Polish names. In this case, Briggs wrote the priest's name as Gerick. This is probably really Father Theodore Gierky who was active at St. Albertus around that time. Briggs also says Mr. Lorkowski said the family attended the "St. Alberta" parish. He must have meant St. Albertus. Briggs says a search of parish records failed to turn up anything to do with the family. It is possible that the staff who helped him, including a number of priests, simply didn't want one of the nation's greatest villains to be associated with their parish.

28. Ibid., 302.

29. Rauchway, *Murdering McKinley*, 124–25.

30. Briggs, *Manner of Man*, 262. Leon had eight brothers and sisters. One other had died in infancy.

31. Ibid., 290.

32. Ibid., 302.

33. Ibid., 290.

34. Ibid., 291.

CHAPTER 4: "THERE WILL BE NO JINGO NONSENSE"

1. "President Takes the Oath," *The New York Times*, March 5, 1896.

2. Leech, *In the Days of McKinley*, 113.

3. "President Takes the Oath," *The New York Times*, March 5, 1896.

4. Hartzell, *Sketch of the Life of Mrs. William McKinley*, 22.

5. Whitcomb and Whitcomb, *Real Life at the White House*, 209.

6. Morgan, *William McKinley and His America*, 311.

7. Leech, *In the Days of McKinley*, 27.

8. Morgan, *William McKinley and His America*, 82.

9. Ibid., 83.

10. Foraker, *I Would Live It Again*, 256–59. Foraker clearly lost no love for Ida and recounts several examples of the First Lady's rudeness and petulance.

11. Whitcomb and Whitcomb, *Real Life at the White House*, 209.

12. Letters from McKinley to Ida, 1880. On file at the McKinley Presidential Library, Canton, Ohio, in the "McKinley Family Letters" binder.

13. Morgan, *William McKinley and His America*, 82.

14. Storer, "How Theodore Roosevelt Was Appointed," 9.

15. "The Inauguration Bible," *The New York Times*, February 16, 1897.

16. "President Takes the Oath of Office," *The New York Times*, March 5, 1896.

17. First Inaugural Address of William McKinley. Lillian Goldman Law Library, Yale Law School, http://avalon.law.yale.edu/19th_century/mckin1.asp.

18. May, *Imperial Democracy*, 3.

19. Porter, "Discipline in the Navy," 410.

20. Stealey, *Twenty Years in the Press Gallery*, 31–32.

21. Morgan, *William McKinley and His America*, 71.

22. Wise, *Recollections of Thirteen Presidents*, 215.

23. Beer, *Hanna* (1929), 110.

24. Wise, *Recollections of Thirteen Presidents*, 216.

25. Offner, *Unwanted War*, 39–40.

26. Macfarland, "William R. Day," 278–79.

27. Storer, "How Theodore Roosevelt Was Appointed," 9.

28. Millis, *Martial Spirit*, 38.

29. Morris, *Rise of Theodore Roosevelt*, 582.

30. Fuess, *Carl Schurz, Reformer*, 349.

31. Hoar, *Autobiography of Seventy Years*, 309.

32. Darwin, *Descent of Man*, 160–61.

33. Fiske, "Manifest Destiny," 588.

34. Strong, *Our Country*, 210–18.

35. Ferreiro, "Mahan and the 'English Club,' " 902.

36. LaFeber, *New Empire*, 89; and Zimmermann, *First Great Triumph*, 99.

37. Zimmermann, *First Great Triumph*, 100.

CHAPTER 5: "THE GOVERNMENT IS BEST WHICH GOVERNS LEAST"

1. Coulter, *Poles of Cleveland*, 9–10.

2. Rauchway, *Murdering McKinley*, 159–60.

3. Ibid., 164–65.

4. Paul operated the bar himself for only a few months before he rented it to the Findlay Beer Company. Briggs, *Manner of Man*, 303.

5. Rauchway, *Murdering McKinley*, 164.

6. Ibid., 162.

7. Ibid., 166.

8. Briggs, *Manner of Man*, 303.

9. Ibid., 304.

10. Ibid., 304–5.

11. Brecher, *Strike!*, 80.

12. Ibid., 82.

13. Briggs, *Manner of Man*, 305.

14. Ibid.

15. Downs, *Books That Changed America*, 102.

16. Ibid., 100–110.

17. Briggs, *Manner of Man*, 314.

18. Seibert, *"I Done My Duty,"* 92–94. See also "Czolgosz Says He Had No Aid," *Chicago Sunday Tribune,* September, 8 1901. Text available on the McKinley Assasination Link: http://74.125.155.132/search?q=cache: mhKFICkGM2gJ:mckinleydeath.com/documents/newspapers/CST60-251b.htm+Anton+Zwolinski+czolgosz&cd=2&hl=en&ct=clnk&gl=us.

19. Donovan, "Man Who Would Not Shake Hands," 111–12.

20. Joll, *Anarchists*, 34.

21. Burke, *Works*, 45.

22. Marshall, *William Godwin*, 99.

23. Conway, *Writings of Thomas Paine*, 69.

24. Rocker, *Pioneers of American Freedom*, 15–16.

25. Emerson, *Emerson's Essays*, 409.

26. Thoreau, *On the Duty of Divil Disobedience*, 7.

27. Jacker, *Black Flag of Anarchy*, 48.

28. Sutton, *Communal Utopias*, 5.

29. Ibid., 6.

30. Ibid., 7.

31. Bailie, *Josiah Warren*, 7.

32. Rocker, *Pioneers of American Freedom*, 61.

33. Jacker, *Black Flag of Anarchy*, 59.

34. Ibid., 60.

35. Bailie, *Josiah Warren*, 60–61. See also Martin, *Men Against the State,* 70–84.

36. Bailie, *Josiah Warren*, 61–62.

37. Martin, *Men Against the State*, 82.

CHAPTER 6: THE HAWAIIAN ANVIL

1. Marquis, *Who's Who in America*, 405.

2. Russ, *Hawaiian Republic*, 130–31.

3. *World Almanac and Encyclopedia*, 1903, 151.

4. Foster, *Diplomatic Memoirs*, 171.

5. Pletcher, *Diplomacy of Involvement*, 241.

6. McCormick, *China Market*, 28.

7. Francisco and Fast, *Conspiracy for Empire*, 26–27.

8. Lamoreaux, *Great Merger Movement in American Business*, 32.

9. Ibid., 34.

10. LaFeber, *Cambridge History of American Foreign Relations*, 30.

11. F. P. Prial, "Trade Outlooks for 1897," *The New York Times*, February 7, 1897.

12. McCormick, *China Market*, 36.

13. "Must Find New Markets," *The New York Times*, January 24, 1896.

14. Williams, *Tragedy of American Diplomacy*, 17.

15. Kohlsaat, *From McKinley to Harding*, 72.

16. Van Alstyne, *Rising American Empire*, 188.

17. Wilcox, *Harper's History of the War in the Philippines*, 393–95.

18. Dennet, *Americans in Eastern Asia*, 49.

19. Morison, *Maritime History of Massachusetts*, 65.

20. Ward, "Fair, Honorable and Legitimate Trade," http://www.american heritage.com/articles/magazine/ah/1986/5/1986_5_49.shtml.

21. Campbell, *Special Business Interests*, 20.

22. Ibid.

23. Daws, *Shoal of Time*, 287.

24. Hoar, *Autobiography of Seventy Years*, 307–8.

25. Pletcher, *Diplomacy of Involvement*, 250.

26. Foster, *Diplomatic Memoirs*, 172.

27. Morgan, *William McKinley and His America*, 295.

28. Fuess, *Carl Schurz*, 350.

CHAPTER 7: AN UNLIKELY ANARCHIST

1. *People of the State of New York vs. Leon F. Czolgosz;* "The Assassin Makes a Full Confession," *The New York Times*, September 8, 1901; "Czolgosz Says He Had No Aid," *Chicago Sunday Tribune*, September 8, 1901. Nowak would visit Czolgosz in prison and try to discover if there had been other plotters.

2. "Assassin Known as Rabid Anarchist," *The New York Times*, September 8, 1901.

3. "Czolgosz Says He Had No Aid," *Chicago Sunday Tribune*, September 8, 1901.

4. Foner, *Autobiographies of the Haymarket Martyrs*, 27.

5. Ibid., 29.

6. Avrich, *Haymarket Tragedy*, 10.

7. Ashbaugh, *Lucy Parsons*, 267–68.

8. Avrich, *Haymarket Tragedy*, 14.

9. Green, *Death in the Haymarket*, 61.

10. Ibid., 60.

11. Pierce, *History of Chicago*, 3:244.

12. Foner, *Autobiographies of the Haymarket Martyrs*, 180.

13. Bruce, *1877: Year of Violence*, 100–107.

14. Beatty, *Age of Betrayal*, 289.

15. Foner, *Great Labor Uprising of 1877*, 151.

16. Avrich, *Haymarket Tragedy*, 28.

17. Ibid., 30.

CHAPTER 8: AN OPEN CASK OF GUNPOWDER

1. Eggert, "Our Man in Havana," 463–85.

2. Ibid., 480.

3. Trask, *War with Spain*, 15.

4. Hamilton, *President McKinley, War, and Empire*, 1:105.

5. Musicant, *Empire by Default*, 57.

6. Foner, *Spanish-Cuban-American War*, 1:106.

7. Musicant, *Empire by Default*, 68.

8. O'Toole, *Spanish War*, 56.

9. Foner, *Spanish-Cuban-American War*, 1:115.

10. Trask, *War with Spain*, 9.

11. Musicant, *Empire by Default*, 70.

12. Brown, *Correspondents' War*, 14–15.

13. Ibid., 78.

14. Ibid., 36.

15. Ibid., 101–2.

16. 54th Cong., 1st sess., *Congressional Record* 28, pt. 3, March 2, 1898: 2349.

17. Hirst, *Life and Letters of Thomas Jefferson*, 540.

18. Grenville and Young, *Politics, Strategy, and American Diplomacy*, 179.

19. O'Toole, *Spanish War*, 38.

20. Mandel, *Samuel Gompers*, 201–2.

21. United States Department of State, *Papers Relating to the Foreign Relations, 1896*, 582.

22. Trask, *War with Spain*, 2.

23. Rubens, *Liberty*, 204–5.

24. Trask, *War with Spain,* 11.

25. Offner, "McKinley and the Spanish-American War," 54. Considerable debate remains about what real effect granting belligerent status would have meant for the insurgents. See Beale, "Recognition of Cuban Belligerency," 406–19.

26. Trask, *War with Spain,* 11.

27. Musicant, *Empire by Default,* 91.

28. Parker, *Recollections of Grover Cleveland,* 248–50.

29. "President McKinley in War Times," 213.

30. Ibid., 214.

31. Whitcomb and Whitcomb, *Real Life at the White House,* 216.

32. Morgan, *William McKinley and His America,* 313.

33. "President McKinley in War Times," 215.

34. Whitcomb and Whitcomb, *Real Life at the White House,* 214.

35. Morgan, *William McKinley and His America,* 305.

36. Whitcomb and Whitcomb, *Real Life at the White House,* 211.

37. Ibid., 213.

38. Foner, *Spanish-Cuban-American War,* 1:212.

39. Pérez, *Cuba and the United States,* 61.

40. Pratt, *Expansionists of 1898,* 237.

41. "Calhoun Back from Cuba," *The New York Times,* June 8, 1897.

42. Foner, *Spanish-Cuban-American War,* 1:117.

43. Palmer, *Bliss, Peacemaker,* 42.

44. Roosevelt to Lodge, September 21, 1897, in Roosevelt and Lodge, *Selections from the Correspondence,* 278.

45. Grenville, "American Naval Preparations for War with Spain," 35.

46. Ibid., 43.

47. Williams, *Tragedy of American Diplomacy,* 34.

48. William McKinley, "Message of the President, December 6, 1897," in United States Department of State, *Papers Relating to the Foreign Relations,* 1897, xx.

49. Ibid., 16.

50. Musicant, *Empire by Default,* 109.

51. Offner, *Unwanted War,* 93.

52. Bonsal, *Real Condition of Cuba,* 36.

53. Pérez, *Cuba Between Empires,* 160.

54. Ibid., 159.

55. "Revolt Feared in Havana" *The New York Times,* January 17, 1898.

56. United States Department of State, *Papers Relating to the Foreign Relations,* 1898, 1024.

57. Ibid.

58. Ibid., 1024–25.

59. Ibid., 1025.

60. Foner, *Spanish-Cuban-American War*, 1:229.

61. Musicant, *Empire by Default*, 190.

62. *Spanish Diplomatic Correspondence*, 64–65.

63. Barrón, "Enrique Dupuy de Lôme and the Spanish-American War," 40.

64. Ibid., 52.

65. Ibid., 55.

66. Long, *Journal of John D. Long*, 214.

67. Herrick, *American Naval Revolution*, 210.

68. Beer, *Hanna, Crane and the Mauve Decade*, 548.

CHAPTER 9: PROPAGANDA OF THE DEED

1. In his autobiography, Parsons gives a different date, July 22, 1877. He also exaggerated the size of the crowd, saying thirty thousand people were on hand. In reality, it was closer to six thousand.

2. Calmer, *Labor Agitator*, 29.

3. Foner, *Autobiographies of the Haymarket Martyrs*, 32.

4. Ibid.

5. Ibid.

6. Ibid., 33.

7. Avrich, *Haymarket Tragedy*, 32–33.

8. Ibid., 30.

9. Ibid., 34.

10. Bruce, *1877: Year of Violence*, 283.

11. Rayback, *History of American Labor*, 135.

12. Gotkin, "Legislated Adjustment of Labor Disputes," 481.

13. Brecher, *Strike!*, 31.

14. Trautmann, *Voice of Terror*, 78–79.

15. Goyens, *Beer and Revolution*, 88.

16. David, *History of the Haymarket Affair*, 65–66.

17. Merriman, *Dynamite Club*, 75.

18. Goldman, *Living My Life*, 1:6.

19. Avrich, *Haymarket Tragedy*, 136.

20. Ibid., 144–45.

21. Ibid., 169.

22. Ibid., 170.

CHAPTER 10: "THE *MAINE* BLOWN UP!"

1. Sigsbee, *"Maine,"* 26–27. There existed some dispute as to the buoy number.
2. Cluverius, "Midshipman on the *Maine*," 245.
3. Rickover, *How the Battleship* Maine *Was Destroyed,* 1–3.
4. Ibid., 4.
5. Ibid.
6. Sigsbee, *"Maine,"* 43.
7. Ibid., 42.
8. Musicant, *Empire by Default,* 129.
9. "The Worst Insult to the United States in Its History," *New York Journal and Advertiser,* February 8, 1898.
10. Sigsbee, *"Maine,"* 64.
11. Ibid., 67.
12. "Night of the Explosion in Havana," 222.
13. Millis, *Martial Spirit,* 104.
14. Ibid., 102.
15. Rickover, *How the Battleship* Maine *Was Destroyed,* 1.
16. "Cruiser *Maine* Blown Up in Havana Harbor," *New York Journal and Advertiser,* February 16, 1898.
17. "Destruction of the Warship *Maine* Was the Work of the Enemy," *New York Journal and Advertiser,* February 17, 1898.
18. "*Maine* Explosion Caused by Bomb or Torpedo?" *The World,* February 17, 1898.
19. "Vizcaya Still at Sea," *The World,* February 19, 1898.
20. Foner, *Spanish-Cuban-American War,* 1:238. The *Journal's* climbed from 416,885 copies on January 9, 1898, to over a million on February 18.
21. Sousa, *Marching Along,* 157.
22. Ibid., 158.
23. Ellis, *To the Flag,* 6.
24. Ibid., 9–19.
25. Rickover, *How the Battleship* Maine *Was Destroyed,* 20.
26. Olcott, *Life of William McKinley,* 2:12–13.
27. Hagedorn, *Leonard Wood,* 141.
28. When exactly Roosevelt made the éclair remark is a matter of some historical debate. See Leech, *In the Days of McKinley,* 628.
29. Gage, *Memoirs of Lyman J. Gage,* 111–12.
30. Leech, *In the Days of McKinley,* 35.
31. McKinley, *Speeches and Addresses,* 1900, 77.

32. Volwiler, "Harrison, Blaine, and American Foreign Policy," 638.

33. James, *Rise and Fall of the British Empire,* 171.

34. Pratt, *Expansionists of 1898,* 258.

35. Beisner, *Twelve Against Empire,* 93.

36. Long, *Journal of John D. Long,* 217.

37. O'Toole, *Spanish War,* 137.

38. Foner, *Spanish-Cuban-American War,* 1:240.

39. Chadwick, *Relations of the United States and Spain,* 1:28–37.

40. Ibid., 37–40.

41. Busbey, *Uncle Joe Cannon,* 186–91.

42. Leech, *In the Days of McKinley,* 169.

43. United States Department of State, *Papers Relating to the Foreign Relations,* 1898, 684.

44. Musicant, *Empire by Default,* 169.

45. Russell, *Illustrated History of Our War with Spain,* 452.

46. "Our Duty to Cuba," *The Washington Post,* March 29, 1898.

47. Morgan, *William McKinley and His America,* 367.

48. Musicant, *Empire by Default,* 150–60.

49. Morris, *Rise of Theodore Roosevelt,* 607–8.

50. William C. Reick to John Russell Young, March 25, 1898, McKinley Papers, reel 3.

51. "Even the Babes in Arms," *The Washington Post,* May 1, 1898.

52. Kohlsaat, *From McKinley to Harding,* 67. Details of this account are disputed.

53. Foner, *Spanish-Cuban-American War,* 1:50.

54. A curious exchange between Day and Woodford in the days prior to the U.S. ultimatum has stimulated a lively debate about whether McKinley changed his policy to demand Cuban independence. In an exchange of notes starting on March 25, 1898, Day told Woodford that the United States wanted Spain to grant the Cubans "full self government," a vague expression that he quickly clarified as meaning "Cuban independence." That would have appeared to have signaled an important shift in McKinley's attitudes toward Cuba. Yet Woodford did not mention Cuban independence when he met with the Spanish, nor did Day when he met with the Spanish minister in Washington. Nor did the president mention Cuban independence in his war message to Congress several weeks hence, an intentional omission for which he was severely criticized. Why Day made the "independence" remarks to Woodford is hard to explain, but in view of the entire thread of American policy it is an anomaly that didn't reflect a change in McKinley's actions.

55. Musicant, *Empire by Default*, 177.

56. Rubens, *Liberty*, 326–27.

57. Gould, *Presidency of William McKinley*, 82–84. Historians have made much of McKinley's refusal to ask Congress for more time, arguing he was too weak to do so. Gould, however, contests that view, arguing rightly that the Spanish peace overture was incomplete.

58. Ibid., 84.

59. Mayo, *America of Yesterday*, 176.

60. 55th Cong., 2nd sess., *Congressional Record* 31, pt. 4, April 11, 1898, 3704–7.

61. "The President's Cuban Message Disappointing to Those Who Want Cuba Freed," *The New York Times*, April 12, 1898.

62. 55th Cong., 2nd sess., *Congressional Record* 31, pt. 4, April 12, 1898, 3732.

63. Halbo, "Presidential Leadership in Foreign Affairs," 1326–32.

64. Palmer, *Bliss, Peacemaker*, 54.

65. Morgan, *William McKinley and His America*, 378.

66. Stoddard, *As I Knew Them*, 252.

CHAPTER 11: "FIRE AND KILL ALL YOU CAN!"

1. Green, *Death in the Haymarket*, 105.

2. Ibid., 116–17.

3. Young, *Art Young*, 80.

4. David, *History of the Haymarket Affair*, 160.

5. Avrich, *Haymarket Tragedy*, 188.

6. Busch, "Haymarket Riot and the Trial of the Anarchists," 250–58.

7. Adamic, *Dynamite*, 72.

8. Calmer, *Labor Agitator*, 91.

9. Lum, *Concise History of the Great Trial of the Chicago Anarchists*, 94.

10. Green, *Death in the Haymarket*, 123.

11. Calmer, *Labor Agitator*, 92.

12. Green, *Death in the Haymarket*, 186.

13. Parsons, *Life of Albert R. Parsons*, 214.

14. "Rioting and Bloodshed in the Streets of Chicago," *The New York Times*, May 5, 1886.

15. McClean, *Rise and Fall of Anarchy in America*, 18.

16. Avrich, *Haymarket Tragedy*, 210.

17. Ibid., 208.

18. Parsons, *Life of Albert R. Parsons*, 215.

CHAPTER 12: DEWEY AT MANILA

1. Dewey, *Autobiogrpahy*, 192.
2. Trask, *War with Spain*, 396.
3. Aguinaldo, *Second Look at America*, 31.
4. Ibid., 33.
5. Karnow, *In Our Image*, 112.
6. Williams, *Tragedy of American Diplomacy*, 36.
7. Kohlsaat, *From McKinley to Harding*, 68.
8. Campbell, *Special Business Interests and the Open Door Policy*, 25–33.
9. Denby, "America's Opportunity in Asia," 33.
10. *The Journal of Commerce and Commercial Bulletin*, January 5, 1898, and January 8, 1898. As quoted in Lorence, *Organized Business*, 4.
11. Karnow, *In Our Image*, 108.
12. Ibid.
13. Alger, *Spanish-American War*, 326.
14. Wolff, *Little Brown Brother*, 61.
15. Leech, *In the Days of McKinley*, 192. Long describes different events, but Crowninshield gives a credible account, rich in detail.
16. Musicant, *Empire by Default*, 202; and O'Tolle, *Spanish War*, 174.
17. West, *Admirals of the American Empire*, 140.
18. Ibid., 75, 80.
19. O'Toole, *Spanish War*, 177. Two additional nonfighting colliers rounded out the American fleet.
20. Conroy, *Battle of Manila Bay*, 34.
21. Stickney, "With Dewey at Manila," 479.
22. Dewey, *Autobiography*, 214.
23. Conroy, *Battle of Manila Bay*, 46.
24. Ibid., 49.
25. Ibid., 53.
26. Harden, "Dewey at Manila," 370.
27. Stickney, "With Dewey at Manila," 476.
28. "The Nation Honors Dewey," *The New York Times*, May 10, 1898. See also "The Admiral Dewey's Sword," *The New York Times*, September 18, 1898.
29. Chadwick, *Relations of the United States and Spain*, 1:208.
30. Millis, *Martial Spirit*, 198.
31. Ibid.
32. Wolff, *Little Brown Brother*, 159.

33. Pritchett, "Some Recollections," 397–98.
34. United States Adjutant-General's Office, *Correspondence Relating to the War with Spain,* 2:635, 644.
35. Dewey to Long, May 13, 1898, McKinley Papers, reel 3.
36. United States Adjutant-General's Office, *Correspondence Relating to the War with Spain,* 2:646.
37. Ibid., 2:676–78.

CHAPTER 13: A RESPECTABLE TRAMP

1. Pierce, *History of Chicago,* 3:280.
2. Whitlock, *Forty Years of It,* 73.
3. Pringle, *Theodore Roosevelt,* 110.
4. Avrich, *Haymarket Tragedy,* 220.
5. Ibid., 216.
6. Ashbaugh, *Lucy Parsons,* 85.
7. Parsons, *Life of Albert Parsons,* 227.
8. Ibid., 216.
9. Ibid.
10. Avrich, *Haymarket Tragedy,* 247–48.
11. Ibid., 250.
12. Zeisler, *Reminiscences of the Anarchist Case,* 20.
13. Parsons, *Anarchism,* 183–84.
14. Lum, *Concise History of the Great Trial,* 49; Parsons, *Life of Albert Parsons,* 222.
15. Calmer, *Labor Agitator,* 101.
16. Avrich, *Haymarket Tragedy,* 270.
17. Green, *Death in the Haymarket,* 226.
18. Ibid., 227.
19. Werstein, *Strangled Voices,* 75.
20. David, *History of the Haymarket Affair,* 316.
21. Green, *Death in the Haymarket,* 241.
22. "The Trial of the President's Assassin," *Saturday Globe* (Utica, N.Y.), September 28, 1901.
23. Green, *Death in the Haymarket,* 243.
24. Ibid., 258–59.
25. Avrich, *Haymarket Tragedy,* 361.
26. Busch, "Haymarket Riot," 252.
27. Parsons, *Life of Albert Parsons,* 249–51.

28. Ibid., 247.
29. Ibid.

CHAPTER 14: THE "LEAST DANGEROUS EXPERIMENT"

1. Millis, *Martial Spirit*, 164; Musicant, *Empire by Default*, 245–46.
2. Musicant, *Empire by Default*, 248.
3. Morgan, *William McKinley and His America*, 383.
4. Carlson and Bates, *Hearst*, 105–6.
5. Millis, *Martial Spirit*, 162–63.
6. Carlson and Bates, *Hearst*, 107.
7. Morris, *Rise of Theodore Roosevelt*, 640.
8. Ibid., 643.
9. Roosevelt, *Rough Riders*, 11.
10. Ibid., 63.
11. Millis, *Martial Spirit*, 208.
12. Cosmas, *Army for Empire*, 193.
13. Musicant, *Empire by Default*, 268.
14. Alger, *Spanish-American War*, 66–68.
15. Musicant, *Empire by Default*, 249.
16. Davis, "Rocking-Chair Period," 132.
17. Brown, *Correspondents' War*, 211.
18. Davis, "Rocking-Chair Period," 132.
19. "Spain's Fleet Steams Toward American Waters," *The New York Herald*, May 1, 1898.
20. Musicant, *Empire by Default*, 291.
21. Roosevelt, *Theodore Roosevelt*, 258–59.
22. Bradford, *Crucible of Empire*, 33.
23. Millis, *Martial Spirit*, 232–35.
24. Graham, *Schley and Santiago*, 149.
25. Pritchett, "Some Recollections," 400.
26. Reid, *Problems of Expansion*, 20.
27. Rogers, *Destiny's Landfall*, 109.
28. Davis, *Our Conquests in the Pacific*, 46.
29. Ibid., 52.
30. Ibid., 52–53. Other writers offer slightly different accounts of the exchange, but the overall story is the same.
31. Ibid., 54–55.

CHAPTER 15: "THE CHILD HAS GONE CRAZY"

1. Goldman, *Living My Life*, 1:10.
2. Ibid.
3. Wexler, *Emma Goldman*, 6.
4. Ibid., 9.
5. Ibid., 18.
6. Goldman, *Living My Life*, 1:60.
7. Wexler, *Emma Goldman*, 21.
8. Ibid., 28.
9. Ibid., 40.
10. Goldman, *Living My Life*, 1:5–6.
11. Ibid., 1:72–73.
12. Falk, *Emma Goldman*, 291.
13. Wexler, *Emma Goldman*, 43–60.

CHAPTER 16: SAN JUAN HILL

1. Alger, *Spanish-American War*, 71.
2. Ibid., 65–74.
3. Miley, *In Cuba with Shafter*, 54.
4. Trask, *War with Spain*, 204.
5. Reno, "General Calixto Garcia," 55.
6. Miley, *In Cuba with Shafter*, 56.
7. Roosevelt, *Rough Riders*, 74–75.
8. Dobson, *Reticent Expansionism*, 87.
9. Atkins, *War in Cuba*, 100.
10. Ibid., 100–101.
11. Musicant, *Empire by Default*, 369.
12. Foner, *Spanish-Cuban-American War*, 2:355.
13. Musicant, *Empire by Default*, 400.
14. O'Toole, *Spanish War*, 300.
15. Millis, *Martial Spirit*, 317.
16. Russ, *Hawaiian Republic, 1894–98*, 240.
17. Musicant, *Empire by Default*, 404.
18. Freidel, *Splendid Little War*, 145.
19. Brown, *Correspondents' War*, 354.
20. Musicant, *Empire by Default*, 414.

21. Roosevelt, *Rough Riders*, 121.

22. Ibid., 123–24.

23. Lee, "Regulars at El Caney," 410.

24. Ibid., 411.

25. Musicant, *Empire by Default*, 409.

26. Davis, *Cuban and Porto Rican Campaigns*, 219–20.

27. Ibid., 220.

28. Parker, "Some Lessons of the War," 430.

29. Freidel, *Splendid Little War*, 162.

CHAPTER 17: LUNCHROOM

1. Goldman, *Living My Life*, 1:82.

2. Ibid., 85.

3. Wolff, *Lockout*, 29.

4. Ibid., 30.

5. Ibid.

6. Brecher, *Strike!*, 53.

7. Brooks, *Toil and Trouble*, 89.

8. Nasaw, *Andrew Carnegie*, 409.

9. Brecher, *Strike!*, 54.

10. Berkman, *Prison Memoirs of an Anarchist*, 1.

11. Goldman, *Living My Life*, 1:84.

12. Ibid., 85.

13. Berkman, *Prison Memoirs of an Anarchist*, 4.

CHAPTER 18: A COUNTRY "FULL OF SWAGGER"

1. Graham, "Destruction of Cervera's Fleet," 405.

2. Ibid., 408.

3. Chadwick, *Relations of the United States and Spain*, 2:136.

4. Brown, *Correspondents' War*, 381.

5. Graham, "Destruction of Cervera's Fleet," 424–31.

6. Goldstein and Dillon, *Spanish-American War*, 152–54.

7. Foner, *Spanish-Cuban-American War*, 2:366–68.

8. Ibid., 2:370.

9. *Spanish Diplomatic Correspondence*, 213.

10. Ibid., 214.

11. "Dewey's Pet Dog," *The New York Times*, August 28, 1899. For details about the "Society of the Dog" see "Biographies in Naval History: Admiral of the Navy George Dewey, USN," Navy Department Library, Department of the Navy, http://www.history.navy.mil/bios/dewey_george.htm.

12. Dewey, *Autobiography*, 246–47.

13. Karnow, *In Our Image*, 113–14.

14. Wolf, *Little Brown Brother*, 69.

15. Karnow, *In Our Image*, 115.

16. Ibid., 120.

17. Ibid., 121–22.

18. Chadwick, *Relations of the United States and Spain*, 2:412.

19. Karnow, *In Our Image*, 124.

20. Millet, *Expedition to the Philippines*, 159.

21. Musicant, *Empire by Default*, 529.

22. Davis, *Cuban and Porto Rico Campaign*, 309.

23. Zakaria, *From Wealth to Power*, 161.

24. Walron, "Commercial Promise of Cuba," 481.

CHAPTER 19: BLOODY HOMESTEAD

1. Wolff, *Lockout*, 104.

2. Ibid., 100.

3. Burgoyne, *Homestead*, 54.

4. Nasaw, *Andrew Carnegie*, 423.

5. Burgoyne, *Homestead*, 78–82.

6. Nasaw, *Andrew Carnegie*, 426.

7. Berkman, *Prison Memoirs of an Anarchist*, 4–7.

8. Goldman, *Living My Life*, 1:88.

9. "Chairman Frick Shot," *The New York Times*, July 24, 1892.

10. Schreiner, *Henry Clay Frick*, 99. There are various accounts of when Berkman tried to detonate the bomb in his mouth. In possibly a second attempt at suicide, Berkman tried to detonate a cap of fulminate of mercury according to "Chairman Frick Shot," *The New York Times*, July 24, 1892. Goldman, in *Living My Life*, vol. 1, page 97, states that Berkman was unconscious after the hammer blow and was revived at the station house, where detectives noticed he had something in his mouth that turned out to be a dynamite cartridge.

11. Schreiner, *Henry Clay Frick*, 100.

12. Goldman, *Living My Life*, 1:98.

13. Ibid., 1:105.
14. Wexler, *Emma Goldman*, 66; Goldman, *Living My Life*, 1:105–6.
15. Wexler, *Emma Goldman*, 76–77.
16. Ibid., 79.

CHAPTER 20: SPOILS OF WAR

1. "Mr. McKinley at Montauk," *The New York Times*, September 4, 1898.
2. Ibid.
3. *New York World*, July 20, 1898. Quoted in Foner, *The Spanish-Cuban-American War*, 2:394.
4. "The Week," *The Nation* 69, no. 1795 (November 23, 1899):382.
5. "Shafter's Opinion of Cubans," *The New York Times*, December 19, 1898.
6. Foner, *Spanish-Cuban-American War*, 2:393.
7. Sams, "Trouble with Cubans," *The New York Times*, August 5, 1898.
8. "A New Era in Cuba," *The New York Times*, August 12, 1898.
9. 56th Cong., 2nd sess., *Congressional Record* 34 (February 26, 1901):3042.
10. "Spain Hauls Down Her Flag in Cuba," *The New York Times*, January 2, 1899.
11. United States Tarriff Commission, *Effects of the Cuban Reciprocity Treaty of 1902*, 374.
12. Foner, *The Spanish-Cuban-American War*, 2:422.
13. Ibid., 2:482.
14. Ibid., 2:476–77.
15. Ibid., 2:481.
16. Ibid., 2:471.

CHAPTER 21: HUNTING RABBITS

1. Rauchway, *Murdering McKinley*, 180.
2. Ibid., 180–82.
3. Briggs, *Manner of Man*, 305, 314. Page and Czolgosz's brother Waldek offer different accounts of when Czolgosz left the factory. Page's account, which is based on the company's records, is probably more reliable.
4. Ibid., 294.
5. Ibid., 307.

CHAPTER 22: "IT IS ALWAYS THE UNEXPECTED THAT HAPPENS, AT LEAST IN MY CASE"

1. United States Department of State, *Papers Relating to the Foreign Relations*, 1898, 907.
2. *Treaty of Peace and Accompanying Papers*, 472–90.
3. McKinley, *Speeches and Addresses*, 1900, 109.
4. Ibid., 105.
5. Karnow, *In Our Image*, 129.
6. "The Danger of Today," *The New York Times*, June 22, 1898.
7. Wolff, *Little Brown Brother*, 195.
8. Ibid.
9. Schirmer and Shalom, *Philippines Reader*, 22.
10. Hay to Day, October 26, 1898, McKinley Papers, reel 63.
11. Hay to Day, November 5, 1898, McKinley Papers, reel 63.
12. Hay to Day, October 26, 1898–November 13, 1898, McKinley Papers, reel 63.
13. Karnow, *In Our Image*, 131.
14. Wolff, *Little Brown Brother*, 175.
15. Karnow, *In Our Image*, 139–40.
16. Wolff, *Little Brown Brother*, 277.
17. Leech, *In the Days of McKinley*, 357–58.
18. Wolff, *Little Brown Brother*, 230.
19. Roosevelt and Lodge, *Selections from the Correspondence*, 391.
20. "President McKinley on the Philippines," *The New York Times*, February 17, 1899.
21. Boot, *Savage Wars of Peace*, 109.
22. Wolff, *Little Brown Brother*, 241.
23. Ibid., 311.
24. "Nation's Capital Welcomes Dewey," *The New York Times*, October 3, 1899.
25. McKinley, *Speeches and Addresses*, 1900, 216.
26. Coffman, *Hilt of the Sword*, 5.
27. Silbey, *War of Frontier and Empire*, 142.
28. Karnow, *In Our Image*, 179.
29. Silbey, *War of Frontier and Empire*, 164.

CHAPTER 23: RED EMMA

1. Wexler, *Emma Goldman*, 85.
2. Falk, *Emma Goldman*, 392.
3. Ibid., 327.
4. Ibid., 385.
5. Ibid., 386.
6. Fine, "Anarchism and the Assassination of McKinley," 777.
7. Merriman, *Dynamite Club*, 69–78.
8. Tuchman, *Proud Tower*, 92.
9. Ibid., 107.
10. Ibid., 102.
11. Ibid., 108.
12. Joll, *Anarchists*, 138.
13. Tuchman, *Proud Tower*, 110.
14. Ibid., 109.

CHAPTER 24: OPEN DOORS

1. "Beresford on China," *The New York Times*, February 11, 1899.
2. Ibid.
3. Dennett, *John Hay*, 288.
4. Murolo and Chitty, *From the Folks Who Brought You the Weekend*, 120.
5. Varg, *Open Door Diplomat*, 22.
6. Ibid., 29.
7. Ibid., 30.
8. Dennett, *John Hay*, 293.
9. Zakaria, *From Wealth to Power*, 163.
10. Preston, *Boxer Rebellion*, 24.
11. Ibid., 26.
12. Ibid.
13. Ibid., 27.
14. Ibid., 48.
15. Hoover, *Memoirs*, 47–48.
16. O'Conner, *Spirit Soldiers*, 143.
17. Ibid.
18. McCormick, *China Market*, 157.
19. Ibid., 158.
20. Dennett, *John Hay*, 301.

21. LaFeber, *Cambridge History of Foreign Relations*, 74.
22. Dennett, *John Hay*, 302.
23. McCormick, *China Market*, 160.
24. Ibid.
25. Briggs, *United States Marines in North China*, 40.
26. Thomas, *Old Gimlet Eye*, 43–53.
27. Hoover, *Memoirs*, 53.
28. Preston, *The Boxer Rebellion*, 209.

CHAPTER 25: *"AVANTI!"*

1. "Assassin's Lot Fell Upon Anarchist Here," *The New York Times*, July 31, 1900.
2. Ibid.
3. Tuchman, *Proud Tower*, 121.
4. Falk, *Emma Goldman*, 422.

CHAPTER 26: THE AMERICAN CENTURY

1. Leech, *In the Days of McKinley*, 467.
2. Jas T. Woodward, "The United States the Envy of the World," *The New York Times*, January 1, 1900.
3. Kent, *America in 1900*, 22.
4. Ibid., 18.
5. Ibid., 22.
6. Carter, *Historical Statistics of the United States*, 2:903.
7. Ibid., 2:898.
8. Lamoreaux, *The Great Merger Movement*, 2.
9. Bryan, "Issue in the Presidential Campaign," 766.
10. Ibid., 767–68.
11. Morris, *Rise of Theodore Roosevelt*, 756.
12. Thayer, *Life and Letters of John Hay*, 342.
13. Morris, *Rise of Theodore Roosevelt*, 763.

CHAPTER 27: WORDS THAT BURN

1. Briggs, *Manner of Man*, 293.
2. Ibid., 307.

3. Ibid., 308.
4. Goldman, *Living My Life*, 1:290.
5. Falk, *Emma Goldman*, 453.
6. "The Curse of Government," *Free Society*, June 30, 1901.
7. "Kings and King-Slayers," *Free Society*, August 26, 1900.

CHAPTER 28: "SURRENDER OR BE KILLED"

1. Bain, *Sitting in Darkness*, 96.
2. Karnow, *In Our Image*, 167.
3. Ibid., 176.
4. Bain, *Sitting in Darkness*, 98.
5. Ibid., 210.
6. Ibid., 219.
7. Ibid., 373.
8. Aguinaldo, *A Second Look at America*, 129.

CHAPTER 29: "HAVE YOU ANY SECRET SOCIETIES?"

1. Channing Papers, 21–24.
2. Channing, *Mental Status of Leon Czolgosz*, 15, gives an alternate spelling of Hauser.
3. Channing Papers, 24. See also Briggs, *Manner of Man*, 308.
4. Channing Papers, 24. See also Briggs, *Manner of Man*, 308.
5. There is no evidence at this point that Czolgosz wanted to commit violent acts.
6. Briggs, *Manner of Man*, 318.
7. Ibid., 309.
8. Ibid., 294.
9. Ibid., 309.
10. Goldman, *Living My Life*, 1:290–91.
11. Everett, *Complete Life of William McKinley*, 84–85.
12. Channing, *Mental Status of Czolgosz*, 18.
13. Ibid., 18–19. Czolgosz claim that he was not an anarchist may be explained in a couple ways. Possibly, Isaak wanted to distance Czolgosz from the ideology. Or, it may be that Czolgosz, as he sometimes did, intentionally gave misleading information in hopes that it would make Isaak more sympathetic.
14. Ibid., 17.

15. Ibid., 19.
16. Everett, *Complete Life of William McKinley*, 87.
17. Channing, *Mental Status of Czolgosz*, 17.
18. Briggs, *Manner of Man*, 321.
19. Ibid., 320.
20. Goldman, *Living My Life*, 1:291.
21. Seibert, *"I Done My Duty,"* 109.

CHAPTER 30: GOING TO THE FAIR

1. Leech, *In the Days of McKinley*, 576.
2. Ibid., 577.
3. Ibid.
4. "Mrs. McKinley in a Critical Condition," *The New York Times*, May 16, 1901.
5. Ibid.
6. *"Ohio* Glides into Sea," *The Washington Post*, May 19, 1901.
7. Leech, *In the Days of McKinley*, 579.
8. "President and His Wife on Their Way to Canton," *The New York Times*, July 6, 1901.
9. "Greets Canton Friends," *The Washington Post*, July 7, 1901.
10. McCullough, *Path Between the Seas*, 254.
11. Ibid., 38.
12. Leech, *In the Days of McKinley*, 583.
13. "The President at Home," *New York Daily Tribune*, August 27, 1901.
14. "President's First Auto Ride," *The New York Times*, July 14, 1901.
15. Leech, *In the Days of McKinley*, 584–85.

CHAPTER 31: "I DONE MY DUTY"

1. Briggs, *Manner of Man*, 275.
2. Ibid., 277.
3. Ibid., 278.
4. Fisher, *Stolen Glory*, 45.
5. Channing, *Mental Status of Czolgosz*, 23.
6. "The Assassin Makes a Full Confession," *The New York Times*, September 8, 1901.
7. Fisher, *Stolen Glory*, 46.

8. "The Assassin Makes a Full Confession," *The New York Times,* September 8, 1901.

9. Ibid.

10. Goldman, *High Hopes,* 8.

11. Leech, *In the Days of McKinley,* 586.

12. Fisher, *Stolen Glory,* 48.

13. Bryan and Halsey, *World's Famous Orations,* 239–48.

14. "The Assassin Makes a Full Confession," *The New York Times,* September 8, 1901.

15. Fisher, *Stolen Glory,* 53.

16. It was stated in the trial that Czolgosz had tracked the president to Niagara. In his confession as recorded by *The New York Times,* Czolgosz, however, said he had waited at the fair all day. He also told reporters on his way to Auburn that he had not gone to Niagara the day of the shooting. *Buffalo Courier,* September 26, 1901.

17. Rauchway, *Murdering McKinley,* 61–62.

18. *People of the State of New York vs. Leon F. Czolgosz.*

19. Ibid. It is almost impossible to fully portray the events immediately following the shooting. Nearly every participant and witness would later tell slightly different versions of what happened. Here, I have attempted to portray an account that most agree upon.

20. Channing, *Mental Status of Leon Czolgosz,* 23. This is according to Czolgosz. None of his attackers would report hearing the remark, though it's possible they could not have in the confusion of the moment.

21. Everett, *Complete Life of William McKinley,* 39.

22. Johns, *Man Who Shot McKinley,* 96.

23. "How the Deed Was Done," *The New York Times,* September 7, 1901.

24. Olcott, *Life of William McKinley,* 2:316.

25. Johns, *Man Who Shot McKinley,* 97–98.

26. "I Hope He Dies. I Hope He Dies!" *The Cleveland Press,* September 8, 1901.

27. *People of the State of New York vs. Leon F. Czolgosz.*

28. "The Assassin Makes a Full Confession, *The New York Times,* September 8, 1901.

29. Channing, *Mental Status of Leon Czolgosz,* 22–23.

30. *Cleveland Plain Dealer,* September 7, 1901. Quoted in Seibert, "I Done My Duty," 116.

31. "Czolgosz Says He Had No Aid," *Chicago Sunday Tribune,* September 8, 1901.

32. *Cleveland Plain Dealer,* September 7, 1901. Quoted in Seibert, "I Done My Duty," 116.

33. "Assassin Known as Rabid Anarchist," *The New York Times*, September 8, 1901.

34. *The Cincinnati Post*, September 7, 1901. Quoted in Seibert, "*I Done My Duty*," 127.

35. *Cleveland Plain Dealer*, September 13, 1901. Quoted in Seibert, "*I Done My Duty*," 127.

36. Ibid.

37. *The Buffalo Enquirer*, September 7, 1901. Quoted in Seibert, "*I Done My Duty*," 128.

38. *Buffalo Courier*, September 11, 1901. Quoted in Seibert, "*I Done My Duty*," 119.

39. "Chicago Anarchists Raided," *The New York Times*, September 8, 1901.

40. Falk, *Emma Goldman*, 467–68.

41. "Emma Goldman Is Arrested in Chicago," *The New York Times*, September 11, 1901.

42. Goldman, *Living My Life*, 1:296–300. It should be stressed that this is only one account of her arrest and others give slightly different details, including Falk's *Emma Goldman*.

43. Goldman, *Living My Life*, 1:312.

44. "Wanted to Kill Anarchists," *The New York Times*, September 7, 1901.

45. Fine, "Anarchism and the Assassination of McKinley," 786.

46. "Universal Rejoicing Over President's Progress," *The New York Times*, September 9, 1901.

47. "Czolgosz Has Told Much, but He Might Tell More," *Buffalo Courier*, September 12, 1901.

48. *Buffalo Evening News*, September 9, 1901. Quoted in Seibert, "*I Done My Duty*," 125.

49. *The Buffalo Commercial*, September 9, 1901. Quoted in Seibert, "*I Done My Duty*," 120.

CHAPTER 32: THE OPERATING THEATER

1. Fisher, *Stolen Glory*, 69.

2. Adler, "Operation on President McKinley," 121.

3. Ibid., 122.

4. Johns, *Man Who Shot McKinley*, 109.

5. "Official Report on the Case of President McKinley," 1030.

6. Ibid., 1029.

7. Fisher, *Stolen Glory*, 77–78.

8. "Official Report on the Case of President McKinley," 1030.

9. Fisher, *Stolen Glory*, 87.

10. "President McKinley Shot," *New York Tribune*, September 7, 1901.

11. Fisher, *Stolen Glory*, 90.

12. Johns, *Man Who Shot McKinley*, 143.

13. "Great Hope for the President," *The New York Times*, September 9, 1901.

14. Fisher, *Stolen Glory*, 99.

15. "President Will Get Well Soon," *The New York Times*, September 11, 1901.

16. "Only Favorable Reports Come from the Bedside of President M'Kinley," *The Cleveland Leader*, September 12, 1901.

CHAPTER 33: A PARK RANGER COMES RUNNING

1. Morris, *Rise of Theodore Roosevelt*, 740–41.

2. "Mr. McKinley Has Sinking Spell," *The New York Times*, September 13, 1901.

3. "Patient's Stomach Fails to Assimilate Solid Food," *Buffalo Courier*, September 13, 1901.

4. *The Washington Post*, September 13, 1901. Quoted in Seibert, *"I Done My Duty,"* 181.

5. "Mr. McKinley's Last Day of Suffering," *The New York Times*, September 14, 1901.

6. Ibid.

7. Seibert, *"I Done My Duty,"* 188.

8. Matthews, "President's Final Days," 943.

CHAPTER 34: THE CHAIR

1. "Another Insanity Expert Examines Leon Czolgosz," *Buffalo Courier*, September 22, 1901. See also Johns, *Man Who Shot McKinley*, 195.

2. "Another Insanity Expert Examines Leon Czolgosz," *Buffalo Courier*, September 22, 1901.

3. "Czolgosz Pleads," *Illustrated Buffalo Express*, September 21, 1901.

4. "The Proceedings in Court," *The New York Times*, September 24, 1901.

5. "Czolgosz to Have Three Lawyers," *Buffalo Courier*, September 22, 1901.

6. "Interesting Facts About Men Who Will Try Czolgosz," *Pittsburgh Dispatch*, September 24, 1901.

7. Johns, *Man Who Shot McKinley*, 198.

8. *Buffalo Courier*, September 18, 1901. Quoted in Seibert, *"I Done My Duty,"* 254.

9. "The Trial of the President's Assassin," *Saturday Globe* (Utica, N.Y.), September 28, 1901.

10. Fisher, *Stolen Glory*, 114.

11. Ibid., 115.

12. Ibid., 149.

13. Seibert, *"I Done My Duty,"* 196–205.

14. "I Do Not Believe I Shall Appear for the Defense," *Buffalo Courier,* September 23, 1901.

15. "Trial of Assassin Begins This Morning," *Buffalo Courier,* September 23, 1901.

16. *Buffalo Courier,* September 25, 1901. Quoted in Seibert, *"I Done My Duty,"* 282.

17. Ibid.

18. *Buffalo Commercial,* September 27, 1901, and *Buffalo Courier,* September 26, 1901. Quoted in Seibert, *"I Done My Duty,"* 287.

19. "Czolgosz Doomed to Die," *The New York Times,* September 26, 1901.

20. Johns, *Man Who Shot McKinley,* 240.

21. Halstead, "Illustrious Life of William McKinley," 461–62.

22. *Buffalo Evening News,* September 27, 1901. Quoted in Seibert, *"I Done My Duty,"* 296.

23. Ibid.

24. *Buffalo Courier,* October 29, 1901. Quoted in Seibert, *"I Done My Duty,"* 302.

25. *Buffalo Evening News,* October 4, 1901. Quoted in Seibert, *"I Done My Duty,"* 298.

26. *Buffalo Express,* September 30, 1901. Quoted in Seibert, *"I Done My Duty,"* 302.

27. "President's Assassin Asks for a Priest," *The New York Times,* October 23, 1901.

28. *Buffalo Courier,* October 29, 1901. Quoted in Seibert, *"I Done My Duty,"* 304.

29. Seibert, *"I Done My Duty,"* 300–301.

30. Briggs, *Manner of Man,* 263.

31. "Assassin Czolgosz Is Executed at Auburn," *The New York Times,* October 30, 1901.

32. Ibid.

AFTERWORD

1. Morris, *Theodore Rex,* 14.

2. Hamilton, *President McKinley, War, and Empire,* 2:109–10.

3. Phillips, *William McKinley*, 104.

4. Ibid., 87.

5. McCullough, *Path Between the Seas*, 266–67.

6. Ibid., 283.

7. LaFeber, *American Age*, 227.

8. Jones, *Crucible of Power*, 32.

9. Ibid., 36.

10. Pérez, *Cuba Between Empires*, 323.

11. Pérez, *Cuba and the United States*, 124.

12. Ibid., 136.

13. Ibid., 139.

14. Ibid., 147.

15. Boot, *Savage Wars of Peace*, 123–24.

16. Ibid., 125.

17. Karnow, *In Our Image*, 197.

18. Ibid., 230.

19. Ibid., 201.

20. U.S. Department of Commerce, Bureau of the Census, *Historical Statistics of the United States*, 903.

21. Hamilton, *President McKinley, War, and Empire*, 2:134.

22. LaFeber, *American Age*, 235.

23. Jones, *Crucible of Empire*, 45.

24. LaFeber, *American Age*, 238.

25. Ibid., 243.

26. Fine, "Anarchism and the Assassination," 788.

27. Ibid., 793.

28. Avrich, *Sacco and Vanzetti*, 130.

29. Wexler, *Emma Goldman*, 108.

30. Ibid., 105.

31. Fine, "Anarchism and the Assassination," 796.

32. Wexler, *Emma Goldman*, 165.

33. Ibid., 166.

34. Ibid., 266.

35. Avrich, *Sacco and Vanzetti*, 100.

36. Ibid., 105.

37. Ibid., 141.

38. Ibid., 146.

39. Ibid., 153–56.

40. Ibid., 192–94. Avrich argues Salsedo surely committed suicide.

41. Avrich, *Anarchist Voices*, 87–92.

42. Seibert, "*I Done My Duty*," 341–42.

43. Ibid., 356.
44. Ibid., 381.
45. Ibid., 397.
46. Rickover, *How the Battleship* Maine *Was Destroyed,* 76–79.
47. Ibid., 75–106.

Bibliography

BOOKS AND PAPERS

Adamic, Louis. *Dynamite: The Story of Class Violence in America.* New York: Viking Press, 1934.

Adams, Henry. *The Letters of Henry Adams.* 5 vols. Edited by J. C. Levenson, et al. London: Belknap Press, 1988.

Aguinaldo, Emilo, with Vicente A. Pacis. *A Second Look at America.* New York: Robert Speller and Sons, 1957.

Alger, R. A. *The Spanish-American War.* New York: Harper and Brothers, 1901.

Anbinder, Tyler. *Five Points: The 19th-Century New York City Neighborhood That Invented Tap Dance, Stole Elections, and Became the World's Most Notorious Slum.* New York: Free Press, 2001.

Armstrong, William H. *Major McKinley.* Kent, Ohio: Kent State University Press, 2000.

Ashbaugh, Carolyn. *Lucy Parsons, American Revolutionary.* Chicago: Charles H. Kerr Publishing Company, 1976.

Atkins, Edwin F. *Sixty Years in Cuba.* Cambridge, Mass.: Riverside Press, 1926.

Atkins, John Black. *The War in Cuba: The Experiences of an Englishman with the United States Army.* London: Smith, Eldee and Company, 1899.

Avrich, Paul. *Anarchist Voices: An Oral History of Anarchism in America.* Princeton, N.J.: Princeton University Press, 1995.

———. *The Haymarket Tragedy.* Princeton, N.J.: Princeton University Press, 1984.

———. *Sacco and Vanzetti: The Anarchist Background.* Princeton, N.J.: Princeton University Press, 1991.

Badaczewski, Dennis. *Poles in Michigan.* East Lansing: Michigan State University Press, 2002.

Bailie, William. *Josiah Warren: The First American Anarchist.* Boston: Small, Maynard, and Company, 1906.

Bain, David H. *Sitting in Darkness.* Boston: Houghton Mifflin Company, 1984.

Balch, Emily Greene. *Our Slavic Fellow Citizens.* New York: Charities Publication Committee, 1910.

Barry, Richard H. *An Historic Memento of the Nation's Loss: The True Story of the Assassination of President McKinley at Buffalo.* Buffalo, N.Y.: Robert Allan Reid, 1901.

Beatty, Jack. *Age of Betrayal: The Triumph of Money in America 1865–1900.* New York: Alfred A. Knopf, 2007.

———, ed. *Colossus: How the Corporation Changed America.* New York: Broadway Books, 2001.

Beer, Thomas. *Hanna.* New York: Alfred A. Knopf, 1929.

———. *Hanna, Crane and the Mauve Decade.* New York: Alfred A. Knopf, 1923.

Beisner, Robert L. *Twelve Against Empire: The Anti-Imperialists, 1898–1900.* New York: McGraw-Hill Book Company, 1968.

Berkman, Alexander. *Prison Memoirs of an Anarchist.* New York: Schocken Books, 1970.

Bobinska, Celina, and Andrzej Pilch, eds. *Employment-Seeking Emigrations of the Poles World-Wide, XIX and XX C.* Krakow: Państwowe Wydawnictwo Naukowe, 1975.

Bogart, Ernest Ludlow. *Economic History of the American People.* New York: Longmans, Green, and Company, 1939.

Bonsal, Stephen. *The Real Condition of Cuba To-Day.* New York: Harper and Brothers, 1897.

Boot, Max. *The Savage Wars of Peace: Small Wars and the Rise of American Power.* New York: Basic Books, 2002.

Boris, Eileen, and Nelson Lichtenstein, eds. *Major Problems in the History of American Workers: Documents and Essays.* Lexington, Mass.: D. C. Heath and Company, 1991.

Bose, Atindranath. *A History of Anarchism.* Calcutta: World Press Private Ltd., 1967.

Bradford, James C., ed. *Crucible of Empire: The Spanish-American War and Its Aftermath.* Annapolis, Md.: Naval Institute Press, 1993.

Brandon, Ruth. *A Capitalist Romance.* Philadelphia: J. B. Lippincott Company, 1977.

Brecher, Jeremy. *Strike!* San Francisco: Straight Arrow Books, 1972.

Briggs, Chester M. *The United States Marines in North China, 1894–1942.* Jefferson, N.C.: McFarland and Company, 2003.

Briggs, Vernon L. *The Manner of Man That Kills: Spencer—Czolgosz—Richeson.* Boston: R. G. Badger, 1921.

Brooks, Thomas R. *Toil and Trouble: A History of American Labor.* New York: Delacorte Press, 1964.

Brown, Charles H. *The Correspondents' War: Journalists in the Spanish-American War.* New York: Charles Scribner's Sons, 1967.

Brown, Ford K. *The Life of William Godwin.* London: J. M. Dent and Sons, Ltd., 1926.

Bruce, Robert. *1877: Year of Violence.* Indianapolis: New Bobbs-Merrill Company, Inc., 1959.

Bryan, William Jennings, and Francis W. Halsey, eds. *The World's Famous Orations.* New York: Funk and Wagnalls, 1906.

Burgoyne, Arthur. *The Homestead Strike of 1892.* Pittsburgh: University of Pittsburgh Press, 1979.

Burke, Edmund. *The Works.* Vol. 1. Boston: Little, Brown, and Company, 1894.

Busbey, White L. *Uncle Joe Cannon: The Story of a Pioneer American.* New York: Henry Holt and Company, 1927.

Butterfield, Roger. *The American Past: A History of the United States from Concord to Hiroshima, 1775–1945.* New York: Simon and Schuster, 1947.

Byington, Margaret. *Homestead: The Households of a Mill Town.* Pittsburgh: University of Pittsburgh Press, 1974.

Cable, Mary. *Top Drawer.* New York: Atheneum, 1984.

Calhoun, Charles W., ed. *The Gilded Age.* Wilmington, Del.: Scholarly Resources, 2000.

Calmer, Alan. *Labor Agitator: The Story of Albert R. Parsons.* New York: International Publishers, 1937.

Camfield, Gregg. *The Oxford Companion to Mark Twain.* New York: Oxford University Press, 2003.

Campbell, Charles. *Special Business Interests and the Open Door Policy.* New Haven, Conn.: Yale University Press, 1951.

Carlson, Oliver, and Ernest Sutherland Bates. *Hearst: Lord of San Simeon.* New York: Viking Press, 1936.

Carnegie, Andrew. *The Autobiography of Andrew Carnegie.* Boston: Northeastern University Press, 1986. First published in Boston by Houghton Mifflin in 1920.

Carrère, John M. "The Architectural Scheme," in *Art Hand-Book: Official Handbook of Architecture and Sculpture and Art Catalogue to the Pan-American Exposition.* Edited by David Gray. Buffalo, N.Y.: David Gray, 1901.

Carter, Susan B., ed. *Historical Statistics of the United States: Earliest Times to Present.* 5 vols. New York: Cambridge University Press, 2006.

Cashman, Sean D. *America in the Gilded Age.* New York: New York University Press, 1984.

Chadwick, French Ensor. *The Relations of the United States and Spain: The Spanish-American War.* 2 vols. New York: Charles Scribner's Sons, 1911.

Channing Papers, Papers of Walter Channing, Channing Family Papers. Boston: Massachusetts Historical Society.

Coffman, Edward M. *The Hilt of the Sword.* Madison: University of Wisconsin Press, 1966.

Coletta, Paolo. *William Jennings Bryan.* Vol. 1, *Political Evangelist 1860–1908.* Lincoln: University of Nebraska Press, 1964.

Conant, Charles. *A History of Modern Banks of Issue.* New York: G. P. Putnam's Sons, 1909.

———. *The United States in the Orient: The Nature of the Economic Problem.* Boston: Houghton Mifflin Company, 1900.

Conroy, Robert. *The Battle of Manila Bay.* New York: Macmillan Company, 1968.

Conway, Moncure Daniel, ed. *The Writings of Thomas Paine,* New York: G. P. Putnam's Sons, 1894.

Cosmas, Graham. *An Army for Empire: The United States Army in the Spanish-American War.* Columbia: University of Missouri Press, 1971.

Coulter, Charles. *The Poles of Cleveland.* Cleveland: Cleveland Americanization Committee, Mayor's Advisory War Committee, 1919.

Croly, Herbert. *Marcus Alonzo Hanna: His Life and Work.* New York: Macmillan Company, 1912.

Dabney, Virginius. *Liberalism in the South.* Chapel Hill: University of North Carolina Press, 1932.

Darwin, Charles. *The Descent of Man, and Selection in Relation to Sex.* New York: A. L. Burt, 1874.

David, Henry. *The History of the Haymarket Affair: A Study in the American Social-Revolutionary and Labor Movement.* New York: Farrar and Rinehart, Inc., 1936.

Davis, Oscar King. *Our Conquests in the Pacific.* New York: Frederick A. Stokes Company, 1898.

Davis, Richard Harding. *The Cuban and Porto Rican Campaigns.* Freeport, N.Y.: Books for Libraries Press, 1898.

Dawes, Charles G. *A Journal of the McKinley Years.* Chicago: Lakeside Press, 1950.

Daws, Gavan. *Shoal of Time: A History of the Hawaiian Islands.* Honolulu: University of Hawaii Press, 1968.

Dennett, Tyler. *Americans in Eastern Asia.* New York: Barnes and Noble, 1922.

———. *John Hay: From Poetry to Politics.* New York: Dodd, Mead, and Company, 1933.

Dewey, George. *Autobiography of George Dewey, Admiral of the Navy.* New York: Charles Scribner's Sons, 1913.

Dobson, John. *Reticent Expansionism: The Foreign Policy of William McKinley.* Pittsburgh: Duquesne University Press, 1988.

Downs, Robert B. *Books That Changed America.* London: Macmillan Company, 1970.

Dulles, Foster R. *The Imperial Years.* New York: Thomas Y. Crowell Company, 1956.

———. *Labor in America: A History.* New York: Thomas Y. Crowell Company, 1949.

———. *The Old China Trade.* Boston: Houghton Mifflin Company, 1930.

Dunn, Arthur W. *From Harrison to Harding: A Personal Narrative, Covering a Third of a Century 1888–1921.* New York: G. P. Putnam's Sons, 1922.

Ellis, Richard J. *To the Flag: The Unlikely History of the Pledge of Allegiance.* Lawrence: University Press of Kansas, 2005.

Emerson, Ralph Waldo. *Emerson's Essays.* New York: Thomas Y. Crowell Co., 1926.

Everett, Marshall. *Complete Life of William McKinley and Story of His Assassination.* 1901.

Falk, Candace, ed. *Emma Goldman: A Documentary History of the American Years.* Vol. 1. Berkeley: University of California Press, 2003.

Fisher, Jack C. *Stolen Glory: The McKinley Assassination.* La Jolla, Calif.: Alamar Books, 2001.

Folsom, Franklin. *The Impatient Armies of the Poor: The Story of Collective Action of the Unemployed 1808–1942.* Niwot: University Press of Colorado, 1991.

Foner, Philip S. *The Autobiographies of the Haymarket Martyrs.* New York:
A.I.M.S. for Humanities Press, 1969.

———. *The Great Labor Uprising of 1877.* New York: Monad Press, 1977.

———. *Reconstruction: America's Unfinished Revolution, 1863–1877.* New York:
Harper and Row, 1988.

———. *The Spanish-Cuban-American War and the Birth of American
Imperialism.* 2 vols. New York: Monthly Review Press, 1972.

Foraker, Joseph B. *Notes of a Busy Life.* Vol. 1. Cincinnati: Stewart and Kidd
Company, 1916.

Foraker, Julia B. *I Would Live It Again: Memories of a Vivid Life.* New York:
Harper and Brothers, 1932.

Foster, John W. *Diplomatic Memoirs.* 2 vols. Boston: Houghton Mifflin
Company, 1909.

Francisco, Luzviminda B., and Jonathan S. Fast. *Conspiracy for Empire: Big
Business, Corruption, and the Politics of Imperialism in America 1876–1907.*
Quezon City, Philippines: Foundation for Nationalist Studies, 1985.

Freidel, Frank. *The Splendid Little War.* Boston: Little, Brown and Company,
1958.

Fuess, Claude Moore. *Carl Schurz, Reformer: 1829–1906.* New York: Dodd,
Mead, and Company, 1932.

Funston, Frederick. *Memories of Two Wars: Cuban and Philippine Experiences.*
London: Constable and Company, 1912.

Gage, Beverly. *The Day Wall Street Exploded: A Story of America in Its First Age
of Terror.* New York: Oxford University Press, 2009.

Gage, Gloria. *Memoirs of Lyman J. Gage.* New York: House of Field, 1937.

Garraty, John A., ed. *Labor and Capital in the Gilded Age.* Boston: Little,
Brown and Company, 1968.

Geisst, Charles R. *Wall Street: A History.* New York: Oxford University Press,
1997.

Glad, Paul W. *McKinley, Bryan, and the People.* Philadelphia: J. B. Lippincott
Company, 1964.

Goldberg, Joyce S. *The Baltimore Affair.* Lincoln: University of Nebraska
Press, 1986.

Goldman, Emma. *Living My Life.* 2 vols. New York: Alfred Knopf, Inc., 1931.

Goldman, Mark. *High Hopes: The Rise and Decline of Buffalo, New York.*
Albany: State University of New York Press, 1983.

Goldstein, Donald M., and Katherine V. Dillon. *The Spanish-American War:
The Story and Photographs.* Washington, D.C.: Brassey's, 2000.

Gould, Lewis L. *The Presidency of William McKinley.* Lawrence: Regents Press
of Kansas, 1980.

Goyens, Tom. *Beer and Revolution: The German Anarchist Movement in New York City, 1880–1914*. Urbana: University of Illinois Press, 2007.

Graham, George Edward. *Schley and Santiago: An Historical Account of the Blockade and Final Destruction of the Spanish Fleet Under the Command of Admiral Pasquale Cervera, July 3, 1898*. Chicago: W. B. Conkey Company, 1902.

Gray, David, ed. *Art Hand-Book: Official Handbook of Architecture and Sculpture and Art Catalogue to the Pan-American Exposition*. Buffalo, N.Y. : David Gray, 1901.

Green, James. *Death in the Haymarket: A Story of Chicago, the First Labor Movement, and the Bombing That Divided Gilded Age America*. New York: Pantheon Books, 2006.

Grenville, John A. S., and George Berkley Young. *Politics, Strategy, and American Diplomacy: Studies in Foreign Policy, 1873–1917*. New Haven, Conn.: Yale University Press, 1966.

Hagedorn, Hermann. *Leonard Wood: A Biography*. Vol. 1. New York: Harper and Brothers, 1931.

Halstead, Murat. *The Illustrious Life of William McKinley, Our Martyred President*. [Chicago, 1901.]

Hamilton, Richard F. *President McKinley, War, and Empire*. 2 vols. New Brunswick, N.J.: Transaction Publishers, 2006.

Hartzell, Josiah. *Sketch of the Life of Mrs. William McKinley*. Washington, D.C.: Home Magazine Press, 1896.

Herrick, Walter R. *The American Naval Revolution*. Baton Rouge: Louisiana State University Press, 1966.

Hirst, Francis. *The Life and Letters of Thomas Jefferson*. New York: Macmillan, 1926.

Hoar, George F. *Autobiography of Seventy Years*. Vol. 2. New York: Charles Scribner's Sons, 1903.

Hoerder, Dirk, and Horst Rössler. *Distant Magnets: Expectations and Realities in the Immigrant Experience, 1840–1930*. New York: Holmes and Meier, 1993.

Hoover, Herbert. *Memoirs*. Vol. 1, *Years of Adventure, 1874–1920*. New York: Macmillan, 1951.

Jacker, Corinne. *The Black Flag of Anarchy: Antistatism in the United States*. New York: Scribner, 1968.

James, Lawrence. *The Rise and Fall of the British Empire*. London: Little, Brown and Company, 1994.

Johns, A. Wesley. *The Man Who Shot McKinley*. South Brunswick, N.J.: A. S. Barnes and Company, Inc., 1970.

Joll, James. *The Anarchists*. Boston: Little, Brown and Company, 1964.

Jones, Howard. *Crucible of Power: A History of U.S. Foreign Relations Since 1897*. Wilmington, Del.: Scholarly Resources, Inc., 2001.

Jones, Stanley L. *The Presidential Election of 1896*. Madison: University of Wisconsin Press, 1964.

Josephson, Matthew. *The Politicos, 1865–1896*. New York: Harcourt, Brace, and Company, 1938.

Kaplan, Justin. *When the Astors Owned New York*. New York: Viking, 2006.

Karnow, Stanley. *In Our Image: America's Empire in the Philippines*. New York: Ballantine Books, 1990.

Kennan, George F. *American Diplomacy 1900–1950*. Chicago: University of Chicago Press, 1951.

Kent, Noel J. *America in 1900*. Armonk, N.Y.: M. Sharpe, 2000.

Knoles, George H. *The Presidential Campaign and Election of 1892*. Stanford, Calif.: Stanford University Press, 1942.

Kohlsaat, H. H. *From McKinley to Harding*. New York: Charles Scribner's Sons, 1923.

LaFeber, Walter. *The American Age: United States Foreign Policy at Home and Abroad Since 1750*. New York: W. W. Norton and Co., 1989.

———. *Cambridge History of American Foreign Relations*. Vol. 2, *American Search for Opportunity, 1865–1913*. Cambridge: Cambridge University Press, 2008.

———. *The New Empire: An Interpretation of American Expansion 1860–1898*. Ithaca, N.Y.: Cornell University Press, 1963.

Lamoreaux, Naomi R. *The Great Merger Movement in American Business, 1895–1904*. New York: Cambridge University Press, 1985.

Lee, Fitzhugh, and Joseph Wheeler. *Cuba's Struggle Against Spain*. New York: American Historical Press, 1899.

Leech, Margaret. *In the Days of McKinley*. New York: Harper & Brothers, 1959.

Lens, Sidney. *The Forging of the American Empire*. New York: Thomas Y. Crowell Company, 1971.

Livezey, William E. *Mahan on Sea Power*. Norman: University of Oklahoma Press, 1981.

Lodge, Henry Cabot. *The War with Spain*. New York: Harper and Brothers, 1900.

Long, John D. *The Journal of John D. Long*. Edited by Margaret Long. Rindge, N.H.: Richard R. Smith Publisher, Inc., 1956.

Long, Priscilla. *Where the Sun Never Shines: A History of America's Bloody Coal Industry*. New York: Paragon House, 1989.

Longworth, Alice Roosevelt. *Crowded Hours: Reminiscences of Alice Roosevelt Longworth*. New York: Charles Scribner's Sons, 1933.

Lorence, James J. *Organized Business and the Myth of the China Market: The American Asiatic Association, 1898–1937.* Philadelphia: The American Philosophical Society, 1981.

Lum, Dyer D. *A Concise History of the Great Trial of the Chicago Anarchists in 1886: Condensed from the Official Record.* Ann Arbor, Mich.: UMI Books on Demand, 2000.

Mahan, A. T. *From Sail to Steam: Recollections of a Naval Life.* New York: Harper and Brothers, 1907.

Mandel, Bernard. *Samuel Gompers: A Biography.* Yellow Springs, Ohio: Antioch Press, 1963.

Marcus, Robert D. *Grand Old Party: Political Structure in the Gilded Age.* New York: Oxford University Press, 1971.

Marcuse, Maxwell F. *This Was New York!* New York: LIM Press, 1969.

Marquis, Albert Nelson. *Who's Who in America, 1908–1909.* Chicago: A. N. Marquis and Company, 1908.

Marshall, Peter. *William Godwin.* New Haven, Conn.: Yale University Press, 1984.

Martin, James J. *Men Against the State: The Expositors of Individualist Anarchism in America, 1827–1908.* DeKalb, Ill.: Adrian Allen Associates, 1953.

May, Ernest R. *Imperial Democracy: The Emergence of America as a Great Power.* Chicago: Imprint Publications, Inc., 1961.

Mayo, Lawrence Shaw, ed. *America of Yesterday as Reflected in the Journal of John Davis Long.* Boston: Atlantic Monthly Press, 1923.

McCormick, Thomas J. *China Market: America's Quest for Informal Empire.* Chicago: Quadrangle Books, 1967.

McCullough, David. *The Path Between the Seas: The Creation of the Panama Canal, 1870–1914.* New York: Simon and Schuster, 1977.

McKinley, William. *Speeches and Addresses of William McKinley, from His Election to Congress to the Present Time.* New York: D. Appleton and Company, 1893.

———. *Speeches and Addresses of William McKinley, from March 1, 1897 to May 30, 1900.* New York: Doubleday and McClure Company, 1900.

McLean, Geo N. *The Rise and Fall of Anarchy in America.* Chicago: R. G. Badoux and Company, 1888.

Merriman, John. *The Dynamite Club: How a Bombing in Fin-de-Siècle Paris Ignited the Age of Modern Terror.* New York: Houghton Mifflin Harcourt, 2009.

Miley, John D. *In Cuba with Shafter.* New York: Charles Scribner's Sons, 1899.

Millet, F. D. *The Expedition to the Philippines.* New York: Harper and Brothers, 1899.

Millis, Walter. *The Martial Spirit: A Study of Our War with Spain.* Boston:
    Houghton Mifflin Company, 1931.

Mitchell, Donald W. *History of the Modern American Navy, from 1883 Through
    Pearl Harbor.* New York: Alfred A. Knopf, 1946.

Morgan, H. Wayne. *William McKinley and His America.* Syracuse, N.Y.:
    Syracuse University Press, 1963.

Morison, Samuel Eliot. *The Maritime History of Massachusetts.* Boston:
    Northeastern University Press, 1921.

Morris, Charles. *The Tycoons: How Andrew Carnegie, John D. Rockefeller, Jay
    Gould, and J. P. Morgan Invented the American Supereconomy.* New York:
    Times Books, 2005.

Morris, Edmund. *The Rise of Theodore Roosevelt.* New York: Modern Library,
    2001. First published in 1979.

——. *Theodore Rex.* New York: Random House, 2001.

Murolo, Priscilla, and A. B. Chitty. *From the Folks Who Brought You the
    Weekend: A Short, Illustrated History of Labor in the United States.* New
    York: New York Press, 2001.

Musicant, Ivan. *Empire by Default: The Spanish-American War and the Dawn of
    the American Century.* New York: Henry Holt and Company, 1998.

Nasaw, David. *Andrew Carnegie.* New York: Penguin Press, 2006.

Nicholson, Philip Y. *Labor's Story in the United States.* Philadelphia: Temple
    University Press, 2004.

Obermann, Karl. *Joseph Weydemeyer, Pioneer of American Socialism.* New
    York: International Publishers, 1947.

O'Connor, Richard. *The Spirit Soldiers: A Historical Narrative of the Boxer
    Rebellion.* New York: G. P. Putnam's Sons, 1973.

Offner, John. *An Unwanted War: The Diplomacy of the United States and Spain
    Over Cuba, 1895–1898.* Chapel Hill: University of North Carolina Press,
    1992.

Olcott, Charles S. *The Life of William McKinley.* 2 vols. Boston: Houghton
    Mifflin Company, 1916.

O'Toole, G. J. A. *The Spanish War: An American Epic—1898.* New York:
    Norton, 1984.

Palmer, Frederick. *Bliss, Peacemaker: The Life and Letters of Tasker H. Bliss.*
    New York: Dodd, Mead, and Company, 1934.

Parker, George F. *Recollections of Grover Cleveland.* New York: Century
    Company, 1909.

Parsons, A. R. *Anarchism: Its Philosophy and Scientific Basis.* Chicago: Mrs.
    A. R. Parsons, Publisher, 1887.

Parsons, Lucy E. *Life of Albert R. Parsons with Brief History of the Labor
    Movement in America.* Chicago: Mrs. Lucy E. Parsons, 1903.

Paterson, Thomas G., ed. *Major Problems in American Foreign Policy.* Vol. 1. Lexington, Mass.: D. C. Heath and Company, 1978.

Pérez, Louis A., Jr. *Cuba and the United States: Ties of Singular Intimacy.* Athens: University of Georgia Press, 1990.

———. *Cuba Between Empires, 1878–1902.* Pittsburgh: University of Pittsburgh Press, 1983.

Phillips, Kevin. *William McKinley.* New York: Henry Holt and Company, 2003.

Pierce, Bessie Louise. *A History of Chicago.* 3 vols. New York: Alfred A. Knopf, 1957.

Pinkerton, Allan. *Strikers, Communists, Tramps, and Detectives.* New York: G. W. Dillingham Company, 1906.

Pletcher, David M. *The Diplomacy of Involvement: American Economic Expansion Across the Pacific, 1784–1900.* Columbia: University of Missouri Press, 2001.

———. *The Diplomacy of Trade and Investment: American Economic Expansion in the Hemisphere, 1865–1900.* Columbia: University of Missouri Press, 1998.

Ponder, Stephen. *Managing the Press: Origins of the Media Presidency, 1897–1933.* New York: St. Martin's Press.

Porter, Robert. *Life of William McKinley, Soldier, Lawyer, Statesman.* Cleveland: N. G. Hamilton Publishing Company, 1896.

Pratt, Julius W. *Expansionists of 1898: The Acquisition of Hawaii and the Spanish Islands.* Baltimore: Johns Hopkins Press, 1936.

Preston, Diana. *The Boxer Rebellion: The Dramatic Story of China's War on Foreigners That Shook the World in the Summer of 1900.* New York: Berkley Books, 1999.

Price, Eva J. *China Journal: An American Missionary Family During the Boxer Rebellion.* New York: Macmillan, 1989.

Pringle, Henry F. *Theodore Roosevelt: A Biography.* New York: Harcourt, Brace, and Company, 1931.

Puleston, W. D. *Mahan: The Life and Work of Captain Alfred Thayer Mahan, U.S.N.* New Haven, Conn.: Yale University Press, 1939.

Rauchway, Eric. *Murdering McKinley: The Making of Theodore Roosevelt's America.* New York: Hill and Wang, 2003.

Rayback, Joseph G. *A History of American Labor.* New York: Macmillan, 1959.

Reeder, Red. *The Story of the Spanish-American War.* New York: Duell, Sloan, and Pearce, 1966.

Reef, Catherine. *Working in America: An Eyewitness History.* New York: Facts on File, Inc., 2000.

Reid, Whitelaw. *Problems of Expansion.* New York: Century Company, 1900.

Rickover, H. G. *How the Battleship* Maine *Was Destroyed.* Washington, D.C.: Naval History Division, Department of the Navy, 1976.

Rocker, Rudolf. *Pioneers of American Freedom: Origin of Liberal and Radical Thought in America.* Los Angeles: Rocker Publications Committee, 1949.

Rogers, Robert F. *Destiny's Landfall: A History of Guam.* Honolulu: University of Hawaii Press, 1995.

Roosevelt, Theodore. *The Rough Riders.* New York: Charles Scribner's Sons, 1923.

———. *Theodore Roosevelt: An Autobiography.* New York: Charles Scribner's Sons, 1925.

Roosevelt, Theodore, and Henry Cabot Lodge. *Selections from the Correspondence of Theodore Roosevelt and Henry Cabot Lodge, 1884–1918.* Vol. 1. New York: Charles Scribner's Sons, 1925.

Rubens, Horatio S. *Liberty: The Story of Cuba.* New York: Ams Press, 1932.

Russ, William A. *The Hawaiian Republic (1894–98) and Its Struggle to Win Annexation.* Selinsgrove, Penn.: Susquehanna University Press, 1961.

Russell, Henry B. *An Illustrated History of Our War with Spain: Its Causes, Incidents, and Results.* Hartford, Conn.: A. D. Worthington and Company, 1898.

———. *The Lives of William McKinley and Garret A. Hobart.* Hartford, Conn.: A. D. Worthington and Company, 1896.

Sandburg, Carl. *Always the Young Strangers.* New York: Harcourt, Brace, and Company, 1952.

Schirmer, Daniel B., and Stephen Rosskamm Shalom, eds. *The Philippines Reader: A History of Colonialism, Neocolonialism, Dictatorship, and Resistance.* Boston: South End Press, 1987.

Schlesinger, Arthur M., Jr. *The Imperial Presidency.* Boston: Houghton Mifflin Company, 1973.

Schreiner, Samuel A. *Henry Clay Frick: A Gospel of Greed.* New York: St. Martin's Press, 1995.

Seibert, Jeffrey W. *"I Done My Duty": The Complete Story of the Assassination of President McKinley.* Bowie, Md.: Heritage Books, 2002.

Semmel, Bernard. *The Rise of Free Trade Imperialism, Classical Political Economy, the Empire of Free Trade, and Imperialism, 1750–1850.* Cambridge: Cambridge University Press, 1970.

Shrock, Joel. *The Gilded Age.* Westport, Conn.: Greenwood Press, 2004.

Sigsbee, Charles. *The "Maine": An Account of Her Destruction in Havana Harbor.* New York: Century Company, 1899.

Silbey, David J. *A War of Frontier and Empire: The Philippine-American War, 1899–1902.* New York: Hill and Wang, 2007.

Sklar, Martin K. *The Corporate Reconstruction of American Capitalism, 1890–1916.* Cambridge: Cambridge University Press, 1988.

Smith, Adam. *An Inquiry into the Nature and Causes of the Wealth of Nations.* New York: Modern Library, 1937.

Smith, Page. *The Rise of Industrial America: A People's History of the Post-Reconstruction Era.* New York: McGraw-Hill Book Company, 1984.

Sousa, John P. *Marching Along: Recollections of Men, Women, and Music.* Edited by Paul E. Bierley. Westerville, Ohio: Integrity Press, 1994.

Spahr, Charles B. *An Essay on the Present Distribution of Wealth in the United States.* New York: Thomas Y. Crowell and Company, 1896.

Spence, Jonathan D. *The Search for Modern China.* London: Century Hutchinson, 1990.

Spencer, David. *The Yellow Journalism, the Press, and America's Emergence as a World Power.* Evanston, Ill.: Northwestern University Press, 2007.

Stealey, Orlando O. *Twenty Years in the Press Gallery.* New York: Publishers Printing Company, 1906.

Steward, T. G. *The Colored Regulars in the United States Army.* New York: Arno Press and *The New York Times,* 1969.

Stoddard, Henry L. *As I Knew Them: Presidents and Politics from Grant to Coolidge.* New York: Harper and Brothers, 1927.

Strong, Josiah. *Our Country.* Cambridge, Mass.: Harvard University Press, 1963.

Sutton, Robert P. *Communal Utopias and the American Experience: Secular Communities, 1824–2000.* Westport, Conn.: Praeger Publishers, 2004.

Taft, Helen Herron. *Recollections of Full Years.* New York: Dodd, Mead, and Company, 1914.

Thayer, William R. *The Life and Letters of John Hay.* 2 vols. Boston: Houghton Mifflin Company, 1908.

Thomas, Lowell. *Old Gimlet Eye: The Adventures of Smedley D. Butler.* New York: Farrar and Rinehart, 1933.

Thoreau, Henry David. *On the Duty of Civil Disobedience.* Radford, Va.: Wilder Publications, 2008.

Timmons, Bascom N. *Portrait of an American: Charles G. Dawes.* New York: Henry Holt and Company, 1953.

Trachtenberg, Alan. *The Incorporation of America: Culture and Society in the Gilded Age.* New York: Hill and Wang, 1982.

Trask, David F. *The War with Spain in 1898.* New York: Macmillan, 1981.

Trautmann, Frederic. *The Voice of Terror: A Biography of Johann Most.* Westport, Conn.: Greenwood Press, 1980.

Tuchman, Barbara. *The Proud Tower.* New York: Bantam Books, 1967.

Van Alstyne, R. W. *The Rising American Empire*. New York: Oxford University Press, 1960.

Varg, Paul A. *Open Door Diplomat: The Life of W. W. Rockhill*. Urbana: University of Illinois Press, 1952.

Ware, Norman J. *The Labor Movement in the United States, 1860–1895*. Gloucester, Mass.: Peter Smith, 1959.

Werstein, Irving. *Strangled Voices: The History of the Haymarket Affair*. New York: Macmillan, 1970.

West, Richard S. *Admirals of the American Empire*. Westport, Conn.: Greenwood Press, 1971. First published in 1948 by the Bobbs-Merrill Company.

Wexler, Alice. *Emma Goldman: An Intimate Life*. New York: Pantheon Books, 1984.

Wheeler, Joseph. *The Santiago Campaign 1898*. Boston: Lamson, Wolffe, and Company, 1898.

Whitcomb, John, and Claire Whitcomb. *Real Life at the White House*. New York: Routledge, 2000.

Whitlock, Brand. *Forty Years of It*. New York: D. Appleton and Company, 1914.

Wilcox, Marrion, ed. *Harper's History of the War in the Philippines*. New York: Harper and Brothers, 1900.

Williams, Charles Richard, ed. *Diary and Letters of Rutherford Birchard Hayes, Nineteenth President of the United States*. Vol. 2. Columbus, Ohio: F. J. Heer Printing Company, 1922.

Williams, William Appleman. *The Tragedy of American Diplomacy*. New York: Dell Publishing, 1959.

Wise, John S. *Recollections of Thirteen Presidents*. New York: Doubleday, Page, and Company, 1906.

Wittke, Carl. *We Who Built America: The Saga of the Immigrant*. New York: Prentice-Hall, Inc., 1939.

Wolff, Leon. *Little Brown Brother: How the United States Purchased and Pacified the Philippine Islands at the Century's Turn*. Garden City, N.Y.: Doubleday and Company, 1961.

———. *Lockout: The Story of the Homestead Strike of 1892—A Study of Violence, Unionism, and the Carnegie Steel Empire*. New York: Harper and Row, 1965.

Woodcock, George. *Anarchism: A History of Libertarian Ideas and Movements*. New York: New World Publishing Company, 1962.

The World Almanac and Encyclopedia, 1903. New York: Press Publishing Company, 1902.

Young, Art. *Art Young: His Life and Times.* New York: Sheridan House, 1939.

Young, Kenneth Ray. *The General's General: The Life and Times of Arthur MacArthur.* Boulder, Colo.: Westview Press, 1994.

Zakaria, Fareed. *From Wealth to Power: The Unusual Origins of America's World Role.* Princeton, N.J.: Princeton University Press, 1998.

Zeisler, Sigmund. *Reminiscences of the Anarchist Case.* Chicago: Chicago Literary Club, 1927.

Zimmermann, Warren: *First Great Triumph: How Five Americans Made Their Country a World Power.* New York: Farrar, Straus, and Giroux, 2002.

GOVERNMENT PUBLICATIONS

Compilation of Reports of Committee on Foreign Relations, United States Senate, 1789–1901. Washington, D.C.: Government Printing Office, 1901.

Congressional Record: Proceedings and Debates, Vol. 21 to Vol. 35. Washington, D.C.: Government Printing Office, 1889–1902.

Mueller, Jose Y Tejeiro. *Office of Naval Intelligence, War Notes No. 1. Information from Abroad. Battles and Capitulation of Santiago de Cuba.* Washington, D.C.: Government Printing Office, 1899.

The People of the State of New York vs. Leon F. Czolgosz. Unpublished trial transcript. Bar Association of Erie County.

The Report of the Naval Court of Inquiry Upon the Destruction of the United States Battleship Maine in Havana Harbor, February 15, 1896, Together with the Testimony Taken Before the Court. Washington, D.C.: Government Printing Office, 1898.

Review of the World's Commerce, Introductory to Commercial Relations of the United States with Foreign Countries During the Years 1895–1896. Washington, D.C.: Government Printing Office, 1897.

Spanish Diplomatic Correspondence: Documents, 1896–1900. Washington, D.C.: Government Printing Office, 1905.

Treaty of Peace and Accompanying Papers. Senate Document No. 62, Pt. 1. Washington, D.C.: Government Printing Office, 1899.

United States Adjutant-General's Office. *Correspondence Relating to the War with Spain, Including the Insurrection in the Philippine Islands and the China Relief Expedition, April 15, 1898, to July 30, 1902.* 2 vols. Washington, D.C.: U.S. Government Printing Office, 1993.

United States Department of Commerce, Bureau of the Census. *Historical Statistics of the United States: Colonial Times to 1970.* 2 vols. White Plains, N.Y.: Kraus International Publications, 1989.

United States Department of Labor, Employment and Training Administration. *200 Years of American Work Life.* Washington, D.C.: Government Printing Office, 1977.

United States Department of State. *Papers Relating to the Foreign Relations of the United States.* Washington, D.C.: U.S. Government Printing Office, 1894–1901.

United States Department of War. *Annual Reports of the War Department.* Washington, D.C.: U.S. Government Printing Office, selected years.

United States Industrial Commission. *Preliminary Report on Trusts and Industrial Combinations.* Vols. 1 and 2. Washington, D.C.: Government Printing Office, 1900.

United States Naval Institute Proceedings 44, no. 2 (February 1918).

United States Tariff Commission. *Effects of the Cuban Reciprocity Treaty of 1902.* Washington, D.C.: Government Printing Office, 1902.

William McKinley Papers. Presidential Papers Microfilm. Washington D.C.: The Library of Congress, 1961.

JOURNALS AND MAGAZINE ARTICLES

Adams, Brooks. "The New Industrial Revolution." *The Atlantic Monthly* 87, no. 520 (February 1901): 157–66.

Adler, Selig. "Operation on President McKinley." *Scientific American* 208, no. 3 (March 1963): 118–30.

"All America vs. All Europe." *The Literary Digest* 15, no. 33 (December 11, 1897): 964–65.

Auxier, George. "The Propaganda Activities of the Cuban Junta in Precipitating the Spanish-American War, 1895–1898." *The Hispanic American Historical Review* 19, no. 3 (August 1939): 286–305.

Barrett, John. "America's Duty in China." *North American Review* 171, no. 525 (August 1900): 145–58.

Barrón, Carlos García. "Enrique Dupuy de Lôme and the Spanish-American War." *The Americas* 36, no. 1 (July 1979): 39–58.

Beale, Joseph. "Recognition of Cuban Belligerency." *Harvard Law Review* 9, no. 6 (1895–96): 406–19.

Bonsal, Stephen. "The Fight for Santiago." *McClure's Magazine* 11, no. 6 (October 1898): 499–518.

Bryan, W. J. "The Issue in the Presidential Campaign." *North American Review* 170, no. 523 (June 1900): 753–72.

Busch, Francis. "The Haymarket Riot and the Trial of the Anarchists." *Journal of the Illinois State Historical Society* 48, no. 3 (Autumn 1955): 247–70.

"Castelar's Views of McKinley." *The Literary Digest* 15, no. 1 (May 1, 1897): 6.

Channing, Walter. "The Mental Status of Czolgosz, the Assassin of President McKinley." *American Journal of Insanity* LIX, no. 2 (1902).

Chapman, John Jay. "The Capture of Government by Commercialism." *The Atlantic Monthly* 81, no. 484 (February 1898): 149–59.

Cluverius, W. T. "A Midshipman on the *Maine*." United States Naval Institute Proceedings 44, no. 2 (February 1918): 237–48.

Conant, Charles. "The Economic Basis of Imperialism." *North American Review* 167, no. 502 (September 1898): 326–41.

Cunningham, William. "English Imperialism." *The Atlantic Monthly* 84, no. 501 (July 1899): 1–7.

Davis, Richard Harding. "The Rocking-Chair Period of the War." *Scribner's Magazine* 24, no. 2 (August 1898): 131–41.

Denby, Charles. "America's Opportunity in Asia." *North American Review* 166, no. 494 (January 1898): 32–40.

Donovan, Robert J. "The Man Who Would Not Shake Hands." *The New Yorker* (Nov. 28, 1953): 105–128.

Eggert, Gerald G. "Our Man in Havana: Fitzhugh Lee." *Hispanic American Historical Review* 47, no. 4 (November 1967): 463–85.

Ferreiro, Larrie. "Mahan and the 'English Club' of Lima, Peru: The Genesis of *The Influence of Sea Power upon History*." *The Journal of Military History* 72, no. 3 (July 2008): 901–6.

Fine, Sidney. "Anarchism and the Assassination of McKinley." *The American Historical Review* 60, no. 4 (July 1955): 777–99.

Fiske, John. "Manifest Destiny." *Harper's New Monthly Magazine* 70, no. 418 (March 1885): 578–90.

Gary, Joseph E. "The Chicago Anarchists of 1886." *The Century* 45, no. 6 (April 1893): 803–38.

"German Socialism in America." *North American Review* 128, no. 269 (April 1879): 372–88.

Gotkin, Joshua. "The Legislated Adjustment of Labor Disputes: An Empirical Analysis, 1880–1894." *Journal of Economic History* 57, no. 2 (June 1997): 481–84.

Graham, George B. "The Destruction of Cervera's Fleet: By an Eye-Witness on the 'Brooklyn.' " *McClure's Magazine* 11, no. 5 (September 1898): 404–21.

Grenville, John A. S. "American Naval Preparations for War with Spain, 1896–98." *Journal of American Studies* 2, no. 1 (April 1968): 33–47.

Halbo, Paul S. "Presidential Leadership in Foreign Affairs: William McKinley and the Turpie-Foraker Amendment." *American Historical Review* 72, no. 4 (July 1967): 1321–55.

Harden, Edward W. "Dewey at Manila." *McClure's Magazine* 12, no. 4 (February 1899): 369–84.

"How He Saved the President's Life." *Leslie's Weekly,* September 21, 1901.

Knoles, George Harmon. "The Presidential Campaign and Election of 1892." *History, Economics, and Political Science* 5, no. 1 (1942).

Lea, Henry Charles. "The Decadence of Spain." *The Atlantic Monthly* 82, no. 489 (July 1898): 36–47.

Lee, Arthur H. "The Regulars at El Caney." *Scribner's Magazine* 24, no. 4 (October 1898): 403–13.

Lee, Fitzhugh. "Cuba Under Spanish Rule." *McClure's Magazine* 11, no. 2 (June 1898): 99–114.

Macfarland, Henry. "William R. Day: A New Statesman of the First Rank." *The American Review of Reviews* 17, no. 3 (September 1898).

Matthews, Franklin. "The President's Last Days." *Harper's Weekly* 45, no. 2335 (September 21, 1901): 943.

McKinley, William. "The Value of Protection." *North American Review* 150, no. 403 (June 1890): 740–49.

Morgan, H. Wayne. "William McKinley as Political Leader." *The Review of Politics* 28, no. 4 (October 1966): 417–32.

Morgan, John T. "What Shall We Do with the Conquered Islands?" *North American Review* 166, no. 499 (June 1898): 641–50.

"The Night of the Explosion in Havana." *Harper's Weekly* 62, no. 2150 (March 5, 1898): 217–40.

North, S. N. D. "The Industrial Commission." *North American Review* 168, no. 511 (June 1899): 708–20.

Offner, John L. "McKinley and the Spanish-American War." *Presidential Studies Quarterly* 34, no. 1 (March 2004): 50–61.

Osgood, Herbert L. "Scientific Anarchism." *Political Science Quarterly* 4, no. 1 (March 1889): 1–36.

Parker, John H. "Some Lessons of the War from an Officer's Standpoint." *The American Monthly Review of Reviews* 18, no. 4 (October 1898): 427–31.

Pite, Rebekah E. "The Force of Food: Life on the Atkins Family Sugar Plantation in Cienfuegos, Cuba, 1884–1900." *The Massachusetts Historical Review* 5 (2003): 58–93.

Pixton, John, Jr. "Charles G. Dawes and the McKinley Campaign." *Journal of the Illinois State Historical Society* 48, no. 3 (Autumn 1955): 283–306.

Porter, David D. "Discipline in the Navy." *North American Review* 150, no. 401 (April 1890): 409–19.

"President McKinley in War Times." *McClure's Magazine* 11, no. 2 (July 1898): 209–24.

Pritchett, Henry. "Some Recollections of President McKinley and the Cuban Intervention." *North American Review* 189, no. 640 (March 1909): 397–403.

"Radical Comment on the President's Assassination." *The Literary Digest* 23, no. 12 (September 21, 1901): 331–60.

"The Rebellion at Homestead." *Harper's Weekly* 26, no. 1856 (July 16, 1892): 674.

Reno, George. "General Calixto Garcia." *The American Monthly Review of Reviews* 19, no. 1 (January 1899): 52–55.

Rixey, P. M., M. D. Mann, H. Mynter, R. Park, E. Wasdin, C. McBurney, and C. G. Stockton. "The Official Report on the Case of President McKinley." *Journal of the American Medical Association,* October 19, 1901, 1029–36.

Smalley, Eugene. "William McKinley—A Study of His Character and Career." *Review of Reviews* 14, no. 1 (July 1896).

Smith, Judson. "The Awakening of China." *North American Review* 168, no. 507 (February 1899): 229–40.

Stickney, Joseph L. "With Dewey at Manila." *Harper's New Monthly Magazine* 98, no. 585 (February 1899): 476–84.

Storer, Mrs. Bellamy. "How Theodore Roosevelt Was Appointed Assistant Secretary of the Navy, a Hitherto Unrelated Chapter of History." *Harper's Weekly* 56, no. 2893 (July 1, 1912).

"The 3 Shake Hands." *The New Yorker.* November 28, 1953, 111–12.

"Topics of the Day." *The Literary Digest* 17, no. 18 (October 29, 1898): 509–36.

Tosti, Gustavo. "Anarchistic Crimes." *Political Science Quarterly* 14, no. 3 (September 1899): 404–17.

Volwiler, A. T. "Harrison, Blaine, and American Foreign Policy, 1889–1893." *Proceedings of the American Philosophical Society* 79, no 4 (November 15, 1938): 637–48.

Walron, George B. "The Commercial Promise of Cuba, Porto Rico, and the Philippians." *McClure's Magazine* 11, no. 5 (September 1898): 481–84.

Ward, Geoffrey. "A Fair, Honorable and Legitimate Trade." *American Heritage* 37, no. 5 (August–September 1986).

"The Week," *The Nation* 69, no. 1795, November 23, 1899.

Index

As a correspondent for *The Wall Street Journal* and Reuters news agency, SCOTT MILLER spent nearly twenty years based in Asia and Europe, reporting from more than twenty-five countries. Miller holds a master's degree in international relations from the University of Cambridge. He now lives in Seattle with his wife and two daughters.